CHILDREN'S LITERATURE

CHILDREN'S LITERATURE

Critical Concepts in Literary and Cultural Studies

Edited by
Peter Hunt

Volume IV
International and Comparative

Routledge
Taylor & Francis Group

LONDON AND NEW YORK

First published 2006
by Routledge
2 Park Square, Milton Park, Abingdon, Oxon OX14 4RN

Simultaneously published in the USA and Canada
by Routledge
270 Madison Avenue, New York, NY 10016-0602

Routledge is an imprint of the Taylor & Francis Group, an informa business

Typeset in 10/12pt Times by Graphicraft Limited, Hong Kong
Printed and bound in Great Britain by
MPG Books Ltd, Bodmin, Cornwall

. *British Library Cataloguing in Publication Data*
A catalogue record for this book is available from the British Library

Library of Congress Cataloging in Publication Data
A catalog record for this book has been requested

ISBN10: 0–415–37228–3 (Set)
ISBN10: 0–415–37227–5 (Volume IV)

ISBN13: 978–0–415–37228–2 (Set)
ISBN13: 978–0–415–37227–5 (Volume IV)

Publisher's note

References within each chapter are as they appear in the original complete work

CONTENTS

CONTENTS

CONTENTS

ACKNOWLEDGEMENTS

The Publishers would like to thank the following for permission to reprint their material:

Anne Pellowski for permission to reprint Anne Pellowski, 'Story in Orature and Literature: Why and How we Make it Available to Children in Different Cultures', in International Board on Books for Young People, *Proceedings, 25th Congress, 12–16 August 1996, Telling the Tale*, Amsterdam: Dutch Section of IBBY, 1997, pp. 81–86.

Taylor & Francis for permission to reprint Marian Koren, 'The Right of The Child to Information and its Practical Impact on Children's Libraries', *The New Review of Children's Literature and Librarianship* 4 (1998): 1–16.

The Société de Stylistique Anglaise for permission to reprint Andy Arleo, 'Do Children's Rhymes Reveal Universal Metrical Patterns?', *Bulletin de la Société de Stylistique Anglaise* 22 (2001): 125–145.

The Centre for Children's Literature for permission to reprint Tony Watkins, 'Homelands: Landscape and Identity in Children's Literature', in Wendy Parsons and Robert Goodwin (eds), *Landscape and Identity: Perspectives from Australia*, Adelaide: Auslib Press, 1994, pp. 3–20.

European Academic Publishers for permission to reprint Riitta Oittinen, 'The Verbal and the Visual: On the Carnivalism and Dialogics of Translating for Children,' *Compar(a)ison: An International Journal of Comparative Literature* 2 (1995): 49–65.

Reinbert Tabbert, 'Approaches to the Translation of Children's Literature: A Review of Critical Studies since 1960', *Target: International Journal of Translation Studies* 14(2) (2002): 303–351. With kind permission by John Benjamins Publishing Company. www.benjamins.com.

Meta and Emer O'Sullivan for permission to reprint Emer O'Sullivan, 'Narratology meets Translation Studies, or, The Voice of the Translator in Children's Literature', *Meta* 48(1–2) (2003): 197–207.

ACKNOWLEDGEMENTS

Taylor & Francis for permission to reprint Roderick McGillis, Extract from the 'Introduction' to *Voices of the Other: Children's Literature and the Postcolonial Context*, New York: Garland, 2000, pp. xix–xxviii.

ARIEL for permission to reprint Heather Scutter, 'Hunting for History: Children's Literature Outside, Over There, and Down Under', *ARIEL: A Review of International English Literature* 28(1) (January 1997): 21–36.

Yale University Press for permission to reprint Clare Bradford, 'The End of Empire? Colonial and Postcolonial Journeys in Children's Books', *Children's Literature* 29 (2001): 196–218. Copyright © 2001 Hollins University.

Cambridge University Press and Elizabeth Cook for permission to reprint Elizabeth Cook, 'Myths, Legends and Fairy Tales in the Lives of Children', in *The Ordinary and the Fabulous*, Cambridge: Cambridge University Press, 1976, pp. 1–9. © Cambridge University Press, reproduced with permission.

'Introduction' by Jack Zipes from *Spells of Enchantment*, edited by Jack Zipes, copyright © 1991 by Jack Zipes. Used by permission of Viking Penguin, a division of Penguin Group (USA) Inc.

Princeton University Press for permission to reprint Maria Tatar, 'Rewritten by Adults: The Inscription of Children's Literature', in *Off With Their Heads! Fairy Tales and the Culture of Childhood*, Princeton: Princeton University Press, 1992, pp. 3–21, 241–244. © 1992 Princeton University Press, 1993 paperback edition. Reprinted by permission of Princeton University Press.

Taylor & Francis for permission to reprint John Stephens and Robyn McCallum, 'Pre-Texts, Metanarratives, and the Western Metaethic', in *Retelling Stories, Framing Culture: Traditional Story and Metanarratives in Children's Literature*, New York: Garland, 1998, pp. 3–23.

Libreria Editrice Cafoscarina for permission to reprint Laura Tosi, 'Did They Live Happily Ever After? Rewriting Fairy Tales for a Contemporary Audience', *Hearts of Lightness: The Magic of Children's Literature*, Venice: Cafoscarina, 2001, pp. 101–124.

The Children's Literature Association for permission to reprint Claire Malarte-Feldman, 'Folk Materials, Re-Visions, and Narrative Images: The Intertextual Games They Play', *Children's Literature Association Quarterly* 28(4) (2003–2004): 210–19. Reprinted by permission of the Children's Literature Association.

Duke University Press for permission to reprint Jack Zipes, 'Political Children's Theater in the Age of Globalization', *Theater* 33(2) (2003): 3–25. Copyright, 2003, Yale School of Drama/Yale Repertory Theatre. All rights reserved. Used by permission of the publisher.

Springer Science and Business Media and Rosemary Ross Johnston for permission to reprint Rosemary Ross Johnston, 'Carnivals, the Carnivalesque, *The Magic Puddin*', and David Almond's *Wild Girl, Wild Boy*: Towards a Theorizing of Children's Plays', *Children's Literature in Education* 34(2) (June 2003): 131–146. With permission from Springer Science and Business Media.

Disclaimer

INTRODUCTION TO VOLUME IV

> It seems to me ... that notions of the 'universality of human experience' need to be handled with great care, since it may amount to no more than a matter of re-presenting the past in our own image.
>
> (Stephens 1992, p. 207)

Internationalism

The idea of a universal childhood and, as a corollary, a universal children's literature is essentially a romantic one, epitomised in Paul Hazard's *Les Livres, les enfants et les hommes* (1932). Hazard's idea that children can be the peace-making, world-uniting force for the future, and that their literature can provide understanding and reconciliation, is also, ultimately, behind a number of successful and entirely admirable international organisations such as IBBY (International Board on Books for the Young) and perhaps even, at the academic level, the IRSCL (International Research Society for Children's Literature). The assumed 'universality' of certain kinds of narratives – myths, legends and fairy tales – also suggests to some that children have shared interests and motivations across the world.

However, it might be argued that, in fact, concepts of childhood and of literature differ so radically from place to place, and the difficulties of meaning-making that are found between individuals or within local classrooms are so magnified internationally (and perhaps especially at conferences), that this idea is self-defeating. (Even the association of folk tales and fairy tales with childhood is highly questionable.) The raw facts of the interchange of books suggests, at best, a commercial homogenisation (see Chapter 66) and, at worst, a neo-colonialism (see Chapters 89–91). Thus, in terms of the written word, the world is dominated by a very few countries; the movement of books across borders is skewed – fewer than two percent of English-language children's books are translations, whereas in very many countries as many as eighty percent of children's books published are translations from English. This even applies in terms of content: 'around eighty percent of books for children set in non-European and non-American cultures are written by European and American authors' (O'Sullivan 2004, p. 20).

Nevertheless, internationalism and multiculturalism are potent ideological forces which Children's Literature studies have to take into account. For example, a multicultural project on war in European children's literature (Batho *et al.*, 1998) found that it was focusing on '*stereotypes, nostalgia, exclusion, Otherness, cultural domination, religious belief,* and, of course, *national identity*' (Fox 2001, p. 44) – all elements of immense importance for children and intercultural relationships. Equally, the power of 'orature' – oral performances (as opposed to 'literature') – discussed by Pellowski (Chapter 82) needs to be taken into account if the 'textual' experiences of child-readers across the world are to be studied adequately. This has hardly been addressed and, as Pellowski has pointed out, unusual international conditions need to be considered: 'And what of those hundreds of thousands of children separated from the physical aspects of their culture by wars, famine and other disasters?' as well as the thousands of minority languages which 'have speakers numbering in hundreds of thousands rather than millions; . . . each group has its own culture and its own distinct Orature. These minority groups are often ignored in professional writing . . .' (2004 Vol. II, pp. 868, 869) (see also Chapters 33, 57, 58)

Translation

Despite the relatively small number of translations into English, translation remains a major part of the dissemination of children's literature. However, there are several practical and theoretical problems (discussed in Chapters 86–88 and see also Chapters 28, 47, 97 and 98) that militate against translation as a road to an intercultural utopia. One is pointed out by Emer O'Sullivan:

> There is a paradox at the heart of translation of children's literature: it is commonly held that books are translated in order to enrich the children's literature of the target language and to introduce children to foreign cultures, yet at the same time that foreign element itself is often eradicated from translations which are heavily adapted to their target culture, allegedly on the grounds that young readers will not understand it.
>
> (2005, p. 74)

This problem is compounded by the commercial pressure for international co-productions that has led to many examples of bland pictorial styles and simplified texts.

Another reason is the suppression of individual styles:

> For a translator, the supreme authority should be the *author's personal style*. But most translators obey another authority: that of

the *conventional version* of 'good French' (or good German, good English, etc.). ... That is the error: every author of some value *transgresses* against 'good style', and in that transgression lies the originality (and hence the raison d'être) of his art.

(Milan Kundera, quoted in Chambers 2001, p. 125)

Colonialism/postcolonialism

Children's literature itself can be seen as a site of colonialism, in that the 'child' is both defined and very often silenced in texts (see Wall on the narrator's voice in Chapter 24). Equally, not only can texts for children never be ideologically neutral, but they have played (and play) an important and sometimes symbiotic part in the development of empires as disparate as those of the British, the Disney Company and the male (see Chapters 66 and 68). As Martin Green put it in *Dreams of Adventure, Deeds of Empire*:

> ... the adventure tales that formed the light reading of Englishmen for two hundred years and more after *Robinson Crusoe* were in fact, the energising myth of English imperialism.
>
> (1980, p. 3)

The literature is the myth, and the myth becomes the norm; in all cases the 'Other' is defined and dominated. As Jack Zipes observed, when discussing the colonisation of the children's book world by the 'Harry Potter' books:

> For anything to become a phenomenon in Western society, it must become *conventional*; it must be recognized and categorized as unusual, extraordinary, remarkable, and outstanding. In other words ... it must conform to the standards of exception set by the mass media and promoted by the culture industry in general. ... And if the phenomenon does somehow contain some qualities that are truly different, they are bound to be corroded and degraded, turning the phenomenon against itself and into a homogenized commodity. ... Difference and otherness are obliterated in the process.
>
> (2001, p. 175)

In the articles reprinted here, we can see the beginnings of a rehabilitation of the suppressed or invisible 'Other', in terms very similar to the rehabilitation of the gender-oppressed (see Le Guin in Chapter 70). This carries with it a danger of neo-colonialism, which may be illustrated by an exchange at an Australian children's literature conference in 1988. James

Moloney, a non-Aboriginal, who had written two books in which the narrator and characters were Aboriginals, posed the question: 'Should non-Aboriginal writers refrain from writing about Aboriginal characters'? He went on:

> It sounds like a fine idea, but I think the effect would be the opposite of that intended. . . . If a group of people are denied a voice . . . they quickly lose heart and then lose interest. I suspect that if *only black were allowed to write about black* non-Aborigines would see the books as black writing for black *alone* . . . a literary ghetto would form . . .'
>
> (Moloney, Lucashenko and Hutchins 1998, p. 80)

The response from Melissa Lucashenko, an Aboriginal, was very direct:

> Your history, our history, is not pretty. And so the cry comes up from white academics and white authors, oh, these stories must be told. And, yes, they do need to be told, but what non-indigenous people don't understand is that you cannot heal yourself through *more* theft and *more* appropriation. . . . Healing can and will occur. But the way to overcome our tragic history isn't by you stealing our indigenous voices. . . . [T]ime's getting on, but it's still not too late for you, the chained people, to learn to listen.
>
> (Moloney, Lucashenko and Hutchins 1998, p. 90)

Myths, folk tales and fairy tales

The inclusion of 'folk' materials under the umbrella of children's literature has been contentious, often on the grounds of content (see also Chapters 9, 28 and 63).

> On the face of it, there seems to be no logical reason why a group of texts of remarkable unpleasantness and crudity, dealing with physical – and very commonly sexual – violence, rape, incest, cannibalism, murder, let alone withdrawal of love, betrayal, loneliness and fear and the machinations of arbitrary and frequently malicious fate, should be placed firmly in the ambit of children.
>
> (Hunt 2001, p. 273)

As J. R. R. Tolkien put it:

> Actually, the association of children and fairy-stories is an accident of our domestic history. Fairy-stories have in the modern lettered

4

world been relegated to the 'nursery', as shabby or old-fashioned furniture is relegated to the play-room, primarily because the adults do not want it, and do not mind if it is misused. It is not the choice of the children which decides this. Children as a class – except in a common lack of experience they are not one – neither like fairy-stories more, nor understand them better than adults do; and no more than they like many other things. They are young and growing, and normally have keen appetites, so the fairy-stories as a rule go down well enough. But in fact only some children, and some adults, have any special taste for them; and when they have it, it is not exclusive, nor even necessarily dominant. It is a taste, too, that would not appear, I think, very early in childhood without artificial stimulus; it is certainly one that does not decrease but increases with age, if it is innate.

(1964, p. 34)

Even if there is a confusion of thought in linking contemporary childhood with the childhood of story, there is a positive element involved here, that of the passing on of both local and world heritage, and re-tellings of tales thrive in the children's book market.

Ultimately, the argument for the validity of non-realistic texts of all kinds may hinge on the perceived limitations of realism as opposed to the supposed freedoms offered by fantasy. G. K. Chesterton, famously, pointed out in an article that presages the ideas about childhood of Rose, Lesnik-Oberstein and others (Chapters 46, 49 and 52) that fantasy actually caters for adults who have lost a sense of wonder:

> . . . when we are very young children we do not need fairy tales: we need only takes. Mere life is interesting enough. A child of seven is excited by being told that Tommy opened a door and saw a dragon. But a child of three is excited by being told that Tommy opened a door.
>
> ('The Ethics of Elfland' (1908),
reprinted in Hunt 1990, pp. 31–32)

However, the prevailing wisdom on both folk tales and fantasy is provided by Terry Pratchett:

> So let's not get frightened when children read fantasy. It is the compost for a healthy mind. It stimulates the inquisitive nodes. It may not appear as 'relevant' as books set firmly in the child's environment, or whatever hell the writer believes to be the child's environment, but there is some evidence that a rich internal fantasy life is as good and necessary for a child as healthy soil is for

5

a plant, for much the same reasons. . . . Like the fairy tales that were its forebears, fantasy need no excuses.

(1993, p. 5)

Theatre

The two articles reprinted here demonstrate, once again, the links that Children's Literature inevitably forms between different genres, internationalism, politics and performance. They also demonstrate that children's theatre has been under-theorised – critics 'rightly recognising that a play is both a printed text and a performed event, the two elements making a whole that must be looked at integrally . . . [have] shied off from assessment and criticism (Chambers 1982, p. 7). That may well be why, as Hollindale has pointed out, 'drama will remain the Cinderella of children's literature, when it is arguably the most important children's art form of all, the one they are sure to live with, through the media of film and television, all their lives' (1996, p. 219).

Nevertheless, the twin elements of text and event appear in all children's interaction with text, and it is this mysterious interaction that all of Children's Literature theory and criticism ultimately addresses.

References

Batho, R., Leysen, A., De Wynck, A., Fox, C., Gutterez, R., and Fonselo, M., (eds) (1998) *War and Peace in Children's Books*, Leuven: University of Leuven.

Chambers, A. (1982) *Plays for Young People to Read and Perform*, South Woodchester: Thimble Press.

—— (2001) *Reading Talk*, South Woodchester: Thimble Press.

Fox, C. (2001) 'Conflicting Fictions: National Identity in Children's Literature About War', in M. Meek (ed.) *Children's Literature and National Identity*, Stoke on Trent: Trentham Books.

Green, M. (1980) *Dreams of Adventure, Deeds of Empire*, London: Routledge and Kegan Paul.

Hazard, P. (1932) *Les Livres, les enfants et les hommes*, Paris: Flammarion.

Hollindale, P. (1996) 'Drama', in P. Hunt (ed.) *International Companion Encyclopedia of Children's Literature*, London and New York: Routledge.

Hunt, P. (ed.) (1990) *Children's Literature: The Development of Criticism*, London: Routledge, pp. 28–32.

Hunt, P. (2001) *Children's Literature: A Guide*, Oxford: Blackwell.

Moloney, J., Lucashenko, M., and Hutchins, E. (1998) 'Whose Dreaming, Whose Story?', in S. van der Hoeven (ed.) *Time Will Tell: Children's Literature into the 21st Century*, Adelaide: Children's Book Council of Australia, pp. 86–92.

O'Sullivan, E. (2004) 'Internationalism, the Universal Child and the World of Children's Literature', in P. Hunt (ed.) *International Companion Encyclopedia of Children's Literature*, 2 edn, London and New York: Routledge.

—— (2005) *Comparative Children's Literature*, London and New York: Routledge.

Pellowski, A. (2004) 'Culture and Developing Countries', in P. Hunt (ed.) *International Companion Encyclopedia of Children's Literature*, 2 edn, London and New York: Routledge.

Pratchett, T. (1993) 'Let there be Dragons', *Books for Keeps* 83: 6–7.

Stephens, J. (1992) *Language and Ideology in Children's Fiction*, London: Longman.

Tolkien, J. R. R. (1964) *Tree and Leaf*, London: Allen and Unwin.

Zipes, J. (2001) *Sticks and Stones: The Troublesome Success of Children's Literature from Slovenly Peter to Harry Potter*, New York and London: Routledge.

Part 16

INTERNATIONALISM

STORY IN ORATURE
AND LITERATURE

Why and how we make it available
to children in different cultures

Anne Pellowski

Source: International Board on Books for Young People, *Proceedings, 25th Congress, 12–16 August 1996, Telling the Tale*, Amsterdam: Dutch Section of IBBY, 1997, pp. 81–86.

Some definitions of terms as I use them:

Education – any process by means of which human beings share or pass on knowledge, belief, information or experience to other human beings.

Pedagogy – the art or science of education in a setting designed specifically for education, such as a school.

Language play – the poetic use of language for the sole purpose of pleasure in word sounds and patterns, such as is found in many nursery rhymes, nonsense rhymes, game rhymes, tongue twisters, etc.

Story – an account of connected series of events, most often (but not always) in a linear order. Story can be factual, fictional or symbolic.

Enhanced information – information (often of a philosophical, moral or religious nature) conveyed by means of short bursts of symbolic, poetic or special language, such as is found in proverbs, sayings, riddles, etc.

Orature for children – oral passing on of story, enhanced information, and language play directed at children; does not include oral recitation or presentation of literature that has been learned chiefly by memorizing or adapting written works.

Literature for children – written (or otherwise recorded) stories, enhanced information, and language play directed at children.

Storytelling – oral performance of stories; these can be stories learned through the processes of orature or literature, or a combination of both.

11

From ancient times onwards, we have evidence that many cultures recognized the power of story. Here we will not go into many situations in which the telling of a story was deemed appropriate or effective or even necessary. These can be found described in the books cited in the first part of the bibliography accompanying this paper.

Let us just cite here a few instances in which storytelling for education are specifically mentioned. One recommendation that stands up to common pedagogical practice even today comes to us from the Greek historian Strabo. About 2,000 years ago he wrote:

> "Man is eager to learn and his fondness for tales is a prelude to this quality. It is fondness for tales, then, that induces children to give their attention to narratives and more and more to take part in them . . . myth is a new language that tells them not of things as they are, but of a different set of things. And what is new is pleasing . . . But if you add to this the marvellous and portentous, you thereby increase the pleasure, and pleasure acts as a charm to incite to learning."
>
> (Geography, Book 1, Part 2,8)

In India, probably in a similar era, the sage who wrote down the great story collection of the Panchatantra introduced it by saying that whether you learned the stories in it by heart, or listened to them from a storyteller, you would always be prepared for life, whatever it brought you. In other words, you would be educated, in the broadest sense.

More recently, Bensen Lewis of the Western Apache stated: "Stories go to work on you like arrows. Stories make you live right. Stories make you replace yourself." (Quoted in Pellowski, 1990, p. 223)

Although there is general agreement that story is universal and powerful, there seems to be less agreement on the meaning of story, its forms, its contexts, its uses. There are those who would insist on the primacy of the playful or recreative effect of story; others would insist that it is the moral or psychological impact it has on reader or viewer or listener that is all-important; still others might express the belief that it is only through story that we learn the contexts of language that enable us to fully communicate with other human beings.

I have cited in Part 2 of the bibliography a few of the works of some theorists on story, but I would like to call attention specifically to one of them, and that is Roger Schank. Sometimes it is illuminating to go outside one's own field to get a new perspective and the literature specialist will certainly get that from Schank, who is a specialist in the field of computers and artificial intelligence. In his book *Tell me a story*, Schank comes right out and says: Knowledge is stories. Intelligence, he believes, is characterized by the ability to get reminded, and the way humans do this best is through story: encountering it, manipulating it, comprehending it, explaining it, communicating it, etc. According to Schank, in much of modern media, "...some of the individuality of that storytelling and receiving process has been lost. We wind up believing the same stories."

Whether we agree or disagree with Schank, or with any others who have speculated on the central meaning and role of story, chances are we all have a common-sense definition of story, at least insofar as it is used in our own culture. We here are all professionals involved in some way with bringing story to children through print media.

So we come to some key questions to be asked and discussed at this Congress:

1) What are the differences between orally composed and written stories?
2) What are the differences (in story itself, in story giver and Story taker) when stories are passed on through orature, when they are told but from written literature, when they are read aloud, when they are read privately?
3) How much does the context (i.e. where and why and how a story is heard, read, seen or experienced) affect perception of the content and meaning of story?
4) Does a wide experience of hearing story affect a person's ability to read and write story and conversely, does the very fact of knowing how to read and write affect a person's attitude to story?
5) Should storytelling be used in pedagogy mostly as an adjunct or lead-in to reading, or should it have its own place in the curriculum, with its own rationale?

To answer question No. 1, we can most emphatically say that there is a difference in the way stories are composed orally and in written form. In my personal telling and writing down of many stories, I have not examined too closely the differences in the two processes, but I have recognized that they are different. Richard Adams has given us a detailed explanation of the processes he used in first telling *Watership down*, over an extended period of time, and then writing it down in book form. Virtually everything he reveals about the two processes corresponds with what scholars have discovered about the orally composed and written sections of such world literature as the Bible, the Iliad and Odyssey, the Ramayana, Grimm's *Märchen*, etc.

Some of these differences are: in the composed-in-telling story there are more repetitive phrases, more rhythmic and onomatopoeic language, more borrowing of plots from already-known stories but putting the borrowed plots and sub-plots into new contexts; in the composed-in-writing story there are more characters, more lengthy descriptions of places and characters, more uses of authentic background information, more conscious attempts to use "poetic" or "literary" language.

In numerous workshops, I have observed the telling of a story, and then, the writing-down and crafting of hand-made picture books of that story. The most dramatic occasion occurred in Venezuela, when I was fortunate enough to be part of the process when Eloina Rossi told her story and then attempted to write it and illustrate it in this cloth picture book, in the Pemon language (first slide). This language is relatively new in its written form, and there is still some disagreement among its speakers as to the "correct" way to write it. Eloina told this story to the linguistics adviser present and to me, first in Pemon and then in a somewhat hesitant Spanish. I will translate these words as best I can, but I have to tell you that I don't believe I can bring to the translation half of the feeling of Eloina's voice as she told it.

It was very obvious that her story meant a great deal to her. She wrote down her first version, corrected it with the linguist, and then prepared her cloth pages with great care, crafting the pictures by using a collage method. But before she could write on the pages the version of the text she had crafted, she was asked by the group (all Pemon speakers) to read aloud her story. There was great discussion and disagreement as to what her story meant. While all were familiar with the story, her poetic vision of it did not satisfy many in the group. They kept asking: "What do you mean by that?" or "Why do you use that word? That is not the right word". It was a very difficult process.

Since this was to be a book for children, and there were some children available, the story text was tested out with them, and they seemed to have little problem with it. But that may well have been because of the beauty and unusual look of the pictures. Pemon children have seen attractive books in Spanish, but, until that workshop, there was not a single children's picture book in their own language.

The end result was that Eloina was asked to make a few changes to the text, to correspond with commonly accepted forms of written Pemon, and then she printed out her text, as I have shown you. I find the book quite beautiful and meaningful, by what some would call "universal" standards. Yet I must admit that some in the Pemon group did not agree.

To get back to further answers to question 2, there are a number of empirical studies that show how differently children respond to told stories, read-aloud stories, silently read stories, stories viewed on a moving picture screen. Khare's dissertation (1992) contrasts the effects of told and read-aloud stories on a fairly small sample of children, but her bibliography cites a number of other studies that could not be listed here due to space constraints. Some of the studies listed in Part 6 of the Bibliography also examined the different responses children have to various ways of presenting story. Smardo and Curry (1982) were among the first to observe the effects of live storytelling, and film and video storytelling, on several groups of pre-school children. Young (1988) tested for listening skills by using live storytelling, a person who read aloud the story, and the same story told on video, and found that listening was most affected by the live storytelling.

But these are only the very beginning stages of such research. Few attempts have been made to replicate any of the studies with larger groups of children. Furthermore, there is disagreement as to what the term "storytelling" means. Many researchers have used it to mean the reading aloud or writing of a story. In some cases, research attempting to document the capacity of children to absorb, understand or retell stories involved reading aloud of the story on the part of the teacher/researcher, but required the child to tell the story without benefit of book or pictures.

Storytelling ability and responses to story among children who live in a culture that still uses mostly orature in the home, but who attend schools where story is presented almost exclusively through print literature, are described only for a few cultural groups. Among the few studies I located were Brady (1984) and Scollon and Scollon (1984).

Question 3, the way in which context affects the telling of a tale, is one of the points we should look at most intently in this congress, because I feel that it comes close to the heart of what Jella Lepman, the founder of IBBY, was getting at when she first introduced the concept of "international understanding through children's books." It is true that we have many translated stories crossing many borders, but has this brought children closer to any real understanding of other children who are different from them? Sometimes, yes, but often, apparently not.

I believe that those of us from countries with large and powerful publishing groups have not been particularly mindful of the content and context of stories. We have, for the most part, taken over the stories, and often changed them just enough so that they fit into our cultural values. This is nothing new. Dominant cultures have been usurping and changing stories for more than two thousand years. But we now have more knowledge and experience of the ways in which cultures can communicate. It should be possible, even in telling the tale to children, to give more of its original cultural context, especially in a pedagogical setting. To give some specific examples: 86

a) Among the folklore from African cultures now available in European, American or Asian versions for children, where are those that capture the stories as they are used in orature: the ebullience, the rhythm and musicality, the give-and-take, the mystery, the ambiguity? Harder yet is it to find examples of books that show the symbolic use of language as practiced so skillfully by African children in their orature, especially in their riddling.

b) Histories of literature, and of the book, are so often slanted to a European point of view that our teachers and librarians have little knowledge of other early forms of literature and books. Yet many of them are passing on stories that come from those earliest eras of writing in other cultures. I find I cannot tell even the simplest of stories from Hindu or Buddhist sources (e.g. *The Blind Men and the Elephant, The Monkey and the Crocodile,* etc.) without first showing examples of storytelling cloths or palm leaf picture books, such as these which were so important in keeping alive those stories. (show slides or actual items)

c) Stories that show changes in social history at the child level are quite fascinating, but they are very hard to locate and for some reason, teachers are reluctant to use them, perhaps because they seem so ephemeral or entertaining. I am truly grateful to one of you here in our host country, namely Cecile Bejk van Daal, of Eindhoven (and her aunt, too) for giving me some of my best clues to handkerchief stories, those funny little tales, with figures, that were meant to get the young European child of past centuries interested in always having a handkerchief in the pocket.

Because Rabbit is our symbol here at the Congress, I can't resist telling you the short handkerchief story of the Rabbit. (The drawings of the folded handkerchief have not been reproduced here).

If you go, not far from here, you would find a little hill, If you dig and dig, and dig, you would find a warm little den. If you look inside that den you would find a dear, sweet, soft, little, white, rabbit, with his two ears sticking up. Now, he is not an ordinary rabbit. Oh, no! He is a pocket rabbit. Every day he comes hopping out of his den, looking for a pocket to spend the day in. When he finds a young gentleman with a pocket, hop, there he jumps in, staying there all day, with his ears sticking out. Every day, he searched out a new pocket. Until one day, the young lady had to sneeze. So she pulled Rabbit out by the ears and "Ka-choo!" she had her handkerchief ready.

Another type I might mention are the *ekaki uta* of Japanese children, little drawing stories that are always accompanied by a kind of chant. As Koizumi (1986) states, these little drawing story chants can give quite a few clues to the changes in Japanese society over the past one hundred years, but at the same time they are pure fun for children.

I find such stories can create a deep sense of intimacy that is full of social meaning. It offends me when adults call such stories merely "cute".

Responses to Question 4: Hearing many stories told or read aloud, and becoming more and more adept at oral language, does affect the child's ability and interests in reading. More than thirty years ago, Loban (1963) made a very direct connection between these activities. Other researchers have found the same results, but the point was expanded much further by Sutton-Smith (1981), Paley (1990), Schu (1993) and others. To paraphrase Sutton-Smith: If you keep asking children to make up stories for you, and show interest in their stories by coming back again and again to ask for more stories, their stories will get better and better, and furthermore, they progress from wanting to tell those stories to wanting to write them down, to wanting to read more stories, or have more read to them.

Some answers to Question 5: As mentioned before, storytelling for general education purposes (passing on of culture) is widely accepted. Storytelling in pedagogy is not, although this is changing. One project that is attempting to transfer the values of orature storytelling, to storytelling in pedagogy, is that being carried out by Wajuppa Tossa in Thailand, among the Isan culture group. She writes: "The integral vibrancy of traditional Isan language and culture is in danger of fading entirely . . . This project is aimed at countering this . . ." (Tossa and MacDonald, 1995).

Many of the North American and European educators who have written about the reasons for including storytelling as a part of the school curriculum justify it as a means of getting children to read better, or with more interest. It is rare to find teachers who advocate making storytelling the core method of teaching, as described by Egan (1989) and Paley (1990).

In a recent survey in the state of Minnesota (Hanson, 1994) it was found that the persons doing the most storytelling in a school setting were the librarians (or media specialists), not the teachers. And the amount of storytelling dropped dramatically for the levels of junior and senior high school. A few schools could afford to bring in storytelling specialists for a day or a week. Based on my experience in doing such work in schools throughout North America, this is a common pattern. I have also observed similar situations in Australia, France and Germany.

There are some documented cases of years of work by storyteller/teachers who have told stories to children, trained children to tell stories, and led clubs of young storytellers who went out into the community to tell stories, as well as telling them to other classes in school. Two notable examples of such long-term storyteller/teachers are Larry Johnson at Pillsbury School in Minneapolis, Minnesota and Robert Rubinstein of Roosevelt Middle School in Eugene, Oregon (Pellowski, 1995).

A few school systems, notably the New York City Public Schools, and the Department of Defense Schools, have had storytelling contests or festivals for many years, in which well over 50,000 children participate annually. In most cases, the storytelling "adviser" to these children is the school librarian.

Which leads to two final questions, in addition to the ones posed above: First, if certain stories (especially myths) have had such power in the past, why have many of them died out or lost their core meaning? Is that truly the result of the human's need to search constantly for new myths and stories, or is it because we lose our capacity to tell or write or depict them in effective ways? In other words, is the method of presentation of the story as important as the content and meaning of the story, in terms of keeping it alive?

Secondly if storytelling is so powerful in its effect, and if so many educators and researchers have attested to its value, why do so few parents and teachers use it? From the comments of those who have participated in my courses and workshops in North America and Europe, it would seem that a chief stumbling block is fear. Fear of not being able to do as well at telling as at reading aloud, fear of not remembering, fear of the large amount of time they believe is needed in order to learn a story, fear (mostly by teachers) that by spending time storytelling, they will not be covering "facts" or "competencies" that children will be asked for on state tests.

But storytelling is also not used much by teachers in many African, Asian and Latin American countries, where community or home storytelling is still remembered by many as having been a chief means of entertainment and education. Yet in many of those communities, although children's books have not arrived yet in great numbers, families have given up on oral storytelling, so the child gets neither orature nor literature. We have to examine why this is so, and find out more of what can be done to change it. We look forward with great interest to the result of Tossa and MacDonald's project in Thailand. Perhaps there are others here at the Congress who can tell of similar projects in other countries.

To summarize what can be culled from all experts:

a) Children have the need to experience orature and orally performed literature; to have literature read to them, and have access to orature and literature that can be read or viewed by them in some way.

b) Children have the need to tell stories and recite playful language from orature and literature, to write stories and poems, and to make books or other media that encase their writings in a culturally meaningful way.

c) Those involved in the education of children need to increase their use of oral storytelling, at all age levels, and in all subject areas.

d) The first stories we share with children should be those common to their culture; soon after being introduced to those stories, children need to hear stories that are from other cultures, along with bits and pieces of the cultural contexts of those stories. Gradually, the complexity of the cultural contexts can be increased.

My personal recommendation will simply be added to that of Aidan Chambers. Once a week, that time set aside for reading aloud should be given over to storytelling–by the teachers and librarians, and by the children and young people.

Many talk of saving habitat for plants and animals, so that we continue to have diversity of life. I feel we must also work to save the intellectual, cultural and social habitat of all the world's children. We must pay special attention to children who come from minority language cultures. The best way to do this is by telling their stories in the many unique ways they express them.

Selective international bibliography

1. History of storytelling

Alvey, Richard Gerald (1974) THE HISTORICAL DEVELOPMENT OF ORGANIZED STORYTELLING TO CHILDREN IN THE UNITED STATES, Philadelphia: University of Pennsylvania (Doctoral dissertation).

Bolte, Johannes and Georg Polivka (1913–1932) ANMERKUNGEN ZU DEN KINDER- UND HAUSMARCHEN DER BRUDER GRIMM, Leipzig: Dieterich.

Mair, Victor H. (1988) PAINTING AND PERFORMANCE; CHINESE PICTURE RECITATION AND ITS INDIAN GENESIS, Honolulu: University of Hawaii.

OP DE STROOM VAN DE RIVIER (1989) ed. by Wendy de Graaff and others, The Hague, Nederlands Bibliotheek en Lektuur Centrum.

Pellowski, Anne (1990) THE WORLD OF STORYTELLING, rev. ed., New York: H. W. Wilson.

Putra Yadna, I. B. and Murti Bunanta (1995) "Mesatua and the Fate of Storytelling in Bali," in BOOKBIRD, Vol, 33, No. 2, pp. 23–27.

See also Jean (1981) in Part 2, below.

2. Philosophy or psychology of story and its role in education

Applebee, Arthur (1978) THE CHILD'S CONCEPT OF STORY, Chicago, University of Chicago Press.

Bettelheim, Bruno (1976) THE USES OF ENCHANTMENT, New York: Knopf (also available in many translations).

Buhler, Charlotte and Josephine Bilz (1958) DAS MARCHEN UND DIE PHANTASIE DES KINDES, Munchen: J. A. Barth.

Coles, Robert (1989) THE CALL OF STORIES: TEACHING AND THE MORAL IMAGINATION, Boston: Houghton Mifflin.

Egan, Kieran (1989) TEACHING AS STORYTELLING, Chicago: University of Chicago Press.

Jean, Georges (1981) LE POUVOIR DES CONTES, Paris, Castermann.

Maranda, Elli Kongas and Pierre Maranda (1971) STRUCTURAL MODELS IN FOLKLORE AND TRANSFORMATIONAL ESSAYS, The Hague: Mouton.

Propp, Vladimir (1928) MORFOLOGIIA SKAZKI, Leningrad: Academia (also available in many translations).

Rodari, Gianni (1973) GRAMMATICA DELLA FANTASIA: INTRODUZIONE ALL' ARTE DI INVENTARE STORIE, Torino: Einaudi (American edition, New York: Teachers and Writers Collaborative, 1996).

Rooth, Anna Birgitta (1976) THE IMPORTANCE OF STORYTELLING: A STUDY BASED ON FIELD WORK IN NORTHERN ALASKA, Stockholm & Uppsala: Almquist & Wiksell International.

Schank, Roger C. (1990) TELL ME A STORY; A NEW LOOK AT REAL AND ARTIFICIAL MEMORY, New York: Scribner's.

3. Differences between storytelling and story writing or storytelling and story reading

Adams, Richard (1989) "To the Order of Two Little Girls: The Oral and Written Versions of Watership Down," pp. 115–122 in THE VOICE OF THE NARRATOR IN CHILDREN'S LITERATURE, ed. by Charlotte F. Otten and Gary D. Schmidt, Westport, Connecticut: Greenwood Press.

Gerbracht, Gloria Jean (1994) THE EFFECT OF STORYTELLING ON THE NARRATIVE WRITING OF THIRD-GRADE STUDENTS, Doctoral dissertation, Indiana University of Pennsylvania.

Khare, Pratibha (1992) EFFECTS OF ORAL VERSUS READ STORIES ON CHILDREN'S CREATIVITY AND SENSE OF STORY STRUCTURE, Doctoral dissertation, University of Alabama.

Ong, Walter J. (1982) ORALITY AND LITERACY: THE TECHNOLOGIZING OF THE WORD, New York and London: Methuen.

Smith, William Ward (1991) THE EFFECTS OF STORY PRESENTATION STRATEGIES ON STORY RECALL AND UNDERSTANDING OF 4TH GRADERS WITH DIFFERENT INFORMATION PROCESSING STYLES, Doctoral dissertation, United States International University.

See also Cooper (1993) in Part 5; also Smardo and Curry (1982) and Young (1988) in Part 6.

4. Reasons for inclusion of storytelling in pedagogy

Cooper, Pamela J. and Rives Collins (1992) LOOK WHAT HAPPENED TO FROG; STORYTELLING IN EDUCATION, Scottsdale, Az: Gorsuch Scarisbrick.

Frommer, Harald (1992) ERZAHLEN: EINE DIDAKTIK FUR DIE SEKUNDARSTUFE I UND II, Frankfurt am Main: Cornelson Scriptor.

Jones, Anthony and June Buttrey (1970) CHILDREN AND STORIES, Oxford: Blackwell.

Loban, Walter (1963) THE LANGUAGE OF ELEMENTARY SCHOOL CHILDREN, Urbana, Illinois: National Council of Teachers of English.

Masaki Ruriko (1987) GENDAI NI OKERU OHANASHI, Tokyo: Jido Toshokan Kenkyukai.

Roney, R. Craig (1996) "Storytelling in the Classroom: some theoretical thoughts," STORYTELLING WORLD, No. 9, p. 8.

—— (1993) "Telling Stories: A Key to Reading and Writing," pp. 9–25 in ONCE UPON A FOLKTALE ed. by Gloria Blatt, New York: Teachers College Press.

See also OP DE STROOM VAN DE RIVIER in Part 1 above; Jean (1981) and Rooth (1976) in Part 2; and Cooper (1993), Maguire (1985), Mallan (1991) Morgan and Rinvolucri (1984) in Parts 5 and 8, below.

5. *Storytelling in education: anecdotal summaries or studies*

Calame-Griaule, Genevieve, ed. (1991) LE RENOUVEAU DU CONTE, Paris: Centre National de la Recherche Scientifique.

Cooper, Patty (1993) WHEN STORIES COME TO SCHOOL: TELLING, WRITING, AND PERFORMING STORIES IN THE EARLY CHILDHOOD CLASSROOM. New York: Teachers and Writers Collaborative.

GIVE A LISTEN: STORIES OF STORYTELLING IN SCHOOL (1994) ed. by Ann M. Trousdale, Sue A. Woestehoff and Marni Schwartz, Urbana: National Council of Teachers of English.

Klotz, Renate (1993) DAS MARCHEN KOMMT: ERLEBNISSE UND ERINNERUNGEN EINER MARCHENERZAHLERIN, Regensburg: Roth.

Levy, Jette Lundbo (1968) HANS I VADESTOVLERNE; EN STUDIE I MUNDTLIG FORTELLETEKNIK, Kobenhavn: Akademisk Forlag.

OHANASHI: OTONA KARA KODOMOE; KODOMO KARA OTONAE (1994), edited by Tokyo Children's Library, Tokyo: Japan Editor School.

Paley, Vivian Gussin (1990) THE BOY WHO WOULD BE A HELICOPTER; THE USES OF STORYTELLING IN THE CLASSROOM, Cambridge: Harvard University Press.

Tossa, Wajuppa and Margaret Read Macdonald (1995) "Storytelling: A Means of Conserving a Dying Language and Culture." Manuscript description of a collaborative research project in Thailand (ongoing).

6. *Storytelling in pedagogy: empirical or statistical studies*

Amoriggi, Helen D. (1981) THE EFFECT OF STORYTELLING ON YOUNG CHILDREN'S SEQUENCING ABILITY. Dissertation, Boston University.

Farrell, Catherine Horne and Denise D. Nessel (1982) EFFECTS OF STORY-TELLING, AN ANCIENT ART FOR MODERN CLASSROOMS, San Francisco: Zellerbach Family Fund and San Francisco Education Fund.

Gerbracht, Gloria Jean (1994) THE EFFECT OF STORYTELLING ON THE NARRATIVE WRITING OF THIRD-GRADE STUDENTS. Doctoral dissertation, Indiana University of Pennsylvania.

Godbole, Anil (1990) STORYTELLING; A WAY FOR DEVELOPING THE CHILD'S PERSONALITY. Doctoral Dissertation, Poona University, India.

Haggberg, Susan Marie (1977) A STUDY OF THE USE OF STORYTELLING IN MINNESOTA PUBLIC ELEMENTARY SCHOOL MEDIA PROGRAMS, Master's thesis, St. Cloud State University.

Hanson, Anne Margaret (1994) ORAL STORYTELLING INSTRUCTION IN MINNESOTA ELEMENTARY SCHOOLS, Master's thesis, Mankato State University.

Jenkins, Jane (1994) USING THE ART OF STORYTELLING TO ENRICH WHOLE LANGUAGE LITERATURE-BASED READING. Dissertation, St. Louis University.

Marchisio, Linda (1983) MOVEMENT ASSISTED STORYTELLING AND READING MOTIVATION, Masters Essay, Wesleyan University, Middletown, Connecticut.

Oscarsson, Kristen (1992) HAITIAN FOLKTALES AS A LITERACY STRATEGY FOR ELEMENTARY HAITIAN ESOL STUDENTS. Fort Lauderdale, Florida, Doctoral dissertation, Nova University.

Smardo, Frances A. and John F. Curry (1982) WHAT RESEARCH TELLS US ABOUT STORY HOURS AND RECEPTIVE LANGUAGE. Dallas: Dallas Public Library.

Young, Yvonne (1988) THE EFFECTS OF STORYTELLING ON CHILDREN'S LISTENING SKILLS, Master's Thesis, University of Oregon.

7. Orature and storytelling by children (its importance; when, why, and how it evolves)

Brady, Margaret K. (1984) "SOME KIND OF POWER." NAVAJO CHILDREN'S SKINWALKER NARRATIVES, Salt Lake City, University of Utah Press.

Chukovsky, Kornei (1925) MALEN'KIE DETI, Moscow (revised and reissued in many editions under title OT DVUKH DO PIATI; English translation: FROM TWO TO FIVE; many other translations available.)

Engel, Susan (1995) THE STORIES CHILDREN TELL: MAKING SENSE OF THE NARRATIVES OF CHILDHOOD, New York: W. H. Freeman.

Koizumi, Fumio (1986) KODOMO NO ASOBI TO UTA, Tokyo, Soshisha. (Children's rhymes and drawing story chants)

Loban, Walter (1963) THE LANGUAGE OF ELEMENTARY SCHOOL CHILDREN, Urbana, Illinois: National Council of Teachers of English.

Magee, Mary Ann and Brian Sutton-Smith (1983) "The Art of Storytelling: How Do Children Learn It?" In: YOUNG CHILDREN, May issue, pp. 4–12.

Pitcher, Evelyn Goodenough and Ernst Prelinger (1963) CHILDREN TELL STORIES; AN ANALYSIS OF FANTASY, New York: International Universities Press.

Schu, Josef (1993) KINDER ALS ERZAHLER, ERWACHSENE ALS ZUHORER, Frankfurt am Main: Lang.

Scollon, Ron and Suzanne B. K. Scollon (1984) "Cooking It Up and Boiling It Down; Abstracts in Athabaskan Children's Story Retellings," in COHERENCE IN SPOKEN AND WRITTEN DISCOURSE ed. by Deborah Tannen, Norwood, N. J.: Ablex.

Stocklin-Meier, Susanne (1975) SPIELEN UND SPRECHEN, Zurich, Orell Fussli Verlag.

Sutton-Smith, Brian et al. (1976) THE ENCULTURATION OF THE IMAGINATIVE PROCESS BETWEEN THE AGES OF FIVE TO SEVEN YEARS AND THE EFFECT UPON CLASSROOM ACTIVITY, Washington, National Institute of Education (available as ERIC document ED 140945).

Sutton-Smith, Brian (1981) THE FOLKSTORIES OF CHILDREN. Philadelphia: University of Pennsylvania Press.

Wellhousen, Karyn (1993) "Eliciting and Examining Young Children's Storytelling," in JOURNAL OF RESEARCH IN CHILDHOOD EDUCATION, Vol. 7, No. 2, pp. 62–66.

8. Storytelling to and by children: guides and manuals for use by teachers, librarians, other educators

Barton, Bob (1990) STORIES IN THE CLASSROOM: STORYTELLING, READING ALOUD AND ROLEPLAYING WITH CHILDREN, Markham, Ontario: Pembroke.

Bauer, Carolyn Feller (1993) NEW HANDBOOK FOR STORYTELLERS, Chicago: American Library Association.

Bryant, Sarah Cone (1980 reprint of 1924 edition) HOW TO TELL STORIES TO CHILDREN, New York, Gordon Press. (available in many translations)

de Vos, Gail (1991) STORYTELLING FOR YOUNG ADULTS: TECHNIQUES AND TREASURY, Littleton, Colorado: Libraries Unlimited.

Ewers, Hans-Heino (1992) KINDLICHES ERZAHLEN, ERZAHLEN FUR KINDER, Basel: Beltz (in cooperation with Arbeitsgemeinschaft Kinder-und Jugendliteraturforschung).

Greene, Ellin (1996) STORYTELLING ART AND TECHNIQUE, 3rd ed., New York, R. R. Bowker.

Hamilton, Martha and Mitch Weiss (1990) CHILDREN TELL STORIES: A TEACHING GUIDE, Katonah, N. Y.: Richard C. Owen.

Hoff, Helga (1989) MARCHEN ERZAHLEN UND MARCHEN SPIELEN; MEHR LEBENSFREUDE FUR KINDER UND ERZIEHER, Freiberg, Basel, Vienna: Herder.

Livo, Norma and Sandra A. Reitz (1986) STORYTELLING – PROCESS AND PRACTICE, Littleton, Colorado: Libraries Unlimited.

MacDonald, Margaret Read (1993) THE STORYTELLER'S START-UP BOOK, Little Rock, Arkansas: August House.

—— (1986) TWENTY TELLABLE TALES, New York, H. W. Wilson Co.

Maguire, Jack (1985) CREATIVE STORYTELLING: CHOOSING, INVENTING AND SHARING TALES FOR CHILDREN, New York: McGraw Hill.

Mallan, Kerry (1991) CHILDREN AS STORYTELLERS, Primary English Teaching Association, Laura St., Newtown NSW 2042, Australia.

Matsuoka, Kyoko (1994) TANOSHII OHANASHI, 2 vols. Tokyo: Japan Editor School.

Merkel, Johannes and Michael Nagel (1982) ERZAHLEN; EIN HANDBUCH, Reinbek: Rowohlt.

Morgan, John and Mario Rinvolucri (1984) ONCE UPON A TIME; USING STORIES IN THE LANGUAGE CLASSROOM, Cambridge University Press.

Sawyer, Ruth (1977) THE WAY OF THE STORYTELLER, rev. ed., New York: Viking Penguin.

Zipes, Jack (1995) CREATIVE STORYTELLING, New York: Routledge.

See also OP DE STROOM VAN DE RIVIER (1989) in Part 1; Cooper and Collins (1992), Frommer (1992), Jones and Buttrey (1970) in Part 4; OHANASHI (1994) in Part 5.

9. Guides and manuals for use by children

JUNIOR STORYTELLER; A NEWSLETTER FOR YOUNG STORYTELLERS (Fall 1994 to present), Quarterly, Storycraft Publishing P. O. Box 205, Masonville, Co, 80451-0205.

Pellowski, Anne (1995) THE STORYTELLING HANDBOOK; A YOUNG PEOPLE'S COLLECTION OF UNUSUAL TALES AND HELPFUL HINTS ON HOW TO TELL THEM. New York, Simon and Schuster.

10. Storytelling periodicals

STORYTELLING MAGAZINE, monthly, National Storytelling Association (formerly NAPPS), P. O. Box 309, Jonesborough, TN 37659.

STORYTELLING WORLD, quarterly, East Tennessee State University, Box 70647, Johnson City, TN 37614.

My thanks to the following persons who gave me specific information on some titles to be included in the bibliography: Erika V. Engelbrechten, Yumiko Fukumoto, Flora Joy, Margaret Read Macdonald, Ruth Stotter, Joke Thiel, Shigeo Watanabe.

THE RIGHT OF THE CHILD TO INFORMATION AND ITS PRACTICAL IMPACT ON CHILDREN'S LIBRARIES

Marian Koren

Source: *The New Review of Children's Literature and Librarianship* 4 (1998): 1–16.

Rights of the child

It took mankind a long time to accept that human rights apply to all human beings without exception. This means a universal understanding that 'the basis which unites us all as citizens of one community can be nothing else than respect for the human being as such. Without that basis a society or a real human community is excluded.'[1] The UN Declaration, of which we celebrate the 50th anniversary this year, emphasises as a final basis for all law and justice, the inherent human dignity and the inalienable rights which every human being possesses by nature.

Article 1
All human beings are born free and equal in dignity and rights. They are endowed with reason and conscience and should act towards one another in a spirit of brotherhood.

'Children's rights are an integral part of human rights. The whole human rights programme of the United Nations is of direct relevance to children inasmuch as the ultimate aim of the programme is the well-being of every individual person in national as well as international society. But even more, the whole human rights endeavour may be said to be built on the foundation of care and love for children and respect for their rights. The special place of children in society is recognised in the Universal Declaration of Human Rights and pervades the whole framework of international human rights standards.'[2]

Childhood

The idea that children have rights is of relatively recent origin and related to the concept of childhood and the notion of a child. 'The question: What is a child? is one answered by adults. Adults impose their conceptions of childishness on beings they consider to be children. There have been different conceptions of the nature of childhood at different periods of history. Childhood is a social construct, a man-made phenomenon.'[3]

In general, children have been silenced in history because they have an insignificant position in social life. In a world, which is dominated by the interests of adults, who also have the power to define, children are considered to *become* autonomous, not to *be* autonomous.

Children have human rights, and they do not have to deserve them, they do not need to be given rights.[4] 'The fact that children are not yet grown up is used as an excuse by parents, social workers, teachers, judges and many other adults to follow their own interpretation of the child's interest and to set demands and make decisions that may have far-reaching consequences for children which no one can foresee. (. . .) Why are adults, who are in a much stronger position in many respects, so afraid to take children seriously and to grant them a large degree of autonomy?'[5]

The child has to be regarded as an individual with rights of his own as a human being. Due to his situation, he also needs rights for protection and to guarantee access to services. Legal protection includes having rights and being informed about them; having the possibility to exercise these rights effectively; protecting one's interests; and, eventually being able to enforce these rights.

Convention on the rights of the child

During the International Year of the Child, 1979, an Open-Ended Working Group was set up on the Question of a Convention on the Rights of the Child. The drafting process took ten years and ended in a UN Convention on the Rights of the Child, adopted unanimously on 20 November 1989.[6] All states in the world (191) have ratified the Convention with the exception of the USA and Somalia. So one can really speak of an international standard.

The right to self-determination stating that children have the right to express their views freely in all matters affecting them, and must be heard in any judicial and administrative proceeding affecting them (article 12) is crucial, as it contains a general principle characteristic of the underlying approach of the Convention: 'that children are not only objects but also subjects of rights, and that a determination of the child's best interests should be based not only on what adults think, but also on what the child thinks.'[7] Evidence is given that in the field of children's rights there are not only obligations for the state, parents and other adults, but also possibilities, and opportunities for children to participate in daily life and at least have a say in their own lives. This points to a child's right to information, which will be considered in more detail.

Right to information

The study of the child's developmental process reveals that information plays an indispensable role. In essence, the child is an information seeker. Information affects the physical, emotional, cognitive and social development of the child and this fact has far-reaching implications for the child's providers of information. It is important that all children have access to information and can benefit from such information processes, regardless of the place and time in which they live. Are children legally protected while they grow up, seek information and develop as human beings? As this question regards *all* children, an international approach is useful.[8]

In tracing a right to information in the Convention on the Rights of the Child, explicit formulations are found in the child's right to freedom of expression (article 13) and his right of access to information (article 17). The latter refers to the role of the mass media in providing information and material from a variety of sources. Implicit formulations of the right to information provide a wider spectrum. They refer to the role of information in the process of upbringing by parents, the development of the child's personality; his freedom to express views in all matters concerning his life; the freedom of thought, conscience and religion; and, the respect for his private life. Other implicit formulations are related to the child's right to information which supports his social participation, such as his freedom of association; the possibilities of the child to participate in cultural life; his access to education; and, his right to know about his rights.

A closer look at the right to information in its most explicit formulations is interesting for librarians because the articles reveal the approach, which has been intended by the drafters of the Convention. Not only States but especially NGOs have contributed a lot to the final version. The actual formulation of article 17 was mainly proposed by the Bahá'í Community, a NGO that promotes international understanding, world citizenship and stresses the importance of this education and supports the work of the United Nations. In a commentary the positive task of the mass media was stressed to convey appropriate information; to support educational programmes; to promote the cultural heritage of the child and to inform the child of the wider world of which he is part.[9] As the provision of information is related to an educational aim, another proposal (article 29) was put forward by Bahá'í as well. Bahá'í considers education as the most important means of improving the human condition, of safeguarding human rights and of establishing peace and justice on earth. But such education 'cannot simply be academic education, or book-learning. The kind of education that is required is education of the character. It is not sufficient, for example simply to tell the child that he has a duty to respect human rights. What is required is guidance and training that will develop in the child qualities that are indispensable if the child is to become a promoter and protector of human rights.'[10]

In this way it is clear that access to information has especially to be provided in view of the educational potential and the understanding of human values protected in human rights.

Children's books

The double provision of article 17, to encourage the positive effects of information, and to protect the child from negative effects, points to the responsibility of all those working in the field of the mass media and providing information and material to children. These include of course, all concerned with the production and dissemination of children's books, as is explicitly mentioned in the Convention.

The IBBY (International Board on Books for the Young) representatives to UNICEF strongly advocated the inclusion of children's right to have access to books in the Convention, and proposed a new subparagraph: 'Encourage, at all levels, literacy and the reading habit through children's book production and dissemination, as well as the habit of storytelling.'[11] The basic idea to encourage literacy was accepted by the Austrian representative and put in legal terms. As a result, the habits of reading and storytelling are not expressly mentioned. France, Italy and the Netherlands supported the proposal which was adopted in the Working Group by consensus.[12] The omission of storytelling, or more importantly, the promotion of books in general, is regrettable. Nevertheless, thanks to IBBY and UNICEF, children's books are expressly mentioned in the Convention, and from the obvious consensus one may conclude that the importance of children's books is acknowledged worldwide. However, further steps are needed.

Implementation in public libraries

The Convention on the Rights of the Child is a special treaty as it not only formulates obligations for the states, but also speaks of the primary responsibility of parents for the upbringing and development of the child. But also other individuals and institutions have obligations if one thinks of the child's right to be heard in administrative and judicial proceedings or the child's right to education. In general, all human beings have a duty to respect each other and each other's rights. As the child for example has a right to express his views in all matters affecting the child, there is a clear obligation for all who are taking decisions, formulating policies or creating the child's environment, either in schools, in the street or elsewhere to organise the participation of children. There is no reason to exempt libraries and librarians from these obligations of human rights. On the contrary, there is ample reason for libraries to show library commitment to children's rights, as they are already committed to the UNESCO Manifesto,[13] the IFLA Guidelines and through their States to general international consensus on human rights. The Universal Declaration and the UN Convention on the Rights of the Child.

As all states (and even the USA has at last signed the Convention) are parties to the Convention and have accepted its obligations, they are committed to implement the various articles and provisions of the Convention. The role and activities of public libraries can be considered as part of this implementation of the Convention. So therefore no public library can maintain that it has nothing to do with the Convention or with children's rights. In fact, nobody can refrain from being concerned with the human rights of children.

The States Parties to the Convention on the Right of the Child are obliged to implement its articles and principles. What are the obligations when speaking of the implementation in the public library as a public institution?

General obligations

To the general obligations formulated in the Convention belong the following ones, which also have to be fulfilled in the public library:

* **Respect**; the child has the right to be respected. The Polish pedagogue and author Janusz Korczak already formulated this and the Convention is a witness of that fundamental acknowledgement. This also includes the principle of non-discrimination: all children must have equal access to information, even if this requires extra measures because they are refugees, disabled, belong to a minority group, live in remote areas or have parents without a job. Paying respect also means to take into account the evolving capacities to the child, thus adapting information and programmes to their understanding, but never underestimating or downgrading children's competence, but challenging them instead.
* **The best interests of the child**; they should be the primary consideration in all measures concerning children. In the library we can think of opening hours, the best place for the children's department, preference for a children's librarian, an adequate budget at least for children.

- **Maximum resources**. Article 4 explicitly mentions that States Parties are obliged to implement to the maximum extent of their available resources, where needed, within the framework of international co-operation. This means that when budget cuts are made, the children's services should be the last to be affected if at all. Rich countries cannot easily maintain that they have used their maximum resources for giving children access to information and cultural participation. Countries in poorer conditions can require help and support in international co-operation.

- **Participation**. Respect for the views of the child refers to the obligation of the state or public libraries to enable children to participate in the creation of services, programmes and activities. The approach that children only have to be protected and are not competent to views, ideas and decision-making is outdated. The Convention obliges us to take a child-perspective and to communicate and cooperate with them. This requires a change of attitude of adults, librarians, and trust in children themselves. Those who have started with paying more attention and giving a follow up to the views and participation of children have been surprised by their competence, creativity and sense of responsibility.

Apart from these general obligations, there are more specific ones, also applicable in libraries.

Specific obligations

To these specific obligations belong the provisions of for example article 17:

- **Access to information**; the child has the right of access to information and material from a diversity of national and international sources, especially those aimed at the promotion of his or her social, spiritual and moral well-being and physical and mental health. It is good to note the type of information that is envisaged and which requires special support and protection. In library collections and activities these sources should be prioritised.

- **Dissemination of information** and material of social and cultural benefit to the child, should also be in accordance with the spirit of the aim of education which includes: the development of the child's personality, talents and mental and physical abilities to their fullest potential; the development of respect for human rights, for other cultures and the natural environment.

The idea that information in the broad sense serves the upbringing and education of the child and aims at high human values is underlying the right to information. Libraries have a special role to play as they have an overview of the variety of sources of information.

- **The production and dissemination of children's books**; thanks to IBBY this obligation is mentioned, now libraries must protect this right of the child by providing a variety of services and a balanced programme for book reading and using information materials. Resources should be created to buy extra children's books, also in other languages, minority languages and in adapted form for disabled children. A good dissemination of books also requires a well-established and spread network of library provisions for children, so that they may travel to and use the library in the highest autonomy. Every child should have a library card of his own, as it establishes the particular relationship between each individual child and the library with its books for free choice. Another provision, which relates to library services, is mentioned in article 31:
- **Support and provide cultural participation**; the library must see to it that children freely participate in cultural life and the arts. Libraries must create appropriate and equal opportunities for cultural, artistic, recreational and leisure activity. To fulfil this obligation libraries may need to contact other cultural institutions and cooperate with them. Children should have information about what is offered and where, on what conditions. Programmes offered should be appropriate to the age of the child, so libraries have to set up a policy of 'life long' cultural programmes, taking into account the various interests and levels of understanding. In fact, it is not enough to offer a general programme for children as a group; the right to cultural participation is a right guaranteed to every individual child.
- **Provide information to prevent children from harm**. In various articles the Convention obliges the State to prevent children from harm or injurious information causing harm. Information can also be used to prevent children from harm. A children's information centre can be established in the library in which all kinds of practical information is collected and made understandable for children.

This may be information in the field of health, technics, media, relationships, environment, and trips. Information about counselling, children's law shops, ombudsworkers, help-lines or contact persons should also be available. Therefore, the library must cooperate in a network of social institutions and provisions for children.

- **Support the implementation and execution of children's rights**. By providing information on all kinds of subjects, by offering programmes for reading and cultural participation, even by doing philosophy with children,[14] libraries can help children to execute other rights of the child. For example their right to education, which includes non-formal education. Very often a human right presupposes a right to information, e.g. the right to freedom of thought, conscience and religion or the right to be heard; in this way the library can help the child to orientate himself in society, in the world around and about his opportunities.

• **Information about the Convention and its Principles.** The Convention explicitly states the obligation to make the Convention, its principles and provisions widely known to children and adults alike. Here, there is a clear task for the library, but it is not enough to hand out leaflets with the text of the Convention. Children and adults should be enabled to understand the content, to monitor their own environment and become sensitive to violations of the Convention, larger and smaller injustices in every day life. Children's rights have not only to do with the rights of children in extreme or poor circumstances sometimes far away, but also with the life of every child here and now, nearby.

Practical recommendations

What measures can be taken by libraries to implement the above mentioned human rights of children. What can they do on their own, what must be done in co-operation, nationally and internationally?

• **Checklist of obligations**; all libraries need a clear view of the obligations derived from the Convention on the Rights of the Child, especially with a view to the right of the child to information. Working groups should scrutinise the Convention, contact NGOs who are familiar with the interpretation of the Convention and set up a checklist of obligations. This checklist makes it possible to trace gaps and omissions in the library policies and practices. An international working group could make a first set up. But it is important that as many librarians as possible are involved in the understanding, interpretation and implementation of children's rights in their services. Besides, co-operation with organisations concerned with children's rights might lead to the conclusion that the public library is an unexpected but useful partner in working with children and promoting their rights.

On the *national and international* level:

• **Draft programme of implementation**; a next step is to set up a draft programme of implementation, which should include the main approach of public libraries and the envisaged priorities, a planning of activities, training and evaluation. The success of the implementation will rely very much on the support which regional library organisations and national associations can give their workers and members by developing tools, working methods and providing research. It would be a great step forwards if libraries would agree to some overall activities for example the individual library card, no fees, or information about the Convention.

- **Research on the conditions for children to use the library**; part of libraries' contribution to the implementation of children's rights in the library field should be to monitor the conditions for children to use the library. How many children are still excluded, for what reason? What collections and materials are lacking? How much can children participate in the set up of programmes? How do they feel about the library, does it meet their needs, concerns, and interests? Are children welcomed by all of the library staff? Public libraries should cooperate with universities and NGOs to have an annual monitoring report including both qualitative and quantitative data, especially views from children. On the international level models for such monitoring could be prepared and proposed.

- **Include library services in the National State Report and the NGO Report** to the UN Committee on the Rights of the Child. An international Committee of experts monitors the implementation of the Convention by discussing the reports, which States Parties have to make every two or five years. Part of these dialogues with the responsible ministers should also be based on reports from the library field. Therefore, the state of the art in information and library services to children should be included in the State Report and the NGO-report submitted to the Committee.

- **Training in children's rights**; both the coming and the settled librarians should know about human rights of children and the implications for the exercise of librarianship and the performance of library services. Therefore, children's rights should be included in the curriculum of library schools, in the same way as this should be the case for teachers, policemen, social workers, lawyers etc. In order to raise the consciousness about respect for children, their views and the need for protection of their rights, additional training and workshops should be held, aimed at new attitudes and innovative programmes.

On the *local level* implementation of the right to information requires for example:

- **Setting up networks with (child) organisations** in the field of children's ombudswork, leisure and sport and culture. These information networks should be aimed at supporting the child in finding the right information and in strengthening the social tasks of public libraries. Part of this policy should also be to consider the library as a part and partner in local youth policy. This does not mean that information services should only be aimed at prevention of criminal activities, but rather should a broader approach be taken, to which the library has much to offer. If needed, the library must be the spokesman for the child when it comes to access to information and participation in society. Librarians must adapt themselves and dedicate themselves to such tasks, which often have to be performed outside the safe four walls of the library.

- **Celebrating 20 November the International Day of the Rights of the Child**; The 20 November has been the International Day of Children's Rights ever since the Declaration of 1959 was proclaimed. In 1989 the special character of this day was continued by the adoption of the UN Convention on the Rights of the Child. So the best way of showing the libraries' commitment to the principles and human rights of children is to celebrate this day in all libraries. It would be most successful if IFLA and all libraries would adopt this day as the central day to put focus on library services to children and their rights, which can be performed by public libraries. Therefore, there should be an attractive programme on this day, which supports the consciousness-raising among children and adults about children's rights, focusing on one or more rights as a theme. This day should be made a tradition in libraries as a clear international statement about children's rights to information and culture. Now the key element in such a day is that the programme should be set up in co-operation with children. It is *their* day; it is about *their* rights. Such participation is in itself a proof of the library taking the rights of children seriously, not symbolically.

Just to give an example of what can be done practically: in the Netherlands the Dutch Library Association has contacted various organisations involved in children and their rights. A package was made available and mailed to all 1150 public libraries containing a poster on various rights of the child, leaflets about rights adapted to children, postcards with a practical survey of the various types of rights, leaflets with background information and a catalogue of UNICEF with contained possibilities for other educational and promotional materials. All librarians received the first Newsletter on the Rights of the Child in the Public Library. The Newsletter included background information on the Convention, useful addresses, and suggestions for activities and the celebration of the 20th of November. For example, make documentation on children's rights available for talks and papers in school, when children are looking for a subject. Set up a children's panel and get them involved in activities and decision-making of the library. Support youth clubs and offer them space and information to discuss their activities. An example of a library branch in Haarlem was given where the library has been transformed into a children's information centre. Children discuss acquisition and activities. They have set up a quiz on literature and are running this in the neighbourhood schools. The librarians have contacted various organisations youth and welfare work, to reach out to other children's groups. Older children volunteer in making the younger ones knowledgeable about new media, making a paper on the computer etc. The papers the children make at school are acquired by the library and can be borrowed. Children are proud and acknowledge that the library is a place where they are respected.

Next year a large conference will take place focusing on innovations in children's library work, based on implementation of children's rights. Training of librarians is needed. They will also get acquainted with various youth organisations, their documentation and information and their activities. In this way they will be better informed about the consequences of the Convention on the Rights of the Child and the impact on public libraries.

Many other conclusions can be drawn from this introduction of the right to information in the Convention on the Rights of the Child. As was mentioned before, much of the realisation of the child's right to information, depends on those professionally involved. These professional groups have to exercise self-discipline and ensure that they perform high quality work. They should set up their own codes of ethics, and verify whether they meet the high aspirations of their craftsmanship and human values like honesty, dignity and respect. The promotion of and respect for children's rights depends on these professionals, and their awareness of rights.

Rights need to be translated into everyday life situations. Therefore, the assistance of living human beings who have a sense of human values, and who can professionally translate this sensitiveness and respect into aspiring stories, is needed. These are the stories a child will benefit from, as they will honestly help him to seek an answer to his question of life. The first priority of a professional is to ensure that no child, wherever he may live, and whatever circumstances he may encounter, is excluded from essential stories. All other motives of professionals should be scrutinised and stripped of their self-serving elements. Let's work on the child's right to information. Let's respect and celebrate the Rights of the Child in libraries!

References

1. SCHELTENS, D. *Mens en menserechten*, Samsom, Alphen aan den Rijn, 1981, p. 15. For the text of the Universal Declaration of Human Rights see: http://boes.org/un/enghr-b.html.
2. BOVEN, Th. van, Children's Rights. Address at the opening meeting of the International Forum on the Rights of the Child, Budapest, Hungary, 1 June 1979, in: Thoolen, H. (ed.), *People matter. Views on International Human Rights Policy by Theo van Boven*, Director of the United Nations Division of Human Rights 1977–1982, p. 157.

3. FREEMAN, M. *The Rights and Wrongs of Children*, Frances Pinter, London, 1983, p. 7.
4. VERHELLEN, C., *Convention on the Rights of the Child*. Background, motivation, strategies, main themes, Garant, Leuven/Apeldoorn, 1994, p. 18.
5. LANGEN, M. de, Children's rights, in: Verhellen, E.F. Spiesschaert (eds.), *Ombudswork for children*, Acco. Leuven/Amersfoort, 1989, p. 487.
6. UN Doc. GA Res 44/25, 1989. See for the full text: http://eurochild.gla.ac.uk/Rights.htm.
7. GOODMAN, D. Analysis of the First Session of the Committee on the Rights of the Child, in: *Netherlands Quarterly of Human Rights*, Vol. 10, 1992, 1, p. 50.
8. See for a thorough study on which also this paper is based: Koren, M., *Tell me! The Right of the Child to Information*, NBLC. The Hague, 1996.
9. UN Doc. E/CN.4/1983/62, Annex II.
10. Letter of Bahá'í International Community, undated, referring to its proposal about the aims of education (UN Doc. E/CN.4/1985/WG.1/WP.2).
11. *Bookbird*, Vol. 28, 1, 1990, and Letter dated 18 November 1985 submitted to the Centre for Human Rights, UN Doc. E/CN.4/1987/WG.1/WP.2, p. 6.
12. UN Doc. E/CN.4/1987/25, p. 7.
13. See for the full text: http://www.ifla.org/documents/libraries/policies/unesco.htm.
14. See the works of M. Lipman and G. Matthews on philosophy and children, and philosophical questions in children's literature.

Annex
United Nations Convention on the Rights of the Child 1989

Article 12

1. States Parties shall assure to the child who is capable of forming his or her own views the right to express those views freely in all matters affecting the child, the views of the child being given due weight in accordance with the age and maturity of the child.
2. For this purpose, the child shall in particular be provided the opportunity to be heard in any judicial and administrative proceedings affecting the child, either directly, or through a representative or an appropriate body, in a manner consistent with the procedural rules of national law.

Article 13

1. The child shall have the right to freedom of expression; this right shall include freedom to seek, receive and impart information and ideas of all kinds, regardless of frontiers, either orally, in writing or in print, in the form of art, or through any other media of the child's choice.
2. The exercise of this right may be subject to certain restrictions, but these shall only be such as are provided by law and are necessary:

(a) For respect of the rights or reputations of others; or
(b) For the protection of national security or of public order (ordre public), or of public health or morals.

Article 17

1. States Parties recognize the important function performed by the mass media and shall ensure that the child has access to information and material from a diversity of national and international sources, especially those aimed at the promotion of his or her social, spiritual and moral well-being and physical and mental health. To this end, States Parties shall:

   (a) Encourage the mass media to disseminate information and material of social and cultural benefit to the child and in accordance with the spirit of article 29;
   (b) Encourage international co-operation in the production, exchange and dissemination of such information and material from a diversity of cultural, national and international sources;
   (c) Encourage the production and dissemination of children's books;
   (d) Encourage the mass media to have particular regard to the linguistic needs of the child who belongs to a minority group or who is indigenous;
   (e) Encourage the development of appropriate guidelines for the protection of the child from information and material injurious to his or her well-being, bearing in mind the provisions of articles 13 and 18.

Article 29

1. States Parties agree that the education of the child shall be directed to:

   (a) The development of the child's personality, talents and mental and physical abilities to their fullest potential;
   (b) The development of respect for human rights and fundamental freedoms, and for the principles enshrined in the Charter of the United Nations;
   (c) The development of respect for the child's parents, his or her own cultural identity, language and values, for the national values of the country in which the child is living; the country from which he or she may originate, and for civilizations different from his or her own;
   (d) The preparation of the child for responsible life in a free society, in the spirit of understanding, peace, tolerance, equality of sexes, and friendship among all peoples, ethnic, national and religious groups and persons of indigenous origin;
   (e) The development of respect for the natural environment. (...)

Article 31

1. States Parties recognize the right of the child to rest and leisure, to engage in play and recreational activities appropriate to the age of the child and to participate freely in cultural life and the arts.
2. States Parties shall respect and promote the right of the child to participate fully in cultural and artistic life and shall encourage the provision of appropriate and equal opportunities for cultural, artistic, recreational and leisure activity.

Article 42

States Parties undertake to make the principles and provisions of the Convention widely known, by appropriate and active means, to adults and children alike.

84

DO CHILDREN'S RHYMES REVEAL UNIVERSAL METRICAL PATTERNS?[1]

Andy Arleo

Source: *Bulletin de la Société de Stylistique Anglaise* 22 (2001): 125–145.

Introduction

Back in the middle of the twentieth century Rumanian ethnomusico-logist Constantin Brailoiu (1984 [1956]) and American linguist Robbins Burling (1966) independently uncovered evidence showing that children's rhymes around the world have strikingly similar metrical patterns and speculated that these may indeed be universal. The first section of this article will review the Brailoiu and Burling models as well as more recent work by Hayes and MacEachern (1998). A revised version of a Hypothesis of Metrical Symmetry (HMS) for children's rhymes, first formulated in Arleo (1997), will be presented in section 2 and then tested for two genres of children's rhymes, English and French counting-out rhymes and English jump-rope rhymes, in section 3. In the conclusion I will offer several explanations as to why symmetry should play such an important role in oral traditions and will place the metrics of children's rhymes in a broader perspective, involving the study of isochrony in language.

Before proceeding to the first section of the paper, it is necessary to clarify the meaning of the terms "universal" and "children's rhymes." As Brown (1991) has shown, the notion of universals has often been controver-sial, especially in anthropology, where cultural relativism reigned during much of the twentieth century. Brown discusses various types and degrees of universality, including formal versus substantive universals, absolute versus near universals, implicational universals (i.e., if a language has fea-ture A, then it will have feature B) and statistical universals. The Hypothesis of Metrical Symmetry that will be presented below falls mainly in this last category, that is, it involves tendencies rather than absolute laws.

Furthermore, universals research does not deny cultural or linguistic diversity, but aims to define the necessary conditions for understanding what is truly different in each culture or language. There is an obvious analogy with biology, where the genetic code underlies tremendous biological diversity. Thus the search for universals in children's rhymes, while emphasizing cross-cultural and cross-linguistic similarities, is in no way an attempt to standardize the rich and diverse traditions around the world.

The second term, children's rhymes, is often used in a confusing way to refer both to rhymes performed by adults for children, what Iona and Peter Opie (1959) call "nursery lore," and rhymes performed by children for children, that is, part of "children's folklore" or "childlore." This paper will argue that when investigating metrical patterns, nursery lore and childlore should not be lumped together, even though there is much overlap between the two. Some specialists of adult literature might wonder why anyone would even bother studying childlore and children's rhymes. This attitude is what play specialist Sutton-Smith (1970) has termed the "triviality barrier," the notion that children's play and folklore is trivial and undeserving of serious academic study. There are however many good reasons for studying childlore. For the linguist, children's verbal folklore is part of language, belonging to a "dialect of childhood" that is used by a substantial part of the world's population, that is, children from roughly four to twelve, and remembered by adolescents and adults. Furthermore, as Jakobson and Waugh (1980: 264–268) have pointed out, although the verbal art of the child and of the adult are different, they form a continuum, making the study of children's rhymes a branch of poetics. Childlore also has an obvious value for psychologists: Piaget (1969 [1932]), for example, observed marble playing in order to study the development of moral judgement in childhood. Finally, childlore is part of the whole culture and is often alluded to in literature, headlines, and advertising, as well as in everyday conversation. Therefore, some familiarity with children's folklore is surely useful for foreign language students, and especially foreign language teachers working with children.

The hypothesis of universal metrical patterns in children's rhymes: a review of previous studies

Brailoiu (1984 [1956])

We now move on to the main topic of this article, the hypothesis that there are universal metrical patterns in children's rhymes. Our story begins in 1956 with the publication of a paper by Constantin Brailoiu in which he claimed that children's rhythms ("la rythmique enfantine") constitute an immediately recognizable autonomous system that is "spread over a considerable surface of the earth, from Hudson Bay to Japan" (Brailoiu

1984 [1956]: 207). Furthermore, "children's rhythms are based on a restricted number of extremely simple principles," which are "constantly concealed by the resources (almost unlimited here) of variation" (ibid. 209). Brailoiu describes what he calls "series" of syllables, which generally correspond to lines. The most frequent series is the equivalent of eight short syllables, that is, in musical terms, quavers (British English) or eighth notes (American English).[2] Example 1 shows lines from various languages of the "series worth eight":

(1a)   J'ai pas-sé par la cui-si-ne (French)
(1b)   Ques-ta ro-sa e Ma-riet-ta (Italian)
(1c)   Wenn du willst e'n Gaul be-schla-gl (German)
(1d)   l-pu-tuy-or-ti-gu-wa-ra (Eskimo)

The series worth eight does not necessarily comprise eight pronounced syllables. In example 2a each line has seven syllables, but a total duration of eight eighth notes. In example 2b the third line has six syllables, but also a total duration of eight eighth notes.

(2a)   Eeny meeny miny mo,
       Catch a tiger by the toe,
       If he hollers, let him go,
       Eeny meeny miny mo.
       (personal recollection, New Jersey, ca. 1960)

(2b)   Eeny meeny miny mo,
       Put the baby on the po,
       When it's done, wipe its bum,
       Eeny meeny miny mo.
       (Webb 1983, recorded in Workington, Cumberland, England in 1960;
       cf. Abrahams 1969: 63)

In his conclusion Brailoiu states that children's rhythms are governed by "strict symmetry" and suggests that "the system proceeds, if not from dance, then at least from ordered movement, which is closely associated with it." He notes that "it remains to be seen how the most diverse languages manage to bend themselves to its inflexibility," a task that can only be accomplished by collaboration between researchers "as numerous as the languages themselves" (ibid. 238).

Burling (1966)

Our story now jumps ahead to 1966, the year that linguist Robbins Burling published a seminal study on the metrics of children's rhymes in several structurally different languages, such as English, Bengkulu, and Chinese. Whereas Brailoiu had focused on the line, Burling examined the stanza, discovering a widespread 16-beat pattern, made up of four four-beat lines. This may be illustrated by the well-known counting-out rhyme "Engine engine number nine":

(3) *Engine, engine, number nine,*
     Going down Chicago line,
     If the train goes off the track,
     Do you want your money back?
     (personal recollection, New Jersey, ca. 1960)

In this example the counter's gestures, used to designate each player, is synchronized with the quarter-note beat. We also note that there is a good fit between the beat and the syllables that are ordinarily stressed in the spoken language. In all the polysyllabic nouns, for example, the beat is aligned with the word stress (e.g., engine, number, Chicago, money), How-ever, there are cases where the syllables aligned with the beat might not be stressed in spoken English: for example, "do" (in "Do you want your money back") is often reduced to "d'ya" in conversation.

Burling also notes that while beats tend to coincide with stressed syllables, this is not always the case. Many nursery rhymes have rests (designated by the letter R), as in example (4):

(4) *Hickory, dickory, dock, R*
     The mouse ran up the clock, R
     The clock struck one, the mouse ran down,
     Hickory, dickory, dock, R

Furthermore, the number of syllables between successive beats may vary, with a maximum of three. In this example there are two weak syllables between beat 1, synchronized with /hɪ/, and beat 2, synchronized with /dɪ/. Burling claims that the odd-numbered beats have slightly greater stress than the even-numbered beats, although the difference is subtle and may vary with the style of recitation. He also observes that this simple English verse has "a peculiar binary character" (ibid. 1423): the 16-beat quatrains are divided into two eight-beat couplets, which are divided into four-beat lines, which are often subdivided into hemistichs marked off by internal rhymes. Like Brailoiu, Burling stresses the semi-autonomy of this model: "The pattern of beats, then, is partially independent of the rest of the language, and the trick of composing simple poetry is to fit the words to the pattern, adjusting them in such a way that their stresses will somehow fit the rhythm of beats that our ear demands" (ibid. 1424). Burling points out that four-beat lines are extremely widespread in popular verse in English, not only in nursery rhymes, but in innumerable popular songs, advertising jingles, and light verse. Furthermore, citing the work of Lehmann (1956), he shows that the four-beat line has great historical depth and appears to be linked to the earliest poetry in the Germanic languages, in which the line is made up of four predominant syllables, "[. . .] two in each half-line, which are elevated by stress, quantity, and two or three of them by alliteration" (Lehmann 1956: 37).

Burling then analyzes examples of the same 16-beat pattern in two other languages, both typologically and geographically divergent from English, the Peking dialect of Chinese and Bengkulu, a Malayo-Polynesian language spoken in southwestern Sumatra. Finally, he gives some "rather random and only partially analyzed" examples from Cairo Arabic, Yoruba, and Serrano, a Southern California Indian language (ibid. 1433–34). In his conclusion Burling states: "If these patterns should prove to be universal, I can see no explanation except that of our common humanity" (ibid. 1435). He suggests that sophisticated verse might be built in part on the foundation of simple verse, the result of modifying rules and adding restrictions. If this is the case, the "comparative study of metrics would then be the study of the diverse ways in which different poetic traditions depart from the common basis of simple verse" (ibid. 1436).

Hayes and MacEachern 1998

Before assessing these two hypotheses, we will discuss briefly an important recent study by Bruce Hayes and Margaret MacEachern that has used Burling's work as a starting point to build a sophisticated model of the quatrain form in English folk verse, which includes children's verse, such as nursery rhymes, as well as traditional authentic folk verse "sung mostly without accompaniment by ordinary people and transmitted orally" (Hayes and MacEachern 1998: 474). Like Burling, Hayes and MacEachern see the folk quatrain as a binary hierarchy, not just a sequence of four lines, but a pair of pairs, that is, the quatrain is made up of two couplets and each couplet is made up of two lines. They propose a grid representation, consisting of a sequence of columns of x's or other symbols, where each column may be associated with an event in time, such as the pronunciation of syllables. The height of a grid column depicts the strength of the rhythmic beat associated with the event. In sung or chanted verse it is assumed that grid rows are performed isochronously, at least in theory, "abstracting away from various structural and expressive timing adjustments" (ibid. 476). This is illustrated in Figure 1 below, using the first line of example 3 (the symbol "0" represents an unfilled metrical position):

Half-note level	x				x		
Quarter-note level	x		x		x		x	
Eighth-note level	x	x	x	x	x	x	x	x
	En-	gine,	En-	gine,	num-	ber	nine	0

Figure 1 Grid analysis of the first line of "Engine engine number nine".

Using this framework, Hayes and MacEachern study patterns of truncation, that is, the non-filling of metrical positions at the ends of lines. They find 26 truncation patterns, each of which defines a verse type. Like Burling, they suggest that the relative simplicity of children's verse is an advantage for studying these patterns: "Art verse and popular verse apparently also normally obey our laws, but since they are the productions of exceptional individuals, they might well be expected to involve greater complexity and idiosyncrasy [. . .]." This position echoes Jakobson (1960: 369): "Folklore offers the most clear-cut and stereotyped forms of poetry particularly suitable for structural scrutiny."

The hypothesis of metrical symmetry

We turn now to a proposal for studying the metrics of children's rhymes first formulated in Arleo (1997). This article points out first of all that the hypotheses put forth independently by Brailoiu and Burling are compatible, at least for the line. Although Burling also deals with the stanza, his four-beat lines are equivalent to Brailoiu's "series worth eight." Secondly, it is noted that in both models children's rhymes are treated globally without looking at specific genres. However, the play function of rhymes often has a direct effect on the metrical pattern, as in the French hand-clapping rhyme shown in example 5, which has five-beat lines:

(5) Beats:	1	2	3	4	5
	La sa-	ma-ri-	tain'	tain',	tain',
	Va à	la fon-	tain',	tain',	tain' . . .

Indeed, these five-beat lines are a direct reflection of the hand-clapping pattern in which players clap their hands three times on the syllable -*tain*. Finally, it is suggested that the Brailoiu and Burling models might be collapsed into a more general hypothesis, termed the Hypothesis of Metrical Symmetry (HMS). The HMS has two versions, which are formulated below:

Hypothesis of Metrical Symmetry (Arleo 1997)
Children's rhymes tend toward symmetry, defined as follows:

1. The number of beats in a given metrical unit (i.e., hemistich, line, stanza) tends to be even.
2. The number of beats in a given metrical unit tends to be a power of two.

Version 2 is stronger and more precise than version 1: if 2 holds, then 1 will automatically apply since all powers of two are even. Furthermore, the Burling and Brailoiu models are not discarded but become special cases of version 2: Brailoiu's series worth eight and Burling's four four-beat lines are examples of metrical units containing numbers of beats that are powers of two. The fact that this is a probabilistic model reflects the expectation that "we will not find ironclad deterministic laws, but rather statistical tendencies that will undoubtedly vary from one tradition to another due to linguistic and cultural factors" (Arleo 1997: 396).

This earlier version of the HMS only concerns the number of beats in a given metrical unit, but we should also consider the number of lines in stanzas. Below is a revised version of the HMS that takes into account both the number of beats and the number of lines. A more accurate definition of "power of two" is also given.

The Hypothesis of Metrical Symmetry (revised version)

Children's rhymes tend toward symmetry, defined as follows:

1a. Beats (version a). The number of beats in a given metrical unit (i.e., hemistich, line, stanza) tends to be even.

1b. Beats (version b). The number of beats in a given metrical unit tends to be a power of two (2^n, where $n > 0$).

2a. Lines (version a). The number of lines in stanzas tends to be even.

2b. Lines (version b). The number of lines in stanzas tends to be a power of two.

Before testing the HMS, let us compare it with the work that has been summarized above. First of all, like Brailoiu and Burling, as well as Hayes and MacEachern, the beat is used as a basic unit in order to compare equivalences between metrical units. Specifically, the beat is viewed as a mental event that is shared between players or performers, which allows the synchronization of body movements, such as hand-clapping, but also phonetic gestures, such as syllable attacks. This conception of the beat is very close to that of Lerdahl and Jackendoff (1983: 18); that is, beats are idealized points in time that do not have duration. On the other hand, time spans, the intervals of time between beats, do have duration. I also assume that, as a mental event, the beat is correlated with temporal patterning in the brain, but will leave this matter to specialists.

Secondly, all these models involve some degree of idealization. In actual performance children may deviate from a regular beat by slowing down or speeding up the tempo, just as they often deviate from regular pitch patterns. Nevertheless, schoolchildren who are used to playing together often achieve a high degree of isochrony in their performances. Two crucial factors are play context and age. A regular beat is often required to synchronize movement patterns between players, as in hand-clapping games, whereas in solitary play there is usually less of a functional need to keep a steady beat. Furthermore, the acquisition of a regular beat is a gradual process that varies from child to child.

Thirdly, children's rhymes usually have several levels of beats, but generally one level is more basic. For example, in "Engine engine number nine" I can clap four beats per line (**Engine engine number nine**, or two beats per line (**En**gine engine **num**ber nine) or one beat per line, and so on. However, the four-beat per line pattern is most salient in this case, and indeed corresponds to the counter's gesture of designation. To describe this basic beat level Lerdahl and Jackendoff (1983) use the Renaissance term *tactus*. We can consider this as the foot-tapping, hand-clapping, or finger-snapping level. This is also the intermediate quarter-note level in Figure 1 above. As can be seen, the stressed syllables tend to be aligned with beats at this level. Beat levels above and below the tactus level become progressively less salient. Hayes and MacEachern's metrical grids, which are derived from traditional musical notation, show four levels of beats, or rhythmic strength, in folk verse, but whether or not all these levels are perceived by all performers and listeners remains an open question.

Finally, as already mentioned, the previous studies have lumped together many different genres so that we might be missing some subtle distinctions. As a research strategy, it seems wise to distinguish between nursery lore, adult folklore for children, and children's folklore (or childlore). Furthermore, within children's folklore, metrical patterns should be studied genre by genre, because function often determines form, at least partially. Having outlined the theoretical framework, we will now examine two childlore genres, counting-out rhymes and jump-rope (or skipping) rhymes.

Testing the hypothesis of metrical symmetry (revised version)

English and French counting-out rhymes

We begin by looking at the metrics of English and French counting-out rhymes. Counting-out rhymes are used by children to choose a central player in a games like tag ("le Loup") or Hide 'n seek ("cache-cache"). They are widespread in different languages and cultures. In 1888 folklorist Henry Carrington Bolton published a collection of 873 counting-out rhymes in nineteen languages or dialects, including Arabic, Basque, Marathi, Turkish, Armenian, and many Western European languages. An Italian website, created by Mauro Presini, gives examples of counting-out rhymes from about fifty countries (see address in reference list). In the counting-out ritual the players are in a circle and a counter chants or sings a rhyme to a regular beat while successively touching each player's foot, usually in a clockwise direction. The player on whom the last syllable falls is eliminated and counting-out resumes until one player is left, who is "It" (in French "le Loup" or "le Chat") (see Arleo 1997: 401). Counting-out rhymes are an ideal genre for testing cross-linguistic hypotheses because they are part of a well-documented and widespread living oral tradition passed on from child to child. Because of their status as a regulatory "meta-game," in which play organizes play, counting-out rhymes are performed both by boys and girls and tend not to go out of fashion from one generation of children to the next, as is often the case for other children's games.

Reanalyzing data in Arleo (1982), we first examine the number of lines per rhyme and then the number of beats per line. Table 1 compares the number of lines per rhyme in two samples of 40 French and 40 English counting-out rhymes. The samples were taken from two major collections, Baucomont *et al.* (1961) for the French rhymes, and Abrahams and Rankin (1980) for the English rhymes. These rhymes are geographically widespread, with a large number of citations, including recent versions at the time of publication.

Table 1 Distribution of 40 English and 40 French counting-out rhymes according to the number of lines.

Number of lines:	1	2	3	4	5	6	7	8
Nb. of Fr. rhymes:	1	1	0	9	7	7	1	0
% of total:	2.5	2.5	0	22.5	17.5	17.5	2.5	0
Nb of Eng. rhymes:	0	6	2	19	2	6	0	2
% of total:	0	15	5	47.5	5	15	0	5

Number of lines:	9	10	11	12	13	Uncertain	Total
Nb. of Fr. rhymes:	4	3	0	0	1	6	40
% of total	10	7.5	0	0	2.5	15	100
Nb. of Eng. rhymes:	0	0	0	0	0	3	40
% of total:	0	0	0	0	0	7.5	100

In both samples there are more rhymes with an even number of lines than rhymes with an odd number of lines. In the English sample the tendency towards an even number of lines is quite strong: 33 rhymes (82.5%) have an even number of lines against only 4 rhymes (10%) with an odd number. Furthermore, 27 (67.5%) rhymes have two, four or eight lines, and 19 out of 40 rhymes have four lines. Therefore, versions 2a and 2b of the HMS are quite strongly supported by the English data.

In the French sample, 20 rhymes (50%) have an even number of lines against 14 rhymes with an odd number of lines (35%) and 10 rhymes (25%)

have two, four or eight lines. In both samples the quatrain is the most frequent pattern. The results are therefore mixed for the French sample. There is a slight tendency for the number of lines to be even; if we discount the six uncertain cases, then the percentage of even-numbered stanzas is 58.8% against 41.2%. However, only 10 of the French rhymes are equal to a power of two, rising to 29.4% of the sample once the uncertain cases are excluded.

We turn now to the number of beats per line. According to the earlier analysis (Arleo 1982), based on the same sample of 40 English counting out rhymes, 118 out of 176 lines, (67%) had four stressed syllables. However, this underestimates the number of beats because lines with three stressed syllables often have a fourth beat that is not aligned with a syllable, as in "Hickory dickory dock" (see example 4 above). A reanalysis of the data brings the percentage of four-beat lines to 73.3%, as shown in Table 2.

Table 2 Distribution of number of beats per line in a sample of 40 English counting-out rhymes.

Number of beats:	1	2	3	4	>4	Uncertain	Total
Number of lines:	0	8	1	129	0	38	176
% of total	0	4.5	0.6	73.3	0	21.6	100

The rather high number of uncertain cases is due mainly to cases where it was difficult to decide whether a line contained a rest, that is a beat not aligned with a syllable. Recordings and musical transcriptions could provide a greater degree of accuracy here, but it would be hard to obtain such a representative sample. Even allowing for a margin of error due to subjectivity in identifying rests, it is safe to conclude that the four-beat line is the predominant model for English counting-out rhymes. Since four is both even and a power of two, both versions of the HMS are therefore confirmed.

Arleo (1994) examines the number of beats per line in 27 French counting-out rhymes recorded in and around Saint-Nazaire. Nearly two-thirds (65.1%) of the lines had an even number of beats versus 34.9% with an odd number of beats. Furthermore, the four-beat line was the most common, accounting for 56.9% of the data. The evidence from French counting-out rhymes therefore supports the HMS for number of beats per line, but not as strongly as in English.

English jump-rope rhymes

We will now test the HMS for a second genre of childlore, jump-rope (or skipping) rhymes in English. The corpus for this analysis is Abrahams

(1969), a large-scale compilation of jump-rope rhymes from the main English-speaking countries, including Britain, Ireland, Australia, New Zealand, the United States and Canada, and used by children from roughly the beginning of the twentieth century until the late 1960s. According to Abrahams (1969: xv), "until relatively recently the ancient pastime of jumping rope was exclusively a boys' activity and had no rhymed games associated with it." The changeover seems to have occurred in the last generation of the nineteenth century, although there are reports that boys still jumped rope as a game in the 1920s in at least one region of the U.S. Furthermore, and this is particularly important for metrics, jump-rope rhymes often use verbal material from other genres, especially counting-out rhymes, but also singing games, taunts, popular songs and so on. As Abrahams (ibid. xix) points out, "counting-out rhymes are the most common source, in fact, because so many jump-rope games involve counting and invoke player elimination of the 'out-goes-she' sort."

Before presenting the data on the metrics of jump-rope rhymes, several methodological issues need to be addressed. The first methodological decision involved the elimination of 79 of the 619 main entries in Abraham's dictionary because they were incomplete or, in a few rare cases, were described as improvisations that did not appear to have metrical structure. The initial corpus was therefore reduced to 540 rhymes.

The second methodological question is more complex, as it involves the theoretical status of the line in oral poetry, an issue that will be discussed below. From a practical viewpoint, in counting the number of lines per rhyme, the line division given by Abrahams was followed except in the following situations. Many rhymes are made up of a main rhyme, often a couplet or a quatrain, followed by a coda (to use the terminology proposed by Arleo 1980 for counting-out rhymes), which is often an enumeration, as shown in examples 6 and 7:

(6) *Charlie Chaplin sat on a pin.*
     How many inches did it go in?
     One, two, three, etc.
     (Abrahams 1969: 25, more than 25 sources listed)

(7) *Teacher, teacher, oh so tired,*
     How many times were you fired?
     One, two, three, etc.
     (Ibid. 186, one source from New Mexico, published in 1961)

As the metrical structure here is clearly a rhymed couplet, examples 7 and 8 were tabulated as having two lines. Furthermore, in a small number of rhymes the line division did not appear to reflect a plausible metrical structure, as in example 8a:

(8a) *Bread and butter,*
      Sugar and spice,
      How many boys think I'm nice?
      One, two, three, etc.
      (Abrahams 1969: 21)

This was reanalyzed as a two-line rhyme followed by a coda, as shown in 8b:

(8b) *Bread and butter, sugar and spice,*
      How many boys think I'm nice?
      + Coda

8b is preferable because there is convergence in two key criteria for line division: the rhyme scheme and the metrical scheme, in this case the number of beats per line. Whereas 8a has an abb rhyme scheme, where line a does not rhyme with another line, 8b has a rhyming aa couplet, a basic pattern in the corpus. In 8a lines 1 and 2 each have two beats, and line 3 has four beats, giving a 2-2-4 metrical scheme, which, by analogy with rhyme scheme, we can call an aab pattern. On the other hand, 8b has two four-beat lines, a 4-4 or aa pattern. Out of the 540 rhymes in the corpus, only 11 (2% of the total) were reanalyzed, so this does not change the general conclusions that will be presented below.

The preceding discussion shows that line division is a major methodological and theoretical issue, especially when dealing with oral tradition. Oral poetry is by definition concerned with the perceptual grouping of auditory events, which is very different from reading written poetry, where the reader is guided by the conventional visual cues of layout and punctuation. Listening to and learning rhymes in an oral tradition is akin to the perception of music, where the listener usually makes unconscious grouping decisions according to preference rules based on various criteria (see Lerdahl and Jackendoff 1983). In the case of children's rhymes the transcriber uses rhyme schemes, metrical patterns, repetition, grammatical parallelism and so on to propose a plausible line division, that is, one that brings out perceived regularities in the text. When these criteria converge, different transcribers will come up with the same line division, as in "Engine engine number nine . . ." (example 3), where each line has four beats and the ends of lines correspond to major syntactic boundaries. But in many cases there may be a conflict between the criteria, as in example 9a:

(9a) *I asked my mother for fifteen cents,*
      To see the elephant jump the fence,
      He jumped so high,
      He reached the sky,

And didn't come back till the Fourth of July.
(Abrahams 1969: 72)

With this line division we have five lines with an aabbb rhyme scheme, and the rhyme between *sky* and *July* is foregrounded. The metrical scheme is 4-4-2-2-4 (aabba), i.e., lines 1, 2 and 5 have four beats each and lines 3 and 4 have two beats each. The total number of beats is therefore 16, but spread over five lines. Although this rhyme was tabulated as five lines, it could very well be reanalyzed as in example 9b:

(9b)   I asked my mother for fifteen cents,
To see the elephant jump the fence,
He jumped so high, he reached the sky,
And didn't come back till the Fourth of July.

This segmentation shows greater regularity: the rhyme scheme is now aabb and the third line has internal rhyme; the metrical scheme is 4-4-4-4, that is aaaa. On the other hand, the rhyme between *high* and *sky* is not highlighted or visually salient. Many of the five-line rhymes in the corpus are of this type, which is reminiscent of the metrical pattern of limericks. Had these five-line rhymes been reanalyzed as quatrains, the proportion of rhymes conforming to the HMS would have been even higher.

We return now to the data on the metrics of jump-rope rhymes. Table 3 shows the distribution of the 540 rhymes in the corpus according to the number of lines.

Out of 540 rhymes, 433 (80.2%) have an even number of lines and 107 (19.8%) have an odd number of lines. This strongly supports version 2a of the HMS: 388 rhymes (71.9%) have a number of lines equal to a power of two, (that is, 2, 4, 8, or 16 lines) versus 152 (28.1%) with a number of lines not equal to a power of two. Thus, version 2b of the HMS is also confirmed. Another interesting finding is that 388 of the rhymes (73.7%) have four or fewer lines.

Table 3 Distribution of 540 jump-rope rhymes according to the number of lines.

Number of lines:	1	2	3	4	5	6	7	8	9
Number of rhymes:	25	108	33	232	36	33	6	47	5
% of total:	4.6	20.0	6.1	43.0	6.7	6.1	1.1	8.7	0.9
Number of lines:	10	11	12	13	14	15	16	24	Total
Number of rhymes:	6	0	4	1	1	1	1	1	540
% of total:	1.1	0	0.7	0.2	0.2	0.2	0.2	0.2	100

There are a number of other aspects of the metrics of jump-rope rhymes that cannot be investigated in detail in the present article, such as the number of beats per line or the characteristic rhyme schemes. However, it should be noted that the four-beat line is very common and that the prevailing rhyme scheme appears to be the rhymed couplet, which works like a fundamental building block. Indeed, many of the quatrains have an aabb rhyme scheme. These results confirm what Iona and Peter Opie (1997: 209) have written about skipping rhymes: "What are the characteristics of the successful chant (successful in the sense of being long-surviving and widespread)? It is likely to be a four-line verse with four trochaic feet in each line, the first, stressed, syllable coinciding with the slap of the rope on the ground and the jump over it."

Another related topic that might be investigated further is the frequency of repeated lines, as in examples 10 and 11:

(10) Ra   *Jelly in the dish,*
      Ra   *Jelly in the dish,*
      b   *Wiggle waggle, wiggle waggle,*
      Ra   *Jelly in the dish.*
      (Abrahams 1969: 99)

(11) Ra   *Minny and a Minny and a ha, ha, ha,*
      a   *Kissed her fellow on a Broadway trolley car.*
      a   *You tell Ma and I'll tell Pa.*
      Ra   *Minny and a Minny and a ha, ha, ha.*
      (Abrahams 1969: 123)

A notation developed by Cornulier (1995: 266) is used here to designate repeated lines. The capital letter R means that the entire line is repeated. Thus, example 10 is a RaRabRa pattern and example 11 is a RaaaRa pattern. Repeated lines are common in oral folk traditions since they ease the burden of memorization. Example 10 shows how minimal textual material can be expanded into a quatrain through repetition.

Conclusion

Do children's rhymes reveal universal metrical patterns? It is obviously too early to answer in terms of absolute universals, e.g. "all cultures or languages have children's rhymes with universal metrical patterns." The question might better be framed in implicational terms: if a culture or a language has children's rhymes, that is, a body of folk verse produced and transmitted primarily among children, then these are likely to have certain metrical patterns or properties. We recall that Brailoiu and Burling provided examples of children's rhymes from around the world to show that there are similar metrical patterns, but they did not deal with the frequency with these patterns compared to other patterns. Furthermore, there was little attempt to distinguish between nursery lore and childlore, to pinpoint specific genres, or to examine the influence of function on metrical form. The present approach attempts to come to terms with these issues by analyzing carefully delimited genres and by formulating a precise hypothesis, the HMS, in relative statistical terms. Although the HMS does not propose an absolute universal law, it does make specific predictions regarding the number of beats per line and the number of lines per stanza that can be tested empirically, language by language and genre by genre. This paper has strongly confirmed that the number of lines in English counting-out rhymes and jump-rope rhymes is generally even and equal to a power of two. Furthermore, English counting-out rhymes also tend to have four beats per line. Evidence from French counting-out rhymes is not as clear, although there is a slight preference for stanzas with an even number of lines and for lines with an even number of beats. Other genres of childlore that could be studied in the future include hand-clapping games and singing games, in English, French and other languages.

Although it is premature to conclude that most children's rhymes around the world are symmetrical, the accumulated evidence from Brailoiu and Burling, the present study, and other sources (Despringre 1997: 194–96) show that many children's rhymes do have elements of symmetry. We would of course like to know why such patterns are so widespread. Hayes and MacEachern (1998: 474) suggest that the striking resemblances among children's verse types from "unrelated, geographically distant languages" may be innate:

> As an explanation for the resemblances Burling makes an appeal (1435) to "our common humanity," which we take to be a somewhat poetic invocation of the view that certain aspects of cognition are genetically coded. This could occur either directly or, perhaps indirectly, at a very abstract level from which the observed systems derive.

In my own view, the relative contributions of nature and nurture to the symmetry of children's rhymes remain an open question. It is clear that children are not born with the ability to keep a steady beat, but acquire it, although they may be aware of regular rhythms in their environment. Children's rhymes also depend of course on the acquisition of language. They are first learned at home, in nursery school and in other play settings, and then truly blossom in the first years of elementary school, with many individual differences among children. We know very little about how the development of children's rhymes and other items of childlore connects with innate cognitive faculties and this is certainly a subject that requires further research.

Among the many possible explanations for symmetry in children's rhymes, I would like to briefly focus on two. The first is that symmetry has great functional value in an oral tradition because it aids memorization. This has been demonstrated at length by cognitive psychologist David Rubin (1995) in relation to epic, folk ballads and counting-out rhymes. Along with imagery and sound patterns, regular metrical schemes contribute to predictability and provide cues for the listener. Imagine, for example, a listener or a singer who doesn't understand or has forgotten the last word of the second line in a song with four-beat lines and an aabb rhyme scheme. By combining the multiple constraints of rhyme, metrics, grammar and meaning, the search can be narrowed down and the missing word more easily retrieved. This is one of the reasons why songs and rhymes are such effective tools for learning foreign languages (Arleo 2000). Written traditions can of course break out of these somewhat stereotyped symmetrical patterns and develop irregular innovations without interrupting the chain of transmission between sender and receiver. Similar questions arise in music. Jazz, for example, which has evolved from oral tradition to become a sophisticated musical genre, continues to exploit the symmetrical 32-bar standard as a favorite form for improvisors; it is doubtful, on the other hand, that twelve-tone serial music could have evolved from a purely oral tradition and it is highly questionable whether humans could learn to improvise dodecaphonic melodies without the support of written music.

A second possible explanation for symmetry in children's verse is related to our bodies. Although the human body is not systematically symmetrical (think of internal organs like the heart or the liver as well as front-back and top-bottom asymmetry), when we are face to face with another human being there is a general impression of left-right symmetry. More importantly, our basic activities, like walking and breathing, are based on regulary binary rhythms. MacNeilage (1998: 503), in an important article on the evolution of speech, notes that such "biphasic cycles are the main method by which the animal kingdom does work that is extended in the time domain" and provides a long list of examples, including locomotion, heartbeat, respiration, scratching, digging, copulating, vomiting, milking cows and cyclical ingestive processes.

From the viewpoint of the linguist, the study of metrical patterns in children's rhymes is part of a broader research project that investigates isochrony in language. Arleo (1995) has suggested that there is a scale of isochrony in speech ranging from relatively "arhythmic" styles (e.g., non-fluid speech involving many hesitations) to genres that are isochronous in nature, including cheers, children's rhymes, chants, light poetry (such as limericks) and songs. Utterances in everyday conversation, not to mention public speeches, are often synchronized with a regular beat, and this is frequently linked to pragmatic and rhetorical purposes. While the present article has focused on the metrics of specific genres of children's folklore, and their possible universality, it also aims to contribute more generally to research on the isochronous properties of language.

Notes

1 This is a revised version of a paper presented at the Atelier de stylistique et de poétique at the XIème Congrès de la Société des Anglicistes de l'Enseignement Supérieur, Université d'Angers, May 19–21, 2000. I wish to thank the participants in this workshop for their comments as well as Jenna Tester for her assistance.
2 In French, "croches." The American English terminology will be used in this article.

Références

Abrahams, R[oger] D. *Jump-rope Rhymes: a Dictionary*. London: University of Texas Press, 1969.

Abrahams, R[oger] D. and L[ois] Rankin. *Counting-out Rhymes: a Dictionary*. London: University of Texas Press, 1980.

Arleo, Andy. "With a dirty, dirty dishrag on your mother's big fat toe: the coda in the counting-out rhyme." *Western Folklore* 39. 3 (1980): 211–22.

Arleo, Andy. "Une étude comparative des comptines françaises et anglaises." Thèse de 3ème cycle, Université de Nantes, 1982.

Arleo, Andy. "Vers l'analyse métrique de la formulette enfantine." *Poétique* 98 (1994): 153–69.

Arleo, Andy. "It don't mean a thing if it ain't got that swing: accentuation, rythme et langue de spécialité." *Les Cahiers de l'APLIUT* 14. 3 (1995): 9–26.

Arleo, Andy. "Counting-out and the search for universals." *Journal of American Folklore* 110, n° 438 (1997): 391–407.

Arleo, Andy. "Music, song and foreign language teaching." *Les Cahiers de l'APLIUT* 19. 4 (2000): 6–19.

Baucomont, Jean *et al. Les Comptines de langue française*. Paris: Seghers, 1961.

Bolton, H[enry] C[arrington]. *The Counting-out Rhymes of Children* [1888]. Detroit: Singing Tree Press, 1969.

Brailoiu, C[onstantin]. "Children's rhythms." *Problems of Ethnomusicology*. Cambridge: Cambridge University Press, 1984: 206–238. Trans. A. L. Lloyd [Original article: "Le rythme enfantin," *Les Colloques de Wégimont*. Paris-Bruxelles: Elsevier, 1956. Reprinted as: "La rythmique enfantine," G. Rouget, ed., *Problèmes d'ethnomusicologie*. Genève: Minkoff Reprint, 1973: 267–299].

Brown, D[onald] E. *Human Universals*. New York: McGraw Hill, 1991.

Burling, R[obbins). "The metrics of children's verse: a cross-linguistic study." *American Anthropologist* 68 (1966): 1418–41.

Cornulier, Benoît de. *Art poëtique: notions et problèmes de métrique*. Lyon: Presses Universitaires de Lyon. 1995.

Despringre, André-Marie, éd. *Chants enfantins d'Europe: systèmes poético-musicaux de jeux chantés (France, Espagne, Chypre, Italie)*. Paris: Éd. l'Harmattan, 1997.

Hayes, B. and M. MacEachern. "Quatrain form in English folk verse." *Language* 74. 3 (1998): 473–507.

Jakobson, R[oman]. "Linguistics and poetics." *Style in language*, ed. by T[homas] A[lbert] Sebeok. Cambridge, Ma.: MIT Press, 1960, 350–77.

Jakobson, R[oman] and L[inda R.] Waugh. *La Charpente phonique du langage*, trans. A. Kihrn. Paris: Minuit, 1980. Original ed. *The Sound Shape of Language*. Brighton: Harvester Press, 1979.

Lehmann, W[infred] P[hilipp]. *The Development of Germanic Verse Form*. Austin: University of Texas Press, 1956.

Lerdahl, F[red] and R[ay] Jackendoff. *A Generative Theory of Tonal Music*. Cambridge, Mass.: 1983.

MacNeilage, Peter F. "The frame/content theory of evolution of speech production." *Behavioral and Brain Sciences* 21 (1998): 499–546.

Opie, I[ona] and P[eter]. *The Lore and Language of Schoolchildren*. Oxford: Oxford UP, 1959.

Opie, I[ona] and P[eter]. 1997. *Children's Games with Things*. Oxford: Oxford University Press.

Piaget, Jean. *Le Jugement moral chez l'enfant* [1932]. Paris: PUF, 1969.

Rubin, D[avid C.] *Memory in Oral Traditions: the Cognitive Psychology of Epic, Ballads, and Counting-out Rhymes*. Oxford: Oxford UP, 1995.

Sutton-Smith, B[rian]. "Psychology of childlore: the triviality barrier." *Western Folklore* 29 (1970): 1–8.

Discography

Webb, D. *Children's Singing Games*, 12-inch LP, Saydisc Records SDL 338, 1983.

Websites

http://kidslink.bo.cnr.it/cocomaro/conteinl.htm
[website on counting-out rhymes created by Mauro Presini, teacher at the Scuola elementare "B. Ciari" di Cocomaro di Cona, Italy]

http://www.humnet.ucla.edu/humnet/linguistics/people/hayes/metrics.htm
[website for Hayes & MacEachern 1998]

HOMELANDS

Landscape and identity in children's literature

Tony Watkins

Source: Wendy Parsons and Robert Goodwin (eds), *Landscape and Identity: Perspectives from Australia*, Adelaide: Auslib Press, 1994, pp. 3–20.

In the Tusitala edition of R. L. Stevenson's works, there appears a fable entitled 'The Persons of the Tale', bound in with that famous landscape of adventure, <u>Treasure Island</u>. I would like to read you the opening section of it.

A FABLE
THE PERSONS OF THE TALE

AFTER the 32nd chapter of Treasure Island, *two of the puppets strolled out to have a pipe before business should begin again, and met in an open place not far from the story.*

'Good morning, Cap'n,' said the first, with a man-o'-war salute and a beaming countenance.

'Ah, Silver!' grunted the other. 'You're in a bad way, Silver.'

'Now, Cap'n Smollett,' remonstrated Silver, 'dooty is dooty, as I knows, and none better; but we're off dooty now; and I can't see no call to keep up the morality business.'

'You're a damned rogue, my man,' said the Captain. 'Come, come, Cap'n, be just,' returned the other. There's no call to be angry with me in earnest. I'm on'y a chara'ter in a sea story. I don't really exist.'

'Well, I don't really exist either,' says the Captain, which seems to meet that.'

'I wouldn't set no limits to what a virtuous chara'ter might consider argument,' responded Silver. 'But I'm the villain of this tale, I am; and speaking as one seafaring man to another, what I want to know is, what's the odds?'

'Were you never taught your catechism' said the Captain. 'Don't you know – there's such a thing as an Author?'

'Such a thing as a Author?' returned John, derisively. And who better'n me? And the p'int is, if the Author made you, he made Long John, and he made Hands, and Pew, and George Merry – not that George is up to much, for he's little more'n a name; and he made Flint, what there is of him; and he made this here mutiny, you keep such a work about; and he had Tom Redruth shot; and – well, if that's a Author, give me Pew.
'Don't you believe in a future state?' said Smollett. 'Do you think there's nothing but the present storypaper?'
*'I don't rightly know for that,' said Silver 'and I don't see what it's got to do with it anyway. What I know is this: if there is sich a thing as **a** Author, I'm his favourite chara'ter. He does me fathoms better'n he does you – fathoms, he does. And he likes doing me. He keeps me on deck mostly all the time, crutch and all; and he leaves you measling in the hold, where nobody can't see you, nor wants to, and you may lay to that. If there is a Author, by thunder, but he's on my side, and you may lay to it!'*

In some ways, the fable seems extraordinarily contemporary: a postmodern text drawing attention to its own fictionality and raising the question of whether such a thing as an 'author' really exists.

[W]e are [. . .] concerned with fictions of landscape and fictions of identity of various kinds[:]

[. . .] I want to talk first of all about how some theorists from cultural geography and from cultural studies are conceptualising the study of landscape and identity. Then I want to suggest how myths of national identity can provide the <u>intertext</u> for understanding the meaning of the use of landscape in some works of children's literature and how both the images of landscape and myths of the nation help shape our children's identity.

I ought to say that my examples are drawn mainly from post-war British writing for children, but I also refer to one or two examples of American culture and American children's literature. [. . .]

I started with fiction because that should remind us how important fiction and narratives are in our lives. It has been argued that what we call social reality is a vast network of narratives that we use to make sense of experience, to understand the present, the past and the future. Narratives constantly shape and re-shape our identity as individuals and as members of a socially symbolic reality. As Barbara Hardy puts it:

we dream in narrative, daydream in narrative... In order really to live, we make up stories about ourselves and others, about the personal as well as the social past and future.

(Hardy 1977: 13)

Narratives help us turn the constant flow of events into intelligible experience. We relate narratives to one another in many forms: from gossip to literature there stretches a continuum of stories. This way of seeing things enables us to give children's literature its proper place: as Fred Inglis puts it, novels, including children's novels, can be thought of as 'the disciplined and public versions of the fictions we must have if we are to think at all.' (Inglis 1981: 310)

Stories contribute to the formation and re-formation in us and in our children of the cultural imagination, a network of patterns and templates through which we articulate our experience. Thus Paul Ricoeur argues that

> *In the same way that our experience of the natural world requires a mapping, a mapping is also necessary for our experience of social reality.*
>
> (Ricoeur 1986)

So the stories we tell our children, the narratives we give them to make sense of cultural experience constitute a kind of mapping, maps of meaning that enable our children to make sense of the world. These maps contribute to children's sense of <u>identity</u>, an identity that is simultaneously personal and social. Some narratives, we might say, shape the way children find a 'home' in the world.

Cultural geography, according to one expert in the field, is being transformed 'as a result of its dialogue with social geography and cultural theory'. I am not an expert in the field, but it appears to be a very fruitful dialogue. For example, some geographers are showing interest in the way that writers and other artists transform 'real' landscapes through the imagination into 'geographies of the mind' (Lowenthal & Bowden 1976; Jackson 1989: 1, 22) The notable examples are, of course, 'Hardy's Wessex' or 'the Constable country' of East Anglia.

But to see <u>something as</u> landscape is already to have constructed it in the mind: it is a cultural text, an image which is 'a construct of the mind and of feeling' (Tuan 1979: 89). So Denis Cosgrove, using a cultural materialist approach in his book <u>Social Formation and Symbolic Landscape,</u> (Cosgrove 1984) argues that even our <u>concept</u> of 'landscape' is 'a social and cultural product, a way of seeing projected on to the land and having its own techniques and compositional forms, but he argues that 'this is a restrictive way of seeing that diminishes alternative modes of experiencing our relations with nature.' (Cosgrove 1984: 269)

Other geographers, following the influence of cultural anthropologists such as Clifford Geertz (Geertz 1975), 'have also begun to "read" the landscape, to refer to its "biography" and to employ the metaphor of

landscape-as-text' (Jackson 1989: 173). The introduction to a 1988 collection of essays entitled <u>The Iconography of Landscape</u> (Cosgrove & Daniels
1988), argues that there are similarities between the work of the art
critic Erwin Panofsky (Panofsky 1970) and the ethnography of Clifford
Geertz, and declares that there is now 'common ground between practitioners from a variety of different disciplines concerned with landscape and
culture: geography, fine art, literature, social history and anthropology',
and that common ground has been established through the 'fertile concept
of iconography: the theoretical and historical study of symbolic imagery.'
(Cosgrove & Daniels 1988: 1)

It is interesting that the metaphor of the landscape as a text, as a book,
is carried through in writing for children, most notably, of course in Alan
Garner's title for his novel, <u>The Stone Book</u>, and in Penelope Lively's
comment that the landscape 'functions in layers, rather as I like a book to
function, the obvious and explicable shrouding the less obvious and accessible.' (Lively 1978: 203)

If we now move from cultural geography to cultural studies generally,
we engage with a debate between cultural materialism and cultural
hermeneutics. I want to sketch out some of the differences between them
and consider the way we can use them for reading the landscapes in children's literature.

Materialist, political approaches deriving from Marxism and feminism
obviously stress <u>power</u> as the major component of cultural text, power
which is often hidden or rendered apparently 'natural' through the process
of ideology. These approaches use what Thompson calls the 'critical' concept of ideology which is

> *essentially linked to the process of sustaining asymmetrical relations*
> *of power – that is, to the process of maintaining domination. It pre-*
> *serves the negative connotation which has been conveyed by the term*
> *throughout most of its history and binds the analysis of ideology to*
> *the question of critique.*
>
> (Thompson 1984: 4)

If ideology is embodied in cultural text, including the representation
of landscapes, the major task of the cultural critic is not only <u>understanding
the meaning</u> of the text but also <u>unmasking</u> what appears as natural as a
social construction which favours a particular class or group in society.
This process of 'ideology critique' or ideological deconstruction is often
carried out in literary studies, in 'a combination of historical context, theoretical method, political commitment and textual analysis' where it takes
the form called cultural materialism. For example, two Shakespeare critics
introduce their collection of essays entitled <u>Political Shakespeare: new
essays in cultural materialism</u> (1985) with the following explanation:

> *Historical context undermines the transcendent significance tradi-*
> *tionally accorded to the literary text and allows us to recover its*
> *histories: theoretical method detaches the text from immanent*
> *criticism which seeks only to reproduce it in its own terms; socialist*
> *and feminist commitment confronts the conservative categories in which*
> *most criticism has hitherto been conducted; textual analysis locates*
> *the critique of traditional approaches where it cannot be ignored. We*
> *call this cultural materialism.*
>
> (Dollimore and Sinfield 1985: vii)

Within this political paradigm, there have been some very interesting articles published recently on the symbolism of class politics in Frances Hodgson Burnett's The Secret Garden and Philippa Pearce's The Minnow on the Say, both novels which are very relevant to a conference such as this, on landscape and identity. (Phillips 1993; Krips 1993)

One of the most exciting works that I have read on ideology and children's literature was published in 1992. I refer, of course, to John Stephens' Language and Ideology in Children's Fiction. He presents a critical study of 'the discourse of narrative fiction' for children as a contribution to an understanding of 'the ideological practices and assumptions which determine a society's sense of meaning and value' and 'how individual selfhood is constructed' and 'what mechanisms govern interpersonal relationships and social hierarchies.' (Stephens 1992: 1)

To do this, he draws together elements of narrative theory, critical linguistics and contemporary thinking about ideology and subjectivity. He demonstrates how ideologies are implicated not only in what is represented but also in the process of representation: that textual structures embody ideologies and, to some extent, predetermine 'the significances readers may find'.

He provides an example very relevant to this conference on landscape and identity by asking 'to what extent is the representation of idyllic pastoral and anti-pastoral' in Milne's Winnie the Pooh and Hoban's The Mouse and His Child affected by different narratives modes and by the very different gap between explicit and implicit ideology in the two novels?' We might go on to develop John Stephens' question and ask, 'in what ways are the ideologies implicit in the representation of the landscape in the two novels – the British "self-contained Arcadia" (Townsend 1990: 135) of the Hundred-Acre Wood and the American quest for "territory" over a landscape of rubbish-dump and violent countryside related to myths of identity in the two countries?' At the same time, of course, we must recognise that such representations are historically located as are our interpretations of the two novels.

Another helpful aspect of John Stephens' work reminds us that ideological meanings of texts cannot be separated from the institutional and pedagogical contexts of their readings, for example, by children. Drawing on critical linguistics, John Stephens shows how texts construct subject positions for readers and thus offer one or more subjective identities which the reader can adopt for the duration of the reading. However, because taking up the subject position may involve subjection to the authority of focalization within texts, Stephens argues that there are important pedagogical implications for the teaching of reading:

> *the present habit of stressing reader-focused approaches to text in combination with advocacy of identification with focalizers, inconsistent as this combination may be, is a dangerous ideological tool and pedagogically irresponsible. It fosters an illusion that readers are in control of the text whereas they are highly susceptible to the ideologies of the text, especially the unarticulated or implicit ideologies.*
>
> (Stephens 1992: 68)

If we turn from critical concepts of ideology to more neutral ones, we move from cultural materialism to cultural hermeneutics.

Fred Inglis's new book entitled Cultural Studies (published in 1993) is dedicated to the cultural anthropologist, Clifford Geertz.

In his collection of essays, The Interpretation of Culture Geertz argues that 'man is an animal suspended in webs of significance he himself has spun'. He argues that those webs are what we call culture, and therefore the analysis of culture will be 'an interpretive one in search of meaning.' (Geertz 1975: 5) In another essay, he calls culture 'an assemblage of texts' and his analysis of a particular cultural text, the Balinese cockfight, leads him to call it 'a story they tell themselves about themselves.' (Geertz 1975: 448)

Geertz is aware of the danger that such cultural analysis may become what opponents call 'sociological aestheticism', and he argues that analyses must not lose touch with the 'hard surfaces of life – with the political, economic, stratificatory realities within which men are everywhere contained' (Geertz 1975, p. 30) But, inevitably, there is criticism of cultural analysts such as Clifford Geertz from those who see power at the heart of culture and society. For example, one critic argues that Geertz 'is mainly silent on the way cultural meanings sustain power and privilege . . . Where feminists and Marxists find oppression, symbolists find meaning.' (Keesing 1987: 166) Again, what Geertz forgets, it is argued, is that 'Cultures are webs of mystification as well as signification. We need to ask who creates and who defines cultural meanings, and to what ends.' (Keesing 1987: 161–2)

Fred Inglis, who has written at length on children's literature in his book The Promise of Happiness: Value and Meaning in Children's Fiction (Inglis 1981) argues in his new work that the subject of Cultural Studies 'is value, or rather, many values and the way in which values themselves are symbolized and rendered tangible by human making.'

The model of cultural analysis he favours is the interpretative one (sometimes called cultural hermeneutics) which aims at understanding intersubjective meanings. Cultural hermeneutics, according to Fred Inglis, is characterised by the following features:

1. 'The ambition of hermeneutics is always towards holistic inquiry, the understanding of a past in terms of its situation in the whole'.
2. 'Hermeneutics is dialogic; it presupposes interpretative exchange.'
3. 'The interpretive model is no more than a refined version of our understanding of other people in everyday life'.
4. 'We have to be part of the action while also capable of enough detachment to place it in a larger narrative. We have ... to make sense of what is happening ...'
5. 'To treat social action as a text is to bring out its configuration of values, its dominant patterns of imagery, its rhetoric, rhythms and form. To reverse the formula, to treat a text as social action is ... to recover the intentions embedded in that action.' (Inglis 1993: 144–7)

Notice that his emphasis is on understanding, and not criticism, using such concepts as ideology or hegemony which aim to deconstruct and demystify ideologies:

> Common or intersubjective meanings and values, therefore, are not only unavailable to hard data and social-survey analysis, they are also unamenable to the rough justice of hegemony – and ideology-criticism. Common meanings are not so much the exercise of hegemony as the presence of ethos, less ideology than structures of being and feeling. Hegemony and ideology are concepts heavy with blame.
>
> (Inglis 1993: 148)

What Inglis is concerned about is the tendency within Cultural Studies to collapse both aesthetics and morality into politics so that 'The study of culture translates into politics without remainder'. (It is ironic that part of the Marxist critique of the Scrutiny group of literary critics included the argument that Leavis and others had collapsed the category of politics into morality.) Inglis quotes Dollimore and Sinfield's statement that cultural materialism 'registers its commitment to the transformation of a social order which exploits people on grounds of race, gender and class' (Dollimore and Sinfield 1985: viii), but asks, using the same phrase which formed the title of his book about Children's Literature, 'What about the promise of happiness held out by art? What about art itself?' (Inglis 1993, pp. 175 & 181)

Taking Geertz's notion of culture, Inglis calls it 'an ensemble of <u>stories</u> we tell ourselves about ourselves' (Inglis 1993, p. 206) and thus argues that our historically changing identity is formed from experience and the 'narrative tradition' of which we are part. It is from this identity that we interpret the world:

'To meet the world I have to interpret it. My interpretation will be grounded in the narrative tradition of which I am a part and which in part constitutes who and what I am . . . My experience, like yours, can only <u>be lived</u> in relation to my (and your) narrative tradition. Neither of us can turn mere events into interpreted experience unless and until we place them in a story. That story, in its many variations, is provided by our narrative tradition. But to talk of 'our' tradition obscures the bloodstains on the traditions which are victorious. A tradition is an argument, sometimes with recourse to weapons (think of the great ideological arguments of the twentieth century). When that happens, of course, tradition becomes a war: between classes, nations, races, sexes.' (Inglis 1993, p. 207)

So, Inglis concludes,

> *the stories we tell ourselves about ourselves are not just a help to moral education; they comprise the only moral education which can gain purchase on the modern world. They are not aids to sensitivity nor adjuncts to the cultivated life. They are theories with which to think forwards . . . and understand backwards.*
>
> (Inglis 1993, p. 214)

How can we move from these debates back to the topic of landscape and identity in children's literature? In these ways, I think:

First, seeing landscape **as** 'landscape' and seeing landscape **as** a text, are both cultural responses to space (and time) that arise from certain historically located cultural frameworks or narrative traditions.

Second, if culture is an ensemble of stories with which to make sense of the world and our identity within it, then the stories we tell our children about landscape are a set of cultural texts which adults provide for children to make sense of themselves and the world. (They are also, of course, symbolic manifestations of the way we as adults regard children and consider what is suitable for them in the process of socialization).

Third, the cultural representations of the landscapes, particularly of home and homeland are articulations of cultural myths, which exist at a deep, unconscious level within culture. If culture is an ensemble of stories then myths exist, perhaps, as <u>proto</u>-narratives because they can be appropriated within different narratives and narrative traditions at different points in history.

Fourth, in looking at the representation of landscape for children, we must ask that question intolerably difficult to answer, what meanings do <u>children</u> take from those representations and how do they shape their identity? John Thompson underlines the importance in cultural analysis of the process of 'reading' or 'appropriation'. It is clear that a message constructed in certain ways may be understood very differently by different readers or 'recipients'. Further, the act of 'reading' is part of the process of self-formation and self-understanding:

> *The process of appropriation is an active and potentially critical process in which individuals are involved in a continuous **effort to understand**, an effort to make sense of the messages they receive, to relate to them and to share them with others ... They are not passively absorbing what is presented to them, but are actively, sometimes critically, engaged in a continuing process of self-formation and self-understanding ...*
>
> (Thompson 1990: 25)

All that, of course, applies to the theme of landscape and identity in children's literature.

Fifth, what about the question of power in such representations? I have two suggestions, neither of them entirely satisfactory.

The first suggestion is the argument that one of the gains of post-structuralism has been to remind us of the polysemic nature of cultural texts: that they have not **a** meaning, but many meanings. It does not <u>necessarily</u> follow from this that the text becomes a site of <u>struggle</u> over meaning. We may have something to learn from what appears to be an emerging paradigm associated with what is called 'the new physics' of relativity and quantum theories. As one enthusiast wrote recently, in physics, the results of Einstein's theory of relative frame of reference and the quantum theorists' inclusion of 'indeterminism, abrupt change and the observer's context in their equations' meant that

> *Hierarchy, absolute certainty and the single point of view were out. A new kind of democracy of perspective, the positive value of ambiguity, of rapid and unpredictable change, and pluralism were in.*
>
> *Just as the old Newtonian science fired the imagination of a whole host of thinkers from other fields, this new science offers us a rich repository of language, metaphor and allusion, a whole new set of images that we can apply to today's experience.*
>
> (Zohar 1994: 14)

or is this simply no more than cultural relativism in a new guise?

The second answer is, that the relevance of the analysis of power in representations will depend upon the specifics of the text and of the contexts of its production and reception.

What we must guard against is, on the one hand, a form of so-called 'sociological aestheticism' that ignores the dimension of power in cultural text, and on the other hand, we must avoid collapsing cultural text into **nothing but** the manifestation of power.

I want to turn now to the most 'felicitous' of spaces: the landscape of home, or rather, of the homeland.

Cultural geographers use what one of them calls 'a simple tripartite classification [which] recognizes sacred, profane and mundane space.' (Norton 1989: 127) 'All sacred spaces vary according to a number of characteristics. They are capable of eliciting a number of emotions such as pride, nostalgia, and spiritual devotion. The intensity of the emotion depends on how 'sacred' the space is.' (Norton 1989: 127) 'Homelands are sacred space because they represent the roots of each individual, family or people.' (Jackson & Henrie 1983: 95 quoted in Norton 1989: 127)

Another geographer, D. W. Meinig, refers to homelands as symbolic landscapes: 'Every mature nation has its symbolic landscapes. They are part of the iconography of nationhood, part of the shared set of ideas and memories and feelings which bind a people together.' (Meinig 1979b: 164)

In Britain, the national myth of a 'real England' or a 'deep England' is powerful and long-lasting: it still strongly shapes the sense of British identity and it forms an important line of imagery in British children's literature. Nevertheless, we have to realise, as some critics have suggested that

> *Englishness has had to be made and re-made in and through history, within available practices and relationships, and existing symbols and ideas. That symbols and ideas recur does not ensure that their meaning is the same. Meaning is not solely a property of genealogy, but a matter of present context and practical life.*
>
> (Colls & Dodd 1986: Preface)

But the same collection of essays also argues that, although since the 1860s, England has become an urban and industrial nation 'the ideology of England and Englishness is to a remarkable degree rural. Most importantly, a large part of the English **ideal** is rural . . . What our rural image does is present us with a "real England". Here men and women still live naturally . . . It is an organic society, a "real" one, as opposed to the unnatural or "unreal" society of the town.' (Howkins 1986: 62–63) But this is not just a way of seeing the countryside. Bound up in the image of 'Englishness' can be cultural values relating to work, to architecture, to gender, and a model of society itself. For some, the real England is 'an organic and natural society of ranks, and of inequality in an economic and social sense, but [also] one based on trust, obligation and even love.' (Howkins 1986: 80)

What stories do children's novelists tell about landscape and how do such stories connect with such larger narratives or myths of our cultural imagination?

A number of British children's writers use rural landscape as central metaphors within their work: for example, since the Second World War, one thinks of Rosemary Sutcliff, William Mayne, Alan Garner, Penelope Lively, Lucy Boston, Philippa Pearce. Particular parts of Britain become associated with them: to set alongside Hardy's Wessex, we have 'Mayne's Yorkshire' and 'Garner's Cheshire'. Some of these novelists concentrate on particular features of the landscape; for example, think of the presence of old houses in the novels of Lucy Boston and Philippa Pearce.

Many of these postwar writers, it seems to me, share a similar 'structure of feeling', to use Raymond Williams' concept (Williams 1977: 128–35) and use their representation of the English landscape to articulate a response to socio-political change. (Stephens 1992, p. 221) But Williams' concept of 'structure of feeling' is a complex one; as one commentator suggests, it 'refers to meanings and values as they are actually lived, not just to formal worldviews or ideologies.' (Jackson 1989: 39) However, most importantly for us, it was the concept that Williams used (Williams 1973) to understand the 'persistent and complex feelings evoked by the symbolic opposition of "country" and "city."' (Jackson 1989: 39)

An important text for understanding the structure of feeling of the particular postwar children's writers I want to talk about, is W. G. Hoskins' The Making of the English Landscape, originally published in 1955 but published in many editions since then. In his book, Hoskins takes the landscape of England as it appears in 1955 and explains how it came to assume its present form. He closes his book with the chapter 'The Landscape Today', in which he laments that 'since 1914, every single change in the English landscape has either uglified it or destroyed its meaning, or both.' He deplores the social process of modernisation and industrialisation which has led to the rise of bureaucratic planning:

'The country houses decay and fall: hardly a week passes when one does not see the auctioneer's notice of the impending sale and dissolution of some big estate.' If the house stands near a town, then the 'political planners swarm into the house, turn it into a rabbit-warren of black-hatted officers of This and That, and the park becomes a site for some "overspill" – a word as beastly as the thing it describes. . . . And if the planners are really fortunate, they fill the house with their paper and their black hats, and their open-cast mining of coal or iron ore simultaneously finishes off the park. They can sit at their desks and contemplate with an exquisite joy how everything is now being put to a good use. Demos and Science are the joint Emperors.' (Hoskins 1955: 231)

Hoskins rails, in ringing tones, against the state of postwar England embodied in what the 'vandals' have done to the landscape:

> *England of the Nissen hut, the 'pre-fab,' and the electric fence, of the high barbed wire around some unmentionable devilment; England of the arterial bypass, treeless and stinking of diesel oil, murderous with lorries; England of the bombing range wherever there was once silence . . . England of high explosive falling upon the prehistoric monuments of Dartmoor. Barbaric England of the scientists, the military men, and the politicians: let us turn away and contemplate the past before all is lost to the vandals.*
>
> (Hoskins 1955: 232)

In the final pages of the book, he does turn away: to contemplate 'an epitome of the gentle unravished English landscape': the view from the room in his house in the Oxfordshire countryside in which he is writing. How does this text, this story of England through its landscape, link with some of the writers for children I mentioned earlier?

In discussing the early Roman-British novels of Rosemary Sutcliff, Fred Inglis argues that what 'comes through as the strongest impulse to feelings is often an intensity of loss and regret, not bitter but intensely nostalgic, for the sweetness of a youth and a landscape intolerably vanished. Rosemary Sutcliff invokes time and again the great images of an organic literature – pure water, oak, ash, may, blackthorn, a cleansed and abundant landscape; . . . she appeals to a symbolism which is largely destroyed and she does so because she needs to disbelieve in the reality of that destruction.'

Her novels 'define a response' which Inglis sees as shared by a <u>group</u> of writers and teachers who hold as their only set beliefs, a 'pale, anxious and rinsed-out liberalism':

> *Rosemary Sutcliff's novels define the response of such a group to the loss of the English landscape both in itself and as a symbol of one version of Englishness; they further define a powerful and unfulfilled longing for a richer moral vocabulary and an ampler, more graceful and courteous style of living such as at the present can only be embodied in a stylized past.*
>
> (Inglis 1971, pp. 71–2)

John Stephens notes that although there was a change of emphasis in Rosemary Sutcliff's novels 'between meaning inhering in Roman civilization and that 'constructed in the depiction of "primitive" Celtic tribal societies ... neither the register employed nor the basic ideology it encodes has undergone any dramatic shift' as he shows in his analysis of <u>Sun Horse, Moon Horse</u>. (Stephens 1992, p. 221) It is significant that the title of Rosemary Sutcliff's autobiography is <u>Blue Remembered Hills</u>, a title taken from the following lines of A. E. Housman's 'A Shropshire Lad':

> *Into my heart an air that kills*
> *From yon far country blows:*
> *What are those blue remembered hills,*
> *What spires, what farms are those?*
> *This is the land of lost content,*
> *I see it shining plain,*
> *The happy highways where I went*
> *And cannot come again.*
> (Housman 1988: 64)

So Rosemary Sutcliff yearns nostalgically for the lost landscape of childhood, the lost landscape of 'real' England, and the lost landscape of values she has cherished.

Penelope Lively also formulates a response to change. In her novels, she is 'concerned with memory' rather than with the past: to write about the past is to write history: 'What I am trying to do is to translate into fictional terms that marvellous process of recollection interpersed with oblivion that goes on inside our own heads. History is another matter altogether; history is linear and chronological and public.' (Lively 1987: 15) Because of her own 'amazed vision', as a child, 'of the layered world', she has used the English landscape in her books to suggest to children 'something of the palimpsest quality both of people and of places, those layerings of memory of which both are composed.' (Lively 1987: 14, 16). The need to relate to landscape, particularly 'man-made landscape' is a need to 'relate to our own past and our future within it'. By doing this, we and our children can escape from isolation of the mind, intellectual egotism, for 'the revelation that there is a collective past is the revelation also that the collective past is composed of myriad private pasts, that the pursuit of social memory is matched by the need for personal memory.' Thus, the presentation of landscape in the stories Penelope Lively tells children, has the important liberal-humanist moral purpose of the exercise of the historical imagination 'to make the imaginative leap into the experience of others'. (Lively 1987: 20–21).

But in 1976, the same year in which she published her novel, <u>A Stitch in Time</u>, a novel which John Stephens calls, 'overtly ideological in its presentation of secular humanism as a position from which to view historical process and to understand being-in-the-world' (Stephens 1992: 214),

Penelope Lively also published an introduction to landscape history entitled <u>The Presence of the Past</u>. The book, although not overtly written for children, is very accessible to teenagers. It opens with an explicit tribute to W. G. Hoskins' <u>The Making of the English Landscape</u>, and in the concluding chapter, there is a significant additional link with Hoskins' book in terms of values and meaning (or, if you wish, in terms of ideology). She too writes from a village in the Oxfordshire countryside and contrasts the rapid social change that has resulted in new houses being built in this small **heart** of a green England, with the centuries of slow peaceful change:

> The village in which I live has around seventy houses: of these, well over half have been built within the last fifteen years. The rest grew, piecemeal, each one presumably a large event in a small place, over four centuries. Today's children are used, as no others have been before, to seeing landscape in a state of flux – to seeing buildings collapse before the bulldozer and fields vanish beneath motorways. We shall need today's photographs in fifty years' time, but just as much, each of us, we shall need those pictures in the head of a land-scape that will be even further bruised and maimed by then. I want to remember, when I am old, that this summer I stood high on an Iron Age hill-fort, with eyebright and milkwort and blue and copper butter-flies at my feet, and watched kestrels hang at eye level against green Dorset . . . That it was still possible to travel west from Oxford through one village after another in which limestone buildings eclipsed the rest.
>
> (Lively 1976: 210–211)

So, again we have landscape used to articulate a response to <u>change</u>. Penelope Lively is concerned about loss but is also fascinated by the complexity of memory layered as a landscape.

Think next of the way the old house motif is used in some English children's books. In Alison Uttley's <u>A Traveller in Time</u> (1939), the farm-house of Thackers that has stood in the countryside since Elizabethan times becomes a symbol of continuity to set against the threat of change, as one commentator puts it,

> Uttley's 'place' is not simply a physical landscape; it is an attitude, a mood, and a position in time as well . . . Thackers is more than the house, the farm. It is also the attitude of the people who have lived there and loved the place and who will live there and love it in coming years. And it is the land itself, which existed before it had a name and will endure after those who loved it are gone.
>
> (Pflieger 1984: ?)

Continuity pervades Uttley's <u>A Traveller in Time</u> but when we get to Philippa Pearce and Lucy Boston, there is an acute sense of loss and change, which is only partly assuaged. Phillipa Pearce wrote <u>Tom's Midnight Garden</u> in 1958 because the house and garden of her childhood in which the novel is set, were 'under threat' of social change. She has said,

> *I wrote the story in the nineteen fifties: that was my personal Present.*
> *However, I set the story slightly in the future – say, the nineteen*
> *sixties. That was because, in the fifties, I thought the house and*
> *garden – hardly changed from my father's childhood – was under*
> *threat, and I wanted to imagine that threat executed – the house split*
> *into flats, the garden built over.*
>
> (Pearce 1990: 72)

The worsening changes brought about by modernisation and industrialisation do not only affect the garden and the house. In a remarkably modern passage (remember the novel was written in 1958), Tom and Aunt Gwen, in present time, walk along the same river that Tom and Hatty had reached through the meadow. Then, it had been flowing out of 'the Eden' of the nineteenth century house and its garden, now it is a surreal wasteland in which the man fishing by the bridge has caught no fish because there are none and the waters have been certified as unsuitable for bathing, wading or paddling 'owing to pollution.' When Tom asks his Aunt what pollution is, she replies, 'It's something to do with all the houses that have been built, and the factories. Dreadful stuff gets into rivers from factories, I believe.' (Pearce 1976: 152).

In Lucy Boston's <u>A Stranger at Green Knowe</u> published in 1961, Hanno the Gorilla escapes from the zoo to the ancient house of Green Knowe, a replica in fiction of Lucy Boston's house, the 900 year old Norman manor house at Hemingford Grey in Huntingdonshire. The house is 'timeless', another symbol of continuity and a sanctuary from the pace of change: as one visitor to the house says,

> *Nowadays everything is changing so quickly we all feel chased about*
> *and trapped . . . And yet here, in the heart of industrial England, is*
> *this extraordinary place where you can draw an easy breath.*
>
> (Boston 1977: 90)

Urban England is represented as a place where modernisation has meant that life is moribund because it has lost touch with the vital force of nature: 'In our big cities there is nothing at all not made by ourselves except the air. We are our context and live by ourselves picking each other's brains. There's no vital force. Electronic Man.' (Boston 1977: 89)

Hanno, on other hand is one of the 'stupendous creatures...elemental stuff packed with compressed vitality, from whom everything is still to come.' (Boston 1977: 88)

But the landscape of the ancient house and its garden prove only a temporary sanctuary for the displaced Hanno: he is shot dead in the garden of Green Knowe. The novel is a tragedy and the tragic hero dies heroically: 'He's dead' [Ping] said clearly and too composedly. 'It's all right. That is how much he didn't want to go back, I saw him choose.'

Alan Garner also uses landscape as a response to social and personal change; but his social and ideological positions are different from some of the other writers I have mentioned. Garner's position is that of the postwar working-class boy enabled by the 1944 Education Act to go to Grammar School and Oxford University: up to that time largely the privilege of the middle-classes. (Incidentally, it would be interesting to compare Garner's response to his experiences with that of other writers like Dennis Potter and Richard Hoggart). Garner was the first of his family's line of working-class rural Cheshire craftsmen to experience the mixed blessing of Grammar School and Oxbridge education. As he said himself, 'gain had been bought with loss' because he was forced to 'suppress, and even to deride', his 'primary native tongue', which he calls 'Northwest Mercian' and 'standard, received English' was <u>imposed</u> on him. But language is not just a medium of communication, it is an embodiment of meanings and values and ideologies and ways of experiencing the world. The suppression and alienation which Garner experienced produced in him 'a fine anger' which makes itself felt, for example, in his novel <u>Elidor</u>, in his description of the suburban landscape surrounding Roland Watson's house. In the novel, Roland's Watson's family have moved to the country because Mrs. Watson wanted her children to grow up there. But what had been a country cottage now stands in a suburban road. In article published some years ago, I wrote

> the sense of values suggested by the English countryside and the implications of its loss are strong in Garner's work: the suburb is growing and engulfing the countryside and instead of real contact with the land, its natural community and seasonal cycles, people are forced to accept a sentimental substitute which expresses itself in the sonorously romantic house names, the respectable but limited gardens:
> 'The street lamps were on when he walked up the road from the station. He plucked leaves off the hedges as he passed. Ivanhoe, Fern Bank, Strathdene, Rowena, Trelawney: respectable houses bounded by privet, each with its square of grass... Whinfield, Eastholme, Glenroy, Orchard Main. What could happen here? thought Roland. Even the toadstools are made of concrete.'
>
> (Watkins 1972: 60–61)

But, of course, the anger goes well beyond this satirical jibe at the bourgeois way of life. His writing, Garner says, is 'prompted by a feeling of outrage – personal, social, political, and linguistic,' which stems partly from the guilt he felt about education that made him 'a stranger to [his] own people'. But the natural landscape of Cheshire and the language associated with it becomes a positive symbol in Garner's work. He says,

> On one square mile of Cheshire hillside, Alderley Edge, the Garners *are*. We know our place. And this sense of fusion with a land rescued me. The education that had made me a stranger to my own people, yet had shown me no acceptable alternative, did increase my understanding of the hill. . . . Until I came to terms with the paradox, I was denied, and I myself denied, the people. But those people had their analogue in the land, and toward that root I began to move the stem of the intellect grown hydroponically in the academic hothouse.
>
> (Garner 1987: 123)

Garner's poetic evocation of landscape, of the relationship of people and land, and of present and past, can be demonstrated by the ending of Tom Fobble's Day, the last of 'The Stone Book Quartet'. William runs, with the two talismanic horseshoes, from the body of his dead grandfather to the top of the hill, :

> The line did hold. Through hand and eye, block, forge and loom to the hill and all that he owned, he sledged sledged sledged for the black and glittering night and the sky flying on fire and the expectation of snow.
>
> (Garner 1977: 72)

It is a feeling for landscape which Garner describes as religious: he claims the land is sacred to him in the same way it is to the Aboriginal peoples of Australia:

> For the Australian the Ancestor exists simultaneously under the earth; in ritual objects; in places such as rocks, hills, springs, waterfalls; as 'spirit children' waiting between death and rebirth; and, most significantly, as the man in whom he is incarnate. It is a world view close to the one I discovered for myself as a child of my family on Alderley Edge.
>
> (Garner 1987: 127–8)

There may be some illuminating parallels too, to be drawn with the work of the adult poet Geoffrey Hill, the author of Mercian Hymns. In an interview, Hill said of one of his sequence of poems: 'The celebration of the inherited beauties of English landscape is bound, in the texture of the sequence, with an equal sense of the oppression of the tenantry.' (quoted in Gervais 1993: 224) and one critic, in commenting on Geoffrey Hill's poetry, uses words which could easily apply to Alan Garner's Stone Book:

> *For the poet who uses a fallen language there are two ways of imagining the past, one nostalgic and the other redemptive, but they are too complementary to be easily told apart.*

(Gervais 1993: 225)

Perhaps landscapes of home and homeland are inevitably nostalgic and nostalgia is certainly deeply rooted within the tradition of English cultural thinking: as David Gervais wrote recently on nostalgia in English intellectual life: 'it has not been just the sentimentalists among us who have yearned for the England before the Great War. It needs no ghost come from the dead to remind us what deep feelings have been sharpened by that watershed, severing for good what continuity had been left untouched by a rampant industrialism.' Indeed, he continues, 'It is, in fact, arguable that, without nostalgia, for many of us the past might not exist at all. The malady is not simply deep-seated – it may even be necessary.' (Gervais 1993: 226)

Perhaps all study of culture, including landscape as cultural text, needs to recognise the importance of nostalgia which can be used critically to criticize the present:

> *Nostalgia is not a swearword. It may be as much a powerful force for good and positive action as it may be a passive or anaesthetic pervasion of the spirit . . . a view of history in which the always fluid present is criticized against the known settlement of a past community pulls towards nostalgia. Cultural Studies are tugged between critical nostalgia and critical policy-making for the future: between longing and hope.*

(Inglis 1993: 46–7)

I want to turn now to American culture and American landscapes in children's literature. Meinig, writing in 1979, saw three symbolic landscapes in American culture which constituted part of 'the iconography of nationhood'.

First is the scene of a village in New England, 'embowered in great elms and maples, its location marked by a slender steeple rising gracefully above a white wooden church which faces on a village green around which are arrayed large white clapboard houses which, like the church, show a simple elegance in form and trim.' (Meining 1979b: 165)

Second, is Main Street of Middle America, 'running east and west, a business thoroughfare aligned with the axis of national development.' It is 'Middle' in several senses: it lies between the frontier to the west and the seaports to the east; it is a commercial centre surrounded by agriculture and local industry; in social class, there are no extremes of wealth or poverty, a genuine community; in size, it is the right size for friendship and familiarity. 'For many people over many decades of our national life' says Meinig, 'this is the landscape of "small town virtues", the "backbone of America", the "real America".' (Meinig 1979b: 167)

Unfortunately, I do not have time in this talk, but I am very interested in analysing popular landscapes for children and adults such as Disneyland and Disneyworld. Meinig points out the conscious link between the symbolic landscape of Middle America and 'the meticulously constructed Main Street' in Disneyland which, he says, 'remains the most popular of the many sections of the massively popular Disneyland . . . a tangible symbolic landscape, a focus for persisting nostalgia for what is imagined to have been a better scale and form of community than most of its visitors now enjoy.' (Meining 1979b: 179) The analysis of Disney's theme parks as cultural text will be even more important now that the Disney corporation has chosen the spot (Haymarket, Virginia) for its third park in the U.S.A. with the theme, 'the history of America.' (Independent (London) 19.1.94)

The third landscape Meinig mentions, is Suburban California which, he argues, is linked to the myth of westward movement in the U.S.A. This landscape also connects to one of America's myths of national identity: that of wilderness and frontier. It has been argued recently that 'Americans are truly American when they (re)create the frontier condition.' (Short 1991: 94) and that in the U.S.A., the frontier has become a 'a major point of reference, a pivot for public debate which not only describes the past but also evaluates the present and contemplates the future.' (Short 1991: 95)

The concept of the frontier leads me to re-consider Frank Baum's novel The Wizard of Oz (1900). The novel was written against the plight and poverty of the farmers of South Dakota in the 1890s, and it was against the background of the Great Depression of 1930s America that MGM's famous film of The Wizard of Oz, starring Judy Garland, was made in 1939. What most people remember about the film, whose 25th anniversary is being celebrated this year, are Dorothy's last lines:

DOROTHY: *'Oh, but anyway, Toto, we're home – home! And this is my room – and you're all here – and I'm not going to leave here ever, ever again, because I love you all! And . . . oh, Auntie Em, there's no place like home!'*

(Langley *et al.* 1989: 132)

75

Home and homeland are central to the mythic status which the novel and, subsequently the film, acquired. The novel opens with an image of home and landscape: Dorothy's small wooden house situated in the middle of the vast Kansas prairies. But it is a grey arid landscape supporting a way of life that has taken all joy and laughter from Dorothy's Aunt Em and Uncle Henry. (Baum 1979: 2) From her Kansas home Dorothy is whirled away by a cyclone to a country that seems to be the very opposite of Kansas: because Oz is small, colourful and fertile (you may recall that the film changes at this point from monochrome to colour), whereas Kansas was grey and arid and Oz is wealthy where Kansas was poor. As Brian Attebury points out:

> *Oz is not plagued with droughts and crop failures, nor with bankers and mortgages, as Kansas most assuredly was.*
>
> (Attebury 1983: 281)

But symbolically, Dorothy has not left America. She has entered a symbolic landscape that, as Attebury argues,

> *[forms] American's image of the western frontier: it is the Garden of the World set in the midst of the Great American Desert.*
>
> (ibid.)

It is an American utopia incorporating elements that draw upon and contribute to the myths of national identity. As an article by Michael Bracewell put it in January this year,

> *one of the functions of Oz has been to offer a kind of secular paradise. To take this argument further, one could say that Dorothy discovers in Oz a prelapsarian paradise, an Eden before the fall, and that this, in turn, is a mirror of the American Dream of an unspoilt land of opportunity.*
>
> (Bracewell 1994: 18)

In the politics of this American utopia, the great and powerful Wizard turns out to be a common man from Omaha. Dorothy, the ordinary girl from Kansas, works to return home in the company of a scarecrow, a tin woodman and a cowardly lion. They all find they have powers that they had not realised they possessed. The 'American myth' of individualism and self-reliance is confirmed: it has been claimed by various critics and commentators, for example, that: 'in Oz, Baum actually added another state to the Union'; that it is 'the first American fairyland' whose characters have become 'part of our language and folklore' (Thompson 1983: 178, 176); and that the virtues of Oz,

are the homely American virtues of family love, friendliness for the
stranger, sympathy for the underdog, practicality and commonsense
in facing life, reliance on one's self for solutions to one's problems.

(Nye 1983: 174)

But the myth of the frontier in the U.S.A. underwent great changes during
the late 1960s and 1970s as a result of the Vietnam war. In his study,
<u>American Myth and the Legacy of Vietnam</u>, John Hellman argues that

Vietnam is an experience that has severely called into question Amer-
ican myth. Americans entered Vietnam with certain expectations
that a story, a distinctly American story, would unfold.

because Indochina had become the new mythic American frontier and
early attempts at American intervention in Vietnam were ways of achieving
an identity and working out a moral purpose. The Vietnam war was 'in
effect a symbolic war in which the true terrain was the American character.'
However, he goes on

When the story of America in Vietnam turned into something unex-
pected, the true nature of the larger story of America itself became
the subject of intense cultural dispute. On the deepest level, the legacy
of Vietnam is the disruption of our story, of our explanation of the
past and vision of the future.

(Hellman 1986: x)

So, when Walter Dean Myers wrote his novel for teenagers about the
Vietnam war, entitled <u>Fallen Angels</u>, (Myers 1990) he was contributing to
changing the myth of American identity that took place during the Vietnam
war and the years after.

However, if the deep national myth of the American frontier has
been disrupted, the myth of Oz, and its articulation in texts, after some
buffeting over the years, lives on. It is true that the story was singled out as
being 'deeply, traitorously "un-American" in its embrace of oddball character and fantasy' (Bracewell 1994: 18) and banned in some parts of the
U.S.A. during the McCarthy campaigns of the 1950s. But during the 1960s,
the story was appropriated by the homosexual community (Bracewell tells
us that 'Homosexuals became known as "friends of Dorothy" because the
only people friendly to Judy Garland on the set [of the 1939] film were
homosexual make-up artists.') and by the subversive counter-cultural
magazine, <u>Oz</u>. In 1992, Salman Rushdie could still make major claims
for the power of the 1939 film. Not only does he say that the film played an
important part in forming his identity as a writer (he says, 'When I first
saw <u>The Wizard of Oz</u> it made a writer of me') (Rushdie 1992: 18), but he
makes this larger claim about Oz and the sense of our identity:

the truth is that once we have left our childhood places and started out to make up our real lives, armed only with what we have and are, we understand that the real secret of the ruby slippers is not that 'there's no place like home', but rather that there is no longer any such place as home: except, of course, for the home we make, or homes that are made for us, in Oz: which is anywhere, and everywhere, except the place from which we began.

(Rushdie 1992: 57)

It seems that Oz itself has acquired a mythic status, or rather that Oz has become a way of exploring what home means today to many people in America and Europe, as the success of the very fine novel for adults, Was by Geoff Ryman perhaps testifies. (Ryman 1992) Ryman's novel, also published in 1992, severely modifies the myth of frontier life as harsh and cruel, but sees Oz as a necessary and critical utopia. As Ryman says in the afterword to the novel,

Tomorrow, we could all decide to live in a place not much different from Oz. We don't. We continue to make the world an ugly, even murderous place, for reasons we do not understand.

(Ryman 1992: 453)

I hope that what has come through in some of the things I have been talking about is, first, that landscape is in a constant state of change: that landscape is a palimpsest, re-written upon through time and history as a result of the work and activity of a range of people. Second, that cultural images of landscape for children have a social and historical location: why this image of this place at this time? Third, that responses to such cultural images of landscapes are forms of re-writing in history: responses by individuals as members of social groups or appropriation by groups themselves, re-writing the images and the meaning of those landscapes. Fourth, that cultural myths of landscape structure and inform the texts of children's literature but that those myths are themselves partly re-formed through their articulation in children's literature.

[. . .]

References

Attebury, B. (1983), 'Oz' in M. P. Hearn (ed.), The Wizard of Oz N.Y.: Schocken Books (1983)

Baum, L. F. (1979), The Wizard of Oz N.Y.: Ballantyne Books

Biersack, Aletta (1989), 'Local Knowledge, Local History: Geertz and Beyond' in Lynn Hunt (ed.), The New Cultural History, Berkeley; University of California Press, pp. 72–96

Boston, Lucy (1977), A Stranger at Green Knowe, Harmondsworth; Puffin (first pub. Faber 1961)

Bracewell, Michael (1994), 'The Never-Ending Story' The Times Magazine, January 29, 1994, pp. 18–19

Colls, Robert & Dodd, Philip (eds.), Englishness: Politics and Culture 1880–1920, London; Croom Helm 1986

Cosgrove, Denis (1984), Social Formation and Symbolic Landscape, London; Croom Helm

Cosgrove, Denis and Daniels, Stephen (eds.) (1988), The Iconography of Landscape: essays on the symbolic representation, design and use of past environments, Cambridge; Cambridge University Press

Dollimore, Jonathan & Sinfield, Alan (1985), Political Shakespeare: New Essays in Cultural Materialism, Manchester, Manchester University Press

Garner, Alan (1977), Tom Fobbles's Day, London; Collins

Garner, Alan (1987), 'Achilles in Altjira' in Barbara Harrison & Gregory Maguire, Innocence and Experience: Essays & Conversations on Children's Literature, New York; Lothrop, Lee & Shepard, pp. 116–128

Geertz, Clifford (1975), The Interpretation of Cultures, London; Hutchinson

Gervais, David (1993), Literary Englands: Versions of Englishness in Modern Writing, Cambridge; Cambridge University Press

Hardy, Barbara (1977), 'Towards a poetics of fiction: an approach through narrative' in M. Meek et al. (eds.) The Cool Web: the Pattern of Children's Reading, London; Bodley Head

Hoggart, Richard (1957), The Uses of Literacy: aspects of working-class life with special reference to publications and entertainments, London; Chatto & Windus

Hoskins, W. G. (1955), The Making of the English Landscape, London; Hodder & Stoughton, pp. 62–88

Housman, A. E. (1988), Collected Poems and Selected Prose (ed. C. Ricks), London; Allen

Howkins, Alun (1986), 'The Discovery of Rural England' in Robert Colls & Philip Dodd (eds.) Englishness: Politics and Culture 1880–1920, London; Croom Helm 1986

Inglis, Fred (1971), 'Reading children's novels: notes on the politics of literature', Children's Literature in Education, 5, 1971, pp. 60–75

Inglis, Fred (1981), The Promise of Happiness: Value and Meaning in Children's Fiction, Cambridge; Cambridge University Press

Inglis, Fred (1993), Cultural Studies, Oxford; Blackwell

Jackson, Peter (1989), Maps of Meaning: An Introduction to Cultural Geography, London; Unwin Hyman

Jackson R. H. & Henrie R. (1983), 'Perception of sacred space', Journal of Cultural Geography, 3, pp. 94–107

Keesing, Roger M. (1987), 'Anthropology as Interpretive Quest', Current Anthropology 28, quoted in Biersack (1989)

Krips, Valerie (1993), 'A Notable Irrelevance: Class and Children's Fiction', The Lion & the Unicorn, 17, 2, pp. 195–209

Langley, Noel et al. (1989), The Wizard of Oz: from the book by Frank L. Baum, London; Faber

Lively, Penelope (1978), 'Children and the Art of Memory: Part II', The Horn Book, Vol. LIV, 2, pp. 197–203

Lively, Penelope (1987), 'Bones in the Sand', in Barbara Harrison & Gregory Maguire, Innocence and Experience: Essays & Conversations on Children's Literature, New York; Lothrop, Lee & Shepard, pp. 13–21

Lowenthal, D. & Bowden, M. J. (eds.) (1976), Geographies of the Mind, Oxford; Oxford University Press

Meinig, D. W. (ed.) (1979a), The Interpretation of Ordinary Landscapes: Geographical Essays, Oxford; Oxford University Press

Meinig, D. W. (1979b), 'Symbolic Landscapes: Some Idealizations of American Communities' in D. W. Meinig (ed.), The Interpretation of Ordinary Landscapes: Geographical Essays, Oxford; Oxford University Press

Myers, Walter Dean (1990), Fallen Angels, London; Harper Collins

Norton, William (1989), Explorations in the Understanding of Landscape: a Cultural Geography, New York; Greenwood Press

Nye, R. B. (1983), 'An Appreciation' in M. P. Hearn (ed.) The Wizard of Oz N.Y.; Schocken Books

Panofsky, Erwin (1970), 'Iconography and Iconology: an introduction to the study of Renaissance art' in Erwin Panofsky, Meaning in the visual arts, Harmondsworth; Penguin, pp. 51–81

Pearce Philippa (1976), Tom's Midnight Garden, Harmondsworth; Puffin Books (first pub. 1958 by Oxford University Press)

Pearce, Philippa (1990), 'Time present' in Barbara Harrison et al., Travellers in Time: Past, Present and To Come, Cambridge; Green Bay Publications, pp. 70–74

Pflieger, Pat (1984), A Reference Guide to Modern Fantasy for Children, New York; Greenwood Press

Phillips, Jerry (1993), 'The Mem Sahib, the Worthy, the Rajah and his Minions: Some Reflections on the Class Politics of The Secret Garden', The Lion & the Unicorn, 17, 2, pp. 168–194

Ricoeur, Paul (1986), Lectures on Ideology and Utopia, New York, Columbia University Press Rushdie, Salmon, The Wizard of Oz (BFI Film Classics), London; BFI Publishing 1992, 27

Ryman, Geoff (1992), Was, London; HarperCollins

Short, John Rennie (1991), Imagined Country: Environment, Culture and Society, London; Routledge

Sopher, David E. (1979), 'The Landscape of Home: Myth, Experience, Social Meaning' in D. W. Meinig (ed.), The Interpretation of Ordinary Landscapes: Geographical Essays, Oxford; Oxford University Press, pp. 129–149

Stephens, John (1992), Language and Ideology in Children's Fiction, London; Longman

Sutcliff, Rosemary (1988), Blue Remembered Hills: A Recollection, Oxford; Oxford University Press

Thompson, J. B. (1984), Studies in the Theory of Ideology, Cambridge: Polity Press

Thompson, R. P. (1983), 'Concerning The Wonderful Wizard of Oz' in M. P. Hearn (ed.) The Wizard of Oz N.Y.: Schocken Books

Townsend, John Rowe (1990), Written for Children: An Outline of English-Language Children's Literature, London; Bodley Head

Tuan, Yi-Fu (1979), 'Thought and Landscape: The Eye and the Mind's Eye' in D. W. Meinig (ed.), The Interpretation of Ordinary Landscapes: Geographical Essays, Oxford; Oxford University Press, pp. 89–102

Watkins, Tony (1972), 'Alan Garner's Elidor', Children's Literature in Education, March 1972, pp. 56–63

Williams, Raymond (1973), The Country and the City, London; Chatto & Windus

Williams, Raymond (1977), Marxism and Literature, Oxford; Oxford University Press

Zohar, Danah (1994), 'Forces of reaction' Sunday Times, 6 February, Section 9 (Culture), pp. 14–15

Part 17

TRANSLATION

THE VERBAL AND
THE VISUAL

On the carnivalism and dialogics
of translating for children[1]

Riitta Oittinen

Source: *Compar(a)ison: An International Journal of Comparative Literature* 2 (1995): 49–65.

We create texts for different purposes, different situations, and different audiences, so any «text» to be translated is much more than a mere text. It is the unity of the original text in words and pictures, the creators, and cultural, social and historical milieu, and text contexts such as the child images, which mirror our cultures and societies. It involves a whole situation with several different perspectives, and includes what the translator brings to the situation as a human being with her/his[2] own background, language, culture, and gender.

Thus translation is not «producing sameness»; it is not what Jacques Attali calls normalized reproduction or repetition, but composing that lies «beyond repetition» and frees us.[3] The pleasure of repetition and similarity is based on a hypnotic effect. Through abstraction, power has been made incomprehensible and conformity to rules and norms «becomes the pleasure of belonging, and the acceptance of powerlessness takes root in the comfort of repetition.» Attali's views could well be applied to translation, too. By tradition, translators are supposed to strive for repetition. If they start composing, re-creating, they are blamed for not being «faithful» to the original. Yet I consider translating an act of composition; I consider it a dialogic, carnivalistic, collaborative process carried out in individual situations.

In this paper, it is my intention to address some fundamental assumptions in the situation of translating for children, taking into account that translators never translate words on paper alone, but whole situations including texts in words and pictures as well as their different readers, writers, and users.

Carnival and children

The Russian philosopher Mikhail Bakhtin's ideas about carnivalism and dialogics apply quite well to translation, especially translating for children: on the one hand, translation is a carnivalistic act as such; on the other, even children's culture can be considered carnivalistic.

In one of his essays, «Discourse in the Novel»[4], Bakhtin deals with the key points of his literary theory: the problematics of the alien word, authoritative discourse, and dialogism. In *Rabelais and His World*[5] Bakhtin discusses the issue of carnivalism, which is closely connected with dialogism and a very interesting phenomenon especially with regard to children and their culture.

In his *Alkukuvien jäljillä* («Tracing the Origin of Images»), the Finnish semiotician Henri Broms characterizes modern children's culture as an underground culture.[6] Here underground is understood as some kind of a carnivalistic culture of laughter outside the establishment described by Bakhtin in *Rabelais and His World*. I, too, see several similarities between children's culture and carnivalism: like carnivalism, children's culture is nonofficial with no dogma or authoritarianism. It does not exist to oppose adult culture as such but rather lives on in spite of it.

Carnivalism originated in Antiquity and had its golden age in the folk cultures of the Middle Ages and the Renaissance. Carnival is «festive laughter», it is «the laughter for all the people», it is ambivalent, triumphant and deeply philosophic, and everybody can join in it. There are no outsiders, there is no audience, as the carnival is universal in scope; it is directed at all and everyone: «footlights would destroy a carnival, as the absence of footlights would destroy a theatrical performance.»[7]

In literature, carnivalism and laughter belong «to the low genres, showing the life of private individuals and the inferior social level», as Bakhtin points out.[8] During the 1980's, there was growing interest and awareness of non-appreciated literature, popular literature, and books written by women authors. The same applies to children's literature. These kinds of literature can be considered «low genres» from a publisher's point of view, for instance, although I do not consider children's literature a genre as such.

The relationship between carnivalism and language is very interesting: for instance, like writing for children, feminist writing has certainly belonged to «low genres» (in the sense of non-appreciation). In feminist writing, we can find attempts to create new (in the sense of non-suppressed) ways of writing and experiencing literature.[9] As Bakhtin points out, «[t]he verbal norms of official and literary language, determined by the canon, prohibit all that is linked with fecundation, pregnancy, childbirth. There is a sharp line of division between familiar speech and 'correct' language.»[10] A new form of culture always evokes a new way of writing. In my own writing I have noticed how the subject and content have influenced my way of expression. Carnivalism frees the language of science, too. A new type of communication always creates new forms of speech or a new meaning given to the old forms:

> The principle of laughter and the carnival spirit on which grotesque is based destroys this limited seriousness and all pretense of an extratemporal meaning and unconditional value of necessity. It frees human consciousness, thought, and imagination for new potentialities. For this reason great changes, even in the field of science, are always preceded by a certain carnival consciousness that prepares the way.[11]

Children, too, use ritualized speech and comic, even vulgar language, which is not considered acceptable in (official) adult language.

In addition to breaking the immovable, absolute, and unchanging norms, carnivalism (folk culture) and children's culture have many other things in common: love for the grotesque (the devil), ridicule of anything that is scary, curses as well as praise and abuse, games, and the mouth and eating. As Bakhtin points out, «[o]f all the features of the human face, the nose and mouth play the most important part in the grotesque image of the body.»[12] The belly is also a central «figure» in carnivalism – and we know how important eating is in all children's literature.

Eating and the names of food are very central issues in children's books in general – Göte Klingberg[13] and Bakhtin note «the companionship of children and food»[14]: the eating child is an idyllic character. Food is magic, it means happiness and safety. It is used as a device, for instance, to rhythmize narration: Carroll's *Alice's Adventures in Wonderland* gets its rhythm from Alice eating and drinking and growing and shrinking and growing again. The whole story is based on eating. As Alice herself points out: «I know *something* interesting is sure to happen [. . .] whenever I eat or drink anything.»[15]

The supper served in Grandgousier's castle, «highly detailed and hyperbolized in Rabelais», like «water-hens, teal, bitterns, curlews, plovers, heath-cock, briganders», has much in common with the picnic meals that the Famous Five eat during their adventures, like «tea, rolls, anchovy paste, a big round jam tart in a cardboard box, oranges, lime juice, a fat lettuce and some ham sandwiches», and, of course, «ginger-beer.»[16]

The Finnish scholar Kaj von Fieandt, who has carried out extensive studies on the child's perception, describes the peculiarity of her/his sense of taste. During her/his first ten years, the child has far more taste-receptors in her/his mouth than the adult. The ability to taste sweet things greatly depends on the amount and function of taste receptors. This means that children tend to prefer all sorts of sweets, while adults favor spices, where smell components are more significant.[17] This may be why food and drink are such popular themes in children's literature (cf. Blyton's *The Famous Five*).

Tastes are part of the child's world of experiences, part of her/his emotional life. Tastes are never «as such», as von Fieandt points out: they always refer to something experienced before, in our childhoods, in some special situation, which is one reason why people taste things differently. On the basis of these early likes and dislikes people remember and feel things in different ways, even if they are «in the same situation» smelling and tasting «the same things.»

But where does the comparison of carnivalism and children's culture take us? In my view it gives us a new point of view on children's culture. It encourages us to acknowledge the value of something other than adult phenomena: this unofficial culture might have something to offer us, as adults, and not just the other way around, as we are used to thinking. The temporal quality of carnivalism makes it easier for the participants to communicate. There is no etiquette, at least not in the adult sense of good and bad manners. Carnivalistic communication is not authoritarian but dialogic, where «you» and «I» meet. Children have their own carnivalistic way of speech, «abusive language», as Bakhtin calls it, but there is no reason to feel strange in this setting: we were part of the culture once, too.

What is also important in carnivalistic laughter is its victory over fear. Rabelais' devils are funny fellows and even hell is a comical place. In the Middle Ages, anything frightening was made grotesque and ridiculous:

> The people play with terror and laugh at it; the awesome becomes a «comic monster». Neither can this grotesque image be understood if oversimplified and interpreted in the spirit of abstract rationalism. It is impossible to determine where the defeat of fear will end and where joyous recreation will begin. Carnival's hell represents the earth which swallows up and gives birth, it is often transformed into a cornucopia; the monster, death, becomes pregnant. Various deformities, such as protruding bellies, enormous noses, or humps, are symptoms of pregnancy or of procreative power. Victory over fear is not its abstract elimination; it is simultaneous uncrowning and renewal, a gay transformation. Hell has burst and has poured forth abundance.[18]

Similar things happen in old fairy and folk tales: when devils, ogres, and witches are ridiculed, they become less dangerous. These evil creatures usually come to an unhappy end, too. In a similar way, Francisco Goya combined the frightening and the comic in his art, especially his graphic arts series about the nobles, priests, doctors, and other well-to-do people, who had money and power and were thus awesome: he depicted them as donkeys and parrots.[19]

In carnivalism, the grotesque is bodily, in a positive sense, since it is not egoistic but universal and dialogic: «The material bodily principle is contained [. . .] in the people, a people who are continually growing and renewed. This is why all that is bodily becomes grandiose, exaggerated, immeasurable.»[20] Grotesque realism is «the lowering of all that is high, spiritual, ideal, abstract; it is a transfer to the material level, to the sphere of earth and body in their dissoluble unity.» The grotesque is a continuous process of re-creation and metamorphosis.[21]

The grotesque is paradoxical, which is well depicted in the birth of Pantagruel, one of Rabelais' characters: «Gargantua [Pantagruel's father] does not know whether to weep over his wife's death or to laugh with joy at the birth of his son. He now laughs <like a calf> (a newborn animal), or moos 'like a cow' (birth-giving and dying).»[22] This paradox, the combination of the grotesque and laughter, makes carnivalism very radical: through victory over fear it reveals the mysteries of power. Laughter is directed against all boundaries, hypocrisy, and adulation, and it liberates a human being from any internal censor:

> [I]t liberates from the fear that developed in man thousands of years: fear of the sacred, of prohibitions, of the past, of power. It unveils the material bodily principle in its true meaning. Laughter opened men's eyes on that which is new, on the future [. . .] Laughter showed the world anew in its gayest and most sober aspects. Its external privileges are intimately linked with interior forces; they are a recognition of the rights of those forces. This is why laughter could never become an instrument to oppress and blind the people. It always remained a free weapon in their hands.[23]

Laughter or pantagruelism means the ability to be happy, gay, and benevolent. It also extends to foolishness, even madness. Like Plato in his *Phaedrus*, Bakhtin underlines the importance of madness, abnormality, drunkenness, and deviation from ordinary language. This is what happens in children's culture and children's language. Bakhtin points out that children's language often deviates from the beaten path: children's speech, free as it is from abstract structures and rules, is life itself.

Our starting point in the discussion of the child and childhood could be positive. We could ask: *what abilities does the child have?* What is typical of a child's thinking? Few people adapting stories for children seem to start from this premise. Jill Paton Walsh, however, appreciates what children bring to the reading experience. She grants that adults have more experience, which makes them to a certain extent «better» readers than children, but as she says, «the other side of the coin» is «the ways in which adults are likely to be *inferior* to children as readers»: While the adult response is «dull» and «weary», children's response is fresh and «sharp» –

carnivalistic. Adults have norms and expectations, but children «just drown», as they «don't know what books are supposed to be like.»[24]

What is most interesting here is that many of our adult abilities turn out to be liabilities, and children's «inabilities» make them better readers and listeners. It is also interesting to note that this conforms to the ideas of the German professor Hans-Ludwig Freese: he asserts that children's abilities are not weaker but different from adult abilities. Children's thinking is not naive, illogical, or «wrong», but mythical and logical in a different way than adult thinking.[25]

As a whole, children's culture could well be seen as one form of carnivalism – imagine the situation where we as translators for children join the children and dive into their carnival, not teaching them but learning from them. Through and within dialogue, we may find fresh new interpretations, which does not mean distortion but respect for the original, along with respect for ourselves and for the carnivalistic world of children.

Dialogue and coming-together

Bakhtin points out that every word is born in a dialogue. Everything in life can be «understood as a part of a greater whole.» He says, «there is a constant interaction between meanings», and all these meanings «have the potential of conditioning each other.» In every translation the reader, as an individual «I», meets the «you» of the text.[26] Dialogue may be described as a kind of context, a situation that occurs between texts and human beings and the world around.

Dialogue is closely connected to «heteroglossia.» All utterances are «heteroglot», which means that «[a]t any given time, in any given place, there will be a set of conditions – social, historical, meteorological, physiological – that will ensure that a word uttered in that place and at that time will have a meaning different than it would have under any other conditions.»[27] To divorce word and dialogue, word and context, would be artificial, because words are always born between the own and the alien. Detached from its context, a word is empty or rather, it simply does not exist; but when a word is in a dialogic interaction with an alien word, it continually takes on different meanings. Thus Bakhtin does not consider languages and texts linguistic systems, but he speaks of metalinguistics instead: «Stylistics must be based not only, and even *not as much*, on linguistics as on *metalinguistics*, which studies the word not in a system of language and not in a 'text' excised from dialogic interaction.»[28] This means that we cannot own meanings, which always escape final definitions. Understanding is always carnivalistic and dialogic interaction.

Dialogue can be both external and internal: it takes place between persons or between persons and things. In reading, for example, it takes place between the reader and a book. The dialogue may also take place within one person. For instance, when a translator translates for the child, she/he also reads, writes, and carries on a discussion with her/his present and former self. She/he also discusses with her/his audience, the listening and reading child.[29] Every text, every translation, is directed toward its readers and listeners. Every listener, every reader, is also directed toward the text. In a dialogue, the reader is active and responsible for what and how she/he reads and understands.

The same thing happens when a text is being translated. If our focus is the purpose of the translation, the original is left in a shadow, and the aim of the new interpretation is to convince readers of its legitimacy. The goal to assure the reader, the internal dialogue of a word, may even become more important than the text material. Thus the translation is a credible whole, a logical entity.

With any translation, and the translation of fiction even more so, we necessarily deal with the issue of reading. The translator always starts out as a reader. Reading is an especially interesting issue within the situation of translating for children, because we need to take both child and adult readers into account. The child as a reader has a key role to play. Where does the child fit into the story, into society? What are the cultural definitions of childhood? Besides the differences between children and adults, other questions also arise, such as the translator as a reader and involvement while reading.

Reading is involvement, as Saskia Tellegen points out.[30] It is an emotional state: the more we read, the more we become attached to the text. Accomplishing something and deriving pleasure are an important part of reading: the more the child gets out of the reading situation, the more the child wants to read. Reading is an active, carnivalistic process, an event, which is guided, to a great extent, by the reader. The reader uses texts; she/he reads for many different purposes. Sometimes she/he needs information, sometimes she/he reads for pleasure; sometimes a parent or translator, for instance, reads for other people, too.

The translator is a very special kind of reader, as she/he is sharing her/his reading experience in one language with readers of another language. The translator is a specialized reader, who travels back and forth in and between texts, the original text and her/his own text. Christiane Nord describes the movements in translation as «looping.» Thus translation «is not a linear, progressive process leading from a starting point [. . .] to a target point [. . .] but a circular, [. . .] recursive process» with feedback loops.[31] While translating, the translator is influenced by previous words and passages – the whole reading and viewing situation – which in their turn influence the words and passages to come, and the other way around. As Mary Ann Caws would describe the situation, «[s]eeing anything twice means reorienting the vision as well as the object seen and ourselves in relation to it.»[32]

Nord's model is not far from Nicole Brossard's, where the movement does not take place within any unbreakable or unbreachable circle (the circle of the «original» and its culture) – it extends in all directions, three-dimensionally. The movement is not center-oriented. It is «sense renewed, through excursions into and explorations of non-sense», as Brossard describes it in her *spiral model*[33]:

Non–sense [unfamiliar, new]

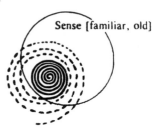

Sense [familiar, old]

(Brossard 1988, 117)

Reading and translation can well be seen as this kind of spiral movement reaching toward what is new in an attempt to understand what is old, dialogically. Thus translation could be described as Brossard describes female culture: «New perspectives: new configurations of woman-[translator]-as-being-in-the-world of what's real, of reality, and of fiction.»[34]

Louise M. Rosenblatt describes reading as *coming-together*. For Rosenblatt, reading is a two-way street: it is transaction between a reader and a text. When a reader reads a text, she/he actively evokes «the poem» out of the text. For Rosenblatt, the poem, the reading experience, is an event in time and place and situation, not an object, but something happening «during a *coming-together* of a reader and a text.»[35]

From a translator's point of view, Rosenblatt's ideas are of great interest. She describes two different reading strategies, aesthetic and efferent reading, which differ in at least two key aspects – time and experience. In aesthetic reading, the reader's whole attention is attached to the experiences she/he has while reading; in efferent reading, on the other hand, what will happen next is important, «what will be the residue *after* the reading», what kind of information, what kind of instructions the reader has internalized.[36]

When a child studies history, the goal is to be able to answer her/his teacher's questions, so the child tries to memorize as many dates, places, and names as possible. The child is thus reading the book in an efferent, non-aesthetic way. Since the same material could be read in an aesthetic way, Rosenblatt always speaks of different kinds of readings, not different text types or text functions.

As a whole, translators are mainly supposed to be thoughtful, analytical readers – but uninvolved. For me, each way of reading makes its own contribution to the translation process. During the first, aesthetic and involved reading, the translator may be fascinated by a story that appeals to her/him emotionally (or she/he may hate it from the very beginning). I believe this happens to some extent every time a translator reads texts, even if she/he usually knows that she/he will be translating the text later on.

During an efferent, more critical reading, the translator starts the translation, reading the text backward and forward, analyzing and synthesizing it; she/he studies the text closely, wanting to be sure of the legitimacy and coherence of her/his own interpretation. She/he is now using the text for a certain purpose. Yet, it is worth pointing out that I do not see these readings as two or more separate events, but, rather, as several successive and overlapping readings, where one reading influences the other. When translating a story, the translator has the memory of the first reading experience constantly in her/his mind, even if it fades, and her/his subsequent readings begin to dominate. So even at the more analytical, critical stages, the first reading experience is always present in the background. The earlier readings can also be seen as parts of the translator's experience, as parts of the whole translation situation.

When translating a story, the translator retains the memory of the first reading experience in her/his mind, even if the memory fades and her/his subsequent readings begin to dominate. So even at the more analytical, critical stages, the first reading experience is always present in the background. The earlier readings can also be seen as parts of the translator's experience, as parts of the whole translation situation. As a whole, translators are mainly assumed to be thoughtful, analytical readers – some writers even consider involvement harmful to the translation process. Yet I find that both of these ways of reading are equally important.

The verbal and the visual

Performance is an essential, quite inseparable, part of art, whether a novel, painting, composition, or film. Performance can also be understood in relation to time, as something happening here and now. Every dialogic situation of translating and writing for children, for instance, is unique and thus ephemeral – the time, place, mood, and the readers involved are different. The reading and listening child and the adult reading the story aloud to the child all bring themselves to the situation. Even the channels used may vary: translations are performed for different media in speech and writing.[37]

In her *Translation Studies* Susan Bassnett considers the performance of translations and uses the terms *performance-oriented* and *reader-oriented*.

Translations may also be *auditive* and *visual*. Bassnett's ideas may well be applied to translation for children: when an adult is reading aloud, she/he is performing, acting, the story to the child. Her/his own interpretation is interwoven in the performance and the listening child is her/his audience. In this situation, as in theater translation, many of the same principles apply. As Bassnett says, «the role of the audience assumes a public dimension not shared by the individual reader whose contact with the text is essentially a private affair.»[38]

As art forms, theater and film are closely related to picture books. In an illustrated book, the reader participates in the dialogue of the rhythm of words and pictures, which gives her/him an idea of the scene, characters, and the whole setting of the story – just like in theater or film. In the same way, we must pay attention to the readability, even «singability» of the text when translating an illustrated text for a small child.

Sharing, performance, and reading aloud are also characteristic of children's books and their translations. The human voice is a powerful tool, and reading aloud is the only way for an illiterate child to enter the world of literature. Jim Trelease, the American reading advocate, points out in his *The New Read-Aloud Handbook* that listening comprehension comes before reading comprehension. He even says that we all become readers because we have seen and heard someone we admire enjoying the experience of reading.[39] Thus the translator is responsible for contributing to the aloud-reader's enjoyment of the story in every way possible. For instance, the translator should use punctuation to give rhythm to the text. I even go as far as to insist that a translator, especially when translating for small children, should not necessarily punctuate according to the rules of grammar, but according to rhythm. The translator of a fairy tale – whether a novel, a poem, or a play – must take into consideration which senses she/he is translating for. When we are translating for children below the school-age (seven in Finland) we should translate, not just for the eye and the ear, but also for the adult's mouth.

Here we also encounter the question of the readability of texts, which is not easy to define. I believe that the «readability of a text» is determined not only by the «text» in the abstract or by the meanings *in* the text, as words on paper, but by the reader's entire situation. The concept «readability of a text» is even misleading, as it often refers to texts being easy or difficult, regardless of how the individual reader responds to them. It would make more sense to speak of the «readability» of the reading situation, which is not far from the idea of «acceptability» advocated by the Israeli scholar Gideon Toury.[40]

In addition, as translators, we must pay attention to the illustrations, which are a kind of set design for the text; as in the theater, they have an effect on the audience, the listening child. In the concrete sense, we, as translators, try to make the text and illustration fit each other, and in another sense, we – either consciously or unconsciously – have internalized the images from our reading of the text and illustrations.

The visual appearance of a book is important for the child and always includes not only the illustrations and selection of scenes, but even the cover, the end- and title pages, the actual typeface, the shape and style of letters and headings, and the book's entire layout. All these elements have an emotional impact on the reader. The illustrator sets the scene and shows what the characters and their situations look like. Illustrations also add to the excitement of the reading experience and give the reader a clue about what may happen on the following pages. Or the illustrations may simply decorate the story. All this enriches and complicates the reader's interpretation of the characters and events in a book. Unconsciously, illustrations both free and capture the dialogics.

Yet an illustrated text, like a picture book, is not just a combination of text and illustration. It has both sound and rhythm, which can also be heard, when books are read aloud. But even if they are read silently, texts also have an inner rhythm that the reader can feel. The American Cecily Raysor Hancock has given «Musical Notes to *The Annotated Alice.*» Referring to the well-known song, Jane Taylor's «Twinkle, Twinkle, Little Star» she points out, «[m]ost English-speaking readers will echo internally Alice's 'I've heard something like it', and for most of them the tune that comes to mind will be the familiar *do do sol sol la la sol* tune [. . .] an international nursery tune with a printing history going back to eighteenth-century France.»[41]

Having read quite a few books aloud to children, the situation is familiar to me: every time there are songs in the stories, I sing the texts – for the songs uncomposed or unfamiliar to me I create tunes of my own. When I read aloud a translation of *Alice's Adventures in Wonderland*, I expect the songs to be singable, too. «[T]he tunes are part of the intended effect», as Hancock concludes her article.[42] Even if I am reading silently, just for pleasure, I may sing the songs in my mind, that is, I audiate them. The music, even inaudible, is part of the emotivity of the reading situation; it is part of the nonverbal text elements, the phonological gestalt, as Christiane Nord describes it.[43]

The translator of a picture book must be able to interpret these auditive and visual messages to understand the dynamics of text and illustration. Just as the translator translating from English into Finnish must be a specialist and know both languages, the translator of illustrated literature must know the language of illustrations. The more prominent the illustrations are, the more important it is for a translator to have the ability to read this language. It is difficult for me to understand why publishers are in the dark about the demands placed on translators of picture books. This also shows up in the publishers' attitudes to children's literature in general: they find it «easier» than literature created for grown-ups. I would describe translating illustrated texts as a special field with its own language. It is a field that requires specialization and training.

Moreover, as interpretative tasks, reading a poem and reading a picture, for instance, are not as different as they may seem at first – much depends on the reader/viewer and her/his point of view. Illustration can be understood as a form of translation, in the sense that it is another channel for interpreting the original, though visually. As Joseph Schwarcz describes the illustrator's work, «[t]he illustrator, consciously or unconsciously, tastefully or crudely, interprets. The illustrator of children's books, like any artist, suggests meanings which he recognizes in the text and wishes to communicate through the content and style of his work.»[44]

As a whole, the issue of the relationship between text and illustration becomes far more complicated when translating is taken into consideration. In an original work, the author, illustrator, source-language readers, and publisher are involved in a dialogic relationship. In a translation, the dialogic constellation expands and involves a translator interpreting the text and illustrations, target-language readers with a different cultural background, a new publisher, and, possibly, even a new illustrator participating in a collaborative dialogue with the translator.

As a reader, the translator has many responsibilities, too: she/he is responsible for her/his reading, not only with respect to her/himself but also with respect to all the participants in each dialogic situation. The good of the future reader of the text is the reason behind the whole translation process: we are translating stories for target-language children to read or listen to.[45] The rights of the original author and those of the future readers of a translation do not conflict. The original author benefits if her/his books are translated in a live, dialogic, and fearless (i.e. carnivalistic) way so that they live on in the target-language culture. This is loyalty, not only to the target-language readers, but to the author of the original, too.

Of course, no speaker or author can be absolutely sure of perfect understanding of her/his messages: the reader and listener always bring along their own personality and background to the reading/viewing/listening situation. On the other hand, authors, including translators, are addressing their words and images to someone, to whom they speak «directly», someone who does not exist in the flesh. This someone might be called a «superaddressee», whom Bakhtin describes as one «whose absolutely just responsive understanding is presumed, either in some metaphysical distance or in distant historical time.»[46]

The child image of the translator for children could be described as this kind of a «superaddressee». The translator is directing her/his words, her/his translation, to some kind of a child: naive or understanding, innocent or experienced; this concept of child influences her/his way of addressing the audience – the choice of words, for instance. Later, in a real dialogue, a real child takes up the book and reads, and new, perhaps unintended, meanings arise. Yet, without any «superaddressee» the book would not be a coherent whole.[47]

Translation as carnivalistic action

To translate well, for her/his target-language audience, the translator needs to encounter the original fearlessly. The lack of fear entails a new kind of attitude, «a free and familiar attitude» that «spreads over everything: over all values, thoughts, phenomena, and things», as Bakhtin describes what happens in carnival.[48] Through carnivalistic laughter, the translator defeats her/his fear of the original. Laughter is therapeutic by nature.[49]

Carnivalism signifies being universal, freedom, and defeat over fear. Carnival is also ephemeral, it is a ritual of crowning and uncrowning. As Bakhtin points out, carnival includes a ritual act, which he calls «the mock crowning and subsequent uncrowning of the carnival king» – or queen. It is a dualistic act, where a carnival queen/king is crowned and given the «symbols of authority». It symbolizes «the joyful relativity of all structure and order». Bakhtin goes on, «[f]rom the very beginning», an uncrowning «glimmers through the crowning».[50]

Translation is in many ways this kind of carnivalistic action: it is crowning and uncrowning. As Bakhtin points out, it is an issue of «shifts and changes, of death and renewal». The idea of uncrowning is immanent in the idea of crowning: today the author is the queen/king, tomorrow she/he is uncrowned and the translator becomes the queen/king; the day after tomorrow the translator loses her/his crown and the target-language reader receives «the symbols of authority». For Bakhtin, the process is never-ending; interpretation is unfinalizable and fearless.[51]

A thought, a sentence, a text, a picture – they are all involved in a never-ending, carnivalistic dialogue. They are continuously changing, moving, and they never meet in a vacuum. In different reading situations, readers interpret these signs in various ways – they turn away from what they read – depending on the situation itself, which involves the text, interpreter, time, place, and so on. Translating, too, always includes the act of turning away from the original, which is the starting point for a new, fearless interpretation based on the translator-reader's reading experience.

All this makes translating rewriting, alteration and positive manipulation. As Hans-Georg Gadamer says, it is adapting a work of art into a new art form: «it is the awakening and conversion of a text into new immediacy».[52] In a dialogic, carnivalistic situation, the translator reads and writes her/his reading in another language for her/his future audience in another culture: the child.

Notes

1 The article is based on two of my books: *I Am Me – I Am Other: On the Dialogics of Translating for Children* (Tampere 1993), where I deal with literary translation within the framework of dialogics and polysystems theory; and *Kääntäjän karnevaali (The Translator's Carnival*, Tampere 1995), where I expand the issue of dialogics and introduce the idea of carnivalism. I trie to demonstrate how the whole situation of translation – text, illustration, different readers – takes precedence over any efforts to discover and reproduce the original author's intentions as a given. Rather than concentrating on the authority of the author, I focus special attention on the intentions of the different readers reading the stories in translation.

2 As a feminine myself, I decided to «put the feminine first», which also conforms to my idea of the individuality and visibility of the translator. See: Susanne DE LOTBINIÈRE-HARWOOD, *Re-Belle et Infidèle. La Traduction comme pratique de réécriture au féminin/The Body Bilingual. Translation as a Rewriting in the Feminine*, Toronto 1991.

3 Jacques ATTALI, *Noise. A Political Economy of Music*, trans. Brian MASSUMI, Minneapolis 1985, 20.

4 Mikhail BAKHTIN, «Discourse in the Novel» (1934–35), in: BAKHTIN, *The Dialogic Imagination: Four Essays*, trans. Caryl EMERSON and Michael HOLQUIST, Austin 1990, 259–422.

5 Mikhail BAKHTIN, *Rabelais and His World*, Bloomington 1984.

6 Henri BROMS, *Alkukuvien jäljillä. Kulttuurin semiotiikkaa*, Juva 1985.

7 BAKHTIN (1984), *op. cit.*, 7; see also: «Introduction», *op. cit.*, 1–58.

8 BAKHTIN (1984), *op. cit.*, 67.

9 Cf. the Canadian literary feminists like Nicole BROSSARD, *The Aerial Letter*, trans. Marlene WILDEMAN, Toronto 1988 and Susanne DE LOTBINIÈRE-HARWOOD, *op. cit.*, and «writing in the feminine».

10 BAKHTIN (1984), *op. cit.*, 320.

11 BAKHTIN (1984), *op. cit.*, 49.

12 BAKHTIN (1984), *op. cit.*, 316.

13 Göte KLINGBERG, *Children's Fiction in the Hands of the Translators*, Studia psychologica et paedagogica, Series altera LXXXII, Lund 1986.

14 Mikhail BAKHTIN, *Kirjallisuuden ja estetiikan ongelmia*, Finnish trans. Kerttu KYHÄLÄ-JUNTUNEN and Veikko AIROLA, The Soviet Union 1979, 390.

15 Lewis CARROLL, *Alice's Adventures in Wonderland and Through the Looking-Glass* (orig. 1865 and 1871), illust. John Tenniel, New York 1981, 23.

16 See: Mikhail BAKHTIN, *The Dialogic Imagination: Four Essays*, trans. Caryl EMERSON and Michael HOLQUIST, ed. HOLQUIST, Austin 1990, 180; and Enid BLYTON, *Five Get into Trouble*, illust. Betty Maxey, London 1981, 26.

17 Kaj VON FIEANDT, *Havaitsemisen maailma*, Porvoo 1972, 85.

18 BAKHTIN (1984), *op. cit.*, 91.

19 Cf. Lauri AHLGREN, «Järjen nukkuminen synnyttää hirviöitä», *Taide* 3 (1975), 26–33. There are endless examples of ridiculing the devil or other evil powers in children's literature and folk tales. For instance, in the Danish folk tale «The Devil's Seven Riddles», a poor man first sells his soul to the devil and, after getting rich, fools the devil by giving correct answers to the devil's riddles, See: «Paholaisen seitsemän arvoitusta», in: *Lasten aarreaitta*, Jyväskylä 1952, 40–45.

20 BAKHTIN (1984), *op. cit.*, 19.

21 BAKHTIN (1984), *op. cit.*, 19–20, 24–25.

22 BAKHTIN (1984), *op. cit.*, 331.

23 BAKHTIN (1984), *op. cit.*, 94.

24 Jill Paton WALSH, Letter from author, 8 March 1992.

25 Hans-Ludwig FREESE, *Lapset ovat filosofeja. Ajatusmatkoja kasvaville ja kasvattajille* (orig. *Kinder sind Philosophen*, Weinheim/Berlin 1989), trans. and ed. Eira WIEGAND, Jyväskylä 1992, 54–55.

26 BAKHTIN (1990), *op. cit.*, 426–427.

27 BAKHTIN (1990), *op. cit.*, 428.

28 Mikhail BAKHTIN, *Problems of Dostoevsky's Poetics*, ed. and trans. Caryl EMERSON, Minneapolis 1987, 202.

29 BAKHTIN (1990), *op. cit.*, 426.

30 Saskia TELLEGEN and Lieven COPPEJANS, «Imaginative Reading. Research into Imagination, Reading Behaviour and Reading Pleasure», Summary of a book published by Dutch centre for Libraries and Literature, The Hague, 1991.

31 Christiane NORD, *Text Analysis in Translation. Theory, Methodology, and Did-actic Application of a Model for Translation-Oriented Text Analysis*, trans. NORD and Penelope SPARROW, Amsterdam–Atlanta 1991, 30; see also: Hans Robert JAUSS, *Question and Answer. Forms of Dialogic Understanding*, trans. and ed. Michael HAYS, Minneapolis 1989, 213–214; and Hans-Georg GADAMER, *Kleine Schriften I Philosophie Hermeneutik (Sammlung)*, Tübingen 1976, 58–59.

32 Mary Ann CAWS, *The Art of Interference. Stressed Readings in Verbal and Visual Texts*, Princeton, New Jersey 1989, 17.

33 Nicole BROSSARD (1988), *op. cit.*, 117.

34 BROSSARD (1988), *op. cit.*, 116–117.

35 Louise M. ROSENBLATT, *The Reader, the Text, the Poem. The Transactional Theory of the Literary Work*, Carbondale and Edwardsville 1978, 12, 75. See also: BAKHTIN (1990), *op. cit.*, 259–422.

36 ROSENBLATT, *op. cit.*, 23.

37 Cf. NORD, *op. cit.*, 56–57.

38 Susan BASSNETT, *Translation Studies*, London and New York 1991, 131–132.

39 Jim TRELEASE, *The New Read-Aloud Handbook*, New York 1989, 2, 10.

40 Gideon TOURY, *In Search of a Theory of Translation*, Tel Aviv 1980, 51ff.

41 Cecily Raysor HANCOCK, «Musical Notes to *the Annotated Alice*», *Children's Literature* 16 (1988), 4–5.

42 HANCOCK, *op. cit.*, 22.

43 NORD, *op. cit.*, 120–121.

44 Joseph H. SCHWARCZ, *Ways of the Illustrator. Visual Communication in Chil-dren's Literature*, Chicago 1982, 104.

45 As Eugene A. Nida has pointed out in his definition of «a good translation», one question clearly takes precedence: «For whom?» See: NIDA and Charles R. TABER, *The Theory and Practice of Translation*, Leiden 1969.

46 BAKHTIN (1979), in: MORSON AND EMERSON, *op. cit.*, 135.

47 Cf. «consistency» in: Wolfgang ISER, *The Implied Reader. Patterns of Com-munication in Prose Fiction from Bunyan to Beckett*, trans. ISER, Baltimore 1990, 285; see also: Jauss's interpretation of «superaddressee» in: JAUSS, *op. cit.*, 215–216.

48 BAKHTIN (1987), *op. cit.*, 123.

49 See: BAKHTIN in: Gary Saul MORSON and Caryl EMERSON, *Mikhail Bakhtin, Cre-ation of a Prosaics*, Stanford 1990, 452.

50 BAKHTIN (1987), *op. cit.*, 124–125.

51 BAKHTIN (1987), *op. cit.*, 124–125; see also: BAKHTIN (1984), *op. cit.*

52 GADAMER, *op. cit.*, 360. See also: André LEFEVERE, *Translation, Rewriting, and the Manipulation of Literary Fame*, London and New York 1992.

APPROACHES TO THE TRANSLATION OF CHILDREN'S LITERATURE

A review of critical studies since 1960

Reinbert Tabbert

Source: *Target: International Journal of Translation Studies* 14(2) (2002): 303–351.

Children's literature, a traditional domain of teachers and librarians, has, in the past 30 years, been made a subject of academic research. Simultaneously, more and more studies have been dedicated to the translation of children's literature. There are four important factors which have prompted such studies: (1) the assumption that translated children's books build bridges between different cultures, (2) text-specific challenges to the translator, (3) the polysystem theory which classifies children's literature as a subsystem of minor prestige within literature, and (4) the age-specific addressees either as implied or as real readers. This review of critical approaches to the translation of children's literature is structured in such a way that the methodological shift from source orientation to target orientation becomes obvious.

Introduction

Children's literature — a new field of research

In the course of the past 30 years new fields of academic research have been defined and established, two of which are Translation Studies (or, in German, *Übersetzungswissenschaft*) and Children's Literature Studies (*Kinderliteraturforschung*). If Translation Studies have a strong bias towards internationalism, this is also true (albeit to a lesser degree) for Studies of Children's Literature, which are concerned with a type of literature that from its very beginnings in the 18th century has tended to cross national and cultural borders. In 1953 the International Board on Books for Young People (IBBY) was founded, an organisation which has actively advanced the quality and distribution of children's books (among other things with the biennial awarding of the Hans Christian Andersen Medal to children's authors and illustrators such as Astrid Lindgren, Erich Kästner, Maurice Sendak or Mitsumasa Anno. The biennial awards are accompanied by certificates for outstanding translations of children's books nominated by the national IBBY sections). In 1970 the more academically oriented International Research Society for Children's Literature (IRSCL), which holds biennial symposia followed. It now has 236 members from 41 countries.

Children's literature, a traditional concern of educationists and librarians, has in some countries gained a foothold in university departments of literature. There are also research institutes in places such as Cologne, Frankfurt, Helsinki, London, Osaka, Paris, Stockholm, Vienna and Zürich, not to mention the International Youth Library in Munich, founded back in 1949 and now a treasure-house of research material in numerous languages. It is true that children's literature is preferably studied in the mother tongue, but scholars of foreign as well as of comparative and general literature have also turned to it (see the surveys by Petzold 1997; Nières 1983; O'Sullivan 1996; 2000), as have special issues of journals addressed at them (*Poetics today* 13:1/1992; *Compara(i)son* 2/1995). International encyclopedias of children's literature have appeared, listing translations of children's books and discussing cross-cultural phenomena including translation (Doderer 1976–84; Hunt 1996; Kümmerling-Meibauer 1999).

The professional interest in children's books has always encompassed a minority's attention to the translation of such books. If the focus of attention is changing, this is due not only to the fact that scholars of literature have taken over from educationists and librarians, but also to the circumstance that their concepts have been influenced by more recent theories of translation. Moreover, a few representatives of Translation Studies have themselves become involved in children's literature (Reiss; Toury; Nord; Oittinen; Puurtinen, etc.).

A shift of focus in the studies of translation

What are the more recent objectives of the studies of translation? On the one hand the process and product of translating are being analysed more precisely, and on the other, corpora of translation literature are being investigated with regard to the historical conditions, particularly norms, which have shaped them. In either case a prescriptive approach (what should a translation be like?) has been replaced by a descriptive one (what is a translation really like?), and exhortations to do justice to the peculiarities of the source text have given way to considerations of the functions of the target text either for the commissioner or for the receiving culture.

This at least is the picture drawn by those who have paved the way for new research: Hans Vermeer (Heidelberg) with his "skopos" theory (which, as the Greek keyword indicates, gives top priority to the "purpose" of a translation) and Gideon Toury (Tel Aviv) with his "descriptive translation studies" (based on history and cultural semiotics). Toury (1995:25) states that in the second half of the 70s both schools contributed independently to a change of paradigm: from "source-orientedness" to "target-orientedness". It is not the source text and the source culture any more which are of primary interest, but the target text and the target culture.

Traditional translation theory is centred on the concept of equivalence: Translators are assumed to match the peculiarities of a source text with equivalent words and structures in their target text. This concept, which is in any case of little help in a particular case of translation, can no longer be taken for granted. If this means the sacrifice of a certain moral obligation to the author, Christiane Nord (Heidelberg/Magdeburg) has attempted to establish a new ethical framework. What matters, she says, is not the "fidelity" to the original text, but the "loyalty" to the initiator of the translation (1989; 1991). However, she asserts that in our culture the purpose of translation must not contradict the author's intention, especially in the case of literary texts (1989: 102).

So target-orientedness is the order of the day; nevertheless in analyses of translation literature the source text retains its importance as a factor of reference, though comparisons now have to be descriptive, not evaluative. It no longer makes sense to differentiate strictly between ("faithful") translation and ("free") adaptation, a stock classification in children's literature criticism (Skjønsberg 1979; 1982; Escarpit 1985; Binder 1985). And in view of the shift of attention towards the target culture translation research imperceptibly passes into (foreign language) reception research. Analyses of translations which were carried out before the change of paradigm may still be valid, if one neglects the usual assumption — specially with regard to literary texts — that there is such a thing as "the" perfect translation.

Scope and perspective of this review

The present article is an extended version of a contribution to the yearbook of the German research society for children's literature (Tabbert 1996). If the original text dealt with critical approaches to the translation of children's literature between 1975 and 1995, either in theoretical works or in significant case studies of children's books written in German (be it as a source or as a target language), the present article attempts to overcome such restrictions in a linguistic as well as a temporal respect. However, this cannot be more than an attempt, as it appears to be impossible to track down all the relevant publications and because I do not have the linguistic prerequisites to read all of those that have passed through my hands.

My perspective is not that of a scholar of translation studies as is the case of Tiina Puurtinen in her chapter on recent theoretical approaches to translation (for children) (Puurtinen 1995:35–62). Though my first academic publication was concerned with a typology of literary translation (Tabbert 1968), my vantage point is that of a German Professor of English who has become more and more involved in Comparative Children's Literature and who is particularly interested in fiction from English- and German-speaking countries. My position may not be too disadvantageous, however, considering the fact that the largest number of children's books are written in English, with quite a substantial amount in German, and that the same seems to be true with regard to published work on the translation of children's literature. Nevertheless I regret that I cannot do justice to all the titles listed in my bibliography, let alone those which have escaped my attention. For some of the titles I am grateful for hints from fellow-researchers: Werner Küffner, Bettina Kümmerling-Meibauer, Isabelle Nières, Maria Nikolajeva, Emer O'Sullivan, Zohar Shavit, Denise von Stockar, Astrid Surmatz, Gideon Toury.

Since the emphasis of this survey is on the change of paradigm in the studies of translated children's literature, no great effort has been made to include more than a fair share of studies from before the mid-seventies. Persson's book from 1962, which crops up as the oldest relevant title in several publications, seems to be a good starting-point. The whole presentation of research work will be structured in a way that helps illustrate the methodological shift from source-orientedness to target-orientedness. Finally a selection of articles is presented in which translators summarise their professional experience so that, despite all the theory, attention is also paid to practice.

It may be worth mentioning in advance that some children's books have been made the subject of several translation studies, an indication of their status as international classics. The titles include: Louisa May Alcott's *Little women* (Skjønsberg 1979; Du-Nour 1995:341–342; Nières 1998:111–113), Wilhelm Busch's *Max und Moritz* (Toury 1980; Görlach 1982a/b; 1993; 1995; 1997; Marx 1997), Carlo Collodi's *Pinocchio* (Koppen 1980; Escarpit 1985:177–179; Marx 1990; 1997; Wunderlich 1992; Gómez del Manzano/ Manila 1996), Astrid Lindgren's *Pippi Långstrump* (Eriksson 1985; Heldner 1992; Even-Zohar 1992; Surmatz 1994; 1998; Camp 1995; Teodorowicz-Hellman 1997; 1999) and A.A. Milne's *Winnie-the-Pooh* (O'Sullivan 1994; 2000:261–264; Fernandez Lopez 1996:285–290; Woodsworth 1996; Weissbrod 1999). In the case of Lewis Carroll's *Alice in wonderland*, likely to be the absolute favourite of translation criticism, there are not only plenty of studies (Parisot 1971; Mango 1977; Lehnert-Rodiek 1988; Nières 1988; Nord

1993; Oittinen 1993; 1997; 2000; Friese 1995; Weissbrod 1996; O'Sullivan 1998a; 2000), but also books which list further translations and further studies of them (Weaver 1964; Guiliano 1980; Jones and Gladstone 1998). Kümmerling-Meibauer's (1999) encyclopedia articles on 534 children's classics from 65 countries are followed by bibliographies which also include analyses of translations. Fairy-tales, though sometimes regarded as children's literature, deserve a chapter of their own in Translation Studies. Here a reference to a recent publication (Sutton 1996) and its review in *Target* (Dollerup 1998) must suffice.

A final remark concerning the following survey of studies is necessary: If a study has been published in English as well as in another language, the English version is preferred; and if it has been published both as an article and as part of a book, it is the book which is quoted.

The import of children's books into various countries

Children's books from foreign countries can be regarded as a political phenomenon. They make critics aware of the fact that they themselves belong to a certain nation, culture or power bloc; and they sometimes make them ask questions about the use, the origin, the quantity and the nature of those books. There are several collections of papers in which authors attempt to answer such questions, either as representatives of countries and institutions or — as the state of the art develops — as distanced scholars.

Persson's collection (1962) is typical of the post-war years up to 1970 in that it appears to show in unquestioned unison the efforts of librarians, editors and translators in pursuit of a sheltered childhood and international understanding. While the Danish librarian Aase Bredsdorf explains that children's libraries in small countries have a special need for translated books in certain categories, the American librarian Virginia Haviland stresses the enrichment given to American children by books from other countries. The Swedish book editor Margareta Schildt points out that every year about 50% of new children's books in her country are translations and she gives aesthetic as well as commercial criteria for the choice of foreign books. Particularly interesting is what the British editor and translator Monica Burns has to say about the work of the translator. In astonishing frankness she agrees with the demand that "Children's books must be tailored to their new country" (Persson 1962:78). She adds that the "tailoring may fall partly on the translator and partly on the editor", and she illustrates this policy with texts which were adapted for religious, political or moral reasons. Rarely will target-language oriented scholars find a less disguised plea for the subjection of translation to conventions, in this case the shared belief, initiated by Rousseau, that children have to be protected against anything culturally unfamiliar or morally unbecoming. This leaves little room for vicarious experience of foreignness.

The volume by Klingberg/Ørvig/Amor (1978), a documentation of the third symposium of the IRSCL, goes beyond Persson (1962) in so far as it is more academically oriented and presents papers from both sides of the Iron Curtain. However, the authors from East Europe appear to be even more officially representative of their countries than those in Persson's volume, stressing their countries' policy of promoting humanistic traditions and international understanding through translated children's books. As opposed to that bias, authors from Western countries uncover the way in which the international production of children's books in capitalist countries determines selection processes with regard to subject-matter and form, and helps to spread Western ideology in the Third World. Two historically oriented studies pursue and explain the predominance of English children's books on the Danish and Swedish book markets since the second half of the 19th century.

The East–West division is also present in Binder's collection of essays (1985), which offers an overview of translated children's books in the countries where German is spoken (at that time four). The impact of the two power blocs on the choice of children's books from foreign countries is particularly evident in an encyclopedia article by Breitinger (1979), who contrasts the share of translated children's books from the USA and the USSR in West Germany (32%/4%) and East Germany (5%/35%). The publication of the few books from the USSR in West Germany is related to events in foreign policy in an article by Seemann (1998; much more detailed and including summaries of the translated books in a 463-page study of 1999). Breitinger's diagnosis of the impact of the political power blocs is confirmed by Tabbert (1998) with regard to translated books which were awarded the (West) German Children's Book Prize between 1955 and 1995. But Tabbert adds that the juries' predilection for books from English-speaking countries, Scandinavia and the Netherlands, which neglects not only East but also South European societies, may also be due to a shared image of childhood, which dates from Rousseau and is favoured by industrialised Protestant countries of the European and the American North. (While that image implies that children should be regarded as human beings in their own right, South European societies tend to consider them as incomplete adults, whilst Communist ideology emphasizes that adults and children live in the same world.) The traditional German reception of children's classics from Britain is exemplified by Petzold (1994), and more recent German imports from various parts of the world are discussed in four contributions to Raecke (1999:196–235).

In Switzerland, a country with four official languages, the question of translation is precariously tied up with national identity, as Elisabeth Külling's contribution to Binder (1985) makes clear. Verena Rutschmann (Rutschmann/von Stockar 1996:6–22) presents interesting conclusions from empirical inquiries into children's reading preferences in the three main language areas of Switzerland: The preferences are shaped by the literary tradition and childhood image of the culture whose language the children share (thus *Pinocchio* comes first for those who read Italian), and additional reading needs are satisfied by translated books not from the other two language areas, but from English-speaking countries.

Denise Escarpit (1985) demonstrates the situation of children's book translation in France in a kaleidoscopic manner, thanks to a great variety of contributors and materials. There are considerations of the problem of translation from the point of view of a semiotician, a librarian and a comparatist; there are statistics of the French import of children's books in the past and in the present; there are case studies of translated children's books from Italy, the USA and Britain; there is the portrait of an influential translator of the 18th century (Arnaud Berquin); and there are statements of one author, five *éditeurs* and four translators. Scholars have the upper hand (as in Klingberg/Ørvig/Amor 1978, from which Klingberg's and Bamberger's contributions are reprinted), but a certain amount of space is conceded to the producers of translated children's books, who are no longer free to tell tales out of school (as they were in Persson 1962), but have to respond to a questionnaire. The methodological bias of the volume is that of source-text oriented philology. Denise Escarpit, the editor, has made herself a name as an Anglicist and as the fourth president of the IRSCL.

Escarpit's French-oriented kaleidoscope on translated children's books has been supplemented by a special issue of a French journal dedicated to translation (*La Revue des Livres pour Enfants* 145. 1992). The contributions to that issue focus on such topics as the translation of French children's books in Norway, problems of translating a Russian folktale, an English alphabet book and poetry in general.

Persson (1962) contains a publisher's report on how American experts in the 50s and 60s chose American children's books for publication in Asian languages, which contrasts with Jörg Becker's criticism of ideological book exports to the Third World (Klingberg/Ørvig/Amor 1978). Ten years later the volume *Development* (1988) documents a UNESCO conference in Tokyo which offered countries of Asia and the Pacific a chance to present their national situation of children's book translation. As one might guess, the range of states of development is very wide. Even the highly developed situation of Japan, which has an enormous import of children's books, is hardly known to most experts in Europe and America. The first translations of Japanese fairy tales and children's books into English and German since the end of the 19th century are outlined by Herring (1988). Glimpses of Japanese culture through translated children's books are provided by Makino (1985). Ueno (1993) gives a survey of the Japanese reception of children's books from German-speaking countries after World War II.

In recent years the national import of children's books has been examined in some academic monographs. Ingeborg Rieken-Gerwing's doctoral thesis (1995) focuses on re-united Germany. The interesting question put forward in the title (Is there a special method of translating children's literature?) does not result in any stimulating analyses or theories; however, the pragmatically oriented chapters provide useful information: on the one hand regarding the quantitative differentiation of translated children's books according to book market statistics and to lists of prize-winning books or of semi-official book recommendations, and on the other hand regarding the working-conditions and methods of the (often part-time) translators, according to 46 questionnaires completed by translators and 14 questionnaires by employees of publishing-houses. The economic factor has been duly taken into account.

Ewa Teodorowicz-Hellman (1999) presents her research on Swedish-Polish relations in the field of children's literature. She has compiled a comprehensive bibliography of translations of Swedish children's books into Polish between 1890 and 1998, which she elucidates in the first chapter of her study. Subsequent chapters, which are based on a variety of methodological approaches, are dedicated to the reception of outstanding works such as Elsa Beskow's picture books and Swedish folktales. While the analysis of the Polish translation of *Pippi Långstrump* proceeds along traditional philological lines, the review of "reception styles" of *Nils Holgersson* represents an interesting variant of target orientation, insofar as the illustrations of the various Polish editions are shown to indicate radically different concepts of the book — from geographical work via adventure novel and fairy-tale to fantasy and *Entwicklungsroman*. Teodorowicz-Hellman's bibliography indicates further studies of the reception of Western children's books in Slavic countries, as for instance an investigation of British children's books in Polish translations by Adamczyk-Garbowska (1988). Unfortunately that study, unlike Teodorowicz-Hellman's has no chapter summaries in English.

Fernandez Lopez (1996) and Zeli (n.d.) are fully aware of the change of translation theory. Therefore their investigations of translated children's books in Spain and Italy respectively will be introduced in Chapter 5 ("The Impact of the Target Culture"). And as Valdivieso (1991) and Beuchat/Valdivieso (1992) are mainly interested in the aspect of culture, their studies of translated children's books in Chile will be considered in Section 4.3 ("Culture-specific Phenomena"). The present chapter will conclude with some ideas concerning the quality and use of imported children's books.

The Austrian Richard Bamberger (1961; 1963; 1978) is a prominent representative of post-war critics of children's literature who believed with Jella Lepman, the founder of the International Youth Library, that children's books may contribute to "building bridges" between foreign cultures. He emphasises that the literary quality of translated children's books is on average much better than the average of children's literature in a given country, [which] is demonstrated by the fact that the percentage of translations on lists of recommended children's books is much higher than the percentage of translations in the number of children's books produced.

(Bamberger 1978:20)

He adds that in Scandinavia and the Netherlands children's writers have been stimulated by the high amount of good imported books to produce work of a comparable standard. Referring to genres, well-known authors and achievements typical of a certain nation, he traces international lines of influence.

The American Maureen White (1992) stresses the importance of children's literature "as a medium for sharing common cultural interests" (261). In an approach which is both pragmatic and systematic she has identified 572 translated children's books which were in print in the U.S. in 1990. From those books she selected 131 titles which she classified as "successful translated children's books" according to the following criteria: at least four years in print and "an award-winner, on a notables list, or the recipient of a favourite review" (264). The list of 131 titles and seven tables interpreting them under various headings are useful material for further investigations. In the table concerning the original language, German comes first with 39 titles (followed by 17 in Swedish) and in the table of favourite authors the Grimms with 10 titles are just ahead of Astrid Lindgren with 9 titles. Similar to the situation in Germany (Tabbert 1998), cultural affinity seems to be a decisive asset in the U.S. for award-winners or otherwise successful books.

Tomlinson (1998), on behalf of the U.S. IBBY section, is more comprehensive than White when he offers an annotated bibliography of over 700 titles from 29 different countries printed between 1950 and 1996, all of which are available in English, many originating in other English-speaking countries. Introductory articles on so-called "international children's books", statistics and tables make this publication a useful source for translation scholars. On a smaller scale this is also true for Susan Stan's *Study of international children's picture books published in the United States in 1994* (1997). Out of 251 picture books originally published in other countries only 42 contain clear "indications in the text or illustrations that they are set in a country outside the U.S." (quoted by Oittinen 2000:150). In spite of such a limited representation of foreignness in "international children's books", educationists such as Rosie Webb Joels are convinced that "the canon of translated children's literary work represents just one resource (but an excellent one) for promoting internationalism" (1999:78).

Deviations from the source text

Göte Klingberg, Swedish educationist and second president of the IRSCL, emphasises the aesthetic quality of children's literature. "My concern is books of literary merit which in translation will mean a valuable addition to the literature available to children and young people" (Klingberg 1986:7). He believes that in translated children's books the integrity of the original work must be touched as little as possible and in a kind of manual for translators of children's books categorises what he regards as typical deviations from the source text. Translations from English into Swedish and Swedish into English provide numerous examples. Most extensively he discusses the question of whether references to the source culture may be adapted to the target culture (his category of "local context adaptation"). In his openly prescriptive manner he tends to demand the preservation of the original references, if necessary with an added explanation, but he also concedes some exceptions (e.g. telling names in a geographical context, 52). Deviations he definitely rejects are "modernisation" (which, in his case, only involves the date and time of a story and explicitly excludes the problem of modernising the classics, 57), "purification" (i.e. the deletion of what adults in the target culture may consider to be taboo for children) and "abridgements" (which, more often than not, according to Klingberg, distort the meaning of a text). Klingberg's book of 1986, which was preceded by two Swedish versions (1974, 1977), may be uninformed as regards new theories of translation, but it gives evidence of the attempt to take children's literature seriously as literature.

Katharina Reiss (1982), the translation scholar, has linked Klingberg's categories with her own early theory of translation based on a typology of texts. The informative, expressive and operative text types, which she deduces from Karl Bühler's functional model of language and supplements with an audiomedial type, may also be found in the field of children's literature, e.g. the informative type in the shape of non-fiction for children. Reiss maintains that each type requires a specific form of equivalence, thus e.g. non-fiction "primarily the correct rendering of content" (1982:9). One may doubt the practical use of the typology for the translation of children's literature, as Tiina Puurtinen does in view of the fact that "most texts are a mixture of various elements" (1995:58). But one may also further differentiate the typology by adding three more functions (aesthetic, phatic and metalingual) as Peter Newmark (1988:39–44) does, following Roman Jakobson. The example Newmark chooses from Christian Morgenstern's *Galgenlieder* to illustrate the aesthetic function is intriguing:

In nonsense poetry, the sound-effect is more important than the sense: 'Ein Wiesel sass auf einem Kiesel inmitten Bachgeriesel'/ 'A ferret nibbling a carrot in a garret'. (42)

Christiane Nord (1995) has demonstrated that text-functions as defined by Jakobson can be fruitfully used as a descriptive tool to compare titles of target and source texts, including the titles of children's books (see e.g. the expressive function in the Spanish picture book title *Donde viven los monstruos* as opposed to the American *Where the wild things are*, 277).

Reiss identifies three factors which in translated children's books frequently lead to deviations from the source text: (1) children's imperfect linguistic competence, (2) the avoidance of breaking taboos which educationally minded adults might want to uphold, (3) the limited world knowledge of young readers. From a sociocritical point of view the publisher's commercial interest may be added as a fourth and perhaps domineering factor. It is this factor which becomes recognisable in Cornelia Krutz-Arnold's (1978) description of how thoroughly Enid Blyton's adventure books have been tailored to the West German market (for comparable alterations in French Blyton editions see Geneviève Bordet in Escarpit 1985:30–31 and Fernandez Lopez 2000:32–34). In some cases nothing is left but "a certain resemblance of motives" between the German and the English version (61), not to mention those German Blyton novels that apparently do not originate in any English text. However, this is by no means a new phenomenon in the history of children's literature. Anne-Lise Mooser (1993) points out that Johanna Spyri's two volumes of *Heidi* were not only stripped of their aesthetic charm by their French translator, but also (because they sold so well) supplemented with three further volumes, the last one entitled *Heidi grand-mère* (see also Abgottspon 2001).

There is a remarkable phenomenon in the diversified English-speaking world which deserves an extra paragraph. In 1990 Mary Hoffman documented the fact that "British publishers are becoming increasingly cautious about how they present American texts to English children. When they buy them at all, they make changes ranging from spellings to culture" (26). This astonishing form of "translation" (or cultural transfer) is a commercially motivated form of concession to "the many adults who mediate the books between writer and reader", though without doubt the young British audience is well acquainted with unchanged American TV, cartoons, films and songs. Yet the interference in the transatlantic children's book transfer is not a one-sided affair. Jane Whitehead has described a possibly even more common "Americanization of British children's books" (1996:687). "Titles, setting, character names, and culturally specific allusions may all be changed in addition to spelling, punctuation, vocabulary, and idiom", and "the younger the child, the heavier the hand." (688).

The Israeli literary historian Zohar Shavit (1986:111–130, earlier version 1981) favours a target-oriented approach to translation, which is based on the notion of literature as a polysystem, and would therefore belong in Chapter 5 ("The impact of the target culture"). Yet in this part of the review it may more suitably elucidate how the deviations from the source text in translated children's literature are interpreted in the light of the new theory. From Shavit's vantage point of cultural semiotics, textual manipulations are symptomatic not only of translated children's literature, but of children's literature in general, in so far as it is considered to be a subsystem of a minor status within the literary polysystem. There are five ways in which a text for children may be manipulated in translation: (1) affiliation to successful models in the target system (*Gulliver's travels*, the satire, is turned into a fantasy story for children), (2) disrespect for the text's integrality (the frequent case of abridgements), (3) reduction of complexity (e.g. by eliminating irony), (4) ideological adaptation (e.g. Campe's adaptation of Defoe's *Robinson Crusoe* to Rousseau's pedagogical system), (5) adaptation to stylistic norms (e.g. to high literary style in Hebrew in order to enrich the child reader's vocabulary).

Deviations from the source text in translated children's literature, which at first glance seem to be caused by the child reader's stage of development (Reiss) and from a sociocritical standpoint by the capitalist market situation (Krutz-Arnold), in Shavit's approach are seen even more generally as symptomatic of the minor cultural status of children's literature. This concept seems to give an answer to a lot of questions, but suggests the unsatisfactory conclusion that anything of cultural value in the field of children's literature (as, for instance, a successful translation) must be regarded as an exception to the rule.

Challenges of the source text

In the wide field of translations of children's literature there is a very special corner occupied by Manfred Görlach. Görlach is a German professor of English philology specializing in the history of the English language and in dialectology, who appears to have a great affection for linguistic metamorphoses of the German children's classic *Max und Moritz*, a picture story composed of rhymed verse and cartoon-like pictures by Wilhelm Busch. Published in 1865, just as *Alice in wonderland*, it enjoys a comparable success in the country of its origin, but not beyond the border (though in the United States it instigated the genre of the comic strip). Görlach has made himself a name as a collector, initiator and editor of both foreign language and dialect versions of *Max und Moritz* (1982a, b, 1986), which he has also adopted as an object of his studies. Thus he has discussed "sociolinguistic determinants for literature in dialects and minority languages" with regard to various versions in German dialects (1993) and five versions in Scots dialects (1995). (Another German Anglicist, Walter Sauer, has published foreign language versions of *Struwwelpeter*, and German dialect versions of *Struwwelpeter, Max und Moritz, Le petit Prince* and *Winnie-the-Pooh* without having the intention of contributing to the theory of translation.)

111

Görlach regards *Max und Moritz* as a challenge which makes the translators (in the case of Scots all of them academics) mobilise the linguistic potential of their dialects. Assuming that not every language is equally equipped to fulfil certain functions, he believes that the source text "provides an excellent opportunity for a successful translation" into European dialects, "having as its subject an uneducated pre-industrial village community of a type that was similar all over 18th–19th-century Europe" (1995:229). Görlach has strong reservations about a Glaswegian version (229) and various versions in German city slang (1993:152) and concludes: "Before translating a text into language X, the translator should make sure that there is an appropriate register for it" (1997:230).

Görlach's criterion for a "successful" translation seems to be equivalence of effect or at least comparability (1993:162). With this criterion in mind he considers the dialect translations according to linguistic levels: sounds (as in onomatopoetic 'half-words', names and rhymes), vocabulary, stylistic and sociolectal variation and localisation. He favours those versions which add "an authentic sound beyond proper spelling, syntax and lexis" so that "Scottish children are likely to recognise in the two laddies or loonies a reflection of themselves" (1995:242). The question of "authenticity" seems to be particularly relevant under the heading of "localisation". Thus e.g. the German dish *Sauerkraut* is replaced by Glaswegian "peas-brose" (1995:241). In a passage in a recent exhibition catalogue which is dedicated to "translations of the drawings" (Görlach 1997:34–36) Görlach points out that in the case of some Yiddish and Hebrew versions of *Max und Moritz* even pictorial representations of culture-specific phenomena have been substituted, e.g. an organ by a piano. There seem to exist no further discussions of the role of illustration in translation with regard to this classic picture story, except maybe in Chmeruk (1990).

While Görlach, the linguist, concentrates on the linguistic challenges a piece of children's literature offers to translators, Emer O'Sullivan, an Irish scholar specialising in children's literature from German- and English-speaking countries, proposes a list of aspects worth considering in translated children's books, which also takes literary categories into account. Constituting structural traits of a text, such categories conspicuously reveal the strengths and weaknesses of a translation. The five traits which O'Sullivan describes as "elements of a seminar on translating children's literature" (1991/92) are: (1) interplay of picture and words in picture books, (2) cultural references, (3) playful use of language, (4) dialect, register, names, (5) the possibility of double address (of child and adult). The following sections of this chapter will discuss studies concerned with the items 1, 3 and 2. A later chapter will deal with item 5. As to item 4, there seem to be no special investigations of the difficult task of translating regional dialect or teenage jargon which tend to crop up in young adult novels (see Klingberg 1986:70–71 on dialect and the brief section on German translations of teenage jargon in Peter Pohl's Swedish *Janne min vän* and in Myron Levoy's American *Alan and Naomi* — in Tabbert 1998:105–106).

Pictures and words

When Birgit Stolt (1978) compared the German illustrations of Astrid Lindgren's Michel books with the originally Swedish ones she must have been one of the first to draw attention to the fact that pictures are an integral part of translating children's literature. Riitta Oittinen (1990) regards the relation between text and illustration as a dialogic one which should be taken into account when a children's book is translated into another language. A thorough treatment of the problem has been attempted by Isabel Maria Moreira da Silva (1991) in her unpublished thesis for a diploma in Translation Studies at the University of Heidelberg. She elucidates the role of children's book illustration as a "latent problem of translation" (176, Peter A. Schmitt's term) from the vantage point of various academic disciplines and applies her insights to a comparison of Alice Vieira's illustrated Portuguese children's book *Flor de Mel* (1986) with its newly illustrated German version *Wenn Melinda kommt* (1991:158–175). If a certain degree of "indeterminacy" (Wolfgang Iser) in the Portuguese descriptions of settings is specified as Portuguese in the original illustrations, the German illustrator redefines some pictorial details as German, thus creating a discrepancy between the ("faithfully" translated) verbal text and its (new) illustrations. While da Silva considers this as due to the German illustrator's ignorance about Portugal (174), examples of "cross-cultural" illustration in other translated children's books seem to indicate conscious assimilation, e.g. the replacement of the "Mad tea party" in *Alice in wonderland* by a German *Kaffeekränzchen* (O'Sullivan 2000:323).

The special case of the picture book has been treated by the author of this review (Tabbert 1991), who in view of the equal importance of pictures and words in that medium, prefers the term "cultural transfer", introduced by Hans Vermeer (1986) as an extension of the term "translation". The point of departure of Tabbert's approach is Bernd Spillner's (1980) semiotic analysis of the *Astérix* comic books, which identifies the interplay of painted situation and pointed speech bubble wording as a comic-specific problem of translation. In most picture books the crucial interplay is that between a narrative text of rather a high degree of "indeterminacy" and the specifying pictures. Indeterminacy tempts the translator into a carefree attitude towards the source text, and since it is short, any deviation may be of greater consequence for its meaning than in the case of a long narration. A frequent disturbance of the original balance between words and pictures is caused by the fact that translators tend to put bits of information into the target text which in the original book is only conveyed by the pictures. This is particularly obvious in the American version of Michel Gay's French picture book *Papa Vroum* (Tabbert 1991a:133; a more detailed comparison in O'Sullivan 1998b:110–113 and O'Sullivan 2000: 287–291). A confrontation of a number of important picture books in three languages with their translations reveals a tendency to turn autostereotypes and heterostereotypes of the source culture into those of the target culture (Tabbert 1991a:134–142). Perhaps this observation can be taken as another proof of the guide-line articulated by an American editor of translated children's books: "The younger the child, the heavier the hand" (Whitehead 1996:688).

An interesting case of both picture-text relation and cultural implications is presented by Ofelia Schultze-Kreft (1998:171–175) in her discussion of the famous Swiss picture book *Schellen-Ursli* (1945, *A bell for Ursli*) and its two sequels, written by Selina Chönz in order to strengthen the minority language of Romansch, and outstandingly illustrated by the Romansch artist Alois Carigiet. Unlike the common practice, the original text, which is Romansch, is more detailed than the German translation, undertaken by the author herself. According to Schultze-Kreft (172) the original text had the additional function of instructing the artist about details concerning the characters and their world, and once these had been realised in the pictures, the author could omit them in her German version of the text. Only the Romansch spring custom of "Chalan-da-marz", which is central to the story and likely to be unknown to German readers, is described more extensively than in the original text.

If in the cultural transfer of picture books the pictures are usually kept intact, whilst the text may be thoroughly altered, in the case of illustrated stories or novels totally new pictures may indicate a specific transformation of the whole work. This phenomenon has been touched upon in studies of the cross-cultural reception of several classics, particularly *Alice in wonderland* (as to illustrations in French editions see Nières 1988:857–901). As has been mentioned before, Teodorowicz-Hellman (1999:49–60, 113) explicitly deduces from the style of illustration in various Polish editions that in her native country *Nils Holgersson* has been received in terms of different genres. A recent article on "anglo-visual" versions of the German children's fairy tale "Hänsel und Gretel" gives evidence that cross-cultural illustrative reception can also be classified according to Bühler's functional model of language (Tabbert 2002), which in the past was applied to a typology of translated poems (Tabbert 1968). Thus the expressive style of Anthony Browne's autobiographically inspired picture book version is very different from Tony Ross's pictorial appeal to the British sense of black humour; and textual manipulations corroborate the respective tendency.

Playful use of language

Wordplay has been one of the attractions of children's literature since Lewis Carroll questioned the dominance of didacticism with his *Alice in wonderland* (1865). As a problem of translation the phenomenon has been systematically and comprehensively investigated in Hans Grassegger's study (1985) of *Astérix* comics, which may not have been produced specifically for young readers, but which seem to belong to their favourite reading material. Grassegger has compared the speech bubble texts of twelve French *Astérix* volumes with the corresponding wording in six European languages, especially German, English and Italian. Similar to the Bühler-Reiss text typology, it is not equivalents of content that translators have to look for, Grassegger says, but equivalents of form. The idea of playfulness (*Spielgedanke*) comes first, and hence the main result of Grassegger's investigation is meant to be seen in a positive light: "For lack of morphological, lexical and syntactic equivalents in the target languages translators have to switch to types of wordplay which are different from those in the original" (100) and are more often than not "shifted about", compared with the original.

It is not only wordplay in a narrower sense (i.e. homophones, taking idiomatic phrases literally, etc.) that Sonia Marx (in Ewers/Lehnert/ O'Sullivan 1994:154–171; 1997:155–178) is concerned with when she confronts Collodi's Italian *Pinocchio* with 16 German variants, or Emer O'Sullivan (1992) when she compares Aidan Chambers's English young adult novels with their respective German versions, but it is all sorts of linguistic humour. Collodi's traditional art favours telling names, bizarre similes, hyperbole, tautologies and intentional break in style. Chambers, who openly shows the influence of James Joyce, has a liking for "the graphic dimension of the text" and for "incongruities between narrative form and content". O'Sullivan's title signals that, in the case of Chambers, cultural transfer means not only "loss", but also "gain", as his innovative use of language could give fresh impulses to children's literature in the target culture.

In a more recent article O'Sullivan (1999b) discusses the specific problem of translating what she calls "intertextual humour" in children's literature. She traces this challenge for translators from novels by Roald Dahl and Aidan Chambers through picture books by Mitsumasa Anno and Janet & Alan Ahlberg ("interpictorial references", Isabelle Nières) back to the parodies in *Alice in wonderland*. The title of her article highlights the successful translation of a spoonerism by Roald Dahl, the inversion of which refers to a prominent English author who in the German translation is replaced by a German one: From 'Dahl's Chickens' to 'Himmels Grausen'.

Lewis Carroll's playful use of language challenges not only the ever new generations of translators, but also critics of resulting translations in various languages. Recent critics (not so Weissbrod 1996:224) tend to neglect the fact that Warren Weaver (1964), an American mathematician and Carroll collector, in a substantial preface to his comprehensive bibliography of translations of *Alice in wonderland*, has already convincingly distinguished five types of challenges, each of which he discusses with regard to translations in 14 languages: (a) parodied verse, (b) puns, (c) manufactured or nonsense words, (d) jokes which involve logic, (e) twists of meaning. Weaver's 14 linguistic "collaborators" were distinguished persons (most of them scientists) who were well-versed in the language in which Weaver sent them Lewis Carroll's chapter "A mad teaparty". They were asked to comment on the peculiarities of the translation they had received and retranslate it into English. Weaver discusses the resulting material with regard to his five types of translational challenges and thus attempts a tentative answer to his question: "How can 'Alice' be translated?"

Naturally, the results tend to be more professional if the analyst is a scholar of Literature or Translation Studies specialising in texts of the language at hand. Christian Enzensberger's German version of the two Alice books, which appeared in 1963, has stimulated several professional studies. Gertrud Lehnert-Rodiek (1988) concentrates on wordplay and parody and then turns to the general question of whether the translation should show foreignness or appear to be a text of the target culture ("documentary" or "instrumental" translation according to Nord 1989:102–103). Lehnert-Rodiek believes that a text such as the Alice book has to be "naturalised" (*eingebürgert*) in order to be understood at all and that Enzensberger has achieved this though in a somewhat strained manner. She contradicts Susan Mango (1977) who considers Enzensberger's equivalents to Carroll's wordplay to be brilliant, but as a native of Britain regrets the translator's target orientation, which she detects in the Germanisation of cultural references, occasional adaptation of the dialogue to child language, replacement of verbal and personal constructions by nominal and impersonal ones and a "slant to negativity" (78) both in syntax and lexis. In further studies of German versions of *Alice* (Friese 1995; O'Sullivan 1998a; 1999b; 2000:296–378), which also include more recent translations, Lehnert-Rodiek's results are duly taken into account, but Mango's subtle linguistic observations seem to find hardly any echo at all.

Concluding from Isabelle Nières's meticulous doctoral dissertation (1988) the reception of the Alice books seems to have been particularly effective in France. Nières dedicates a whole chapter (399–508) to a systematic outline of challenges to the translator, most of which are varieties of *jeux de langage*, which she names according to traditional rhetoric and structural linguistics, collects in lists and explains to her French readers. Of the five translators, whose Alice versions she discusses in another chapter (510–669), the last one, Henri Parisot, has published a detailed commentary on his translations of wordplay under the telling title "Pour franciser les jeux de langage d' 'Alice'" (1971:67–82).

Riitta Oittinen, though concerned with the three Finnish translations of *Alice*, does not treat the specific challenges of wordplay, at least not in her books published in English (1993; 2000). Rachel Weissbrod (1996) examines the problem in three Hebrew translations, and she does it in a norm-oriented manner, which can be more suitably summarised in Chapter 5.

Culture-specific phenomena

As has been shown, cultural references as a challenge of the source text are discussed and catalogued by Klingberg (1986, "local context adaptation") and also reflected upon by Görlach (1993; 1995, "localisation"). Klingberg's demand for the preservation of the original references is shared by Cecilia Beuchat and Carolina Valdivieso (1992) in their comments on Spanish translations of children's books read in Chile. "From an educational point of view" they emphasise that translated children's books contribute "to the improvement of relations between different nations" and provide "knowledge about their unique and peculiar characteristics" (9). From a number of modern British classics they quote examples of translation problems posed by both material and (more difficult) non-material cultural differences and propose the kind of solution which means that "the reader will have the feeling of being 'transported' into another world" (12). In a book publication of the Chilean research group around Valdivieso (1991), excerpts from English, German and French children's books are reprinted together with their respective Spanish versions which are commented upon.

Tanya Christa (1998) presents an interesting case study in her consideration of the German translation of Beth Roberts's Australian children's novel *Manganinnie* (1979), which introduces the reader into the world of Aboriginal culture in the 19th century. The Aboriginal words, which in the source text essentially contribute to the impression of "otherness" and are subtly elucidated by the context, are explicitly explained in the target text, thus destroying the air of authenticity. Another observation worth mentioning is the fact that due to "political correctness" the translator suppresses the German equivalent of the adjective "black", with regard not only to the Aboriginal characters, but even to animals, and that she "whitewashes" war activities of the Aborigines.

There are also semiotic approaches to the problem of coping with cultural differences. Maria Nikolajeva, a Swedish Anglicist of Russian origin, who supports Riitta Oittinen (1993) in her plea for reader-oriented translation of children's books, draws on Yuri Lotman's concepts of cultural context and semiosphere in order to heighten awareness of the systemic implications of cultural differences (Nikolajeva 1996:27–34). She presents translation as a "scheme of interaction of contexts" (28): There is an overlap of the "semiotic space of the source-text reader" and of the "semiotic space of the target-text reader", which constitutes "the zone of mutual under-standing or translatability" (29). Referring to modern children's books, Nikolajeva gives a number of examples of confrontations between three cultural contexts: the Swedish, the Soviet Russian and the American. Thus caviar, as cheap cod paste on sandwiches familiar to Swedish child readers, would make Russian children associate members of a privileged class; and just like this "everyday sign", "relationship signs" may also cause misunder-standing by foreigners, e.g. Swedish school children's habit of addressing their teachers by their first names. Though it may seem that "children's literature is basically non-translatable, since children's semiotic experience does not allow them to interpret the signs of an alien semiosphere", Nikolajeva emphasizes that "Lotman's model of cultural interaction is dynamic and provides for an approach to cultural understanding" (34).

Noriko Shimoda Netley (1992) demonstrates in a case study of the Jap-anese version of Roald Dahl's boisterous children's book *Matilda* (1988) the degree to which the character of a story may be changed if the codes used in the target text are totally different from those constituting the source text. Netley's methodological key is Roland Barthes's concept of a text as a network of various codes (195). Dahl's colloquial style is turned into formal written style in Japanese and, as Netley elaborates with regard to pragmalinguistic possibilities, narrative situation and depicted school life, this "seems to have been caused partly by the difference between the languages, partly by the difference in cultural codes and reference systems" (196). The Japanese *Matilda* is a serious and moral book, and its author, controversially judged by British critics, is praised in Japan for his "morality" (201).

The approach to the problem of cultural references which has been intro-duced by Christiane Nord (1993) may well be the most fertile one, as far as methodology is concerned. The book selected as a test case is *Alice in wonderland* which, from a French point of view, has justifiably been called "un texte totalement ethnocentrique" (Nières 1988:408). Nord compares translations of the book in five languages with the help of Els Oksaar's semiotic concept of "cultureme", a term for "the abstract units of commun-icative human action and behaviour" (Nord 1993:397). With this concept in mind, Nord singles out units in those three dimensions of the world of the source text, which are determined by culture: "background situation" (e.g. English eating-habits: "orange marmalade"), "current situation" (e.g. lower-class accent of the footman) and "references of action" (e.g. in phatic communication, the address "my dear"). In the target text the pinpointed culture markers may be preserved, neutralised or adapted, and thus create or avoid the impression of cultural distance. The Alice version in Brazilian Portuguese turns out to be the only consistent one insofar as it adapts the culture markers throughout; all the other translations are irritating mixtures of foreign and familiar elements. Enzensberger's German translation, for instance, "tends to adapt the situation, but to leave the action — especially communicative action — marked as foreign" (413). As a representative of the skopos theory Nord claims that a translator should decide whether to strive for cultural distance (perhaps in order to convey knowledge about foreign cultures) or to aim at a reading experience motivated by identification. In any case, a translator should create a coherent text.

The impact of the target culture

A considerable number of critical studies have accumulated to be dealt with in this chapter and a subdivision seems advisable. As it is difficult to find clearly defining categories for such a framework, the following attempt can only claim to be of temporary value. There is a recognizable group of studies by Gideon Toury and scholars who refer to his notions of Descriptive Translation Studies. Tiina Puurtinen (1995:43) talks of a "Tourian approach" (which she adapts for her own research project). It is the concept of "norms" of the target culture which those scholars seem to share. Yet before and after Toury's elaboration of the concept the impact of the target culture on the translation of children's books has been acknowledged, too, more or less in the sense of a forming (or rather: deforming) ideology. So the term "ideology" will be used to cover those otherwise heterogeneous studies (including some which are unmistakably source-text oriented). Linguistic aspects are involved when the impact of norms or ideology is pursued into the grammatical structure of the language used in the target text. Investigations of this type, almost exclusively represented by Puurtinen, will make up a third section of this chapter.

Norms

The intellectual home of the norm-oriented approach within Translation Studies appears to be Tel Aviv University, where "Itamar Even-Zohar first introduced the term 'polysystem' for the aggregate of literary systems (including everything from 'high' or 'canonised' forms ... such as poetry to 'low' or 'non-canonised' forms [e.g. children's literature and popular fiction] in a given culture" (Gentzler 1993:105). Gideon Toury, a younger colleague, took up Even-Zohar's notion of the importance of translated literature in literary history and developed a theory of "norms" that influence translation decisions in the target culture (Toury 1980; 2000). Translation activity takes place "in socioculturally relevant settings" (2000:198) governed by norms, the effect of which can only be reliably studied in the products of that activity: in written translations, though "semi-theoretical or critical formulations" about them may be worth taking into account (2000:207). The main distinction Toury makes is that between "adequacy" and "acceptability" of translations: "Whereas adherence to source norms determines a translation's adequacy as compared to the source text, subscription to norms originating in the target culture determines acceptability" (2000:201).

Theory-oriented case studies

In the case of translated children's literature, the choice of norms depends on the position of translated literature in the target literary system (Toury 1980:142). According to Even-Zohar, translations are usually regarded as being of secondary importance and constituting a "peripheral system" inside the polysystem. Their "foremost aim is acceptability in the target system". However, there are also the rarer cases when they might serve to strengthen the weak centre of the target polysystem by aiming for adequacy. Toury exemplifies that "the history of literary translation from German into Hebrew . . . is a motion from the center of Hebrew literature to its periphery" (142). His test case are the four Hebrew versions of *Max und Moritz*. The first version of 1898 strives for adequacy to such a degree that it even risks violation of religious norms. "The wish to introduce into Hebrew children's literature something that it was lacking was stronger than the translator's necessity to subject himself to some of the norms that were already established in it" (144). The fourth version of 1965, on the other hand, is "based on previous translations and adaptations" and shows a high rate of conformity to "the norms prevalent in the Hebrew system" (141).

Even more meticulously, Toury (1995:147–165) demonstrates a tendency towards acceptability in a Hebrew translation of a German *Schlaraffenland* text. The original fairy tale of the land of milk and honey, which had been recorded by Ludwig Bechstein, was tightened by Tom Freud in 1921 to become a children's story and then transformed into a characteristically Hebrew text by the national Hebrew poet Chaim Nahman Bialik, who introduced as a mediating model an accepted Russian narrative structure. In his conclusion Toury emphasizes that though translation is a free decision-making process, even the renowned (and innovative) poet preferred to adhere to the norms existing in the ruling system of Hebrew literature when he did translation.

Zohar Shavit (1992; a variant: 1997) has investigated the beginnings of Jewish-Hebrew children's literature in the early 19th century. As she illustrates with several titles, representatives of the Jewish-Hebrew Enlightenment (*Haskalah*) Movement translated Joachim Heinrich Campe's didactic German children's books as textual models for originally Hebrew children's books. Even more fundamentally than in the case of the first Hebrew translation of *Max und Moritz*, an endeavour for adequacy of translation is indicative of attempts to introduce something new into a literary system. So that endeavour is recognisably caused by the target culture.

Nitsa Ben-Ari (1992) in a much quoted study elucidates the translational reception of German children's literature in Israel after World War II. She formulates as a principle of literary translation "that considerations of adequacy . . . will always come second to considerations of acceptability in the Target Literature" (1992:221), and she exemplifies succinctly that in her test case acceptability is brought about by "three sets of norms: (1) the universal patterns of translation . . . ; (2) the didactic norms pertaining to children's literature per se; and (3) the delicate and intricate didactic attitude [in Israel] to the German culture in particular" (222).

The constraints of the target culture for the translation of children's literature are graphically conspicuous when Basmat Even-Zohar (1992) confronts Astrid Lindgren's preference for authentic current Swedish vernacular with the demands in Israel to use "the 'correct' and 'rich' form of traditional literary Hebrew" in the production of children's literature (1992:244). She also hints at a certain similarity between Hebrew and Russian translations of Lindgren (242; see Skott 1977). However, she is aware of a development of Hebrew children's literature "in the direction of the modern tongue", which will continue to be reflected in translated children's literature (244).

Rachel Weissbrod (1996) reveals the impact of Jewish-Hebrew culture on translation in the handling of wordplay, just as Even-Zohar (1992) traces it in the responses to the printed vernacular. The three complete Hebrew translations of *Alice in wonderland*, separated by periods of about 30 years, represent different varieties of impact. The first two versions strive for acceptability, one (1926) at a sociocultural, the other (1951) at a stylistic level. The third (1987) is intent on adequacy, which was at that time adhered to even in children's literature. In another article Weissbrod (1999) shows that the demands for employing an elevated Hebrew style in the translation of humorous texts may result in mock epic, an 18th-century English genre which presents trivial characters and incidents in the elevated language of the classical epos. One of Weissbrod's four examples is the Hebrew version of the children's classic *Winnie-the-Pooh*, a translation of 1943 which, in its mock-epic dimension, is amusing, but only for adults and in a way different from the humour of the original.

Miryam Du-Nour (1995) sums up earlier analyses of the effect of target culture norms on the translations of children's literature into Hebrew, but differentiates the "Tourian approach" by incorporating Vermeer's and Nord's notion of the purpose (*skopos*) of a translation for a commissioner. She concentrates on the specific purpose "to bring the book closer to the child's heart", which proves "to be the main justification given by 'commissioners' of retranslations and revisions of translated children's books" (1995:332). In her linguistically oriented review of Hebrew retranslations of some children's classics over a span of 70 years Du-Nour reveals that this purpose vies with ideologically motivated and didactically oriented demands to teach children the traditional elevated Hebrew style.

If Du-Nour is concerned with a purpose which, with regard to child readers, might be defined as psychological, the Canadian Judith Woodsworth (1996) considers a purpose which is clearly political: the promotion of national identity by means of translating successful literature into a minority language. One of Woodsworth's two test cases is a 1994 translation of *The house at Pooh corner* (a sequel to *Winnie- the-Pooh*) into Romansch (one of the four official languages of Switzerland, also promoted by the picture book *A bell for Ursli*, see Schultze-Kreft 1998). It is not only the making of the Romansch translation by a Canadian linguist and some of its linguistic results which are documented, but also its institutional support and its distribution. Similar translation activities at a European level in favour of children's books in minority languages have been pointed out in a published interview with the Scottish Gaelic writer, translator and editor Finlay Macleod (Tabbert 1991b).

The reception of post-1968 "emancipatory" German children's books in Turkey has been outlined by the Turkish scholars Selahattin Dilidüzgün and Turgay Kurultay (1992) and analysed in terms of intercultural communication by Kurultay alone (1994), who is familiar with the target-oriented approach of Toury (1980) and Shavit (1981). His discussion of translation in the context of Turkish culture (his test case is Peter Härtling's children's book *Ben liebt Anna*) appears to be more concerned with potential conflicts than most of the Israeli studies. The fundamental difference between the cultures involved may be comparable, insofar as it is rooted in religion, but instead of attending to the reception of children's books as a completed fact of literary history, Kurultay observes the open situation for an imported type of book which is approved of by only a (liberal) minority of his compatriots. It seems to be this very limitation of the potential audience which is the reason why on the one hand (with regard to the liberal minority) the German children's love story was deliberately translated in an "adequate" manner and on the other hand (in spite of breaking essential Turkish taboos) it was not publicly prohibited. Kurultay also addresses the problem of children's restricted ability to participate in intercultural literary communication, which according to him cannot be solved principally, but only casuistically. In the case of Härtling's love story he does not believe Turkish children to be overtaxed by the confrontation with unfamiliar situations, because the translator has found compromises for the crucial passages, which preserve the impression of foreignness and yet grant readability (two options between which Nord [1993] expects a translator to decide). Kurultay's approach resembles that of Woodsworth and of Du-Nour insofar as he seems to combine notions of the Tel-Aviv and of the Heidelberg representatives of translation theory in what could be regarded as a fruitful synthesis (see also Kurultay 2000).

Nation-oriented period studies

In a sense the Israeli case studies introduced in the preceding section are components of a diachronic description of translated children's books in Hebrew. Translated children's books in Spanish and Italian have been examined in two research projects which attempt to explore a specific period of translation policy in the respective countries, namely the most recent one. In her doctoral dissertation written in Spanish, Marisa Fernandez Lopez (1996) investigates twentieth-century English-language children's literature in Spain between 1940 and 1984. Books of that origin constitute more than 50 per cent of translated children's books, which in turn represent 45 per cent of all the books published for young Spanish readers (1996:94, 81). Isabella Zeli is concerned with foreign children's literature in Italy from 1987 on, the year of "the 'explosion' of the children's book market" in her country (Zeli n.d.: 7). In 1996 almost 47 per cent of the published children's books in Italy were translations (10). Both scholars explore their field of research not only through the polysystem concept of literature and case studies of translations, but also through statistics, tables and diagrams.

Fernandez Lopez points out that the Spanish reception of twentieth-century children's literature in the English language began after the Civil War, and she distinguishes three periods of reception between 1940 and 1984, triggered by important events of political history. The development is described concisely and documented by book market statistics and lists of publishers and translators. The second half of the 340-page volume comprises analyses of translated literature, divided into three groups: (1) popular, (2) canonised, (3) high quality books [(2) referring to high quality books before, (3) after the First World War]. In her analyses Fernandez Lopez concentrates on four possible tendencies of translated literature (1996:61) as defined by other scholars: stylistic elevation, stylistic homogeneity (Toury 1980), simplification (Shavit 1986) and cultural context adaptation (Klingberg 1986). Her final generalisation that the translation of canonised texts tends towards "adequacy" and the translation of popular texts towards "acceptability" (322) may be no surprise, but what counts are the carefully differentiating analyses from which this conclusion is drawn. Indeed, the methodologically sound and consistent study deserves attention from both scholars of Translation Studies and scholars of Comparative Children's Literature.

Fernandez Lopez has published essay versions of some of her case studies (on Kenneth Grahame, J. M. Barrie, Scott O'Dell, Roald Dahl) elsewhere, and in a recent article written in English she draws an interesting picture of the nature of ideology in Spanish translations of popular British children's books (Fernandez Lopez 2000). It may be all too obvious that the censorship under Franco's dictatorship (1939–1975) caused textual manipulations as regards sex, religion and politics. Yet striking is the observation that there is a "Spanish norm of fidelity to the original text" (33) which is even effective with regard to Enid Blyton's popular children's books, as Fernandez Lopez demonstrates by contrasting the Spanish translations with the French and Portuguese ones. That norm also appears to make Spanish publishers and translators stick to first editions of British texts, though "political correctness" may have caused them to be purified of racist and xenophobic elements in their country of origin (as in the cases of Blyton, Dahl and Lofting). Over the past few years the ("adequate") translations of more recent English-language children's books have contributed to the strengthening of the Spanish system of children's literature and to making it similar to that of western countries such as France, which have proved to be less "permeable".

Isabella Zeli (n.d.: 7) is concerned with "the impact that imported children's literature has on the national tradition" in Italy. She presents her research in a 50-page thesis, supplemented by 21 documentary attachments. The work, which was written for the Catholic University of Leuven (Belgium) and the Università Cattolica del Sacro Cuore, Milan, has not been published as a book, but is available in the International Youth Library, Munich.

If, according to the statistical material reproduced by Zeli, 1987 marks the beginning of an astonishing increase in the number of books for children in Italy (20 years later than in North European countries), then the publisher Salani played an important role in that development, insofar as he introduced a special *collection* and by doing so paved the way for a growing number of translations, especially of English authors (13), led by Roald Dahl, a best-selling children's writer in Italy. So there is good reason for Zeli's decision to focus her research on that publishing house, its *collections* and translation policy (which is itself of special methodological interest), and to dedicate a case study of cultural transfer to Roald Dahl. She shows that, compared with France and the Netherlands, four main books of his were translated relatively late in Italy, as the Italian system was not prepared for that type of children's literature. A detailed analysis of the layout and the language of the Italian version of Dahl's book *The twits* reveals that it tends to be close to the original, as opposed to the French translation which adapts the book for French child readers (a justification for which is provided by the translator Marie Raymond-Farré in Escarpit 1985:148–151). Zeli's final conclusion is reminiscent of Fernandez Lopez's research concerning Spain: "The position of children's literature in the Italian literary system is very marginal, at the periphery, consequently the foreign production has easily gained the centre" (45). Zeli refers to an interesting statement by Salani's influential editor-in-chief Donatella Ziliotti, which would be worth an additional comparative study: "The few interesting [Italian children's writers] belong to the new generation of Italian authors, influenced by the new trend coming from the North European countries, not concerned with moral or pedagogical goals" (16).

Ideology

The concept of norms controlling translation, introduced by Toury (1980; 2000), is carefully related to sociology and social psychology. The term "ideology", which is mentioned in some of the studies discussed in this section and applied to all of them, is used in the somewhat vague sense of a dictionary definition: "a body of ideas that reflects the beliefs and interests of a nation, political system etc" (*Collins English Dictionary* 1991:771). In none of the studies is ideology linked with the polysystem theory of literature, as is the case with Fernandez Lopez (2000). No matter whether the word is used or not, the fact of ideology manifests itself as a semantic difference between source text and target text. As far as the translation of historical children's books is concerned (mostly so-called "classics"), historical distance tends to set off ideological difference. In the case of contemporary children's books, the difference is solely that which exists per se between two cultures.

The French comparatist Isabelle Nières is familiar with translations of both historical and contemporary children's books. Following a graphic sketch (1992) of the European interchange of didactic children's literature in the 18th century, and of the classic mythological, Christian and oral heritage shared by children's literature in various languages, she attempts a new approach to the question of translation (Nières-Chevrel 1998), one which she had already treated earlier (in Escarpit 1985:35–54). On the one hand she gives examples of an ideological impact of the target culture, with special regard to the transfer of children's books between Protestant and Catholic cultures, whilst on the other hand she demonstrates the "creative" force of translation, in France e.g. by recently paving the way for a new type of picture book (106–107) or for nonsense literature à la Lewis Carroll (120–121). The function of translation which she calls "contourner des situations idéologiques bloquées et renouveler les motifs littéraires" (107) is reminiscent of that which in a systemic approach has been called "modelling the centre of the [target] polysystem" (Toury 1980:142).

Historical children's books abroad

A good deal of those historical children's books which are known as classics are (in the traditional sense of the word) "adaptations" of books written for adults. Frequently this age-specific adjustment coincides with the process of translation or, more correctly: cultural transfer. In order to limit the scope of the present article, the numerous translation analyses concerning that border-line case of adult and children's literature will be mentioned here only by a few titles, for which the ideology of the target culture is of major importance.

Margareta Winqvist (1973) in her tracing of the reception of Defoe's *Robinson Crusoe* in Sweden, and Dieter Petzold (1982) in his summarising studies of German versions of the book for children, concur in drawing attention to variations of didactic reduction of a complex work of world literature. A distinct political component can be identified in the ideological implications of German adaptations of Cooper's *Leatherstocking tales* for young readers, as shown by Irmgard Egger (1991) and Philipp Löser (1998). And if the Danish *Ugly duckling*, a quintessential Andersen story, is a miniature *Bildungsroman* for both children and adults, Andrew Lang's English version brings it close to the prototype of fairy tale for children, including restrictive Victorian norms, as revealed by Viggo H. Pedersen (1990).

The ideological content of 19th-century children's books may be strongly determined by religion. David Blamires (1994) reminds us of the German author Christoph von Schmid, who, though a Catholic priest, wrote widely read children's stories in which the "presentation of Christianity . . . is remarkable in that it contains little that is specifically Catholic" (73). Attractive to the Sunday school market, Schmid's best known story *Das Blumenkörbchen* has been translated into English at least five times, and what is particularly significant is the fact that the first two versions were made to conform to Evangelical dogmatism by means of added authorial comments and quotations, which appear to have granted them a much higher print run than two later translations which were quite "faithful".

While Schmid was "evangelised" through additions, the American Louisa M. Alcott was secularised through omissions, as Kari Skjønsberg (1979: 37–77) points out in the four Norwegian versions of the novel *Little women* (1868). What is deleted in all the versions are the explicit intertextual references to John Bunyan's *Pilgrim's progress*, which constitute a religious framework in the Puritan tradition. In her Norwegian collection of essays Skjønsberg (1979) is concerned with the various meanings of the term "adaptation", and in the somewhat different Swedish edition of her essays (1982) she also includes a quantitative analysis of the Swedish classic *Nils Holgersson* in five West European languages. This analysis could be supplemented by studies of its reception in Russia and Poland (Nikolajeva 1991; Teodorowicz-Hellman 1999). Skjønsberg's conclusion is also applicable to other children's classics: "It seems that though *Nils Holgersson* is known the world over, not two countries know the same story" (1982:149). International variants of *Alice in wonderland* are referred to elsewhere in this article (Sections 4.2, 4.3, 5.1, 6), and contributions on multilingual transformations of Johanna Spyri's *Heidi* and of Erich Kästner's children's books will be collected in forthcoming proceedings of commemorative symposia (Böhler/Rutschmann; Dolle-Weinkauff/Ewers 2002. As to *Heidi* see also Abgottspon 2001).

Carlo Collodi's *Pinocchio* has proved to be one of the busiest border crossers, since he was created in 1880 to help promote Tuscan Italian as the standard language of a new nation state. There are at least 38 translations into German alone (Richter 1996:125). The Austrian linguist Sonia Marx has dedicated her doctoral thesis (Marx 1990) to a fair selection of these translations, after the comparatist Erwin Koppen (1980) elucidated how, in an early attempt of 1905, the German author O. J. Bierbaum deliberately transformed the fairy tale novel with a Tuscan setting into a satire on Wilhelminian Germany. Marx has traced the German-language editions (added and slightly corrected data in Richter 1996 and O'Sullivan 2000:405–414) and analysed selected passages in terms of categories proposed by Klingberg ("context adaptation" in Klingberg/Ørvig/Amor 1978:84–89) and Reiss (1982). A glance at the first and the last of the examined versions (Anton Grumann 1913/Christine Nöstlinger 1988) reveals to what degree each of the new Pinocchios is a child of his time, in those two cases as far as the educational style which is vicariously applied to the hero is concerned (antiauthoritarian versus authoritarian). Analyses of the vocabulary show that there may also be a strong dialect or regional component in the impact of the target culture, which is particularly obvious in the Swiss version and the older Austrian ones.

Marx's approach is not explicitly target-oriented, though a more recent presentation of her results in German under the heading "produktive Rezeption" tends in that direction (Marx 1997:179–201), as do two chapters by other scholars, who take up some of her results (Richter 1996:125–137; O'Sullivan 2000:405–419). American sociologist Richard Wunderlich (1992) has related the success of various *Pinocchio* adaptations in his country to phases of social history, and perhaps it takes a sociologist to consider so convincingly the ideological impact of a target culture on the reception of a literary symbol. But then one must not expect discussions of linguistic subtlety.

More than any other figure in children's literature Pinoccio has become a national symbol (Richter 1996:146) and as such seems to be supported by the "Fondazione Nazionale Carlo Collodi di Pescia". That institution has not only sponsored Marx's book about *Pinocchio* in the German-speaking countries, but also a similar bibliographic and linguistic investigation of *Pinocchio* in Spain, where he emerges in five languages spoken in the country (Mercedes Gómez del Manzano/Gabriel Janer Manila 1996). Publications sponsored earlier trace the Italian child hero to Czechoslovakia, France and the U.S. (Richter 1996:183–184).

Contemporary children's books abroad

If there is one literary figure who surpasses Pinocchio's popularity with children all over the world, it must be Astrid Lindgren's Pippi Longstocking, who, since she entered the public stage in the crucial year of 1945, can also be regarded as a herald of contemporary children's literature. It took quite a while for the untutored spirit of independence, incorporated by the Swedish enfant terrible, to be accepted without reservations by adult mediators of children's literature, especially beyond the Swedish border. Translations of the book into various languages and their revisions testify to this hesitant approval, as shown in several studies.

The most comprehensive study so far, also informed by modern translation theory, is the unpublished doctoral dissertation of the German Scandinavist Astrid Surmatz on the German reception of Astrid Lindgren and its international context (1998). Germany has proved to be a gateway to Europe for Lindgren's books, as it has for modern Scandinavian literature in general. In a chapter which modifies a previous article written in Swedish (1994), Surmatz focuses on a number of passages in the German translation of *Pippi Långstrump* of 1949, in which Pippi's behaviour is modified in order not to deviate from predominant educational norms. In the 1980s the publisher of that edition responded to the criticism of a Scandinavist and had Pippi's original form of independence more or less restituted, also in accordance with current educational trends. In another chapter Surmatz considers translations of the "modern classic" into other languages. The sequence of reception follows a line from the North West of Europe to the South and finally to the East and to Asia. In France, Surmatz notes a process of translational revision comparable to that in Germany: from "acceptability" to "adequacy", one might say in Tourian terms. From her own and other analyses of foreign versions of Lindgren's children's books, Surmatz concludes: The more avant-garde or subversive a text is and the more it fuses narrative forms of realism and of fantasy, the more conspicuous are the translators' interferences. These, however, have been decreasing since the 1960s when Lindgren was widely acknowledged as a major writer.

Lindgren in French seems to be particularly challenging for critics. There is a survey article by Anna Birgitta Erikson (1985) and an analysis of the *Pippi* translation by Christina Heldner (1992), which focuses on the French fear of "subversive education" and on reservations about an oral style of narration (also to be found among Israeli editors, Even-Zohar 1992). Denise von Stockar points out the suppression of emancipatory elements in the French translation not only of *Pippi*, but also of Christine Nöstlinger's *Conrad*, a quite explicit model of antiauthoritarian education, and furthermore the elimination of nuances of child psychology in the translation of Maurice Sendak's *Where the wild things are* (Rutschmann/von Stockar 1996: 35–65. Her positive evaluation of the German translation of *Wild things* is in contrast to that in Schelbert 1975). Karin van Camp (1995) feels stimulated by Lindgren's own criticism of the French version of *Pippi* to plead for a revision of the Dutch version, in which quite a few instances of Swedish wordplay remained untranslated, rendering the heroine less funny.

Ewa Teodorowicz-Hellman, who has analysed the Polish translation in a Polish and in a Swedish contribution (1997; 1999:61–81), finds the transformed heroine "more vociferous and less rebellious" (1999:114). The problem of translating the humour of the book is thoroughly examined in terms of linguistics, reader psychology and Klingberg's and Reiss's translation theory. Lindgren's *Karlsson* in Russian and *Ronja* in Icelandic have been analysed by Skott (1977) and Hauksson (1985) respectively.

Just like *Pippi Långstrump* a number of other excellent children's books, which originated in a liberal world-view in post-war Germany, were subjected to more conservative and restrictive norms, as pointed out by several critics: Leo Lionni's American picture book *Swimmy* (Meckling 1975), Tove Jansson's Finno-Swedish Moomin books (Bode 1995; Jendis 2001, in accordance with the "Tourian" approach of target-oriented translation analysis, including illustrations), and Michael Bond's English Paddington stories (Osberghaus 1997). Monika Osberghaus, in her unpublished M.A. thesis, is explicitly target-oriented insofar as she relates the translated stories to children's literature in the target culture of the same period (she talks of *Zeitgebundenheit*, "period dependence", of translation), in a way similar to Fernandez Lopez (1996) and Surmatz (1994; 1998). In this case the critic herself has made practical use of her attentive reading of the target text, producing a revised and more "adequate" version which attempts to reconstruct the humour of the original (Jung 1996:19).

In the West German translations of the Soviet Russian children's books by Jurij Korinec, the distance between source and target cultures is particularly wide, as the two cultures are based on contrasting political systems. As a predictable consequence there are drastic abbreviations and alterations, which Wolfram Eggeling (1994) reveals with regard to *Dort, weit hinter dem Fluss* [*Tam, vdali, za rekoj*], Korinec's best-known novel, and Iris Seemann (1987), in her unpublished doctoral dissertation, with regard to all West German translations of his books. In the meantime Seemann (1999) has published an encyclopedic presentation of all traceable West German versions of Soviet Russian children's books between 1945 and 1989, target-oriented insofar as it is related to six phases of foreign relations between West Germany and the U.S.S.R., though evaluative rather than descriptive in its considerations of translation. Certainly it is a most useful volume for practical work with children's literature, primarily in the area of intercultural education. As far as the publishing aspect of intercultural relations is concerned three facts are worth mentioning: The West German reception of Soviet Russian children's books is dominated by one single translator, the author Hans Baumann (Seemann 1999:36–39); his translation of Korinec's main work *Dort, weit hinter dem Fluss* is paralleled by a more "faithful" East German version, and is the basis for all the other translations in the capitalist West, except the Danish one (Seemann 1987:263). The two phenomena, personal dominance in cultural transfer between two countries and translated translations, both of which are not uncommon in children's literature, would be worth studying in their own right.

Sentence structure

As far as the language of translated children's books is concerned, it is usually considered in terms of lexis, semantics or semiotics, and sometimes pragmatics. Very rarely are questions of grammar touched upon, only when two languages as distant as English and Japanese are involved, as in the case of the Japanese version of Roald Dahl's *Matilda* (Netley 1992). The German linguist Judith Macheiner (1995, i.e. Monika Doherty) — who does not focus on children's literature, but draws quite a few examples from Enzensberger's German version of the two *Alice* books — bases her theory of translation on a major difference between English and German sentence structures: In English the informational climax is in the middle of a sentence, in German at the beginning or at the end. Macheiner's main criterion for the quality of a translation is its "adequacy" to the grammatical and stylistic rules of the target language, such as those concerning the sentence structure. "Adequacy" in this sense she claims to be more important than concurrence between source and target text with regard to form (which she calls "analogy"), and content ("equivalence").

In the field of translated children's books it is the Finnish scholar of Translation Studies Tiina Puurtinen who uses sentence structure as a vantage point of her research, the results of which she has published in her doctoral dissertation (Puurtinen 1995) and in preceding and subsequent articles (1989; 1994; 1997). Puurtinen, who is well-versed in both the Tel Aviv and the Heidelberg theories of translation, hopes to explain the linguistic acceptability of translated children's books by the readability (and corresponding speakability) of a text, which in turn she sees as depending on its dominant sentence structure. This objective requires a variety of research methods.

Linguistic analysis is the basis for empirical tests. The target texts which Puurtinen chooses are two Finnish translations of Frank L. Baum's American fantasy novel *The wizard of Oz* (1900). Both versions appeared in 1977, but whereas one of them shows a predilection for nonfinite constructions (such as contracted sentences or premodified participial attributes), which results in a static style, the other is characterised by frequent use of finite constructions, which results in a dynamic style. As contemporary Finnish children's literature unmistakably favours a dynamic style (as Puurtinen deduces from her syntactic analysis of 40 originally Finnish children's books and 40 translations into Finnish), the dynamic translation can be expected to be more acceptable than the static one. Comparative cloze tests with children (filling in gaps in excerpts from the two translations) and speakability tests with both children and adults (all of which are carefully recorded) lead to differentiating conclusions. These are summarised in the final chapter of the dissertation (1995:214–232) and in a separate article in *Target* (1997). In the present review the quotation of one concluding paragraph must suffice to convey an impression of the methodological scrupulousness of Puurtinen's research:

> The definition of linguistic acceptability in translated children's literature can now be reformulated as follows: the degree of linguistic acceptability is determined by the readability and speakability level appropriate to a particular group of readers (e.g. of a certain age), conformity to the linguistic norms of the relevant genre and literary subsystem (of translated literature or original TL literature), and/or conformity to the expectations of a particular group of readers (or even to the unique expectations of individual readers). As became evident from the findings of this study, measurements of these three dimensions do not always correlate. There are different kinds of acceptability, and therefore the initial unitary notion of acceptability must be replaced by a more complex, flexible concept, which allows of such heterogeneity.
>
> (1995:230)

If the last sentence refers to the concept of acceptability as introduced by the Tel Aviv theory of translation, the polysystem notion of literature which is also echoed in this paragraph (as indeed in the whole study), Puurtinen is self-critical enough to also realise the limited validity of her own research project:

> One of the shortcomings of the present dissertation likely to arouse criticism is its concentration on one linguistic aspect — the contrast between finiteness and nonfiniteness — and one kind of children's literature — fantasy stories and fairy tales.
>
> (1995:231)

Consciousness of incompleteness is an indication of reliability of results and a stimulant for further research.

Translating for children

Emer O'Sullivan (1991; 1992) has emphasised the importance of the literary communication structure for the translation of children's literature. In stories such as *Alice in wonderland*, which Shavit (1986:63) calls "ambivalent" because they are part of both the children's and the adult system of literature, O'Sullivan distinguishes at least two types of implied readers, child reader and adult reader, and she raises the question of what happens to such multiple addressed stories in translation. In a detailed case-study of two German translations of A.A. Milne's children's classic *Winnie-the-Pooh* she points out that in one of the target texts the multiplicity of the implied reader has been preserved and in the other it has been reduced to an implied child reader, a fact which is by no means uncommon in translated children's literature (O'Sullivan 1994). With regard to adults and children Isabelle Nières (1988), in her French dissertation, explicitly distinguishes two types of editions and of reception of *Alice in wonderland* in France.

In a more recent article O'Sullivan (1999a) has differentiated her approach by taking up ideas from Hermans 1996 and Schiavi 1996. The implied communication situation of a target text is represented by a complex model (O'Sullivan 1999a:47, also 2000:247). The model helps us to realise that in a target text three different voices may be distinguished: the voice of the fictitious narrator of the source text, the voice of the implied translator and the voice of the fictitious narrator of the target text. In two brief case-studies O'Sullivan outlines to what degree the narrator's voice in a target text may break away from that of the fictitious narrator of the source text: in the German version of Roald Dahl's *The Vicar of Nibbleswick* the narrator turns a passage of wordplay into a language lesson and in Irina Korschunow's German version of John Burningham's picture book *Granpa* a sparse dialogue between a girl and her grandfather, who finally dies, has been replaced by a sentimentalised narration from the girl's point-of-view.

O'Sullivan has expanded on her model of translational communication in a key chapter of her recent treatise on Comparative Children's Literature (2000:241–274). More examples from earlier analyses have been well integrated in that chapter. Unfortunately, she hardly ever refers to the concepts of her model in two subsequent chapters on the translation of picture books and the comprehensive history of German versions of *Alice in wonderland*. Surely those concepts could have lent more precision to her results. It would be of particular interest to see how, in the case of picture books, the visual element could be fitted into the model of translational communication.

The Finnish translation scholar Riitta Oittinen appears to be concerned primarily with the child reader — the real one, not the implied one. In her dissertation, subtitled "On the dialogics of translating for children" (1993; a brief variant: 1995), she draws on Mikhail Bakhtin's dialogic theory of literature and on Christiane Nord's modification of the skopos theory of translation, and passionately asserts that especially with regard to children, it is more important to be "loyal" towards the target language readers than "faithful" to the source text. She rejects the traditional idea of the "invisibility" of the translator and stresses the impact which a translator's child image has on his or her translation of children's literature. She herself favours the "carnivalistic" traits which Bakhtin ascribes to the child's world picture.

There is a clear dividing-line which Oittinen draws between her own attitude towards translating for children and the attitudes of Klingberg and Shavit. This is made explicit with regard to versions of *Gulliver's travels* for children in which so-called indecent passages have been deleted. While for Klingberg the deletion shows a lack of respect for the integrity of the original work of art, and for Shavit it is a symptom of the inferior status of children's literature, Oittinen regrets that "the adaptor has not dived into children's carnivalism" (1993:105), which includes fascination of human excretions.

Oittinen's plea for liberating the translator from the fetters of the source text becomes understandable when one considers the communicative situation she envisages and the examples of translation she prefers. Reading aloud to preschoolers is the situation she is herself familiar with, undoubtedly a dialogic event, in which the impact of a text and the feedback of the audience is very direct; and the examples of texts which she discusses in some detail are either adaptations of children's rhymes or reworkings of stories by Roald Dahl, Lewis Carroll and Tove Jansson. In either case poetic license is traditionally conceded. But it is a daring conclusion from case studies like these to demand a change of copyright laws so that a translator, as an "author translator", is on an equal footing with the author. With this aim in mind "the publisher should be included in the dialogic constellation contributing to the translation" (182). But which translator is really equal to a Dahl, Carroll or Jansson and which publisher might be willing to concede "carnivalistic" freedom to a translator as a dialogic negotiator with children? Sometimes the voice of the artist seems to gain the upper hand in the translation scholar: Riitta Oittinen is also a practising illustrator and film maker.

One may well ask if Oittinen overtaxes the meaning of the term "loyalty". Christiane Nord, whom she quotes, uses it with regard to an *Auftraggeber* (i.e. "commissioner", Nord 1989:102; "initiator" in Nord 1991:93). However, children could only be commissioners of translations in a figurative sense; it is the publishers who are normally the real commissioners. The difference itself is a potential source of controversy concerning translations for children which can be solved neither by idealising the listening child in a Bakhtinian or Rousseauist manner nor by demonising publishers, possibly from a Marxist point of view. It is doubtful whether there is a better approach but Turgay Kurultay's casuistic realism to be of help in this question. Oittinen's fresh impulses could perhaps lead to new insights if her model situation of reading out ad hoc translations to preschoolers were to be investigated empirically.

Oittinen herself did not go in that direction when she published a slightly enlarged and bibliographically updated version of her dissertation in 2000. The main addition is a chapter on the three Finnish translations of *Alice in wonderland* dating from 1906, 1972 and 1995, a chapter based on her

Finnish book *Liisa, Liisa ja Alice* (1997). In her comparison of the three versions she seems to come close to the Tel Aviv school of descriptive translation studies by considering the changes of the target culture which have had an impact on the respective translations. She uses Lawrence Venuti's (1995) terms, though, when she sums up her comparison as follows: "While Swan and Kunnas have domesticated their translations and deleted anything strange for Finnish readers, Martin has solved the problem otherwise, she has foreignised her text so that the reader can feel the otherness of the story" (139). It is still the situations she is interested in, though now in historical terms, and not systems of literature: "The three Finnish *Alices* clearly show that translations are always created in unique situations that influence translators' ways of reading and understanding texts" (142).

Translators' experiences

Theorists should not ignore the experiences of those whose practice they reflect upon. In fact some of those who have dealt with theoretical questions concerning the translation of children's books, have themselves translated such books (e.g. Ben-Ari, Even-Zohar, Görlach, Krutz-Arnold, Oittinen, Osberghaus, Shavit, Toury). Of the many professional statements put into print, only a few can be referred to in this chapter, grouped according to the translators' native language. Although English may not be important as a target language in the *International encyclopedia of children's literature* (Hunt 1996:519–529), Ronald Jobe illustrates "the translation process" with telling statements by American, Canadian and British translators, who perceive themselves to be searching for "the most evocative equivalent word" (Fenton), trying "to be true to the artist in the author" (Crampton), believing that the translator must "be a writer herself" (Poluskin) or that "one is interpreting as an actor does" (Bell). Patricia Crampton (1990) has written on her experiences with Lindgren's Swedish and Anthea Bell (1985 a, b, 1986) on translating Nöstlinger's German, Andersen's Danish and the French of the *Astérix* comics. Two topics deserve special mention because they are rarely focused upon: verse for children (Bell 1998) and picture books (Tate 1990).

The compendium on French translations of children's literature contains a special section (Escarpit 1985:147–160) in which the translators are explicitly represented by four practitioners (Farre, Poslaniec, Faucompre, Vassallo). Their statements follow a questionnaire aimed at elucidating the relation between translator, literary work, child reader and *éditeur*. *Éditeurs* seem to have a strong influence on translated children's books in France and it makes sense that the contributions of five editors to the compendium, also subjected to a questionnaire, precede those of the translators. Two renowned translators, Odile Belkeddar and François Mathieu, have written articles in which they describe the professional situation of French translators of children's literature, including the financial aspect (*La Revue des Livres pour Enfants* 1992:57–64).

In the international volume edited by Klingberg/Ørvig/Amor (1978:46–50) it is a Spanish voice which represents the practising translators: Carmen Bravo-Villasante, known for her translations of English and German classics. The fact that she emphasizes the criterion of "faithfulness" is in accordance with what, many years later, Fernandez Lopez (2000:33) says about "the Spanish norm of fidelity to the original text", even in the case of children's literature. Spanish translators of children's books in the English language are listed in Fernandez Lopez's dissertation (1996:177–178).

The situation of translators in West Germany is described by Gerda Neumann (1979) and, following the reunification with East Germany, elucidated with the help of questionnaires by Rieken-Gerwing (1995:113–142). If Neumann also discusses linguistic items in the light of her work with young adult novels from Scandinavia, France and the U.S., the more unusual problems of cultural transfer between Japan and Germany are touched upon by Mariko Sato (Krebs 1990), and those between Nigeria and Germany by Martini-Honus/Martini (1997/98). An interesting experiment was carried out and documented by the editors of the East German journal *Beiträge zur Kinder- und Jugendliteratur* ("Literatur des Auslands" 1983). The editors asked four professional translators to produce German versions of a Russian children's story by Juri Kowal and invited them to discuss the results. The German versions and the justifications and objections in the course of the discussion clearly show that a translation is not a replica in another language, but rather an implied interpretation.

The Austrian Wolf Harranth (1991), known for award-winning translations of children's books from English-speaking countries, lists and exemplifies typical language problems which he has come across as a translator and as a critical reader of translations. With reviewers of children's books in mind he points out symptoms which might be indicative of a successful or an unsuccessful translation, even if the source text is not at hand. His specifications are useful. For in the practical work of reviewing or recommending children's books, selecting them for prizes or for teaching purposes assessment of translational quality cannot be ignored (see Tabbert 1998:108–110 about the jury for the German Children's Book Prize).

However, the present survey of theoretical approaches to the translation of literature in general and children's literature in particular may have brought home the fact that it is not enough to simply focus on linguistic problems. The function a translated children's book is expected to fulfil has also to be taken into account, and the norms determining the translation of such a book may well change from culture to culture and from period to period. French Fifi Brindacier and Israeli Alizza may be stepsisters of Swedish Pippi Långstrump and British Alice respectively, but would they be more acceptable for their time and their culture if they were twins? And if of the two Finnish grandnieces of Dorothy, the American girl who meets the Wizard of Oz, one is static and the other dynamic, both have proved to be acceptable as Finns, albeit for different people and different groups of people.

References

Abgottspon, Elisabeth. 2001. "'Heidi' — übersetzt und verändert von Charles Tritten". Ernst Halter, ed. *Heidi — Karrieren einer Figur.* Zürich: Offizin, 2001. 221–235.

Adamczyk-Garbowska, Monika. 1988. *Polskie tłumaczenia angielskiej literatury dziecięcej. Problemy krytyki przekładu.* Wydawnictwo, Wrocław: Zaklad Narodowy im. Ossolinskich.

Bamberger, Richard. 1961. "Das Jugendbuch in aller Welt: Europa im Spiegel der Jugendbuchübersetzungen im deutschen Sprachraum". *Jugend und Buch* 10:1. 28–43.

Bamberger, Richard.1963. *Übersetzung von Jugendbüchern.* Wien: IBBY.

Bamberger, Richard. 1978. "The influence of translation on the development of national children's literature". Klingberg/Ørvig/Amor 1978:19–27.

Bell, Anthea. 1985a. "Translator's notebook: The naming of names". *Signal* 46. 3–11.

Bell, Anthea. 1985b. "Translator's notebook: On approaching the traditional tales". *Signal* 48. 139–147.

Bell, Anthea. 1986. "Translator's notebook: Delicate matters". *Signal* 49. 17–26.

Bell, Anthea. 1998. "Translating verse for children". *Signal* 85. 3–14.

Ben-Ari, Nitsa. 1992. "Didactic and pedagogic tendencies in the norms dictating the translation of children's literature: The case of post-war German — Hebrew translations". *Poetics today* 13. 221–230.

Beuchat, Cecilia and Carolina Valdivieso. 1992. "Translation of children's literature: Intercultural communication". *Bookbird* 30:1. 9–14.

Binder, Lucia. 1985. *Illustrieren, Bearbeiten, Übersetzen: Arbeit an und mit Texten.* Wien: Internationales Institut für Jugendliteratur und Leseforschung. [Schriften zur Jugendlektüre 36.]

Blamires, David. 1994. "Christoph von Schmid's religious tales for children: German and English versions". *Bulletin of the John Rylands University Library of Manchester*76:3. 69–82.

Bode, Andreas. 1995. "Ausländische Wörter aus dem Hut des Zauberers: Die Übersetzungen der Muminbücher ins Deutsche". *Literatuur zonder leeftijd* 34. 189–203.

Böhler, Michael and Verena Rutschmann, eds. forthcoming. *Collection of essays on the international reception of Spyri's "Heidi".*

Breitinger, Eckard. 1979. "Übersetzungen in der Kinder- und Jugendliteratur". Doderer 1979.3: 603–607.

Camp, Karin van. 1995. "Een halve eeuw Pippi Langkous: Suggesties voor een nieuwe vertaling". *Literatuur zonder leeftijd* 34. 165–188.

Chmeruk, Chone. 1990. "Yiddish adaptations of children's stories from world literature". Ezra Mendelssohn, ed., Richard I. Cohen, guest ed. *Art and its uses: The visual image and modern Jewish society*. New York — Oxford: Oxford University Press, 1990. 186–200. [Studies in Contemporary Jewry: An Annual.]

Christa, Tanya. 1998. "'Manganinnie' auf Deutsch: Authentizität oder Kreativität bei der Übersetzung eines australischen Romans für Kinder". *Volkacher Bote* 63. 6–8.

Collins English Dictionary. 1991. Glasgow: Harper Collins.

Compar(a)ison 2/1995 (special editor: Bettina Kümmerling-Meibauer).

Crampton, Patricia. 1990. "Translating Astrid Lindgren". *Swedish book review* 83–86.

Development of children's book translation. 1988. Report of the 20th Training Course on Book Production in Asia and the Pacific, Tokyo 17 September–3 October 1987. Tokyo: Asian Cultural Centre for Unesco.

Dilidüzgün, Selahattin and Turgay Kurultay. 1992. "Emanzipatorische deutsche Kinderliteratur und ihre Übersetzung ins Türkische im Hinblick auf die Kinderemanzipation". *Diyalog: Interkulturelle Zeitschrift für Germanistik* (Ankara). 89–106.

Doderer, Klaus, ed. 1976–84. *Lexikon der Kinder- und Jugendliteratur*. 4 vols. Weinheim: Beltz.

Dolle-Weinkauff, Bernd and Hans-Heino Ewers, eds. 2002. *Erich Kästners weltweite Wirkung als Kinderschriftsteller*. Frankfurt etc.: Peter Long.

Dollerup, Cay. 1998. Review of Sutton (1996). *Target* 10:2. 371–377.

Du-Nour, Miryam. 1995. "Retranslation of children's books as evidence of changes of norms". *Target* 7:2. 327–346.

Eggeling, Wolfram. 1994. "Zwischen Angleichung und Eigengewichtung: Zur Frage der Übersetzung sowjetischer Kinder- und Jugendliteratur ins Deutsche (am Beispiel von Jurij Korinetz' Roman 'Dort weit hinter dem Fluß')". *Beiträge Jugendliteratur und Medien* 46. 14–25.

Egger, Irmgard. 1991. "*Lederstrumpf*" — *ein deutsches Jugendbuch: Untersuchung zu den Bedingungen und Strukturen literarischer Transformation*. Wien: VWGÖ.

Eriksson, Anna Birgitta. 1985. "Astrid Lindgren på franska: varning för Fifi och Zozo". *Barnboken* 6. 44–48.

Escarpit, Denise, ed. 1985. *Attention!: Un livre peut en cacher un autre . . . traduction et adaptation en littérature d'enfance et de jeunesse*. Pessac: Nous voulons lire!

Even-Zohar, Basmat. 1992. "Translation policy in Hebrew children's literature: The case of Astrid Lindgren". *Poetics today* 13:1. 231–245.

Ewers, Hans-Heino, Gertrud Lehnert and Emer O'Sullivan, eds. 1994. *Kinderliteratur im interkulturellen Prozess*. Stuttgart, Weimar: Metzler.

Fernandez Lopez, Marisa. 1996. *Traducción y literatura juvenil: Narrativa anglosajona contemporanea en España*. León: Secretariado de Publicaciones de la Universidad de León.

Fernandez Lopez, Marisa. 2000. "Translation Studies in contemporary children's literature: A comparison of intercultural ideological factors". *Children's literature association quarterly* 29–37.

Friese, Inka. 1995. "Alice im Wörterwald — Lewis Carrolls 'Alice im Wunderland' und die Probleme bei der Übersetzung". Bettina Hurrelmann, ed. *Klassiker der Kinder- und Jugendliteratur*. Frankfurt: Fischer, 1995. 107–130.

Gentzler, Edwin. 1993. *Contemporary translation theories*. London, New York: Routledge.

Görlach, Manfred, ed. 1982a. *Wilhelm Busch: Max und Moritz polyglott*. München: Deutscher Taschenbucb Verlag.

Görlach, Manfred, ed. 1982b. *Wilhelm Busch: Max und Moritz in deutschen Dialekten, Mittelhochdeutsch und Jiddisch*. Hamburg: Buske. [With a bibliography of 123 translations into various languages and German dialects. 164–177.]

Görlach, Manfred, ed. 1986. *Max and Moritz in English dialects and Creoles*. Hamburg: Buske.

Görlach, Manfred. 1993. "Sprachliche Voraussetzungen für Dialektdichtung und Literatur in kleinen Sprachen". Maria Bonner *et al.*, eds. *Nachbarschaften: Festschrift für Max Mangold*. Saarbrücken, 1993. 134–167.

Görlach, Manfred. 1995. "Sociolinguistic determinants for literature in dialects and minority languages: *Max and Moritz* in Scots". Manfred Görlach. *More Englishes*. Amsterdam: John Benjamins, 1995. 221–245.

Görlach, Manfred. 1997. *Max und Moritz in aller Munde: Wandlungen eines Kinderbuches*. Köln: Universitäts- und Stadtbibliothek. [With a bibliography of 281 translations into foreign languages.]

Gómez del Manzano, Mercedes and Gabriel Janer Manila. 1996. *Pinocchio in Spagna*. Firenze: La Nuova Italia.

Grassegger, Hans. 1985. *Sprachspiel und Übersetzung: Eine Studie anhand der Comic-Serie Asterix*. Tübingen: Stauffenburg.

Guiliano, Edward. 1980. *Lewis Carroll: An annotated international bibliography 1960– 77*. Charlottesville: University Press of Virginia.

Harranth, Wolf. 1991. "Das Übersetzen von Kinder- und Jugendliteratur". *JuLit* 1. 23–27.

Hauksson, Thorleifur. 1985. "Vildvittor och Mattisrövare i islandsk drakt: ett kaseri kring en översättningen av Ronja Rövardotter". *Islandska sallskapets årbok* 36. 35–45.

Heldner, Christina. 1992. "Une anarchiste en camisole de force: Fifi Brindacier ou la métamorphose française de 'Pippi Långstrump'". *La Revue des Livres pour Enfants* 145. 65–71. [rep. in *Moderna språk* 87 (1993). 37–43.]

Hermans, Theo. 1996. "The translator's voice in translated narrative". *Target* 8:1. 23–48.

Herring, Ann King. 1988. "Early translations of Japanese fairy-tales and children's literature". *Phaedrus: An international annual for the history of children's literature* 13. 97–112.

Hoffman, Mary. 1990. "Separated by the same language?" *Books for keeps* 64. 26– 27.

Hunt, Peter, ed. 1996. *International companion encyclopedia of children's literature*. London, New York: Routledge.

Hurrelmann, Bettina and Karin Richter, eds. 1998. *Das Fremde in der Kinder- und Jugendliteratur: Interkulturelle Perspektiven*. Weinheim, München: Juventa.

Jendis, Mareike. *Mumins wundersame Deutschlandabenteuer: Zur Rezeption von Tove Janssons Muminbüchern*. Umeå Universitet: Institutionen för moderna språk. [Skrifter fran moderna Språk 1.]

Jobe, Ronald. 1996. "Translation". Hunt 1996:519–529.

Joels, Rosie Webb. 1999. "Weaving world uderstanding: The importance of translations in international children's literature". *Children's literature in education* 30:1. 65–83.

Jones, J. Elwyn and J. Francis Gladstone, eds. 1998. *The Alice companion: A guide to Lewis Carroll's Alice books*. London: MacMillan. ["Translations of Alice".]

Jung, Christiane. 1996. "Tea-time oder Kaffee und Kuchen?: Von den Schwierigkeiten des Übersetzens". *Bulletin Jugend + Literatur* 2. 13–20.

Klingberg, Göte. 1986. *Children's fiction in the hands of the translators*. Lund: CWK Gleerup.

Klingberg, Göte, Mary Ørvig and Stuart Amor, eds. 1978. *Children's books in translation*. Stockholm: Almqvist & Wiksell.

Koppen, Erwin. 1980. "Pinocchio im Reich des Simplicissimus: Otto Julius Bierbaum als Bearbeiter Collodis". Gerhard Schmidt and Manfred Tietz, eds. *Stimmen der Romania*. Wiesbaden: Heymann, 1980. 225–241.

Krebs, Susanne. 1990. "Zashikibokko oder vom Zaubern mit Wörtern: Mariko Sato über die Schwierigkeiten des Übersetzens". *Die Zeit* 5.10.1990. 41.

Krutz-Arnold, Cornelia. 1978. "Die deutschen Übersetzungen der Blyton-Bücher". *Informationen (des Arbeitskreises für Jugendliteratur)* 3. 53–67.

Kümmerling-Meibauer, Bettina. 1999. *Klassiker der Kinder- und Jugendliteratur: Ein internationales Lexikon*. 2 vols. Stuttgart, Weimar: Metzler.

Kurultay, Turgay. 1994. "Probleme und Strategien bei der kinderliterarischen Übersetzung im Rahmen der interkulturellen Kommunikation". Ewers, Lehnert and O'Sullivan 1994:204–214.

Kurultay, Turgay. 2000. "Wie fremd ist die Übersetzung einer fremden Literatur?: Erscheinungsweisen deutscher Kinder- und Jugendliteratur in türkischer Übersetzung". Nassen and Weinkauff 2000:49–58.

La Revue des Livres pour Enfants 145. 1992 (on translation).

Lehnert-Rodiek, Gertrud. 1988. "Alice in der Klemme: Deutsche 'Wonderland'-Übersetzungen". *Arcadia* 23. 78–90.

"Literatur des Auslands/Gespräch mit Übersetzern". 1983. *Beiträge zur Kinder- und Jugendliteratur* 68. 54–68.

Löser, Philipp. 1998. "Chingachgook zwischen Indianerspiel und Klassenkampf: Amerikas Ureinwohner in den 'Leatherstocking tales' und ihren deutschen Bearbeitungen". Beata Hammerschmid and Hermann Krapoth, eds. *Übersetzung als kultureller Prozess*. Berlin: Erich Schmidt, 1998. 150–177. [Göttinger Beiträge zur Internationalen Übersetzungsforschung 16.]

Macheiner, Judith. 1995. *Übersetzen: Ein Vademecum*. Frankfurt: Eichborn.

Makino, Yasuko. 1985. *Japan through children's literature*. Westport/London: Greenwood Press.

Mango, Susan. 1977. "Alice in two wonderlands: Lewis Carroll in German". *Sub-Stance* 16. 63–84.

Martini-Honus, Helmi and Jürgen Martini. 1997/8. " 'Soup', 'bottlies' und 'teapots' oder: Fallstricke des Übersetzens aus der 'Dritten Welt' ". *Guck mal übern Tellerrand* 7–8.

Marx, Sonia. 1990. *Le Avventure tedesche di Pinocchio*. Firenze: La Nuova Italia.

Marx, Sonia. 1997. *Klassiker der Jugendliteratur in Übersetzungen: 'Struwwelpeter', 'Max und Moritz', 'Pinocchio' im deutsch-italienischen Dialog*. Padova: Unipress.

Meckling, Ingeborg. 1975. "Gemüt statt Solidarität: Ein englisches Kinderbuch und seine deutsche Übersetzung". *Der Deutschunterricht* 27:5. 42–52.

Mooser, Anne-Lise. 1993. " 'Heidi' et son adaptation française ou l'aliénation d'une liberté". Jean Perrot and Pierre Bruno, eds. *La littérature de jeunesse au croisement des cultures.* Paris: CRDP d'Île de France, Académie de Créteil, 1993. 101–116.

Nassen, Ulrich and Gina Weinkauff, eds. 2000. *Konfigurationen des Fremden in der Kinder- und Jugendliteratur nach 1945.* München: Iudicium.

Netley, Noriko Shimoda. 1992. "The difficulty of translation: Decoding cultural signs in other languages". *Children's literature in education* 23:4. 195–202.

Neumann, Gerda. 1979. "Probleme beim Übersetzen von Kinder- und Jugendliteratur". Margareta Gorschenek and Annamaria Rucktäschl, eds. *Kinder- und Jugendliteratur.* München: Fink, 1979. 115–128.

Newmark, Peter. 1988. *A textbook of translation.* New York *et al.*: Prentice Hall.

Nières, Isabelle. 1983. "Cultures d'enfance". Daniel-Henri Pageaux, ed. *La recherche en littérature générale et comparée en France. Aspects et problèmes.* Paris: Société Française de Littérature Générale et Comparée. 181–196.

Nières, Isabelle. 1988. *Lewis Carroll en France (1870–1985): Les Ambivalences d'une reception littéraire.* Université de Picardie. [Unpublished PhD dissertation.]

Nières, Isabelle. 1992. "Une Europe des livres de l'enfance?" Isabelle Nières, ed. *Livres d'enfants en Europe.* Villa Pontivy. COOB, 1992. 9–17.

Nières-Chevrel, Isabelle. 1998. "Traduction et création". Christiane Abodic-Clerc, ed. *Mythes, Traduction et Création: La Littérature de Jeunesse en Europe.* Paris: Centre Georges Pompidou, 1998. 103–123.

Nikolajeva, Maria. 1991. *Selma Lagerlöf ur ryskt perspektiv.* Stockholm: Lagerlöf-sällskapet.

Nikolajeva, Maria. 1996. *Children's literature comes of age: Towards a new aesthetic.* New York: Garland.

Nord, Christiane. 1989. "Loyalität statt Treue: Vorschläge zu einer funktionalen Übersetzungstypologie". *Lebende Sprachen* 3. 100–105.

Nord, Christiane. 1991. "Scopos, loyalty and translational conventions". *Target* 3:1. 91–109.

Nord, Christiane. 1993. "Alice im Niemandsland: Die Bedeutung von Kultursignalen für die Wirkung von literarischen Übersetzungen". Justa Holz-Mänttäri and Christiane Nord, eds. *Traducere Navem: Festschrift für Katharina Reiss zum 70. Geburtstag.* Tampere: University of Tampere, 1993. 395–416. [Studia translatologica ser. A, vol. 3.]

Nord, Christiane. 1995. "Text-functions in translation: Titles and headings as a case in point". *Target* 7:2. 261–284.

Oittinen, Riitta. 1990. "The dialogic relation between text and illustration: A translatological view". *TEXT con TEXT* 5: 40–53.

Oittinen, Riitta. 1993. *I am me — I am other: On the dialogics of translating for children.* Tampere: University of Tampere. [Acta Universitatis Tamperensis ser. A, vol. 386.]

Oittinen, Riitta. 1995. "The verbal and the visual: On the carnivalism and dialogics of translating for children". *Compar(a)ison* 2. 49–65.

Oittinen, Riitta. 1997. *Liisa, Lisa ja Alice.* Tampere: University of Tampere.

Oittinen, Riitta. 1999. "Kinderliteratur". Mary Snell-Hornby *et al.*, eds. *Handbuch Translation.* Tübingen: Stauffenburg Handbücher, 1999. 250–253.

Oittinen, Riitta. 2000. *Translating for children.* New York, London: Garland Publishing. [Children's literature and culture 11.]

Osberghaus, Monika. 1997. *Die Zeitgebundenheit kinderliterarischer Übersetzung-spraxis: Analyse eines exemplarischen Falles*. Frankfurt: Johann-Wolfgang-Goethe-Universität. [MA Thesis.]

O'Sullivan, Emer. 1991/92. "Kinderliterarisches Übersetzen". *Fundevogel* 93/94. 4–9.

O'Sullivan, Emer. 1992. "Transportverluste — Transportgewinne: Anmerkungen zur Übersetzung von Komik im Werk Aidan Chambers". Hans-Heino Ewers, ed. *Komik im Kinderbuch*. Weinheim, München: Juventa, 1992. 201–221.

O'Sullivan, Emer. 1994. "Winnie-the-Pooh und der erwachsene Leser: Die Mehr-fachadressiertheit eines kinderliterarischen Textes im Übersetzungsvergleich". Ewers, Lehnert and O'Sullivan 1994:79–100.

O'Sullivan, Emer. 1996. "Ansätze zu einer komparatistischen Kinder- und Jugendliteraturforschung". Bernd Dolle-Weinkauff and Hans-Heino Ewers, eds. *Theorien der Jugendlektüre*. Weinheim, München: Juventa, 1996. 285–315.

O'Sullivan, Emer. 1998a. "Alice über Grenzen: Vermittlung und Rezeption von Klassikern der Kinderliteratur". Hurrelmann and Richter 1998:45–57.

O'Sullivan, Emer. 1998b. "Translating pictures: The interaction of pictures and words in the translation of picture books". Penni Cotton, ed. *European children's litera-ture* II. *Papers presented in Austria May 1998*. Kingston Hill: School of Education, Kingston University, 1998. 109–120.

O'Sullivan, Emer. 1999a. "Der implizite Übersetzer in der Kinderliteratur: Zur Theorie kinderliterarischen Übersetzens". *JuLit* 4: 41–53 (correction: *JuLit* 1/2000:67).

O'Sullivan, Emer. 1999b. "Von Dahl's Chickens zu Himmels Grausen: Zum Übersetzen intertextueller Komik in der Kinderliteratu". *1000 und 1* Buch 4: 12–19.

O'Sullivan, Emer. 2000. *Kinderliterarische Komparatistik*. Heidelberg: C. Winter.

Parisot, Henri. 1971. "Pour franciser les jeux de langage d'Alice". Henri Parisot, ed. *Lewis Carroll*. Paris: Editions de l'Herne, 1971. 67–82.

Pedersen, Viggo Hjørnager. 1990. *Oversaettelse eller Parafrase? / Translation or Para-phrase? An evaluation of various versions of "The Tinder Box", "The Ugly Duckling" and "The Little Mermaid"*. H. C. Andersen-Centret Odense Universitet.

Persson, Lisa-Christina, ed. 1962. *Translations of children's books*. Lund: Bibliotekstjänst.

Petzold, Dieter. 1982. *Daniel Defoe: "Robinson Crusoe"*. München: Fink, 1982. 42–54. ["Robinson Crusoe" als Kinderbuch.]

Petzold, Dieter. 1994. "Die Rezeption klassischer englischsprachiger Kinderbücher in Deutschland". Ewers, Lehnert and O'Sullivan 1994:78–91.

Petzold, Dieter. 1997. "Anglistik und Kinderliteratur". *Anglistik* 8:1. 75–90.

Poetics today 13:1. 1992 (special editor: Zohar Shavit).

Puurtinen, Tiina. 1989. "Assessing acceptability in translated children's books". *Target* 1:2. 201–213.

Puurtinen, Tiina. 1994. "Dynamic style as a parameter of acceptability in translated children's books". Mary Snell-Hornby, Franz Pöchhacker and Klaus Kaindl, eds. *Translation Studies: An Interdiscipline*. Amsterdam — Philadelphia: John Benjamins, 1994. 83–90.

Puurtinen, Tiina. 1995. *Linguistic acceptability in translated children's literature*. Joensuu: University of Joensuu.

Puurtinen, Tiina. 1997. "Syntactic norms in Finnish children's literature". *Target* 9:2. 221–234.

Raecke, Renate, ed. 1999. *Kinder- und Jugendliteratur in Deutschland*. München: Arbeitskreis für Jugendliteratur.

Reiss, Katharina. 1982. "Zur Übersetzung von Kinder- und Jugendbüchern: Theorie und Praxis". *Lebende Sprachen* 27. 7–13.

Reiss, Katharina and Hans J. Vermeer. 1984. *Grundlegung einer allgemeinen Translationstheorie*. Tübingen: Niemeyer.

Richter, Dieter. 1996. *Pinocchio oder Vom Roman der Kindheit*. Frankfurt: Fischer.

Rieken-Gerwing, Ingeborg. 1995. *Gibt es eine Spezifik kinderliterarischen Übersetzens? Untersuchungen zu Anspruch und Realität bei der literarischen Übersetzung von Kinder- und Jugendbüchern*. Frankfurt *et al.*: Peter Lang.

Rutschmann, Verena and Denise von Stockar. 1996. *Zum Übersetzen von Kinder- und Jugendliteratur*. Lausanne: Centre de traduction littéraire de Lausanne.

Schelbert, T. 1975. "Die gehörnte Eigenheit der Sprache: Linguistische Überlegungen zu Maurice Sendaks 'Where the Wild Things Are' ". *Sprache im technischen Zeitalter* 53. 59–74.

Schiavi, Giuliana. 1996. "There is always a teller in a tale". *Target* 8:1. 1–21.

Schultze-Kreft, Ofelia. 1998. "Flurina und Schellen-Ursli: Die 'Engadiner-Trilogie' von Selina Chönz und Alois Carigiet". Heidy Margrit Müller, ed. *Dichterische Freiheit und pädagogische Utopie: Studien zur schweizerischen Jugendliteratur*. Bern: Peter Lang, 1998. 159–186.

Seemann, Iris. 1987. *Das erzählende Werk des sowjetischen Jugendschriftstellers Jurij Korinetz im Spiegel der deutschen Übersetzung*. Würzburg. [Unpublished PhD dissertation.]

Seemann, Iris. 1998. "Jugendlektüre zwischen interkultureller Information und entpolitisierter Unterhaltung: Übersetzungen sowjetischer Kinder- und Jugendliteratur in der Bundesrepublik Deutschland 1945 bis 1989". Hurrelmann and Richter 1998:141–153.

Seemann, Iris. 1999. *Jugendlektüre zwischen interkultureller Information und entpolitisierter Unterhaltung: Übersetzungen sowjetischer Kinder- und Jugendliteratur in der Bundesrepublik Deutschland 1945 bis 1989*. Frankfurt *et al.*: Peter Lang. [Kinder- und Jugendkultur, -literatur und -medien 6.]

Shavit, Zohar. 1981. "Translation of children's literature as a function of its position in the literary polysystem". *Poetics today* 2:4. 171–179.

Shavit, Zohar. 1986. *Poetics of children's literature*. Athens, London: University of Georgia Press.

Shavit, Zohar. 1992. "Literary interference between German and Jewish-Hebrew children's literature during the Enlightenment: The case of Campe". *Poetics today* 13:1. 41–61.

Shavit, Zohar. 1997. "Cultural agents and cultural interference: The function of J. H. Campe in an emerging Jewish culture". *Target* 9:1. 111–130.

Silva, Isabel Maria Moreira da. 1991. *Das Bild im Kinderbuch und seine Bedeutung für die Translation*. Heidelberg University. [Unpublished thesis in Translation Studies.]

Skjønsberg, Kari. 1979. *Hvem Forteller?: Om adaptasjoner i barnelitteratur*. Oslo: Tiden Norsk Forlag.

Skjønsberg, Kari. 1982. *Väm Berättar?: Om adaptioner i barnlitteratur*. Stockholm: Rabén och Sjögren.

Skott, Staffan. 1977. "Karlsson på taket i rysk översättning". Mary Ørvig, ed. *En bok om Astrid Lindgren*. Stockholm: Rabén och Sjögren, 1977. 84–132.

Spillner, Bernd. 1980. "Semiotische Aspekte der Übersetzung von Comic-Texten". Wolfram Wilss, ed. *Semiotik und Übersetzen*. Tübingen: Narr, 1980. 73–85.

Stan, Susan. 1997. *A study of international children's picture books published in the United States in 1994*. Ann Arbor, Michigan: UMI Dissertation Services.

Stolt, Birgit. 1978. "How Emil becomes Michel: On the translation of children's books". Klingberg/Ørvig/Amor 1978:130–146.

Surmatz, Astrid. 1994. "Ingenting för barn under fjorton ar!: Pippi Långstrump i Tyskland". *Barnboken* 17:1. 2–11.

Surmatz, Astrid. 1998. *Pippi Långstrump als Paradigma: Die deutsche Rezeption Astrid Lindgrens und ihr internationaler Kontext*. Göttingen. [Unpublished PhD dissertation. To be published by Francke Verlag, Tübingen — Basel, 2002.]

Sutton, Martin. 1996. *The sin-complex: A critical study of English versions of the Grimm's 'Kinder- und Hausmärchen' in the nineteenth century*. Kassel: Brüder Grimm-Gesellschaft.

Tabbert, Reinbert. 1968. "John Keats' 'Ode on Melancholy' in deutschen Übertragungen: Versuch einer Typologie der dichterischen Übersetzung". *Germanisch-romanische Monatsschrift* 18:1. 38–58.

Tabbert, Reinbert. 1991a. "Bilderbücher zwischen zwei Kulturen". Reinbert Tabbert. *Kinderbuchanalysen* II. Frankfurt: Dipa, 1991. 130–148.

Tabbert, Reinbert. 1991b. "Children's books in lesser used languages: An interview with the Gaelic writer Finlay MacLeod". *Bookbird* 29:1. 10–12. [German translation in Tabbert 1991a.]

Tabbert, Reinbert. 1996. "Forschungen zur Übersetzung von Kinderliteratur (1975–1995)". *Kinder- und Jugendliteraturforschung 1995/96*. Stuttgart, Weimar: Metzler, 1996. 97–108.

Tabbert, Reinbert. 1998. " 'Swimmy', 'The BFG' und 'Janne min vän': Bücher aus fremden Sprachen, ausgezeichnet mit dem Deutschen Jugendliteraturpreis". Hurrelmann and Richter 1998:93–113.

Tabbert, Reinbert. 2002. "Hänsel und Gretel anglo-visuell: Amerikanische und englische Illustrationen eines deutschen Kindermärchens". Helge Gerndt and Kristin Wardetzky, eds. *Die Kunst des Erzählens: Festschrift für Walter Scherf*. Potsdam: Verlag für Berlin-Brandenburg, 2002. 301–311.

Tate, Joan. 1990. "Translating Picture Books". *Swedish Book Review*. Supplement. 80–82.

Teodorowicz-Hellman, Ewa. 1997. "Komizm w przekładzie prozy dla dzieci (Pippi Ponczoczanka Astrid Lindgren po polsku)". Piotr Fast, ed. *Komizm a przekład*. Katowice: Śląsk, 1997. 197–212. [The comic in translation of children's fiction: On Polish translation of "Pippi Longstocking".]

Teodorowicz-Hellman, Ewa. 1999. *Svensk-Polska Litterära Möten: Tema: Barn-litteratur*. Stockholm: Svenska institutet. [Summary: "Swedish-Polish literary relations: Children's literature".] [Skrifter utgivna av Svenska barnbokinstitutet 69.]

Tomlinson, Carl. 1998. *Children's books from other countries*. Lanham Maryland: Scarecrow Press.

Toury, Gideon. 1980. *In search of a theory of translation*. Tel Aviv: The Porter Institute for Poetics and Semiotics.

Toury, Gideon. 1995. *Descriptive Translation Studies and beyond.* Amsterdam — Philadelphia: John Benjamins.

Toury, Gideon. 2000 [¹1978]. "The nature and role of norms in translation". Venuti 2000:198–211.

Ueno, Yoko. 1993. "Die Rezeption deutschsprachiger Kinder- und Jugendliteratur in Japan. Teil II". *Symposium Kinderliteratur in Japan und Deutschland 1992.* 22–39. [Veröffentlichungen des Japanisch-deutschen Zentrums, Berlin 18.]

Valdivieso, Carolina, ed. 1991. *Literatura para Niños: Cultura y Traducción.* Santiago (Chile): Pontificia Universidad Católica de Chile.

Venuti, Lawrence. 1995. *The translator's invisibility: A history of translation.* London: Routledge.

Venuti, Lawrence, ed. 2000. *The Translation Studies reader.* London — New York: Routledge.

Vermeer, Hans J. 1986. "Übersetzen als kultureller Transfer". Mary Snell-Hornby, ed. *Übersetzungswissenschaft: Eine Neuorientierung.* Tübingen: Francke, 1986. 30–53.

Vermeer, Hans J. 2000. "Skopos and commission in translational action". Venuti 2000:221–232.

Weaver, Warren. 1964. *Alice in many tongues: The translations of "Alice in wonderland".* Madison: University of Wisconsin Press.

Weissbrod, Rachel. 1996. "'Curiouser and curiouser': Hebrew translations of wordplay in *Alice's adventures in wonderland". The translator* 2:2. 219–234.

Weissbrod, Rachel. 1999. "Mock-epic as a byproduct of the norm of elevated language". *Target* 11:2. 245–262.

White, Maureen. 1992. "Children's books from other languages: A study of successful translations". *Journal of youth services in libraries* 5:3. 261–275.

Whitehead, Jane. 1996/1997. "'This is NOT what I wrote!': The Americanization of British children's books", I — II. *The horn book magazine* 1996:687–693; 1997:27–34.

Winqvist, Margareta. 1973. *Den engelske Robinson Crusoes sällsamma öden och äventyr genom svenska spraket.* Stockholm:Bonnier.

Woodsworth, Judith. 1996. "Language, translation and the promotion of national identity: Two test cases". *Target* 8:2. 211–238.

Wunderlich, Richard. 1992. "The tribulations of *Pinocchio*: How social change can wreck a good story". *Poetics today* 13:1. 197–219.

Zeli, Isabella [n.d.; 1997 or 1998]. *Foreign children's literature in Italian translation: A systemic approach.* Leuven: Katholieke Universiteit, Milano: Università Cattolica del Sacro Cuore.

88

NARRATOLOGY MEETS TRANSLATION STUDIES, OR, THE VOICE OF THE TRANSLATOR IN CHILDREN'S LITERATURE

Emer O'Sullivan

Source: *Meta* 48(1–2) (2003): 197–207.

When scholars or critics identify "changes," "adaptations" or "manipulations" in translations of children's literature, they often rightly describe and analyse them in terms of the differing social, educational or literary norms prevailing in the source and the target languages, cultures and literatures at that given time.[1] *A rich source of such observations are the many translations of Astrid Lindgren's Pippi Långstrump (1945), which give a good indication of what was perceived by the target cultures, at the time of translation, to be inacceptable for child readers. In a scene in the novel* Pippi, Tommy and Annika are playing in the attic when Pippi finds some pistols in a chest. She fires them in the air and then offers them to her friends who delightedly accept. In the German translation Pippi doesn't give the pistols to her friends, instead she instructs them – and the readers – by changing her mind, putting them back in the chest and declaring "Das ist nichts für Kinder!" (Lindgren 1965, 205) ("that's not right for children"), a sentiment totally out of character. She herself had made fun of such moralising just a few moments previously when firing the pistols. A possible explanation for this change in the German translation could be that post-war Germany didn't want its children to be encouraged to use weapons.[2]

The point of focus of this article will not be changes and manipulations in translated children's literature and the reasons motivating them, whether social, educational or aesthetic. Instead I want to concentrate on the agency of such changes, the translator, in order to identify her/his presence in the translated text.

The translator's visibility has been a much discussed issue in translation studies since Lawrence Venuti used the term "invisibility" to describe both the illusionistic effect of the translator's discourse and the practice by publishers, reviewers, readers, etc. in contemporary Anglo-American culture of judging translations acceptable when they read fluently.[3] His "call to action" to translators has been for visibility by use of nonfluent, nonstandard and heterogeneous language, by producing foreignized rather than domesticated texts. He rightly insists on talking about translators as real people in geopolitical situations and about the politics of translation and ethical criteria (cf. Venuti 1995). But the translator's discursive presence can, I submit, also be identified in texts which aren't nonfluent, nonstandard and "foreignized"; it can be located on a theoretical level in a model of narrative communication as shown by Giuliana Schiavi in 1996, and on the level of analysis of the text based on such a model, where the translator's presence is evident in the strategies chosen, in the way s/he positions her/himself in relation to the translated narrative.

My guiding questions are: What kind of translator is making her/himself felt in the text? Where can s/he be located in the act of communication which is the narrative text? How does the implied reader of her/his translation (the target text) differ from that of the "original" (the source text)? To do this, I will present a theoretical and analytical tool, a communicative model of translation which links the theoretical fields of narratology and translation studies. Before doing so, however, I have to emphasise two points. Firstly, the model applies to *all* fictional literature in translation. Due to the asymmetrical nature of the communication in and around children's literature where adults act on behalf of children at every turn, the translator as s/he becomes visible or audible as a narrator is often more tangible in translated children's literature than in literature for adults (where Venuti likes to talk about visibility, my preferred metaphor is audibility, the voice that is heard in the text[4]). I will, secondly, be talking about narrative texts only. A model for drama or poetry would call for appropriate modifications.

Narrative communication: a model

The point of departure for the model to be presented in three steps is the basic narrative structure proposed by Seymour Chatman in *Story and Discourse* (1978) (Fig. 1). In this well-known and commonly applied model six different parties form three pairs. The narrative text – indicated by the box in the middle – is the message transmitted from the *real author* to the *real reader*, from the one who physically wrote the text of the book to the one who holds it in her/his hands and reads it (or has it read to her/him). These parties are not to be found within the book itself, nor does the real author communicate directly with the real reader, the communication takes

Figure 1 Six part model of narrative communication based on Chatman 1978.

place between the constructed pairs within the narrative text. The first of these pairs is the *implied author* and the *implied reader*.

The real author, according to Chatman (1990, 75), "retires from the text as soon as the book is printed and sold," what remains in the text are "the principles of invention and intent" (ibid.). The source of the work's invention, the locus of its intent is the implied author, whom Chatman calls a silent instructor, the "agency within the narrative fiction itself which guides any reading of it" (ibid.). The implied author, an agency contained in every fiction, is the all-informing authorial presence, the idea of the author carried away by the real reader after reading the book. The implied reader is the implied author's counterpart, "the audience presupposed by the narrative itself" (Chatman 1978, 149f), the reader generated by the implied author and inscribed in the text.

The asymmetrical nature of the communication in children's literature is reflected in this model as follows: an adult implied author creates an implied reader based on her/his (culturally determined) presuppositions as to the interests, propensities and capabilities of readers at a certain stage of their development. The implied author is thus the agency in children's literature which has to bridge the distance between "adult" and "child."[5]

The next, innermost, pair in the model is the *narrator* and the *narratee*. The narrator is the one who tells the story, hers/his is the voice audible when a story is being told. The narratee, in the words of Barbara Wall, is "the more or less shadowy being within the story whom . . . the narrator addresses" (1991, 4). The narrator is not always sensed as a persona in the text; Chatman distinguishes between the "overt" and "covert" type. Overt are the narrators who feature as figures in the narrative, an example being Oswald Bastable in Edith Nesbit's *The Treasure Seekers*,

> "There are some things I must tell before I begin to tell about the treasure-seeking, because I have read books myself, and I know how beastly it is when a story begins, " 'Alas!' said Hildegarde with a deep sigh, 'we must look our last on this ancestral home' " . . ."[6],
>
> (Nesbit 1899, 3f)

or Christopher Robin's father who tells the stories and features in the frame in Milne's *Winnie-the-Pooh* (1926). Equally overt are narrators who don't feature as characters but as an authorial presence in the text, such as the one who declares in Nesbit's *The Enchanted Castle*: "the sensible habit of having boys and girls in the same school is not yet as common as I hope it will be some day" (Nesbit 1907, 7). The overt narrator has become less common in children's literature over the past few decades, but even without saying "I," s/he can be no less revealing of character and attitude.[7]

The narratee, too, can be a character in the novel – Christopher Robin in the frame of Milne's *Winnie-the-Pooh* is an obvious example, or the social worker for whom Hal writes the account of his story in Aidan Chambers' *Dance on my Grave* (1982); more often s/he isn't actually portrayed but evoked. The overt first-person, authorial narrator occasionally addresses her/his narratees with questions or appeals like "You know the kind of house, don't you?" or "You may imagine their feelings" (both examples from Nesbit's *The Enchanted Castle*).

The narrator is created by the implied author and is not to be confused with that agency. Similarly the narratee should not be identified with the implied reader. In some cases there will be some overlap. If we again take *Winnie-the-Pooh* as our example: Christopher Robin of the frame is the narratee, but the implied reader or rather implied readers include older children and adults reading the story to children. There are elements in the text which appeal to and can be understood only by them, indeed which are written specifically with an older audience in mind. In this case we can speak of a text with dual or even multiple address.[8]

Translation and narrative communication

The second of the three steps, moving from general narrative theory to the specifics of translation, looks at translation in terms of narrative communication. The model in Fig. 1 applies to an original (non-translated) text and its readers. Taking Erich Kästners *Emil und die Detektive* (1929) as an example: the real author is Kästner, the real reader is someone who reads the original novel in German. Only those who read German can be real readers of that specific text. Where does this leave those who read Kästner's *Emil* in Spanish, Swahili or Swedish? They aren't accounted for in Chatman's model, which can only represent an original text.[9] In the case of a translated text, however, the message transmitted by the real author in the source language is read by the real reader in the target language. Kästner wrote *Emil* in German but a Spaniard reads it in Spanish. To account for what has happened in translation the model has to be expanded.

Translation is depicted in Fig. 2 as two sequential processes of communication. On the left side of Fig. 2 is the source text (the "original") with the already familiar parties. Where the real reader was situated at the end of the process illustrated in Fig. 1, we now have the translator. The translator acts in the first instance as the real reader of the source text.

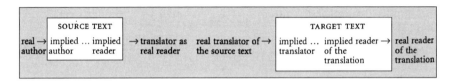

Figure 2 Translation in narrative communication, incorporating the implied translator and the implied reader of the translation ["..." denotes narrator and
narratee].

As someone familiar with the source language as well as the conventions
and norms of that culture, s/he is in a position to slip into the role of the
implied reader of the source text. Above and beyond that s/he tries to
identify "the principles of invention and intent" of the text – the implied
author and the implied reader. (This is particularly significant for the process of translating children's literature. As an adult, the translator does
not belong to the primary addressees of most children's books. S/he has
to negotiate the unequal communication in the source text between adult
(implied) author and child (implied) reader in order to be able to slip into
the latter's role.)

Parallel to the source text is the target text (the translation). As the
creator of the translation, the translator acts, in the second half of
the process shown on the right side of Fig. 2, as a counterpart to the real
author of the source text; s/he is the one who creates the target text in
such a way that it can be understood by readers in the target culture with
language, conventions, codes and references differing from those in the
source culture. However, the translator does not produce a completely new
message, as Giuliana Schiavi who identified the translator's presence in
narratological terms writes, s/he "intercepts the communication and transmits it – re-processed – to the new reader who will receive the message"
(1996, 15). By interpreting the original text, by following certain norms,
and by adopting specific strategies and methods, the translator, according
to Schavi, "builds up a new [. . .] relationship between what we must call
a 'translated text' and a new group of readers" (ibid., 7); in doing so s/he
also creates a different implied reader to the one in the source text; *the
implied reader of the translation*.[10] This implied reader can be equated with
the implied reader of the source text to different degrees but they are not
identical. The implied reader of the translation will always be a different
entity from the implied reader of the source text. This statement applies to
all translated fictional texts.

If the implied reader of the translation differs from her/his counterpart in
the source text. Then the question has to be asked: what is the agency which
creates the difference? The implied reader of the source text, the reader
inscribed in the text, is generated by the implied author. By the same token

the implied reader of the target text is generated by a similar agency: *the implied translator*.

Based on these deliberations, the final, complex model of the translated narrative text[11] and all its agencies (Fig. 3) can be described as follows:

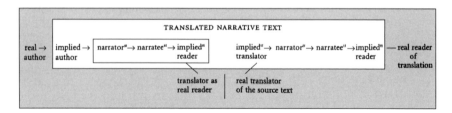

Figure 3 Communicative model of the translated narrative text
(st = source text, tt = target text).

The communication between the *real author of the source text* and the *real reader of the translation* is enabled by the *real translator* who is positioned outside the text. Her/his first act is that of a receptive agent, who then, still in an extratextual position, transmits the source text via the intratextual agency of the *implied translator*. The *narrator*, *narratee* and *implied reader* of the target text, all generated by the implied translator, can be roughly equivalent to their counterparts in the source text; however they can also differ greatly, as the following examples will reveal.

In translated texts, therefore, a discursive presence is to be found, the presence of the (implied) translator. It can manifest itself in a voice which is not that of the narrator of the source text. We could say that two voices are present in the narrative discourse of the translated text: the voice of the narrator of the source text and the voice of the translator.

The voice of the translator

The translator's voice can be identified on at least two levels. One of them is that of the implied translator as author of paratextual information such as prefaces or metalinguistic explanations such as footnotes. Here "the translator" can be heard most clearly. When, for example, s/he tells the readers of the German translation of Barbara Park's *My Mother Got Married (and other disasters)* (1989) that *Thanksgiving Day* is a harvest festival which takes place on the fourth Thursday in November (Park 1991, 115), it is clearly not in translation of an explanation to be found in the source text (American readers hardly need to be told what Thanksgiving Day is). It is information composed for readers of the target text by the translator and proffered in her/his own voice.

In his "companion piece" to Schiavi's with concrete examples of the implied translator, Theo Hermans locates the translator's voice as an "index of the Translator's discursive presence" (Hermans 1996, 27) in situations where s/he has "to come out of the shadows and directly intervene in a text which the reader had been led to believe spoke only with one voice" (ibid.). These are primarily moments of paratextual intervention where explanations are crucial, self-reflexive references to the medium of communication itself, moments where (the source) language itself is the theme and "when 'contextual over-determination' leaves no other option" (ibid., 23). Hermans' Voice of the Translator is therefore primarily a metalinguistic one, in principle "wholly assimilated into the Narrator's voice." I would argue that the translator's voice is not only heard in such interventions, it can also be identified on another discursive level, on the level of the narration itself as a voice "dislocated from the one it mimics" (ibid., 43), one which is not assimilated into the voice of the narrator of the source text. This specific voice, hitherto largely unrecognised by translation studies or narratology, is what I call the *voice of the narrator of the translation*.[12] Two examples will illustrate how this voice can manifest itself and the consequences it has for communication within the text.

The first is a passage from the classic Swiss children's novel first published in 1881/2, Johanna Spyri's *Heidi*. It occurs in the novel just after Heidi has completed the difficult task of teaching the young goatherd Peter to read, so that he can be a source of comfort to his blind grandmother by reading her beloved hymns aloud when they are snowed in during the winter and Heidi is unable to visit. The grandmother nonetheless prefers Heidi's rendering of the hymns, and the following reason is given:

> "Das kam aber daher, weil der Peter sich beim Lesen ein wenig einrichtete, daß er's nicht zu unbequem hatte. Wenn ein Wort kam, das gar zu lang war oder sonst schlimm aussah, so ließ er es lieber ganz aus, denn er dachte, um drei oder vier Worte in einem Vers werde es der Großmutter wohl gleich sein, es kämen ja dann noch viele. So kam es, daß es fast keine Hauptwörter mehr hatte in den Liedern, die der Peter vorlas."
>
> (Spyri 1978, 276)

The manner in which Peter shortcuts his reading and how he justifies it to himself is related by a third-person narrator briefly focalising Peter's point of view. This is reflected in the use of colloquial language ("er's"), the particles "gar" and "wohl gleich," the subjunctive case relating his thoughts as indirect speech ("werde" "kämen") and in the uncommented report of his naïve logic. The authorial description of the result is understated and mildly ironic but the narrator neither remarks upon nor judges Peter's actions or thoughts.

In an anonymous translation published in 1949,[13] the voice of the narrator of the translation tries, largely, to emulate that of the narrator of the original, even though the colloquial tone is muted.

> "The reason (. . .) was that Peter used to tamper with the words a little, so as to make the reading slightly less trouble. When he came to a word that was too long, or in some other way seemed difficult, he simply left it out; for he thought that Grannie wouldn't notice the absence of two or three words in a verse – after all, there were so many of them. The result was that the hymns, as read aloud by Peter, had scarcely any nouns."
>
> (Spyri 1949, 224)

The version of the same passage in M. Rosenbaum's popular and much issued translation is compressed, with the final authorial dictum omitted:

> "The reason was, of course, that Peter was rather lazy about reading for the grandmother, and if a word were too difficult or too long he just skipped over it thinking it would not matter very much to the grandmother seeing there were so many words!"
>
> (Spyri 1955, 210)

The narrator of this passage, unlike the one of the source text, passes judgment on Peter ("rather lazy"). With the phrase "of course" a bond of agreement is insinuated between the narrator of the translation and implied reader and the final exclamation mark is a comment on Peter's thoughts, signalling to the reader that they should be regarded as hilarious. The narrator of this translation therefore appeals directly to the implied reader and makes what s/he has to say more explicit. The implied translator obviously has a reader in mind who may not grasp the subtle irony of Spyri's narrative, whose reading of the text has to be guided with authorial asides and exclamation marks, thus transforming the laconic explanation of the source text into an overstatement.

Less subtle is the amplification to be found in a German translation of Lewis Carroll's *Alice in Wonderland*, published in 1949[14] in the passage in which the "Mock Turtle" is first introduced. In the original it reads as follows:

> "Then the Queen left off, quite out of breath, and said to Alice, 'Have you seen the Mock Turtle yet?'
> 'No,' said Alice. 'I don't even know what a Mock Turtle is.'
> 'It's the thing Mock Turtle Soup is made from,' said the Queen.
> 'I never saw one, or heard of one.'
> 'Come on, then,' said the Queen, 'and he shall tell you his history.'"

Franz Sester, one of thirty-two translators to have produced unabridged German versions of *Alice in Wonderland*, apparently found this too short on explanation. What were his young readers supposed to think a Mock Turtle was? He therefore added a lengthy passage with no equivalent in the English original in which Alice is, culturally adapted, a well-behaved German girl who learns English at school. In the course of the explanation of what a Mock Turtle is, the reader is introduced to Alice's teacher and Alice's aunt and is given a recipe for Mock Turtle soup:

"'Wie kann man mich zu einem Tier führen,' so dachte Alice, 'das es doch gar nicht gibt?' Alice hatte schon im zweiten Jahre Englisch. Die Lehrerin hatte den Kindern bereits beigebracht, daß 'turtle' auf deutsch 'Schildkröte' bedeutet, während 'mock' auf deutsch 'nachgemacht' heißt. Mock-Turtle-Suppe war also nichts anderes als eine 'nachgemachte' Schildkrötensuppe, die gar nicht mit Schildkrötenfleisch zubereitet war. Die Folge des guten englischen Unterrichts, den die Lehrerin gab, war also, daß alle Mädchen der Quinta genau wußten, was eine Mock-Turtle war und aus Dankbarkeit der Lehrerin gleich den schönen Spitznamen 'Die Mockturtle' gaben.

Bei der Hochzeit ihrer Tante hatte Alice auch einmal in der Küche zugesehen, wie die Mock-Turtle-Suppe zubereitet wurde. Sie erinnerte sich noch genau, daß in die Suppe ein halber Kalbskopf, ein Ochsengaumen, Suppengrün und andere Zutaten kamen. Später bei Tisch hatten der kleinen Alice die Kalbskopf- und Ochsengaumen-würfelchen in der Suppe besonders gut geschmeckt, denn, wißt ihr, wenn es sich um Essen handelte, hatte Alice immer ein besonders großes Interesse und ein ausge-zeichnetes Gedächtnis. So etwas behielt sie immer viel besser als englische oder französische Vokabeln."

(Carroll 1949, 69)

("How can I be brought to an animal which doesn't even exist?," thought Alice. This was Alice's second year learning English in school. The teacher had already told the children that "turtle" was "Schildkröte" in German and that "mock" meant "nachgemacht." So Mock Turtle Soup was nothing other than an imitation turtle soup which wasn't made with turtle meat at all. Thanks to the excellent English instruction by their teacher, each girl in the sixth class knew exactly what a Mock Turtle was, and out of gratitude to their teacher they gave her the lovely nickname "the Mockturtle."

At her aunt's wedding Alice had also seen how Mock Turtle soup was made in the kitchen. She could remember exactly that half a calf's head, an ox's gum, some carrots, onion, celery, leeks and parsley and other ingredients were used to make the soup. Later, during the meal, little Alice especially savoured the small pieces of calf's head and ox's gum in the soup because, you know, when it came to eating, Alice was always very interested and remembered anything to do with that much better than English or French vocabulary.

(my translation – eo's)

The voice of the narrator of this translation overrides that of the narrator of the source text, the tone is heavy-handed and pedantic. The work of the implied translator was informed here, as always, by the time and place in which the translation was carried out (the detailed descriptions of food and eating must have been particularly attractive to readers during the hungry post-war years in Germany) and especially by his notion of the implied reader based on assumptions as to the interests, propensities and capabilities of readers at that stage of their development. He obviously envisaged the implied reader of his translation as a child devoid of the fantasy necessary to imagine what a mock turtle might be, a child to whom everything had to be explained. His implied reader can't cope with a "foreign" setting, any action has to be transported to familiar, German, territory. It could be claimed that this implied translator missed the point of the book and produced a nanny translation devoid of nonsense. Unlike the source text, it holds absolutely no attraction for adults, any incidental humorous effect is involuntary. The implied translator of this *Alicens Abenteuer im Wunderland* and the implied author of Carroll's *Alice in Wonderland* come from entirely different planets in the universe of children's literature, and the implied translator is sure that his is a safer place for child readers than Carroll's one.

The discursive presence of the translator can be located in every translated narrative text on an abstract level as the implied translator of the translation. The translator's voice can make itself heard on a paratextual level as that of "the translator" and inscribed in the narrative as what I have called "the voice of the narrator of the translation." This particular voice would seem to be more evident in children's literature than in other bodies of literature due to the specific, asymmetrical communication structure which characterises texts which are written and published by adults for children. In these texts, contemporary and culture-specific notions of childhood play some part in determining the construction of the implied reader: what do "children" want to read, what are their cognitive and linguistic capabilities, how far can/should they be stretched, what is suitable for them – these are only some of the questions implicitly answered by the assumptions evident behind the "child" in children's literature and behind the child in any specific children's book. The same questions are asked again by the translator and by the publisher of the translation. The strategies chosen by translators for children are, as Riitta Oittinen reminds us, primarily dictated by their child image.[15] Assumptions about "the child" and the ensuing construction of readers of specific children's books and of their translations can lead to vast divergences between implied readers of source and target texts for children, as the few examples here have illustrated. Using a model of narrative communication it is possible to locate and name the place and agent of this divergence, to identify exactly where "changes" and "manipulations" happen and how these can be described in terms of narrative strategy, in terms of the construction of implied readers of the translation.

André Lefevere and Susan Bassnett describe translation as one of the most obvious, comprehensive, and easy to study "laboratory situations" for the study of cultural interaction, because a comparison of original and translation "will not only reveal the constraints under which translators have to work at a certain time and in a certain place, but also the strategies they develop to overcome, or at least work around those constraints. This kind of comparison can, therefore, give the researcher something like a synchronic snapshot of many features of a given culture at a given time." (1998, 6). One of these features is doubtlessly child image as one of the most influential factors determing the strategies developed by translators of children's literature. The model of narrative communication presented here offers a tool with which varieties of implied readers of source and target texts at certain times and in certain places can be identified by analysing the narrative strategies chosen by the translator as indicitive of her/his idea of the reading child and the kind of literature appropriate for that child. These strategies manifest themselves in audible form in the voice of the translator in children's literature.

Notes

1 Good examples of this approach can be found in Ben-Ari 1992, Wunderlich 1992 or Du-Nour 1995.

2 The first edition of the German translation of 1949 actually translates the scene as it is in the source text; it was altered in a subsequent edition. Cf. Surmatz 1998.

3 Theo Hermans calls this illusion of transparency and coincidence "the ideology of translation" (1996, 27), it is the illusion of a single voice which blinds critics to the presence of the other voice, the translator's one.

4 As do Hermans (1996), and Schiavi (1996). Barbara Wall (1991) speaks of "The Narrator's Voice" in children's literature.

5 I am deliberately simplifying the case here by omitting adult implied readers also to be found in some children's texts. See Barbara Wall's extensive study on the different addressees in children's literature (Wall 1991).

6 Oswald is a particularly tantalising narrator because he plays with the conventions of the first-person narrative. Although speaking as "I," he doesn't identify himself outright and lets the reader guess which of the six Bastable children is narrating: "It is one of us that tells this story – but I shall not tell you which" (Nesbit 1899, 4).

7 Cf. for example the opening of *Harry Potter and the Philosopher's Stone*: "Mr. and Mrs. Dursley, of number four, Privet Drive, were proud to say that they were perfectly normal, thank you very much." (Rowling 1997, 7).

8 How some of these addressees can go missing in translation is shown in O'Sullivan 1993.

9 The main narratological models available fail to distinguish between original texts and translations. As Theo Hermans rightly says, they "routinely ignore the translator's discursive presence" (1996, 26).

10 This term, and that of *the implied translator*, was introduced by Guiliana Schiavi (1996) who theoretically located these agencies in the translated text. She did not, however, provide examples of the discursive presence of the implied translator in actual translations.

11 This model is loosely based on the diagramme in Schiavi 1996, 14 but has been further developed, for example by placing the real translator in an extratextual position (cf. O'Sullivan 2000, 247).

12 The term was first introduced, in German, as "die Stimme des Erzählers der Übersetzung" in O'Sullivan 2000, 246, where the theoretical context is presented in greater detail and several examples of different manifestations of the voice of the narrator of the translation are presented and analysed.

13 There are, in total, 15 different, unabridged English translations of *Heidi* (cf. O'Sullivan (forthcoming)).

14 A brief account, in English, of *Alice in Wonderland* in German can be found in O'Sullivan 2000a; a bibliography of all German translations of Lewis Carroll's novel is in O'Sullivan 2000.

15 Oittinen describes the influence of the child image of the translator for children (and her/his time and society) thus: "she/he is directing her/his words, her/his translation, to some kind of child: naive or understanding, innocent or experienced; this influences her/his way of addressing the child, her/his choice of words, for instance." (1993, 68).

References

BEN-ARI, N. (1992): Didactic and Pedagogic Tendencies in the Norms Dictating the Translation of Children's Literature: The Case of Postwar German-Hebrew Translations. In: *Poetics Today* 13, 1, 221–230.

CARROLL, L. (1865): *Alice's Adventures in Wonderland*. Ill. John Tenniel. London: Macmillan.

CARROLL, L. (1949): *Alicens Abenteuer im Wunderland*. Aus dem Englischen übertragen von Franz Sester. Ill. Charlotte Strech-Ballot. Düsseldorf.

CHAMBERS, A. (1982): *Dance on my Grave*. London: Bodley Head.

CHATMAN, S. (1978): *Story and Discourse. Narrative Structure in Fiction and Film*. Ithaca, London: Cornell University Press.

CHATMAN, S. (1990): *Coming to Terms. The Rhetoric of Narrative in Fiction and Film*. Ithaca, London: Cornell University Press.

DU-NOUR, M. (1995): Retranslation of Children's Books as Evidence of Changes of Norms. In: *Target* 7, 2, 327–346.

HERMANS, T. (1996): The Translator's Voice in Translated Narrative. In: *Target* 8, 1, 23–48.

KÄSTNER, E. (1929): *Emil und die Detektive. Ein Roman für Kinder*. Ill. Walter Trier. Berlin: Williams & Co.

LEFEVERE, A. and S. BASSNETT (1998): Where are we in Translation Studies? In: Bassnett, Susan (Ed.): *Constructing Cultures. Essays on Literary Translation.* Clevedon: Cromwell, 1–11.

LINDGREN, A. (1945): *Pippi Långstrump.* Ill. Ingrid Vang Nyman. Stockholm: Rabén & Sjögren.

LINDGREN, A. (1949): *Pippi Langstrumpf.* Deutsch von Cäcilie Heinig. Ill. Walter Scharnweber. Hamburg: Oetinger.

MILNE, A. A. (1926): *Winnie-the-Pooh.* With Decorations by E. H. Shepard. London: Methuen.

NESBIT, E. (1907): *The Enchanted Castle.* London: Fisher Unwin.

NESBIT, E. (1899): *The Story of the Treasure Seekers.* Being the adventures of the Bastable Children in search of a fortune. London: Fisher Unwin.

OITTINEN, R. (1993): *I Am Me – I Am Other: On the Dialogics of Translating for Children.* Tampare: University of Tampare.

O'SULLIVAN, E. (1993): The Fate of the Dual Addressee in the Translation of Children's Literature. In: *New Comparison* 16, 109–119.

O'SULLIVAN, E. (2000): *Kinderliterarische Komparatistik.* Heidelberg: Universitätsverlag C. Winter.

O'SULLIVAN, E. (2001): Alice in Different Wonderlands: Varying approaches in the German translations of an English children's classic. In: Meek, Margaret (Ed.): *Children's Literature and National Identity.* London: Trentham, 23–32.

O'SULLIVAN, E. (1989): The Little Swiss Girl from the Mountains: Heidi in englischen Übersetzungen. In: Rutschmann, Verena (Ed.): *Johanna Spyri und ihr Werk.* Zürich: Chronos (forthcoming).

PARK, B.: *My Mother Got Married (and other disasters).* New York: Knopf.

PARK, B. (1991): *Charly und drei Nervensägen.* Aus dem Amerikanischen von Ulla Neckenauer. Würzburg: Arena.

ROWLING, J.K. (1997): *Harry Potter and the Philosopher's Stone.* London: Bloomsbury.

SCHIAVI, G. (1996): There is Always a Teller in a Tale. In: *Target* 8, 1, 1–21.

SPYRI, J. (1978): *Heidi.* Vollständige und ungekürzte Ausgabe in einem Band. Ill. Paul Hey. 2. Aufl. Frankfurt: Insel.

SPYRI, J. (1949): *Heidi.* With Drawings by Janet & Anne Johnstone. London: The Heirloom Library.

SPYRI, J.: *Heidi.* A New Translation by M. Rosenbaum. Glasgow: Collins Clear-Type Press: 1955.

SURMATZ, A. (1998): Kannibalen und Pistolen: die übersetzte Pippi Langstrumpf. In: *Der Rabe* 52, 136–140.

VENUTI, L. (1995): *The Translator's Invisibility. A History of Translation.* London, New York: Routledge.

WALL, B. (1991): *The Narrator's Voice: The Dilemma of Children's Fiction.* London: Macmillan.

WUNDERLICH, R. (1992): The Tribulations of "Pinocchio": How Social Change Can Wreck a Good Story. In: *Poetics Today* 13, 1, 197–219.

Part 18

COLONIALISM/ POSTCOLONIALISM

89

Extract from the
'INTRODUCTION' TO *VOICES OF THE OTHER: CHILDREN'S LITERATURE AND THE POSTCOLONIAL CONTEXT*

Roderick McGillis

Source: *Voices of the Other: Children's Literature and the Postcolonial Context*, New York: Garland, 2000, pp. xix–xxviii.

"Western in yu arse, boy, Western in yu arse!" and Joe was recreating the climax with a lively pantomime: "'ey boy, forty-million o'them against the star-boy and the rest o'them ridin comin and then he bullets run-out. . . ."

"An' then the other guys reach, an' then, ol'-man, then ya jus' see Red-Indian fallin—dong all over the place—ba-da-da-da-da—pretty, boy, pretty!" mused Krishna.
> —MERLE HODGE, *CRICK CRACK, MONKEY* [8]

The cavalry came riding over the hill again, and just as they got to where the Indians were waiting in the river, they disappeared. The Indians charged out of the river and massacred John Wayne and Richard Widmark.
> —THOMAS KING, *GREEN GRASS,*
> *RUNNING WATER* [330]

For much of the last century, young boys in North America and around the world learned to cheer the cowboy hero, first in popular fiction dubbed "dime novels," and later in Hollywood films. Films, especially, brought this figure to audiences in far-flung places, and in doing so perpetuated the activity of the cowboy whom they depicted. Both the films and the cowboys they celebrate participated in a colonial enterprise; they represent a continuing desire on the part of a white Eurocentric people to claim superiority and space throughout the globe. In the two passages I begin with, we have versions of the familiar white man (cowboy) versus native ("Red-Indian"), but in both cases we experience a jolt, a revision of what came to be taken as a natural encounter of the superior white colonist bringing civilization to a savage land and to a savage people, and in doing so defeating the native forces of primitivism, mystery, and violence. These two passages invoke a powerful image of colonialist activity in order to cast this image in a revisionary light. Despite the apparent difference in presentation, both passages ask us to rethink a familiar, even stereotypical plot.

In the passage from Merle Hodge's *Crick Crack, Monkey* (1970), young Trinidadian boys who go by names such as Audie Murphy, Gary Cooper, and Rock Hudson are re-enacting scenes from the films they see, films depicting the slaughter of "forty-million" Native Americans by their cow-boy heroes. We know these boys idolize the cowboy stars because they assume the names of prominent actors who often play cowboys on screen. The success of American culture amounts to a colonizing activity that these boys appear to accept readily and unquestioningly. What gives us pause is that we see these boys from the point of view of the young narrator, Tee, and from this vantage point the boys' play is juvenile. She recounts how their play moves easily into fighting when a girl happens by. And we know that the narrative moves out to an implied author whose silence marks an ambiguous—maybe even an ambivalent—acceptance of the boys' assump-tion of cowboy actions. In this early novel about adolescent girlhood in the Caribbean, we can detect a desire to fling off the colonial influence of Hollywood films. The term "Red Indian," here nicely attributed to the boy, Krishna, reminds us that native American's are not "Indians." So much depends on a name, and here the boys' desire to name themselves after Hollywood stars indicates their immaturity. Red Indians are not Indians, and Audie Murphy, Gary Cooper, and Rock Hudson are not actors at all. Instead, Indians are a colonized people, pushed to the edge of extinction; and Audie, Gary, and Rock are Caribbean boys in danger of losing their cultural heritage by abandoning it to another from away.

But I exaggerate. The passage is more subtle than I have indicated. These boys are not so easily abandoning their culture and replacing it with another. How could they, when the language they speak is distinctly their own? The manner in which these boys speak marks their speech as "other," at least other to those readers outside the cultural milieu in which these boys live. The way they talk indicates that they are neither cowboys nor "Red Indians." They incorporate the culture of the American cowboy into their own lingo, and in doing so claim it as their own. Something similar takes place in the Jamaican film, *The Harder They Come* (1972; directed by Perry Henzell), only here the ironies multiply because the young hero, played by Jimmy Cliff, emulates a cowboy hero who hails, not from America, but from Italy. The Italian western *Django*, starring Franco Nero, is what motivates Cliff's character to act, to become the desperado who stands up to corrupt record producers and hypocritical churchmen. What we see is an appropriation of American culture, not a simple acquiescence to it.

The passage from Thomas King's *Green Grass, Running Water* (1993) is more direct in its revisioning of the American western. Throughout the novel, a film starring John Wayne and Richard Widmark plays continually on a TV set in a small-town furniture store. For most of the film, the same familiar scene of Wayne and Widmark killing faceless savages in a riverside shoot-out plays repeatedly. Then, near the end of the novel, something surprising happens: an arrow pierces John Wayne's thigh and then two bullets "ripped through his chest and out the back of his jacket"; Widmark finds an arrow in his throat and he collapses "face down in the sand" (322). The cavalry does not appear in the nick of time; the two cowboy heroes bite the dust—or in this case, the sand. The reversal announces changing times; the Indians are taking charge. In King's novel, the Native people have taken back, reclaimed, their sense of identity, and their colonialist "civilizers" diminish in importance.

In both of these passages, we hear the voice of the other, the people more written about than writing, more spoken about than speaking, these past so many decades. What these passages speak is a desire for recognition on the part of people who have been either invisible or unfairly constructed or both. The connection with children and women seems inevitable. The culturally invisible or diminished have something in common with women and children in that they, too, have been powerless to take part in the conversations of cultural and other forms of political activity. Now that we are beginning to hear voices of the other, however, we begin to realize that we have not heard these voices before, not because they were silent, but rather because our own ears were closed to all but that which we wished to hear. And by "we," I refer to those of us conditioned by the Eurocentric heritage of the colonizers of North America. But habits are difficult to change, and the fact that I set out to introduce a set of essays on the opening of ears to voices not often enough heard in the past contains its own irony. Is this another colonialist gesture? Do we steal the voices of others in the very act of providing a medium for those voices? These are difficult questions that I hope this volume raises.

This book consists of a series of essays that enact a postcolonial criticism. This kind of criticism is an activity rather than a method. Critical methods refer to the various ways we can approach the interpretation of a text; interpretation can take a formal or a historical or an ethical or a psycho-analytical or a feminist focus (this is not an exhaustive list), all of which may or may not be postcolonial in impetus. The postcolonial critic directs his or her attention to resisting "colonialist perspectives" (Boehmer 3). I'll turn to Simon During for clarification: "post-colonialism is regarded as the need, in nations or groups which have been the victims of imperialism, to achieve an identity uncontaminated by universalist or Eurocentric concepts and images" (125). The activity I have in mind, then, is deeply committed to hearing the voices of those who have been silenced by various forces in our culture. Postcolonialism as an activity of mind is quite simply intent on both acknowledging the history of oppression and liberating the study of literature from traditional and Eurocentric ways of seeing. Postcolonial may refer either to primary works of literature or to commentary on that literature. In other words, we can have a postcolonial literature and a postcolonial criticism. The former derives from writers who are members of groups or nation states that once suffered under the mantle of colonialist control, whereas the latter may be the product of anyone sensitive to the need for recognition on the part of all peoples.

First a word about terms: colonialism, postcolonialism, neocolonialism, multiculturalism, diasporic writing, and the literature of postindependence. Colonialism is, of course, the term we use for an activity among peoples that involves one group assuming priority and authority over another group. Often the word accompanies the notion of imperial expansion, and refers most obviously to the expansion into far-flung areas of the globe of such European countries as Belgium, France, Spain, the Netherlands, and pre-eminently England, especially as these countries established colonies in the nineteenth century. Colonialism is not only a political and economic activity, but it also affects cultures and it assumes a certain mind-set: a colonial mentality. The colonial mentality assumes that the colonizer represents a more advanced state of civilization than the colonized does, and therefore that the colonizer has a right to assume a position of dominance. In terms of English-language literature, the colonialist mentality manifests itself in works that portray expansion "by way of myth and metaphor while at the same time masking suffering" (Boehmer 21). As Elleke Boehmer goes on to say: "Colonial writing is important for revealing the ways in which that world system could represent the degradation of other human beings as natural, an innate part of their degenerate or barbarian state" (21). In English children's literature, the best-known colonialist writers include Rudyard Kipling, G. A. Henty, R. M. Ballantyne, Captain Marryat, Bessie Marchant, and Hugh Lofting. Some critics argue, however, that the colonialist mind-set continues to manifest itself well into the twentieth century in seemingly innocent works such as the Babar books or the Curious George series (see Cummins, Kohl).

Postcolonialism in literature refers to a self-consciousness on the part of emerging peoples of a history, a culture, and an identity separate from and just as important as those of the imperial "masters." The literature of the past twenty years or so in countries such as Canada, Australia, South Africa, India, the islands in the Caribbean, and so on reveals an interest in national identity and pride separate from an attachment to England. The literature "critically scrutinizes the colonial relationship. It is writing that sets out in one way or another to resist colonialist perspectives" (Boehmer 3). The postcolonial writer desires to take his or her place as a historical subject. Some important postcolonial writers of children's literature include: Mordecai Richler, Barbara Smucker, Brian Doyle, Monica Hughes, James Houston (Canada); Patricia Wrightson, Gary Crews, Caroline Macdonald, Nadia Wheatley, John Marsden (Australia); Marguerite Poland, Jenny Seed, Lesley Beake, Diane Hofmyr (South Africa); Ruskin Bond, Satyajit Ray, Jamila Gavin (India); James Berry, Michael Anthony (Jamaica), Sam Selvon, Merle Hodge, Floella Benjamin (Trinidad). Issues of national identity are often at the forefront of the themes such writers take up. What complicates things is that within some national borders postcolonial positioning is itself conflicted. The postcolonial writer confronts directly the forces of cultural domination and racial intolerance. In a country such as Canada, for example, the writers I mentioned above often maintain a Eurocentric sense of things even as they try to articulate something distinctly Canadian. At the same time, others within the country write from positions of subalternity: First Nations writers such as Thomas King or C. J. Taylor resist the dominance of Eurocentric literary patterns, as do other writers (in their own way) from differing cultural and racial backgrounds. I think of Afua Cooper, Himani Bannerji, Lillian Allen, Nazneen Sadiq, Vinita Srivastava, and Ramabai Espinet.

The issues dealt with by writers such as the ones I have listed bring questions of race and culture sharply into focus. Since these issues are sensitive and easily threaten some of those who occupy the center or the dominant culture and race in multicultural and multiracial societies, we might expect some reaction. And in fact, it is necessary to report that a neocolonial sensibility does appear in many books for the young. Neocolonialism is simply a renewed drive on the part of the dominant social and cultural forces to maintain their positions of privilege. We might see the global activities of such American corporations as Disney or McDonalds as examples of neocolonialism in action. Popular culture is an important site for neocolonial activity. Whereas earlier colonialist activity had a political and territorial bias, neocolonialism is more deeply economic and cultural.

In books for children, neocolonialism manifests itself as both a depiction of minority cultures as inveterately other and inferior in some ways to the dominant European or Eurocentric culture, or as an appropriation of other cultures—that is, an assimilation of minority cultures into the mainstream way of thinking. The first of these—the depiction of the subaltern as inherently inferior—is examined in a recent book by Yulisa Amadu Maddy and Donnarae MacCann, *African Images in Juvenile Literature* (1996). Maddy and MacCann demonstrate how "imperialism still flourishes in the 1990s" (137). They examine, for example, the award-winning book by Nancy Farmer, *Do You Know Me* (1993), and conclude that her depiction of people in Mozambique and Zimbabwe shows "only derision and the misunder-standing of a people's culture" (60).

The assimilation of cultural difference is strikingly evident in a book such as Susan Jeffers's *Brother Eagle, Sister Sky* (1991). As Jon Stott notes: "no matter how well-intentioned Susan Jeffers is, no matter how great her respect for traditional and contemporary Native Americans, her book is another example of the creation of a 'white man's Indian,' a construct which reflects not realities but a view of what a white author, painter, motion picture director, actor, politician, missionary, activist, or conservationist believes Native peoples to be, wants them to become, or wishes they already were" (18). Stott carefully examines the errors and manipulations both in text and illustration that Jeffers perpetrates in order to present a view of the world "more in accord with the author's own (worthwhile) views on gender equality and the environment." Jeffers creates a portrait of the Native American "to reinforce her own agenda" (22).

Both the postcolonial and neocolonial enterprises are, in part, a reaction to what we now refer to as multicultural societies. Countries such as the United States, Canada, Australia, South Africa, and England are now in the late twentieth century fully multicultural in their social makeup. This fact of national demographics based on cultural and racial origins has re-sulted in books that deal directly with the relationship between people from differing cultural backgrounds. For example, the work of Paul Yee takes up both the history of the Chinese in Canada and the interaction between the Chinese community and the non-Chinese community, especially on Canada's west coast. The final chapter of Elwyn Jenkins's *Children of the Sun* (1993) deals with race relations and reconciliation as depicted in books for chil-dren in South Africa. In essence, multiculturalism in books for the young surfaces in books that try to deal sensitively and accurately with cultures other than the dominant Anglo-European culture that has until recently assumed unquestioned priority over much of the English-speaking world. The con-temporary promotion of multiculturalism gives rise to what Charles Taylor calls a "politics of recognition" (25), a desire evident in individual groups of people to be recognized as different from other groups, but at the same time equal to other groups. This is the impetus behind such works as Srivastava's *A Giant Named Azalea* (1991) or Bannerji's *Coloured Pictures* (1991).

Two other terms deserve consideration: diaspora and postindependence. Some of the writers I have referred to above do not live in their country of birth. Indeed, in the current multicultural situation many writers write from what used to be thought of as positions of exile. Exile is perhaps not the most efficient word because of its sense of enforced departure from home. Diaspora is the more accurate term here. According to Victor J. Ramraj:

> there are two bodies of writing that could he designated as diasporic.
> The first comes from the descendants of peoples uprooted from

their homelands in the eighteenth and nineteenth centuries and trans-ported from one region of the globe to another to serve British economic needs: Africans as slaves to the West Indies, and Indians, Chinese, and Portuguese as indentured labourers to such far-flung corners of the Empire as the West Indies, Fiji, and Mauriturius. The second is by those from English-speaking regions of the Indian subcontinent, Asia, Africa, and the diasporic communities of the West Indies and Fiji, who for economic, political, cultural, and familial or personal reasons left their homelands for London, England, which many, as citizens of the Empire, considered their capital, and for North America and Australia, continents that long had provided living space for peoples from over-crowded Europe. (214)

Ramraj goes on to explain that "the term diasporic writing has come to be associated with works produced by globally dispersed minority communit-ies that have common ancestral homelands" (214).

Writers of the diaspora write from positions of emergence—an emergence from a culture and place left behind that forms a crucial aspect of their identity, and from the culture and place in which they now live that inevit-ably must affect the identity they once located in their place of origin. In effect, diasporic writing does not set out to preserve cultural identity so much as it works to negotiate that identity (see Chow 25). Negotiation differs from an assimilation into the new culture; it resists acceptance of universal patterns of behavior and thinking. The pressure to universalize experience—what Chow calls the "rhetoric of universals"—"ensures the ghettoized existence of the other, be it in the form of a different culture, religion, race, or sex" (101). Truly diasporic writing sets out to bring people together not by homogenizing experience or history, but rather by focus-ing on "historical forces in their indivisible or *irreducible relations with one another*" (Chow 97; italics in original). A novel such as Bette Bao Lord's *In the Year of the Boar and Jackie Robinson* (1984) is a case in point. The protagonist, young Shirley Temple Wong, learns to cherish her heritage and embrace her new country and its customs. As the title of the novel and the protagonist's name indicate, this book's interest is in drawing differing cultures into conjunction without erasing one or the other. Another example is Paul Yee's *The Curses of Third Uncle* (1986) in which Yee combines both the history of the Chinese community in Canada with the struggle of fourteen-year-old Lillian to come to terms with her diasporic identity.

Finally, we have the term "postindependence." Meena Khorana, in a recent article, reflects on the difference between the terms "postcolonial" and "postindependence." The first of these terms carries with it the sense of an ongoing struggle against the forces of colonialism—the "post" does not indicate a struggle over and done with. On the other hand, postindependence clearly refers to a time when a nation has achieved its freedom from a colonialist power. The postcolonial writer is preoccupied, Khorana indicates, "with a hybrid identity" (19). Writers from "newly independent nations" (e.g., Sri Lanka, India) "are developing national identities, free of the ambivalences of the colonial period" (19). This may be true of a country such as India, but for other countries such as Canada or Australia independence did not bring and end to "the ambivalences of the colonial period." Indeed, the intricacies of colonialism and postcolonialsm are such that it is difficult to see these as truly separate from each other.

Ultimately, then, we have two related notions: colonialism and postcolonialism. In terms of primary creative vision, writers who give us visions of expansion in which a dominant group appears superior morally, intellectually, and socially to an other group are colonialist writers. Perhaps the best known of these writers in English is Daniel Defoe, whose *Robinson Crusoe* (1719) set the pattern for colonialist fiction. The nineteenth century especially saw a whole spate of "Robinsonades" that perpetuated the myth of European superiority over natives in many parts of the world. But the kind of thing these books expressed finds renewed expression in contemporary works that continue to suggest a version of human interaction in which the white person is somehow privileged. A prime example is the 1991 Newbery Medal–winning book by Jerry Spinelli, *Maniac Magee* (1990). In this novel, young Jeffrey Lionel Magee runs into the stuff of myth; he becomes a hero. Along the way, he lives with a black family and brings to the life of African-Americans a sense of the rightness of things. Invested in this boy's goodness is the whiteness of things good.

Writers who self-consciously interrogate the enforced diminishment of indigenous peoples or minorities of any sort write from positions of postcoloniality. The postcolonial creative writer need not focus exclusively on political matters, but her interest in emerging identity and self-determination inevitably brings to her work political concerns. Take, for example, Jamaica Kincaid's *Lucy* (1990) or Jamila Gavin's *The Wheel of Surya* (1992). Both of these novels deal with young people coming to terms with displacement. Lucy leaves the West Indies for North America where she strives to find a place for herself and make an independent living. Marvinder and Jaspal, in *The Wheel of Surya*, leave India for England where they, too, strive to find stability. Both books implicitly question a social, economic, and political system that places barriers against immigrants of such obviously minority and racially "other" backgrounds. Lucy remains in her new land determined to find accommodation there, even if this involves discomfort; Jaspal expresses his desire to return to India at the end of *The Wheel of Surya*, and in the sequels to this novel, we see that he does.

But what of the postcolonial critic? The position of the critic in postcolonial studies differs somewhat from the position of the creative writer in that the critic can bring a postcolonial perspective to works that themselves are not postcolonial. In other words, postcolonialism provides the opportunity for revisionary readings of canonical texts. For example, we have readings of writers such as Frances Hodgson Burnett and George MacDonald that are frankly postcolonial. Obviously, Burnett's evocation of India in both *The Secret Garden* and *A Little Princess* has a colonialist aspect that has remained unnoticed until recently. We can now see how the appropriation of the garden in the first of these books mimics the colonialist enterprise as first articulated in Defoe, and the depiction of Ram Dass in the second book perpetuates stereotypes of the person from India that can only continue misunderstanding rather than lead to acceptance through sensitivity to other cultures and peoples. The postcolonial critic, then, has a responsibility to read works of literature for their stated and unstated assumptions about the other. To put this another way, the activity of the postcolonial critic is political; he or she intervenes in the ways cultures construct persons.

But before I can close this survey of postcolonial activities, I must acknowledge an irony in what I write. If postcolonalism denotes a liberatory activity through recognition of uniqueness, then children themselves as postcolonial subjects are in an odd situation. They neither write the books they read, nor write critical commentary on those books. As Jacqueline Rose and others have noted, children are colonial subjects. Adults are the colonizers; children the colonized. Writers, critics, none of us, as Perry Nodelman has argued, can escape the role of colonizer. Speaking of his own "imperial tendencies," Nodelman admits: "in order to combat colonialism, I am recommending a benevolently helpful colonising attitude towards children" (34). I think, however, the patronizing of children here is unnecessary. What postcolonial activities on the part of adult writers and critics offer is not merely a discourse for gathering in children and forming them in the image adults desire; it is also a discourse that allows for a greater variety in versions of history and social and cultural constructions than was available to earlier generations of children. The young reader has the opportunity to choose between narratives that force questions and choices upon him or her.

Postcolonial narratives—whether fictional or critical—open space for the reader to see and hear peoples from a variety of backgrounds and cultural practices. This can only open possibility, not close it. The closing of the American (or Canadian or Australian or Indian, etc.) mind is the enterprise of colonialist and neocolonialist writers, but postcolonial activity seeks to open that mind. Tolerance and understanding are, in fact, the aim of postcolonial writing; tolerance and understanding can only come through opposition to prevailing conventions of belief and behavior. Opposition in this sense does not mean thoughtless refusal to accede to convention, but rather a critical examination of convention. As I have said elsewhere: "children and their literature are always postcolonial, if by postcolonial we mean that which stands outside and in opposition to tradition and power" (8). Respect for children and their right to inherit a world in which the possibilities for being are open is the mark of the postcolonial writer.

[. . .]

References

Bannerji, Himanni. *Coloured Pictures.* Toronto: Sister Vision Press, 1991.

Boehmer, Elleke. *Colonial & Postcolonial Literature.* New York: Oxford UP, 1995.

Chow, Rey. Writing Diaspora: Tactics of intervention in Contemporary Cultural Studies. Bloomington: Indiana UP, 1993.

Cummins, June. "The Resisting Monkey: 'Curious George,' Slave Captivity Narratives, and the Postcolonial Condition," *ARIEL* 28 (January 1997): 69–83.

During, Simon. "Postmodernism or Post-Colonialism Today," *The Post-Colonial Studies Reader*, Ed. Bill Ashcroft, Gareth Griffiths, and Helen Tiffin. London: Routledge, 1995. 125–129.

Farmer, Nancy. *Do You Know Me.* Illus. by Shelley Jackson. New York: Orchard Books, 1993.

Gavin, Jamila. *The Wheel of Surya.* London: Methuen, 1992.

Hodge, Merle. *Crick Crack, Monkey.* London: Heinernann, 1970.

Jeffers, Susan. *Brother Eagle, Sister Sky: A Message from Chief Seattle.* New York: Dial Books, 1991.

Jenkins, Elwyn. *Children of the Sun: Selected Writers and Themes in South African Children's Literature.* Johannesburg: Ravan, 1993.

Khorana, Meena. "Postcolonial or Postindependence?" *ARIEL* 28 (January 1997): 16–20.

King, Thomas. *Green Grass, Running Water*: Toronto: HarperCollins, 1993.

Kincaid, Jamaica. *Lucy.* New York: Farrar, Straus & Giroux, 1990.

Kohl, Herbert. *Should We Burn Babar? Essays on Children's Literature and the Power of Stories.* New York: The New Press, 1995.

Lord, Bette Bao. *In the Year of the Boar and Jackie Robinson.* New York: Harper & Row, 1984.

Maddy, Yulisa Amadu, and Donnarae MacCann. *African Images in Juvenile Literature: Commentaries on Neocolonialist Fiction.* Jefferson, N.C.: McFarland, 1996.

McGillis, Roderick. "Postcolonialism, Children, and their Literature," *ARIEL*, 28 (January 1997): 7–15.

Nodelman, Perry. "The Other: Orientalism, Colonialism, and Children's Literature," *ChLA Quarterly* 17(1992): 29–35.

Ramraj, Victor J. "Diasporas and Multiculturalism," *New Literatures in English*. Ed. Bruce King. Oxford: OUP 1996. 214–229.

Spinelli. Jerry. *Maniac Magee.* New York: Harper Collins, 1990.

Srivastava, Vinita. *A Giant Named Azalea.* Illus. by Kyo Maclear. Toronto: Sister Vision Press, 1991.

Stott, Jon C. *Native Americans in Children's Literature.* Phoenix: Oryx Press, 1995.

Taylor, Charles. *Multiculturalism: Examining the Politics of Recognition.* Ed. Amy Gutman. Princeton. NJ: Princeton UP 1994.

Yee, Paul. *The Curses of Third Uncle.* Toronto: James Lorimer, 1986.

90

HUNTING FOR HISTORY

Children's literature outside, over there, and down under

Heather Scutter

Source: *ARIEL: A Review of International English Literature* 28(1) (January 1997): 21–36.

How are we to write histories of children's literature now that the world has turned on its axis? The cultural maps we write can no longer assume imperial supremacies by emptying out huge portions of the written world, rendering them alien, irrelevant, invisible, and inscrutable. Is it possible any longer to construct a global history, to survey the parameters of a "field" of literature in space and time, synchronically and diachronically? We have learnt some hard theoretical lessons in children's literature. Yet, while there has been a proliferation of guides, companions, and compilations, there have been precious few disruptive histories. Two antipathetic but deeply linked urges seem evident: the one, the need to collect, amass, substantiate a body of evidence to demonstrate the existence of the discipline and to make material available to scholars and enthusiasts; the other, the drive to disturb that very body of evidence, to dismember it, to produce, if not a corpse, then a corpus whose reason for being has gone missing in action.

Thus, while the past few years have seen the publication in England of Peter Hunt's *An Introduction to Children's Literature* (1994), and of revised editions of F. J. Harvey Darton's *Children's Books in England: Five Centuries of Social Life* (1982) and of *The Oxford Companion to Children's Literature* (1984), they have also seen the more disruptive publication of Jacqueline Rose's *The Case of Peter Pan, or The Impossibility of Children's Fiction* (1984), of Jeffrey Richards's edited collection, *Imperialism and Juvenile Literature* (1989), of Peter Hunt's *Criticism, Theory and Children's Literature* (1991), and of Karin Lesnick-Oberstein's *Children's Literature: Criticism and the Fictional Child* (1994). Against the Eurocentric pattern, I want to set an Australian comparison. The 1980s have seen the publication of Brenda Niall's critical history, *Australia Through the Looking Glass:*

Children's Fiction 1830–1980 (1984), Kerry White's bibliographical study, *Australian Children's Fiction: The Subject Guide* (1992), Pam Macintyre and Stella Lees's *Oxford Companion to Australian Children's Literature* (1993), and Maurice Saxby's survey, *The Proof of the Puddin': Australian Children's Literature 1970–1990* (1993); they have also seen the publication of Barbara Wall's *The Narrator's Voice: The Dilemma of Children's Fiction* (1991) and John Stephens's *Language and Ideology in Children's Fiction* (1992). Both of the latter, incidentally, were published internationally.

The way we write about children's literature needs to move in directions informed more thoroughly by the understandings and practices of postcolonialism, new historicism and cultural studies. We need fewer Oxford guides, stamped with the authority of the centre, designed to provide an assumed (but virtual) pathway through that which is always and already known and understood. The most radical approaches are those which refuse to classify and categorize in the old way, which ask questions to confuse textual and contextual boundaries, which examine the intersections and interdependencies of discourses, and which enable innumerable stopped voices a speaking position. Contradiction, ambiguity and babel/babble are, to my mind, welcome co-travellers.

In "Missed Opportunities and Critical Malpractice: New Historicism and Children's Literature," a very rich article that should gradually transform critical practices, Mitzi Myers lays down a challenge to orthodoxies of children's literature. She stresses the dynamic production and reproduction of meaning between literary and extraliterary contexts, the "fault-lines" that demand attention for their exposure of connected discourses of time, gender, class, age, and race, the conditions of material production, the reception history and the question of canonicity. Most specifically, Myers challenges conventional organizations of historical material in a way that allows for a postcolonial decentring and destabilizing of received wisdoms. Speaking of the New Historicism in literary studies, she writes:

> Recognizing that human subjectivity itself, much less its literary expression, is culture-bound, it couldn't reify or essentialize The Child and Children's Literature (or even Literature) and What Children Like . . . What a New Historical orientation could not make central to its program is what most historically-based study of children's literature still does: organize material within preconceived patterns implying an evolutionary view of historical progress. Linearly organized, always *toward*, most literary histories aren't analytic history, but teleology.

> (42)

We have come to understand that history is a kind of narrative, its structure, plot, closure, and point of view contributing to and comprising its fictionality and textuality. And, as Myers argues, history organized in linear fashion always implies an end point and goal which seem to explain the *meaning* of the connections among events, things, and people. Teleologies thus are a version of metanarrative, and metanarratives are dangerous stories when it comes to the representation and construction of difference.

So it is an occasion both for anticipation and no little scepticism to read, and decode, the long-awaited Oxford *Children's Literature: An Illustrated History* (1995), edited by Peter Hunt, vigorous as a theorist, critic, and historian in England, Europe, America, and, during a visiting fellowship, in Australia. But ironically, while Hunt's history signals radical shifts in critical and historical theory, these are imperfectly embodied in the narratives told. The editorial preface problematizes the practical difficulties of collecting the impedimenta of such a history, the parameters of children's literature, the notion of childhood as a moving target, the aesthetics of popular and unpopular culture, and the intransigence of didacticism. The use of different specialist historians and critics augurs well for the inclusion of different and contestatory approaches.

But overall, there is a resistance to grappling with the complex and subtle imbrications of ideology and a perceptibly controlling and homogenizing editorial stance and voice. The sheer weight of such a project and the manifold editorial difficulties of co-ordinating, directing, overseeing a diverse range of views, in themselves without doubt create a kind of inertia, a reactionary tendency. Ultimately, this is a traditional linear history informed by numerous teleologies. The occasional disruptive moment has the effect of appliqué rather than a good honest tear to the fabric.

This history book is in large part a celebration of how far children's literature has developed from narrow religious and pedagogical beginnings. There is a teleology inherently linked with the Western myth of progress (every day in every way things are getting better, rosier, and truer) and the post-Darwinian theory of recapitulation (like children, natives, colonies, national cultures, and the working classes, children's literature had to grow up, repeat the stages of the adult/race).

Strangely, this dominant teleological drift is undercut by that recurring feature of conventional histories: most attention is paid to writers who, or literary phenomena which, are neither exactly contemporary nor too historically distanced, either in time or space. Thus, Lewis Carroll gets three pages, including this sharp summation of Alice by Briggs and Butts:

> Alice's constant interrogation of the creatures she meets reflects her childish ignorance of widely accepted rules, while their interrogation of her may reflect Carroll's own search for greater intimacy with the object of his desire. These exchanges also reflect the contended-for and shifting dynamics of power between adult and

child, controller and controlled: although full of self-doubt ("I'm not myself, you see"), Alice finds herself surrounded by strange and often childishly atavistic creatures.

(Hunt 141)

Kingsley gets more than two pages, along with a sustained comparison between his Tom and MacDonald's Diamond; but *Tom's Midnight Garden* gets only a paragraph, and Mary Norton is barely glossed. Felice Holman and Norton Juster are absent.

As the saying goes, and Peter Hunt quotes it in his preface, "What's hit's history; what's missed's mystery" (ix). That is the case, of course, if you do not know what you do not know. But for those of us who know sweeps of these books, what is missed becomes an unsaid which is judged as lacking against the status of the "hit-upon" history. The effect of all of this is to canonize precisely the perceived Golden Age of children's literature, and to consign to a booming buzzing confusion those texts in the unclassifiable miasma of the present. The perspective lent by time is specifically that which needs deconstructing.

There are several other teleological narratives threaded through the history. One is instigated by Hunt in his preface, where he argues that, since women have been involved from the outset in the field of children's literature, and since "the male hegemony exercised in 'adult' literary history has not established itself quite so strongly in this sphere," there is less need for "revisionist readings." Hunt follows this with an immediate qualification which sounds like a disclaimer—"but that does not mean that the children's book world is in any sense a cosy or complacent one" (xiii).

Now I can hardly recognize this as the same voice which spoke so challengingly to a conference in Wollongong, Australia, in 1991, of the "ambivalent relationship with male culture" that exists within a field "dominated by women, on behalf of children" ("The Decline and Decline" 11). What is more, Hunt's controlling arguments, then, regarding a plateauing of the quality of children's books, the necessity for radically "childist" criteria and the sorry persistence of monolithic cultural values in selection and judgment, stand oddly against the meliorist tenor of this history.

In feminist terms, a great deal more could have been revised; for the most part, Hunt extrapolates from feminism to develop his notions of "childism." This is a fine comparison. Hunt applauds the paradigms, but a much more complex scrutiny of the dynamics of en-gendering within patriarchy is demanded. It is an understood wisdom that "the child" is a feminized construct, and that children's literature is feminized in relation to "grown-up" literature. I am not satisfied, however, with readings, such as Butts's, which claim that Marryat's "stereotypical portrayal of female characters is inevitably influenced by the historical situation when he wrote" (Hunt, *Children's Literature* 99). Such readings simply defer to a notionally synthesized ideology, and fail to engage with the complex of discourses which support gender stereotypes.

Nor am I impressed with the apparent glibness of Peter Hollindale's vacillations, especially given his pioneering role in ideological criticism. Referring to the stock contents of *Girl* magazine—boarding school girls, nurses, dancers, and ponies—he states: "Whether such tastes are the sinister product of gender conditioning, or simply evidence of what girls like is a controversy that rages fiercely in the 1990s but, as the history of *Girl* demonstrates, is nothing new" (Hunt, *Children's Literature* 261). The first alternative implies a kind of paranoia in those who dare to detect gender role stereotypes (the term "sinister" is evidently meant for the perceivers rather than the "products"); the second is reductive and essentialist, and, with its reference to "nothing new," suggests a rehearsal of the cyclic and repetitive. As is very frequent in this history, and the more so the more contemporary the material and critique become, the contributors hedge, evade, and equivocate over their judgements.

I would like to have seen larger questions asked of gender-inflected shifts within particular historical and cultural contexts. Why, for example, was the first Golden Age of male fantasists in nineteenth-century England so preoccupied with eroticized images of the female child and with recuperation of the perceived "feminine"? And why are the acerbic female fantasists of the period (like Jean Ingelow, whose fairy Mopsa displaces the young male protagonist Jack in stature and status, and yet is so heavily contained by a recessive narrative frame) virtually overlooked and certainly underestimated?

Why was the second Golden Age of fantasists in post-World War II England so preoccupied with little boys being given a glimpse of glorious heritage by old women (for example, Tom in Pearce's *Tom's Midnight Garden*; Tolly in Boston's *The Children of Green Knowe*; the Boy in Norton's *The Borrowers*)? What cultural inflections determine differences in representations of the female child? As Brenda Niall questions in a review of the Oxford *History*, with regard to the American Pollyanna stories,

> Is that relentless optimism an essentially American quality—or at least a quality American adults like to foster? I can't see Anne of Green Gables playing the Glad Game, nor any of the Seven Little Australians, and it would be worth asking why.
>
> (Niall, "Once Upon" 7)

And can we imagine Carroll's Alice managing and imagining out on the prairie as Laura Ingalls did? Or being represented in such a way?

With regard to critical readings of individual texts, there are some "classic" novels of which I would like to see feminist revisionist readings: Tolkien's *The Hobbit* (peculiarly, Hunt reads the fantasy in purely archetypal terms, and yet he is a critic who typically resists what he calls the "speculative" fiction of the psychoanalytic reading); Garner's *The Owl Service* (whose woman of owls or flowers bears more than a passing resemblance to that old dichotomy, virgin or whore, and whose maddened and silenced older women are grim testimony to a patriarchal construction of the sexualized woman as vagina dentata, consuming and deadly); L'Engle's *A Wrinkle in Time* (whose domestication of the intellectualized and spiritualized feminine reinforces the old binaries); even, dare I say it, Avi's *The True Confessions of Charlotte Doyle* (whose dutiful daughter turned mutineer undertakes a boys' own adventure on the high seas in a narrative which sacrifices race in the cause of whited gender; not unexpectedly, the frontier seems to blow east and out to sea, where the winds take it altogether out of history, by way of myth, into the realm of male fantasy). Further, I would like to see some feminist revision with regard to the conditions of production of children's books, the development of pedagogies, the metonymic association with family and domesticity, and notions of writing the body of the child.

So we have two teleologies thus far: the myth of progress and the myth of the already revised female. Another teleological subplot concerns the narrative of a common culture. Now if you think organic communities, commonalities of culture and great traditions have gone the way of all Leavisites, scrutinize Oxford's *Children's Literature: An Illustrated History*. Common culture is an essential selection criterion, or, as the editor puts it, "a certain cultural cohesion" (revealing almost instantly a crucial slippage when he moves on to "narrative norms") dictates whether or not a national literature is included (xiii).

A most telling aspect of the tenacity of the notion evinces itself when regret is expressed several times in the later chapters of the book that classics are not being kept in print, that backlists are not being kept up, that single print runs are becoming the norm. The fear is that there will be no literary heritage to pass on from one generation to another. The book is thus iconic of that "common culture," just as "Literature" used to signify "Life," no mere cultural baggage but a precious artefact in danger of a sort of technological implosion. This is one more of the ways, incidentally, that "the child" has been constructed as a crucial mediating emblem of universalization (no less than was done in the Sunday School reward books that allowed the child figure to move between class boundaries). When a concern is articulated for cultural continuity, we always have to ask on whose behalf, with what exclusions, within what model of cultural integrity, and for fear of what change.

A fourth teleological sub-text is made manifest in the increasing use of the term "political correctness." Hunt himself appears to be the first to use a variation on the term ("political incorrectness") in his chapter, "Retreatism and Advance," when he discusses George Orwell's critique of the *Greyfriars* stories. The increasing use of the term in Chapters 10 and 11 disguises a strongly naturalized set of "correct" values belonging to the writers. Teleologically, the history suggests the sophisticated acceptance of a narrative of conflict-denial, compromise, civilized balance, witty tolerance. This narrative undoes itself without blinking early in Chapter 10, when we are informed that in post-1970 there were, as Hollindale and Sutherland note, the beginnings of "problems of race . . . and of class and gender." The period between 1950 and 1970, they argue, was "singularly free of prescriptive ideologies"—a free space, that is, in comparison with pre-war propaganda and the post-1970s rule-book, "the new agenda of political correctness" (Hunt, *Children's Literature* 253, 259).

This chapter thus mythicizes the second Golden Age as a kind of inter-regnum between the tyrannies of respective discrete ideologies, without attempting to deconstruct the urgent impulse among children's writers, educators, and parents to naturalize "traditional" values and to recuperate what was perceived as a nearly-lost cultural arcady. The discussion of the W. E. Johns's Biggles books brings matters to a head. In the 1950s, the Biggles books flourished amid attempts at prescription and proscription, as Hollindale observes:

> But among professionals such as teachers and librarians the mood of the peacetime years was hostile to many features of the "Biggles" books: their military values, cult of heroism, and propagation of racist stereotypes—as well as their unquestionably modest literary qualities. The books appeared to educated adult readers to be out-of-touch with the egalitarian, internationalist, post-colonial mood of the new Britain.
>
> (Hunt, *Children's Literature* 262)

The double use of the word "mood" signifies a muting of what is really an ideological cluster. Also, these "educated adult readers" are not accused of "political correctness" in this instance, but instead are accorded the triple crown. Only within the field and discourses of children's literature could post-colonialism be yoked with a mood, such is the romanticism of its paradigms.

Zena Sutherland takes an apparently neutral stance when she discusses historical American texts which deal with slavery and African-American experiences. She tags this section with what has become a disclaimer of commitment in this history: "Many of these books have been controversial, dealing as they do with areas where political correctness is at a premium" (Hunt, *Children's Literature* 264). There are those of us who think that more than "political correctness" is at a premium. William Armstrong's *Sounder*, for example, has a "merciless impact" upon me fundamentally because of its awful fatalism inscribed with teleological echoes of the biblical exodus. The land promised is mythically displaced for the political purposes of the dominant culture.

The "political" seems so feared in *Children's Literature: An Illustrated History* that analysis of it is absent even with respect to the most strikingly explicit texts. For example, Sutherland praises Madeleine L'Engle's A *Wrinkle in Time* as "a most inventive fantasy, complicated in its intricate weaving of science, philosophy, religion and familial relationships" (273). No mention is made of its highly politicized dystopian elements, its invocation of a roll-call of freedom fighters, its responses to the Cold War, even its rewriting of Orwell's *1984*.

Ultimately, the structure of Hunt's history serves as a paradigm of imperialism itself. There are four chapters to tell the history of English children's literature from its beginnings until 1850, and one for America to catch up and sneak ahead to 1870. Three English chapters cover the period between 1850 and 1945, and one more American chapter brings the two together neck and neck. With the advent of what is termed "Internationalism" the English and American histories are conjoined for two chapters in a sort of literary two-step that takes the book up to the present. The British contribution is always represented as having more substance and density, as being a kind of gold standard or control.

When the two cultures meet, they recognize each other's imperial status with a degree of mutual self-congratulation (although with a hint of anxiety that England might be subject to colonization by the USA). Dancing a troika at the end are the three colonial literatures perceived as most mimetic of, least different from, the colonizing powers. Ironically the colonies of Canada, Australia, and New Zealand are those which took in the very cultures that had become marginalized and impoverished within Britain— the Irish, the Scots, the Welsh, and the English underclass itself, including its convicts.

Throughout the history, there are highly ambiguous constructions of imperialism from the British point of view. As Briggs and Butts say, there is more than a whiff of frustrated militarism in the description of boys' own adventure narratives promising "the possibility of exciting adventure within the hegemony of British imperialism" (Hunt, *Children's Literature* 149). But more is made of the fact that other lands were perceived as "exotic," than of the assumption of British mastery that enabled colonial subjection. In Briggs's comments in a later chapter, a plangent note enters the fray:

> There is a strong heroic ethos in much of the writing for children between 1890 and 1914, as if the generation doomed to die on the battlefield had been reared with exactly the ideals needed to persuade them to volunteer as soon as they could. To what extent did their childhood reading help to determine the fate of a whole generation?
>
> (Hunt, *Children's Literature* 187)

What is not said here is that this childhood reading matter was not restricted to the English but was sent out in massive quantities to the colonies,
especially in the form of reward books. The result was that more young
Australian and New Zealand men per capita of gross population died on the
European battlefields than did young Englishmen; the young colonials were
doubly subjected.

Perhaps, as Watkins states, the insistent Anglocentricity of the history
explains why there has always been a hedging response to such a writer
as William Mayne and his "ability to explore the importance of other cultures' perception of the world and the often limited quality of the European
view" (Hunt, *Children's Literature* 309). Such hedging will be less when we
refer to the "mixed ethnic origins" of an Englishman rather than of an
African-American boy (as Watkins does of Arthur in Mayne's *The Jersey
Shore*). Intimations of race and blood purity are never far away. It is
fascinating, and significant, that Watkins's account of children's writers
working "Across the Genres" (so the subheading goes) actually deals more
specifically with writers working across and between cultures. This slippage
is also enshrined in the title of the previous chapter, "Internationalism,
Fantasy, and Realism."

Writings of history are these days very often re-writings, revisions. But
Hunt's history still represents England as the imperial and cultural centre.
His project, as stated in the preface, is to tell the history of children's
literature among English-language countries, but he immediately discounts
two enormous former colonial regions, India and the African possessions.
His argument is that these literatures do not share the same "cultural cohesion" as the chosen ones. Hunt is thus working from a model of integrity
and homogeneity that *must* suppress cultural difference and specificity. Those
"Other" cultures are erased more effectively by slight(ing) reference than by
complete silence. This manoeuvre is politically shocking: in the very terms in
which the history is set up, the pedagogical intent of children's literature for
the far-flung colonies was profound. Indeed, the very growth of English
literature as a humanities discipline was intimately linked to the growth and
extension of the British public service in the reaches of the Empire. And, as
Jo-Ann Wallace has argued, that Empire was only conceivable, imaginable,
through the reciprocal development of certain discourses of childhood. The
literature produced for and on behalf of the "child-like" colonies cannot
be separated from the literature produced for the children of the Empire.

There are even more adroit manoeuvres performed closer to home(s). The
terms "British" and "English" are conflated tellingly. The cultures grafted
to the English, often with unhealed scars, are almost completely eliminated
as cultural sources or influences. The Welsh, the Scottish, and the Irish earn
reference as timeless and dehistoricized fonts of Celtic myth, legend, and
oral tradition. Watkins has a brief mention of contemporary novels about
"the troubles":

179

[Gillian Cross's *Wolf*] is a complex novel with many layers of meaning which combines an exciting thriller about the IRA with the exploration of the psychological maturation of a thirteen-year-old girl.

(302)

However, apart from almost anecdotal references such as this (which recalls that earlier reference to "the possibility of exciting adventure within the hegemony of British imperialism"), the history elides the specific politics and cultures of the other members of the UK. There is, thus, a covert back-sourcing which hides the tensions of recent and immediate historic contexts.

Ironically, the first mention of the Welsh in *Children's Literature: An Illustrated History* occurs in Chapter 10, "Internationalism, Fantasy, and Realism [1945–1970]," and that mention occurs in the context of an American fantasy text that plumbs Celtic sources of myth and legend—Lloyd Alexander's *Prydain* chronicles. Given that English is the language of the conquerors, the language through which cultural literacy is negotiated, how do contemporary Welsh authors write for children? I, as an Australian of Scottish descent, am curious as to the very sparse references also to Scottish writers for children, especially contemporary ones. There are missed opportunities for cultural analysis and interpretation here and there, sometimes asked and unanswered, sometimes begging the question. In Chapter 6, Briggs and Butts say:

Like MacDonald, Stevenson and James Barrie, Crockett was a Scot, and the large Scottish contribution to writing for children from the 1860s might suggest that the concept of childhood north of the border was in key respects significantly different.

(Hunt, *Children's Literature* 174)

This is the beginnings of a very valuable point in a history, and yet it is left untested, unexplored. Earlier, Briggs and Butts claim that Stevenson was "less interested in imperialism than other writers," with mention in the next breath of his Scottish nationality and upbringing (152). A cultural connection might have been made here. Ireland is a terribly divided country, as we know. The history refers to Irish myth and legend (or at least to English re-workings of it) but it tells us precious little about literature for children coming from that divided culture. Why have Eire's contributions not been included? This absence is stunning. It seems that Irish literature is celebrated and discussed more freely further from home, perhaps because so many of the colonies became another home to the Empire's waste (see Hillel, "From Dubbo to Dublin").

Something similar happens with the American colossus, so that reference to English-language colonies is swallowed up. What of the massive

180

distribution of American texts for children to American colonies? Within the colonies themselves, which often imitated their imperial source, there is a further replication so that indigenous cultures are overlooked in significant ways. Certainly something is made of the attempts by native cultures to speak their own experiences and literatures, and reference is made to Inuits, American Indians, Maoris, and Aborigines. But nothing is made editorially of the ideological inconsistencies that become evident in the colonial/postcolonial chapter.

While the Canadian Roderick McGillis problematizes nominalism, explaining that the terms "Indians" and "Inuits" "misleadingly homogenize many peoples" (Hunt, *Canadian Literature* 338), Australia's Michael Stone comfortably refers to "the true Aboriginal voice" and to "authenticity" (332), and New Zealand's Betty Gilderdale elides the issue by concentrating on the theme of rapprochement between races. Overall, there is an appalling gap as far as the imposition of English-language literatures upon subject peoples in the name of assimilation. The historical impact of master-literatures upon infantilized races and cultures cannot be so breathtakingly ignored.

Hunt's history sets up a meta-narrative that is imitated in microcosm in each of the three colonial histories. It is time that the telling of the history of children's literature, a history which is so bound up with the formation and promulgation of imperialism, be deconstructed. "[T]he history of strategic colonialist investment in [the child] figure" (Wallace 182) exposes an intricate nexus between ideologies of childhood, race, class, and gender that demands postcolonial analysis and interpretation. The postcolonial cannot be consigned to a hybrid cultural set constrained within a chapter-as-coda (which is just what Hunt's history does in its textual practices and in its index entry: "Colonialism and postcolonialism, 322–51." There is no separate entry or cross-indexing for postcolonialism, which can only be accessed through the precedent sign).

As Edward Said argues in *Culture and Imperialism*:

> No one can deny the persisting continuities of long traditions, sustained habitations, national languages, and cultural geographies, but there seems no reason except fear and prejudice to keep insisting on their separation and distinctiveness, as if that was all human life was about. Survival in fact is about the connections between things. . . . It is more rewarding—and more difficult—to think concretely and sympathetically, contrapuntally, about others than only about "us." But this also means not trying to rule others, not trying to classify them or put them in hierarchies, above all, not constantly reiterating how "our" culture or country is number one (or *not* number one, for that matter). For the intellectual there is quite enough of value to do without *that*.
>
> (408)

But *that* is not quite that. The trouble is that for many of us, our hypotheses and theories change more rapidly than our mindsets and cultural assumptions. There seems always to be a degree of lag between new ways and old ways. It is not possible to write global histories in the old coherent way informed by imperialist structures and beliefs. Instead we will see a growing split in the critical marketplace between two forms: encyclopedic miscellanies, and writings from a cultural studies and new historicist stance, worrying at the edges of traditional categories, reframing the discourses and enabling an ongoing dialogic engagement between constitutive and contestatory elements. Nearly two decades ago, Walter Arnstein classified, somewhat whimsically, four common approaches to the writing of history:

1. The Whig interpretation of history, the "every day in every way we are getting better and better" point of view.
2. The Tory approach, the "since Adam and Eve in the Garden of Eden it has been downhill all the way" point of view.
3. The cyclical approach, the "here we go again but haven't we been this way before?" approach to the past.
4. History as just one doggone thing after another, as a miscellany column in a newspaper, involving neither rhyme nor reason. (44)

It seems to me that there is more than a touch of all of these approaches in Peter Hunt's history. His inclination is towards the fourth but elements of the three other approaches are evident. Now is the time for a powerful renegotiation of the status of otherness and difference within all those "doggone" things while we re-imagine our field without the secure authority of controlling metanarratives.

Works cited

Armstrong, William. *Sounder.* London: Victor Gollanz, 1969.

Arnstein, Walter. "Reflections on Histories of Childhood." *Research About Nineteenth-Century Children and Books.* Ed. Selma K. Richardson. Urbana-Champaign, IL: U of Illinois Graduate School of Library Science, 1980: 41–60.

Carpenter, Humphrey, and Mari Pritchard. *The Oxford Companion to Children's Literature.* Oxford: Oxford UP, 1984.

Darton, F. J. Harvey. *Children's Books in England: Five Centuries of Social Life.* Cambridge: Cambridge UP, 1982. 3rd edn., rev. Brian Alderson. 1982.

Hillel, Margot. "From Dubbo to Dublin: Some Themes and Issues in Australian and Irish Children's Literature." *Towards Excellence in Children's Literature.* Ed. C. Hill and L. Strain. Melbourne: Deakin UP, 1992: 63–74.

Hunt, Peter. "The Decline and Decline of the Children's Book?" *Children's Literature and Contemporary Theory.* Ed. Michael Stone. Wollongong, NSW: New literatures Research Centre, U of Wollongong, 1991: 1–14.

——. *Criticism, Theory and Children's Literature.* Oxford: Blackwell, 1991.

——. *An Introduction to Children's Literature.* Oxford: Oxford UP, 1994.

——, ed. *Children's Literature: An Illustrated History.* Oxford: Oxford UP, 1995.

Lesnick-Oberstein, Karin. *Children's Literature: Criticism and the Fictional Child.* Oxford: Clarendon Press, 1994.

Macintyre, Pam, and Stella Lees. *The Oxford Companion to Australian Children's Literature.* Melbourne: Oxford UP, 1993.

Mayne, William. *The Jersey Shore.* London: Hamish Hamilton, 1973.

Myers, Mitzi. "Missed Opportunities and Critical Malpractice: New Historicism and Children's Literature." *Children's Literature Association Quarterly* 13–1 (1988): 41–3.

Niall, Brenda. *Australia Through the Looking Glass: Children's Fiction 1830–1980.* Melbourne: Melbourne UP, 1984.

——. "Once Upon a Time." Review of Peter Hunt's *Illustrated History of English Literature. The Australian Weekend Review*, 9–10 Sept. 1995: 7.

Richards, Jeffrey, ed. *Imperialism and Juvenile Literature.* Manchester: Manchester UP, 1989.

Rose, Jacqueline. *The Case of Peter Pan, or, The Impossibility of Children's Fiction.* London: Macmillan, 1984.

Said, Edward. *Culture and Imperialism.* London: Vintage, 1993.

Saxby, Maurice. *The Proof of the Puddin: Australian Children's Literature* 1970–1990. Sydney: Ashton Scholastic, 1993.

Stephens, John. *Language and Ideology in Children's Fiction.* London: Longman, 1992.

Wall, Barbara. *The Narrator's Voice: The Dilemma of Children's Fiction.* London: Macmillan, 1991.

Wallace, Jo-Ann. "De-Scribing *The Water-Babies*: 'The Child' in Post-colonial Theory." *De-Scribing Empire: Post-Colonialism and Textuality.* Ed. Chris Tiffin and Alan Lawson. London: Routledge, 1994: 171–84.

White, Kerry. *Australian Children's Fiction: The Subject Guide.* Sydney: ALIA/Thorpe, 1992.

91

THE END OF EMPIRE?

Colonial and postcolonial journeys in children's books

Clare Bradford

Source: *Children's Literature* 29 (2001): 196–218.

To read children's books of the nineteenth and twentieth centuries is to read texts produced within a pattern of imperial culture. Works of the past, such as *Tom Brown's Schooldays, The Water-Babies*, and *The Secret Garden*, readily disclose the imperial ideologies that inform them. Thus, Hughes's depiction of schoolboy life at Rugby is framed by imperialism, not merely because Rugby's régime constitutes a training-ground for imperial adventures, as in the case of Tom's great friend East, who leaves the school to join his regiment in India, but also because the conceptual world in which the boys are located comprises two parts: home and abroad, center and margins, as Hughes's depiction of the tribe of Browns demonstrates: "For centuries, in their quiet, dogged, homespun way, [the Browns] have been subduing the earth in most English counties, and leaving their mark in American forests and Australian uplands" (13). In *The Water-Babies*, Kingsley's mobilization of imperial ideologies is distinguished by its convergence of categories of race and class. When Tom climbs down the wrong chimney to arrive in Ellie's room and catches sight of himself in a mirror, he sees "a little ugly, black, ragged figure, with bleared eyes and grinning white teeth" (19). Here, the grime of the chimney, a signifier of Tom's lowly position within the domestic economy, is mapped onto the blackness of peoples colonized by British imperialism.[1] Conversely, Tom's ascent to the middle class is coterminous with his transformation into a white imperial man: "[he] can plan railroads, and steam-engines, and electric telegraphs, and rifled guns, and so forth" (243–44). And in *The Secret Garden*, Frances Hodgson Burnett represents India as a space marked by disorder, danger, and sickness, so that Mary's return to Britain restores her to physical and psychic health (see Cadden; Phillips).

In these texts, the lands and indigenous peoples "out there" in the far reaches of the British Empire are "Othered" in order to produce and sustain an idea fundamental to colonial discourse: that Europe (and, in these three texts, Britain) is the norm by which other countries and peoples are judged. Not that the process of "Othering" is an unproblematic one—indeed, colonial discourse is shot through with anxieties concerning what Peter Hulme calls "the classic colonial triangle, . . . the relationship between European, native and land" (1). Thus, for example, discourses of Christianity, some of which promote the equality of all people as children of God, frequently clash with colonial discourse, which promotes the superiority of white over colored peoples, and so validates the appropriation of land (see Bradford). Nevertheless, despite their moments of uncertainty and their occasional resistance to dominant ideologies, colonial texts are by and large organized through such binary oppositions as self and other, civilized and savage, white and black.

Postcolonial texts are marked by a more complex and contradictory set of discursive practices, some of which this discussion seeks to identify and analyze. Although the *post* of *postcolonial* is sometimes read merely as a temporal marker separating a period of colonial rule from the time after it, many theorists have pointed to the cultural and historical differences that are concealed by such a monolithic term, and to the fact that in countries with colonial histories (such as North America, South Africa, India, Australia), the consequences of colonial rule are played out in contemporary struggles over power and especially over land (McClintock 9–14; Dirlik 503–4; Ghandi 1–5). Accordingly, my use of the term *postcolonial* recognizes the shifting and uncertain significances that attend references to the imperial project.

A feature common in newly independent states after colonialism is what Leela Ghandi terms "postcolonial amnesia" (4), in which painful events of the colonial period are "forgotten." After Australia achieved nationhood in 1901, for example, there followed what the anthropologist W. E. H. Stanner described in 1968 as "a cult of forgetfulness practised on a national scale" (25), an eloquent silence regarding Aborigines and the violence and dispossession that they endured following white settlement. Most Australian children's texts produced in the first few decades of the twentieth century omit Aborigines from accounts of Australian history or reconfigure historical events to produce stories of white heroism and black savagery, thus positioning child readers to see themselves as citizens of a white Australia and the inheritors of a tradition of pioneer endeavor. Such strategies seek to elide aspects of the past in order to produce a new national identity. But the past is not so easily forgotten, especially by peoples formerly colonized. For as Edward Said notes, interpretations of the present frequently involve the rereading of the past in an attempt to discover "whether the past really is past, over and concluded, or whether it continues, albeit in different forms" (*Culture and Imperialism* 1). The colonial past is variously rehearsed, reinscribed, and contested in postcolonial children's texts, and it is increasingly a site of tension, producing different and conflicting significances. There are two reasons for this: first, the influence of subaltern writing, which seeks to recover the voices of colonized people and tell their stories; and, second, the fact that strategies of silence and forgetting merely repress colonial memories, the recovery of which is frequently painful and confrontational.

Tropes of journeying and travel are prominent in postcolonial texts, many of which rehearse, reexamine, and parody the historical journeys of colonialism. In this discussion I consider two British texts: Roald Dahl's *Charlie and the Chocolate Factory* (first published in 1964) and Penelope Lively's *The House in Norham Gardens* (1974), books as far apart from each other as can be imagined but that thematize aspects of the relations between empire and colonies. As instances of "the Empire writing back," I have selected two Australian texts, Pat Lowe and Jimmy Pike's *Jimmy and Pat Meet the Queen* (1997) and Tohby Riddle's *Royal Guest* (1993), and a New Zealand text, Paula Boock's *Sasscat* (1994). In all five texts, characters undertake journeys to or from Britain: the Oompa-Loompas, in *Charlie and the Chocolate Factory*, travel from Loompaland to the imperial center, located in Willy Wonka's chocolate factory; in *The House in Norham Gardens*, fourteen-year-old Clare becomes obsessed by the journey of her anthropologist great-grandfather to New Guinea in 1905. Both *Jimmy and Pat Meet the Queen* and *The Royal Guest* focus on visits by Queen Elizabeth to Australia, and in *Sasscat*, Win, a young New Zealander, travels to London, and her sister, Sass, dreams of becoming an astronaut. These journeys rework the themes of place and displacement that are so common in postcolonial literatures (see Ashcroft, Griffiths, and Tiffin 9), but the ideologies of the five texts are far from uniform. For although *postcolonialism* might seem to be invested with notions of progressivism and transition to a brave new world, in fact postcolonial texts display the heterogeneity of postcolonial cultures, with their traces of colonialism, their mix of complicitness with and resistance to colonial ideologies (Hodge and Mishra xi–xii), and their spasmodic irruptions of neocolonialism.

As Bob Dixon pointed out in his groundbreaking work *Catching Them Young* (1977), *Charlie and the Chocolate Factory* works as "a paradigm of imperialism" (110), with Willy Wonka exercising imperial power over the colonized Oompa-Loompas.[2] Dixon is quite correct to see *Charlie and the Chocolate Factory* as adhering to the ideologies of nineteenth-century novels of colonial adventure, but there are important distinctions to be made: Dahl wrote *Charlie* in the 1960s, well after the disintegration of the British Empire; and though the heroes of Haggard, Marryat, and Henty travel from Britain to the strange and barbaric lands "out there" in the empire and back again to the safety of Britain, the Oompa-Loompas are brought from their home in Loompaland to work in Willy Wonka's chocolate factory. Dahl's version of the journey thus involves the displacement of colonized people and their mass transportation to the imperial center, to be commodified as cheap labor. Indeed, the Oompa-Loompas signify two kinds of displacement: they displace the local workforce sacked by Willy Wonka, and they themselves are displaced from Loompaland. Dahl sidesteps the first kind of displacement by treating workers as mere cogs in Willy Wonka's machine, not as people and even less as individuals. And the Oompa-Loompas' displacement from their homeland is elided through Dahl's representation of Loompaland, in whose jungles lurk dangerous creatures such as hornswogglers, snozzwangers, and whangdoodles, and where the Oompa-Loompas can find nothing but green caterpillars to eat. In this way, Dahl constructs the home of the colonized as a place characterized by absence and poverty (specifically of cacao beans), so that the Oompa-Loompas' voyage to Willy Wonka's factory, smuggled in "large packing cases with holes in them" (68), is an insignificant price to pay for the privilege of working for Willy Wonka and of being supplied with cacao beans and alcoholic beverages such as butterscotch and buttergin.

Dahl's treatment of the Oompa-Loompas exactly conforms with Edward Said's description of the ways in which the West has rationalized colonial processes with claims that colonized people were "provided with order and a kind of stability that they haven't been able . . . to provide for themselves" (*Culture* 23). Within this fiction of Western benevolence and generosity, colonized peoples are represented as recipients of largesse; homogenized and robbed of individuality, they exist as a discursive figure, "them" as distinct from "us," whose duty it is to appreciate the magnanimity with which they have been treated. Such a "leap to essences and generalizations" (*Culture* 24) effectively elides the variety and specificity of colonial experience, suppressing, for example, the histories of colonized peoples sold to the slave trade or exploited as cheap labor in various parts of the British Empire. Willy Wonka's Oompa-Loompas are effectively enslaved, but through the mediating figure of Willy Wonka, Dahl positions children to read their enslavement as reward and privilege.

This strategy can be seen most clearly in the episode in which Willy Wonka relates the story of his discovery and "liberation" of the Oompa-Loompas. The children and adults who are taken on their tour of the factory first see the Oompa-Loompas from a distance, in a narrator-focalized sequence. The following exchange serves as a transition to Willy Wonka's first-person narrative:

> "Oompa-Loompas!" everyone said at once. "*Oompa-Loompas!*"
> "Imported direct from Loompaland," said Mr Wonka proudly.
> "There's no such place," said Mrs Salt.
> "Excuse me, dear lady, but . . ."
> "*Mr Wonka*," cried Mrs Salt. "I'm a teacher of geography . . ."

"Then you'll know all about it," said Mr Wonka. "And oh, what a terrible country it is. . . ."

(66)

Whereas Mrs Salt is incontrovertibly an adult, Willy Wonka, an "extraordinary little man" (57), his face "alight with fun and laughter" (57), is attributed with qualities intended to persuade child readers that he is one of them, aligned with them against adults (and specifically teachers) such as Mrs Salt. The contrast between Mrs Salt and Willy Wonka is an epistemological one as well: whereas Mrs Salt knows theory (the "facts" of geography), Willy Wonka's knowledge is based on his practical experience of Loompaland. Through these strategies, Willy Wonka is established as a figure who speaks authoritatively to implied child readers about the Oompa-Loompas and their land.

Wonka's depiction of the Oompa-Loompas (66–68) proposes a series of oppositions between himself (as ideal and idealized imperialist) and his colonized workforce. Wonka is, first of all, *knowing*, whereas even the leader of the tribe of Oompa-Loompas is unable to understand anything beyond his physical symptoms of hunger. Contrasting values attach to place: Wonka's pride in the glories of his factory, compared with the Oompa-Loompas' readiness to leave their homeland. Wonka is an adult, the Oompa-Loompas perpetual children; Wonka an amused observer, the Oompa-Loompas objects of his colonizing gaze. Above all, the Oompa-Loompas are promoted to child readers as ideals of how colonized peoples should behave toward their imperial lords: they are satisfied, hardworking, and grateful; moreover, they never forget their colonial place, wearing the clothing that marks them as primitives: "They still wear the same kind of clothes they wore in the jungle. They insist upon that" (68). Racialized and objectified as Others, the Oompa-Loompas are thus distinguished from the book's implied readers, who are positioned as "normal" subjects, citizens whose clothing and way of life mark them as being *at home* in Britain in a way the Oompa-Loompas are not. Dahl's representation of colonized peoples suggests, by inference, that native peoples who turn against imperial rule, or who reject the subservience modeled by the Oompa-Loompas, contravene a model of social and imperial interactions naturalized as correct and appropriate. *Charlie and the Chocolate Factory*, produced in the decade following a dramatic increase in the migration of West Indian, African, and Asian people to Britain, and six years after the anti-black riots in Notting Hill and Nottingham, thus proposes a social and economic structure that treats colonial workers as unskilled and poorly paid factory fodder.

In its promotion of colonialism, its homogenization of the colonized, and its strategies of Othering, *Charlie and the Chocolate Factory* harks back to texts of the nineteenth century; in contrast, Penelope Lively's *House in Norham Gardens* displays many of the tensions and uncertainties of postcolonialism, within a complex and subtle narrative. Both texts play with what Mary Louise Pratt refers to as the "contact zone," the "space of colonial encounters" (6) where colonizers and those colonized meet and negotiate relations of power and influence. *Charlie and the Chocolate Factory* promotes the idea that colonial hierarchies are maintained "at home"—that is, in Willy Wonka's factory—just as they were "out there" in Loompaland. *The House at Norham Gardens*, in contrast, sets one contact zone against another through its shifts in time and place, between 1970s Britain and colonial New Guinea. Clare Mayfield, the protagonist of the novel, lives with her two great-aunts in an Oxford house that constitutes a time capsule of imperialism, for it is filled with the objects and records of Clare's great-grandfather, an anthropologist who "went to queer places and brought things back" (21). Clare discovers in the attic a tamburan, a carved shield from New Guinea, and becomes absorbed by the historical and cultural significances of this object, finally donating it to the Natural History Museum, where it is incorporated into the collection named after her great-grandfather. The tamburan is the central symbol within the novel's exploration of cultural and historical difference, a strand of meaning that intersects with two others: Clare's own sense of becoming an adult who is both like and unlike her fourteen-year-old self, and themes of aging, physical change, and death, centered on "the aunts."

Within its contrapuntal organization, *The House in Norham Gardens* circles around symbols and ideas connected with space and time. The house itself, a nineteen-room Victorian marooned among new buildings and old buildings converted into flats, is remote from modernity, since Clare's aunts live quietly in their library, reading and observing; the house is replete with the past in the form of old photographs, china, books and a lavatory "in brown mahogany with the bowl encircled in purple flowers and a cistern called 'The Great Niagara'" (18). While the narrative chronologically follows a few months (from winter to spring) in Clare's life, a series of flashbacks at the beginning of each chapter traces the process of colonization in the New Guinea village from which the tamburan originates: the coming of Europeans to the village in 1905, the destabilization of an ancient culture, the destruction of forests, the loss of cultural identity, the tribe's journey to modernity. Or, rather, this is how the narrative represents colonization, and the *how* of Lively's representation discloses the limitations of the epistemology on which it relies.

Whereas Dahl's treatment of the Oompa-Loompas trumpets the inferiority of the colonized, Lively's depiction of the New Guinea tribe is tinged with regret and nostalgia, as can be seen in the first of the novel's descriptions of the valley:

> There is an island. At the heart of the island there is a valley. In the valley, among blue mountains, a man kneels before a piece of wood. He paints on it—sometimes with a fibre brush, sometimes

with his finger. The man himself is painted: bright dyes—red, yellow, black—on brown skin. . . . The year is 1900: in England Victoria is queen. The man is remote from England in distance by half the circumference of the world: in understanding, by five thousand years.

(7)

The island, the valley, the mountains, the kneeling man, are objects of a Eurocentric gaze that describes and evaluates them in relation to their remoteness from England. The narrative itself, implying the existence of a knowing observer, inscribes the valley, and the painted man, as vulnerable to the encroachment of modernity. At the same time, the mobilization of a temporal contrast ("The man is remote from England . . . by five thousand years") enacts a vast and unbridgeable gap between the narrator and the painted man. In its authoritativeness, its knowingness, its emphasis on difference, this passage mobilizes the discursive strategies of Orientalism, which, in Said's terms, defines itself through "the whole complex series of knowledgeable manipulations" (*Orientalism* 40) through which it orders the study of the Orient. In Lively's descriptions of the village, the New Guinea tribesmen are represented, in their pre-colonized state, as living in a coherent and ordered society—they "celebrate the mystery of life with ritual" (37). But their culture is defined and fixed through its difference. They have "known no influences, learned no skills" (37)—that is, they have known no influences and learned no skills defined as such by the narrator, whose knowledge and ideological stance are naturalized as normative.

The system of knowledge invoked here is that of anthropology—more specifically, the model of social anthropology prominent in 1974, when *The House in Norham Gardens* was published. The following comments by the Australian anthropologist Gillian Cowlishaw describe how anthropology was mobilized in Australia to "manage" what was commonly called "the Aboriginal problem," but they refer more broadly to the uses to which it was put in former colonies: "From its establishment as a university based discipline there was an underlying, unstated moral task associated with studies of [indigenous] culture. This was that anthropology would supply expert knowledge about that culture that would be used to develop appropriate policy. . . ." (22). In exactly the same way, Lively's description of the New Guinea tribe constructs an "expert knowledge" of what is in the best interests of the tribe. Here is the final episode in the story of the tribe's colonization:

Houses are built for the tribe, and roads. They learn how to drive cars, use telephones, tin-openers, matches and screwdrivers. They are given laws that they must obey: they are not to kill one another and they must pay their taxes. They listen to the radio and they make no more tamburans, but their nights are rich with dreams. The children of the tribe learn how to read and write: they sit at wooden desks with their heads bent low over sheets of paper, and make marks on the paper. One day, they will discover again the need for tamburans, and they will make a new kind of tamburan for themselves, and for their children, and their children's children.

(165)

The underlying assumptions of this passage are that Western laws will prevent bloodshed ("they are not to kill one another") and that the members of the tribe will embrace the icons of the Western lifestyle (houses, cars, telephones, tin-openers). If their entry into modernity precludes the making of tamburans, the gift of literacy will eventually enable the children of the tribe to "make a new kind of tamburan," but this will be possible only because of their deployment of Western systems of knowledge.

This story of colonization intersects with a series of dreams in which Clare observes the tribesmen seeking the return of their tamburan. As her dreams increase in urgency and intensity, they symbolize Clare's own groping after subjectivity; more important for this discussion, they expose the error of her great-grandfather in taking the tamburan from the tribesmen, who had at first believed that their European visitors were tribal ancestors. Significantly, Clare seeks a solution through an appeal to anthropological knowledge. Her Ugandan friend John Sempebwa is established within the text as an authority on native peoples: he is himself, he says, a "detribalized African" (75); moreover, he is a student of anthropology. When he tells Clare that the New Guinea tribes "stop making tamburans ... as soon as they've jumped into the twentieth century. ... They seem to forget how, or why they did it" (99), the principle of cultural discontinuity is promoted: that colonialism has effected a decisive split from the traditional culture of the painted man who created the tamburan. Clare's conclusion that "If it can't be where it belongs, then a museum is the best place" (169) implies that there is no longer any "where," so that the museum, and the disciplinary formations of anthropology, become custodians of the object and its cultural meanings.

Lively's representation of the New Guinea tribe is, of course, a far more progressive representation of colonial relations than that encoded in *Charlie and the Chocolate Factory*. But twenty-five years after its publication, its faultlines are clearly visible. The New Guinea tribesmen (and the figures of Clare's dreams are, true to the phallocentric traditions of anthropology, always male) are consigned to the past of primitivism; the sense of loss and regret that permeates Lively's depiction of the tribe enacts the meaning, implied throughout the novel, that the painted man represents the true and authentic culture of the tribe, a culture preserved only through anthropological knowledge, and specifically by museums. In Lively's descriptions of the colonization of the tribe, the New Guineans are attributed no agency, no capacity for reflexivity or adaptability, but wait passively for the return of the ancestors. Gillian Cowlishaw's summary of anthropological models of the 1960s and 1970s is strikingly close to the mood and tone that permeate Lively's depiction of the tribe: "The metaphor of destruction became intrenched, fixing the complex, ongoing events of colonisation into a one way process of collapse to which the appropriate response is passive sorrow" (25). The novel is thus caught between its contestation of the imperial past (exemplified by Clare's great-grandfather) and its privileging of modernity as a dynamic, protean, complex state that, paradoxically, *needs* primitivism as its opposite term, objectified as the embodiment of stillness, simplicity, and fixedness. *The House in Norham Gardens* concludes with Clare looking intently at her aged and beloved aunts and realizing that what she is doing is "learning them by heart," memorizing them against the time when they are dead. For the New Guinea tribesmen, on the other hand, there are dreams, but no memories; there is a dim consciousness of tradition and a nostalgia for it, but the culture is incapable of adapting and transforming itself.

In *Jimmy and Pat Meet the Queen*, written by Pat Lowe and illustrated by Jimmy Pike, colonization does not effect a rift of memory; instead, traditional knowledge, tested against the land of its production, constitutes a proof of tribal identity in contemporary Australia. Jimmy is "a Walmajarri man," from the Great Sandy Desert in Western Australia; Pat, his wife, "comes from England." The conjunction of histories and traditions exemplified in the partnership of Jimmy and Pat allows for broad comedy based on contrasted modes of speaking and thinking, but *Jimmy and Pat* is a hybrid text in other respects as well. It is at once a tract on land ownership in Australia and an illustrated book; its implied readers constitute a combination of older children, adolescents, and adults; its narrative combines the standard English of Pat with the Creole used by Jimmy in conversational exchanges; its illustrations draw on traditions of Aboriginal art but depict aspects of contemporary life. In these ways it exemplifies "transculturation," the term used by Pratt to describe how colonized and formerly colonized people engage in negotiations between their own culture and that of their colonizers (6).

As I've noted, an important line of resistance to earlier literary and cultural studies of colonialism is embodied in subaltern studies, described by Leela Ghandi as "an attempt to allow the 'people' finally to speak . . . and, in so doing, to speak for, or to sound the muted voices of, the truly oppressed" (2). *Jimmy and Pat Meet the Queen* alludes to the dispossession experienced by Aboriginal people, but its insouciance and subversive wit are anything but muted. On learning that the land of his people is regarded by kartiya (white) law as Vacant Crown Land, Jimmy invites the queen to prove her ownership by one concrete and decisive test: that she knows where to find water in "her" desert. The queen agrees to travel to Walmajarri country, and after a long search she concludes that she is indeed unable to locate any waterholes and that the land belongs to "the Walmajarri mob" (29).

In *The House in Norham Gardens*, tribal knowledge and traditions are represented as failing to survive colonization, so that they can be preserved only within systems of Western knowledge; in *Jimmy and Pat*, in contrast, Western epistemologies are pitted against the ancient and continuous traditions of the Walmajarri, whose knowledge is based on the land itself and on ritual journeys undertaken over many thousands of years. The nostalgia that informs Lively's depiction of the New Guinea tribe derives from an Orientalist emphasis on the primitive nature of their culture, which is quarantined in a past that is discontinuous with modernity. The Aboriginal culture promoted in *Jimmy and Pat* combines traditional beliefs and knowledge with elements of contemporary Western culture: Jimmy and Pat's letter asserting Walmajarri ownership of the land makes the sly suggestion that the queen "may be glad to get away from [her] family for a while" (9); the Walmajarri people follow their traditional journey in a Suzuki and a Toyota. This hybridity is a marker of a set of cultural forms at once fully Aboriginal and selectively modern.

Jimmy and Pat displaces colonial hierarchies through its juxtaposition of standard and Aboriginal English and its mobilization of intertextual references. Here, the queen meets Jimmy and Pat at their desert camp:

> Then a door in the [helicopter] opened, and out stepped the Queen of England.
>
> Jimmy and Pat walked forward to greet her. Jimmy held out his hand while Pat tried to do a curtesy in her King Gees.
>
> "Hello old woman," said Jimmy, and Pat gave him a hard nudge in the ribs.
>
> The Queen took Jimmy's hand. "How do you do?" she said, with her gracious smile.
>
> "Do what?" Jimmy asked Pat.
>
> "She means how are you going," Pat explained, on tenterhooks in case either of them said the wrong thing.
>
> Jimmy turned back to the Queen. "I'm right," he said.
>
> (12)

For Australian readers, this episode evokes the newsreels, photographs, news reports, and verbal commentaries that have always surrounded royal visits to this country. In particular, it recalls the iconic moments when the queen emerges from car, plane or train, to be greeted by her Australian subjects. Usually, such moments are pictured within the broader context of a watching crowd or a line of dignitaries awaiting their turn to be blessed by the royal presence; here, the queen walks alone into the desert, so that the book's implied readers are interpellated as the observers of a scene at once familiar and strange. The queen enacts the rituals of royal visits through the "gracious smile" that strategically ignores Jimmy's "Hello old woman" and through the greeting "How do you do?," but in taking the final "do" as a transitive verb, and responding "Do what?," Jimmy subverts the queen's reliance on a formulaic phrase intended to maintain social hierarchies and insists on locating speech within a context of interpersonal relations.

Jimmy Pike's illustration of the camp where the trio sleep deploys an aerial perspective. For all its apparent artlessness, this picture subverts hierarchies of power and race through its positioning of the queen, in her swag,[3] placed alongside the figures of Jimmy and Pat in their shared swag, and against the white ground of the page. If the queen is at the same level as Jimmy and Pat within a democracy of desert life, she is allowed a signifier of royalty in the tiara that is placed neatly by her, but this is not the only sign that distinguishes her from her companions: her two corgis sleep near her, while Jimmy and Pat's hunting dog sleeps at Jimmy's feet; and her high-heeled shoes, so inappropriate to desert use, invite comparison with the serviceable footwear of Jimmy and Pat. Pike's deployment of a limited number of forms and participants is a feature common in traditional art, which "[uses] a minimalist system of classification to establish a complex network of connections that in Western traditions is associated with metaphor" (Hodge and Mishra 96). In this picture, the key elements are the human and animal participants, seen within a set of relations that displace Western notions of social status. The figure of the queen is smaller than those of Jimmy and Pat, suggesting that despite her tiara she is young in the ways of the desert and in need of the guidance of her companions.

When, finally, the moment of testing comes, and the queen must identify the waterholes that will prove whether she is the owner of the land, the broad humor of the following exchange relies on slippages and contrasts between registers:

> The Queen put her lorgnette up to her eyes and gazed out over the country, but for the life of her she couldn't see any water.
> "There *are* no waterholes!" she declared.
> "Bullshit!" said Jimmy, and Pat grimaced into the bushes. "There's a waterhole that way, and another waterhole that way, and another waterhole right there!" He flung out his arm in different directions as he spoke.
> "And cowpoo to you too!" said the Queen. "There's not a drop of water to be seen! This is a desert!"
> "Well, I'll show you!" said Jimmy.
>
> (27)

The queen's declarations "There *are* no waterholes!" and "This is a desert" insist on the primacy of Western (and queenly) knowledge, but her invention of "And cowpoo to you too," in response to Jimmy's "Bullshit!" traces a shift from "high English" to a demotic register, enacting a destabilization of hierarchies.[4] Following the group's collective action of digging in the region of a waterhole, her response to the discovery of water is a thoroughly colloquial one: "'Well, I'll be buggered!' said the Queen" (29).[5]

The quest for water, with its associated competition between the queen and the Walmajarri people, can be understood within *schemata* of Western folk literature; but the outcome of the quest, and the narrative's validation of Walmajarri ownership of the land, are loaded with ironies that undercut notions of an ending in which all live "happily ever after." This is signaled on the inside front cover of the book, where conventional statements concerning the truth or otherwise of narratives are parodied in the following words: "All the people and places in this book are real. The story is true, although most of it hasn't happened yet." With considerable lightness of touch, Lowe here alludes to the historical and political contexts to which the narrative relates: the stories of dispossession and appropriation that it evokes and the long struggle by indigenous Australians for recognition as the original owners of the land and for continuing rights to it. Most of all, *Jimmy and Pat Meet the Queen* insists on the capacity of Aboriginal culture to transform its repertoire of textual and artistic forms. This is a far cry from Lively's representation of an indigenous culture reliant for its preservation on Western systems of knowledge.

Tohby Riddle's *The Royal Guest* also tells the story of a visit by Queen Elizabeth to Australia, but this text discloses another set of postcolonial significances that refer to Australia's history as a settler colony. Colonial distinctions between white settlers and Aborigines relied on hierarchies of value that placed Aboriginal people at the lower end of the Chain of Being and, following Darwin's *Origin of Species*, as a race locked into an early stage of human evolution. But distinctions of a different sort always attended comparisons between British people who settled in Australia and who gradually came to see themselves as "Australians," and inhabitants of the imperial center. Some of these distinctions manifest themselves in comparisons between the culture and refinement of Britain and a rough-and-ready Australian culture; others insist on the vitality and health of the New World, compared with an effete and exhausted Old World. Riddle's story, which comprises an account of "the last visit of the Queen," when "times were tough" and "people were wondering if the costs of such a visit could be managed," alludes to these comparisons and dismantles them.

The queen in *The Royal Guest* is parodically represented as a collection of features: she wears a sensible blue coat, serviceable brown shoes, white gloves, and a benign expression, and she carries a handbag. Riddle's narrative, unfolded in a deadpan style, tells how "a Mrs. Jones of Padstow" offers to billet the queen during her visit to Sydney: "She had plenty of room and a comfortable inflatable mattress that the Queen was welcome to. She need only bring her sleeping bag." The *faux-naïve* quality of Riddle's text is replicated in the accompanying illustration, which shows the figure of Mrs. Jones performing a deictic function by pointing to her house, which is defined by the details of its exterior as a working-class home of the 1950s: its neat, bungalow-type style, the featured cactus in a pot near the door, the decorative butterfly under the house number, the diamond-shaped panes of glass set in the front door, and the metal gate behind which Mrs. Jones stands.

In the narrative that follows, the queen, carrying her rolled-up sleeping bag, arrives by plane and proceeds to the bus stop, where she catches the bus to Padstow, "go[ing] over her speeches to the nation in her head" during the trip. She spends the evening playing cards with Mrs. Jones and her friend; on the following day, after some moments of anxiety occasioned by the illness of Mrs. Jones's cat, the queen gives a public address before returning by train to Mrs. Jones's home. She is awoken the next morning by "the sound of cartoons on the television," but the Jones children are sent outside to play so as not to disturb her. To thank Mrs. Jones for her hospitality, the queen gives her one of her old crowns, and the narrative concludes with the queen continuing the royal tour to Melbourne, "where she would be staying with the Bradley family of Footscray," another working-class suburb. The comedy of *The Royal Guest* derives from the incongruities that it implies, particularly those between the queen's wealth, fame, and social class and her relocation within the habitus of working-class life. Catching a bus to Padstow, and seated behind a small boy licking an ice cream and in front of a sleeping elderly man, the queen is represented as neither more nor less than an elderly woman, connected to the other participants in the illustration by their common use of bus travel, in which social status is subordinated to the physical organization of the public transport system. Similarly, the queen is incongruously incorporated into the Jones household, whose physical and social interactions are wildly different from those customarily associated with royal life. Thus, Mrs. Jones, her friend, and the queen sit cozily around the kitchen table playing cards; the queen is obliged to hold the family's sick cat on her knee as Mrs. Jones takes her to meet the prime minister; and the Jones children perch on the end of the queen's inflatable mattress as they watch their morning cartoons.

In different but related ways, *Jimmy and Pat Meet the Queen* and *The Royal Guest* construct ironic reversals of other journeys, colonial and postcolonial. In *Jimmy and Pat*, the queen is thrust into a landscape and culture that are alien to her and that expose the shallowness of her knowledge in comparison with the deep knowledge of the "Walmajarri mob"; shadowing the queen's displacement are the colonial stories in which Aboriginal people were removed from their lands and forced to live in alien country. *The Royal Guest* builds its understated comedy out of the queen's insertion into the frugal world of the Jones family, but through his deployment of 1950s settings, Riddle collapses two journeys: the triumphant progress of the young queen throughout Australia in 1954, following her coronation, and "the last visit of the Queen," when "times were tough." The scenes of adulation that surrounded the queen in 1954 thus shadow the surreal comedy of her visit to Padstow, plotting the social change that has seen a move toward republicanism and away from traditional associations with Britain. Nevertheless, the failure of Australians to approve the 1999 referendum on whether Australia would become a republic with an Australian head of state exemplifies the extent to which the colonial past signifies values such as "safety" and "reliability" at a time of rapid social change.

Most of all, both books insist on the radical instability of the sign "queen" in contemporary Australia. In *Jimmy and Pat*, the queen is associated with the legal category "Vacant Crown Land," a phrase that reflects Australia's dependence on the British legal system. In Jimmy's terms, the land is not vacant (being occupied by the Walmajarri people), and the idea that it belongs to the queen is patently silly in the face of her inability to locate waterholes, so that the sign "queen" signifies powerful tensions between colonial history and Aboriginal traditions. In both *Jimmy and Pat* and *The Royal Guest*, the queen is relocated in settings devoid of signifiers of royalty, power, and social class, except for the tiara that she discards for her desert journey and the "old crown" that she gives Mrs. Jones. Without such signifiers, she becomes merely a person—a somewhat inept tourist in *Jimmy and Pat* and, in *The Royal Guest*, a temporary member of the Jones family. And this separation of the sign "queen" from signifiers relating to Australia's historical links with Britain argues for a redefinition both of "queen" and of "Australia." Whereas Dahl's Oompa-Loompas are figures of fun within a schema that locates them at the margins of British culture, the Queen is displaced from the metropolitan center and reconstrued as a figure marginal to Australian and Aboriginal cultures.

Paula Boock's *Sasscat* thematizes a journey from New Zealand to Britain that involves another form of postcolonial displacement. Sass and Win Abbott have always preferred to believe that they are adopted; their parents Madge and Pete, whom they call "the Pets," seem to them to be so utterly ordinary, so devoid of sophistication and good taste, that the girls have invented for themselves elaborate histories to account for their sense of having been "cruelly planted in a low income, low IQ family in the backblocks of New Zealand" (8). In fact, Win turns out to have been adopted as an infant, whereas Sass finds, to her consternation, that she is the natural daughter of "the Pets." Accordingly, Win journeys to London to search for her mother, while Sass remains at home through her summer holidays, which are a time of waiting: for Win to return, for the results of her School Certificate examination, for her developing sense of a subjectivity that does not depend on her relationship with Win. These months of apparent hiatus,

COLONIALISM/POSTCOLONIALISM

like the similar period during which Clare dreams of New Guinea tribesmen in *The House in Norham Gardens*, involve a sequence of significant moments when through empathy, self-assertion, and reflection Sass becomes an active subject in her world.

The narrative see-saw between Sass and Win, signaled through the letters and stories they exchange, enacts a set of comparisons and contrasts between New Zealand and Britain, Arawa (where Sass lives) and London, the Abbotts and the Lowells, Win's "other" family. Sass's sense of imprisonment with "the Pets" is metonymic of her imprisonment within a New Zealand that seems parochial, backward, remote from the metropolitan center. Conversely, Win's flight to discover her mother is that most postcolonial of quests, a search for origins and beginnings that promises her a sense of her own reality. In the following excerpts, Win writes of her discovery of her mother, and Sass responds:

> They [the Lowells] live in Chelsea—it's very posh there. All I know is that Edward works in 'the City'—that's finance, and the twins go to public (that's private) school. Eleanor said of course you understand I was very young and it seemed the Right Thing to Do. . . . I love the name Lowell—don't you think it's much more literary than Abbott? Maybe it could be my pen name. . . . Anyway, I'll write more about the E-Lowells after tomorrow. You can pass this on to the Pets if you like—it saves me writing twice.
>
> (42)

> I am thrilled your mother is infinitely superior to all other mothers you've endured in the past. . . . Lowell is indeed a far more literary, aristocratic and intelligent, cultured, English, snooty bloody polo-playing surname than the lowly Abbott you've suffered for the past eighteen years. It is of course the name of nobody remotely related to you, but then neither is Abbott . . . Sasha Catriona Abbott (another pretentiously named peasant from the colonies.)
>
> (46)

Win's description of the Lowells discloses a set of implied contrasts with her New Zealand family: their "posh" Chelsea setting against the Abbotts' humble home in Arawa; their wealth and privilege against Madge and Pete's occupations (respectively, cleaner and bus driver); the "literariness" that Win projects onto the name "Lowell," against the "appalling Woolworths paintings" (13) with which Madge and Pete decorate their home. And, of course, this cluster of contrasts constitutes part of the larger contrast between Britain as metropolitan center and New Zealand as colonial outpost. Sass's response ironically accords with Win's view but dismantles it through her insistence on the slipperiness of signifiers. Thus, the "poshness" that Win admires is re-visioned by Sass, who sees "Lowell" as a "snooty, bloody polo-playing surname." And Sass's treatment of the signifier "mother," which carries the colonial associations of "mother England" as well as of Win's discovery of her birth mother, insists on Madge's role as adoptive mother (guiltily sidestepped by Win) and, most tellingly, on Win's appropriation of a name (that of her birth mother's husband) to which she has no connection. Sass's self-description as "another pretentiously named peasant from the colonies" is a characteristically postcolonial ploy, simultaneously acknowledging the marginality of the colonial and mocking the center's pretensions. This exchange dismantles the colonial idea that self-realization can be achieved through a return to the ancestral certainty of Britain; moreover, Sass's subversive reading of the name Lowell undermines the very notion of "center" and "margins."

At the end of the novel, Win returns to Arawa, though temporarily, since she has obtained employment in London (ironically, through an old friend of Pete's). To Sass's question concerning which name she will use (Abbott or Lowell), Win responds as follows:

> "Abbott," she said, "Abbott, Abbott, Abbott."
> Sass gave a half-smile. "What's wrong with Lowell?"
> "What's wrong with Lowell?" Win repeated. . . . "Lowell means classist, sexist, racist. Lowell means stiff upper lip and hide the illegitimate daughter. Lowell means what a shame about your accent dear, and here's a nice, fat cheque to keep you at a safe, unembarrassing distance. . . . All in all, I think I had a lucky escape."
>
> (115)

Win's revised reading of the name Lowell accords with Sass's earlier interpretation and so privileges the latter's view from the margins. But whereas previously the comparisons between center and margins (focused on the opposition of Lowell to Abbott) was incorporated into larger oppositions between England and New Zealand, Win's decision to return to Britain discloses another possibility—that her return will not constitute a journey "home," to a lost mother, but to a site where Win will develop a subjectivity no longer limited to a choice between opposites. This type of subjectivity involves a mixture and fluidity of elements: that is, Win can be an Abbott, and a New Zealander, at the same time that she lives in London and embarks on a career.

Sass's realization of agency and self-determination involves a revisioning of herself and her world through her interactions with Win, her parents, her new neighbors, Hester and Jonathan, and a local "rich boy," Trent. The closure of the narrative enacts a mix of significances, centered around the moment when Sass receives her School Certificate results, which reassure her that she is intellectually capable of achieving her dream of becoming a scientist and of gaining a place in NASA's space course for young achievers: "There was a small smile appearing at the edges of Sass's mouth. Win grinned. 'I'll come visit you at NASA, promise.' And the whoops that followed had the entire neighbourhood, including Hester, looking skyward" (108). In one sense, the closure of *Sasscat* affords a quite conventional resolution in that a gifted but insecure adolescent learns to value herself, but Sass's projection of herself as an astronaut also constitutes a contemporary version of the postcolonial journey. While her dream of gaining a place at NASA seems to signal the substitution of one set of imperial relationships for another, the idea of space travel symbolizes a definitive escape from the smallness and remoteness of New Zealand, as well as from the fiction that Britain is the true psychological center for post-colonial subjects.

Colonialism is never over and done with, despite Dahl's attempt to persuade his readers that the Oompa-Loompas love the chains that bind them and Lively's nostalgic representation of a people who have lost their culture. There is thus no possibility of "the end of empire," so influential and pervasive are the effects of imperial rule on its former colonies; and children's books will inevitably continue to rehearse and revisit the events of colonization. Most significantly, the indigenous peoples of Britain's former colonies continue to experience the effects of their displacement and of the appropriation of their land, and it is highly likely that subaltern voices will continue to provide child readers with stories formerly suppressed or elided.

Notes

1 Such intersections of race and class were common during the second half of the nineteenth century: "T. H. Huxley compared the East London poor with Polynesian savages, William Booth chose the African pygmy, and William Barry thought that the slums resembled nothing so much as a slave ship" (McClintock 54). When visiting Ireland, Kingsley commented on the chimpanzee-like appearance of the Irish poor: "to see white chimpanzees is dreadful; if they were black, one would not feel it so much, but their skins, except where tanned by exposure, are as white as ours" (McClintock 216). Apes were commonly seen as figures straddling the margins of race and class; blackness "naturally" distinguished black people from white, but a special horror surrounds the figure of the hybrid who is both white and notwhite, enough like "us" to serve as a reminder about how "we" might descend to this level.
2 Dixon points out that the original American edition of 1964 and the first British edition of 1967 depict the Oompa-Loompas as black and as "imported direct from Africa" (112), whereas the revised 1973 edition removes these references.
3 The word *swag* is derived from a British dialectal term and refers to a bundle or roll containing the bedding and personal belongings of a traveler through the bush.
4 *High English* is glossed in *Jimmy and Pat* as "a form of English spoken by kartiya people, using long words and difficult expressions" (30).
5 "I'll be buggered" is a colloquial expression that means "I'll be damned."

Works cited

Ashcroft, Bill, Gareth Griffiths, and Helen Tiffin. *The Empire Writes Back: Theory and Practice in Post-Colonial Literatures.* London: Routledge, 1989.

Boock, Paula. *Sasscat.* Melbourne: Hyland House, 1994.

Bradford, Clare. " 'Providence Designed It for a Settlement': Religious Discourses and Australian Colonial Texts." *Children's Literature Association Quarterly* 24, no. 1 (1999): 4–14.

Cadden, Mike. "Home Is a Matter of Blood, Time, and Genre: Essentialism in Burnett and McKinley." *Ariel* 28, no. 1 (1997): 53–67.

Cowlishaw, Gillian. "Studying Aborigines: Changing Canons in Anthropology and History." In *Power, Knowledge, and Aborigines.* Ed. Bain Attwood and John Arnold. Melbourne: La Trobe University Press, 1992. Pp. 20–31.

Dahl, Roald. *Charlie and the Chocolate Factory.* 1964. Harmondsworth: Penguin, 1973.

Dirlik, Arif. "The Postcolonial Aura: Third World Criticism in the Age of Global Capitalism." In *Dangerous Liaisons: Gender, Nation, and Postcolonial Perspectives.* Ed. Anne McClintock, Aamir Mufti, and Ella Shohat. Minneapolis: University of Minnesota Press, 1997. Pp. 501–28.

Dixon, Bob. *Catching Them Young: Political Ideas in Children's Fiction.* London: Pluto Press, 1977.

Foucault, Michel, "The Order of Discourse." In *Untying the Text: A Post-Structuralist Reader.* Ed. Robert Young. Boston: Routledge & Kegan Paul, 1981. Pp. 52–64.

Ghandi, Leela. *Postcolonial Theory: A Critical Introduction.* Melbourne: Allen & Unwin, 1998.

Hodge, Bob, and Vijay Mishra. *Dark Side of the Dream: Australian Literature and the Postcolonial Mind.* Sydney: Allen & Unwin, 1991.

Hughes, Thomas. *Tom Brown's Schooldays.* 1856. Harmondsworth: Penguin, 1971.

Hulme, Peter. *Colonial Encounters: Europe and the Native Caribbean 1492–1797.* London: Routledge, 1986.

Kingsley, Charles. *The Water-Babies.* 1863. London: J. M. Dent, 1973.

Lively, Penelope. *The House in Norham Gardens.* 1974. Harmondsworth: Penguin, 1986.

Lowe, Pat, and Jimmy Pike. *Jimmy and Pat Meet the Queen.* Broome: Backyard Press, 1997.

McClintock, Anne. *Imperial Leather: Race, Gender, and Sexuality in the Colonial Contest.* New York and London: Routledge, 1995.

Phillips, Jerry. "The Mem Sahib, the Worthy, the Rajah and His Minions: Some Reflections on the Class Politics of *The Secret Garden*." *Lion and the Unicorn* 17, no. 2 (1993): 168–94.

Pratt, Mary Louise. *Imperial Eyes: Travel Writing and Transculturation.* London and New York: Routledge, 1992.

Riddle, Tohby. *The Royal Guest.* Sydney: Hodder & Stoughton, 1993.

Said, Edward. *Culture and Imperialism.* London: Vintage, 1993.

——. *Orientalism.* New York: Vintage, 1979.

Stanner, W. E. H. *After the Dreaming: Black and White Australians—An Anthropologist's View.* Sydney: ABC, 1968.

Part 19

MYTHS, FOLK TALES
AND FAIRY TALES

92

MYTHS, LEGENDS AND FAIRY TALES IN THE LIVES OF CHILDREN

Elizabeth Cook

Source: *The Ordinary and the Fabulous*, Cambridge: Cambridge University Press, 1976, pp. 1–9.

Past and present fashions

Once upon a time, and not so very far away or long ago, there would have been no need to give reasons for reading to children the stories that are commonly known as fairy tales, legends and myths. It is a pity that there is no one name that can be used for all of them. In rough and ready phrasing myths are about gods, legends are about heroes, and fairy tales are about woodcutters and princesses. A rather more respectable definition might run: myths are about the creation of all things, the origin of evil, and the salvation of man's soul; legends and sagas are about the doings of kings and peoples in the period before records were kept; fairy tales, folk tales and fables are about human behaviour in a world of magic, and often become incorporated in legends. Critics take an endless interest in the finer differences between them, but the common reader is more struck by the ways in which they all look rather like each other, and indeed merge into one another, and by the much more obvious differences that separate them from nineteenth-century novels, or stories about a family of children living in the East End in 1966. They are not realistic; they are almost unlocalized in time and space; they are often supernatural or at least fantastic in character; and the human beings in them are not three-dimensional people with complex motives and temperaments. These stories do hold a mirror up to nature, but they do not reflect the world as we perceive it with our senses at the present moment. J. R. R. Tolkien, who has written fairy tales and legends, sees them as works of 'sub-creation': in reading them we live in a Secondary World which is internally consistent and intricate, and is related to the Primary World (in which we all live for most of the time) by the human prerogative of generalization and abstraction. 'The mind that thought of *light*, *heavy*, *grey*, *yellow*, *still*, *swift*, also conceived of magic that would make heavy things light and able to fly, turn grey lead into yellow gold, and the still rock into swift water.'

Until the end of the eighteenth century traditional 'fairy tales' formed, almost by accident, the greater part of storytelling for very young children: uneducated nurses and servants told children the old stories they had been told themselves, because they were the only stories they knew. In the second half of the nineteenth century the work of men like Charles Kingsley and Andrew Lang was diverting the reading of eight- to twelve-year-olds away from drably realistic, moralising Victorian stories into the world of myth and 'faerie'. The Greek and Northern myths had become standard class-room reading by the 1920's. Most educated people of fifty can't remember not knowing who Perseus or Athene or Thor or the Marquis of Carabas were; the stories had 'got into the bloodstream'. Then the impact of the revival lost its force. As more and more convincingly realistic and not at all moral stories for children appeared year by year, the tale of Perseus, as Kingsley told it, looked drab in its turn: it dropped out of the syllabus. Many people of twenty who went to the same schools, and come from similar homes, have never heard of Perseus. Only the other day a student going into a primary school 'on practice' reported to her supervisor, with unfeigned enthusiasm, 'They seem to be doing a story about someone called Odysseus. It's really rather good; have you ever heard of it?'

At the moment there does seem to be a second revival. Since the last war many fresh versions of myths and legends have been made by accomplished and imaginative writers for children; people who love this kind of literature and hope that their children will love it owe a considerable debt to Roger Lancelyn Green, Barbara Leonie Picard and Ian Serraillier. The original work of C. S. Lewis in *The Chronicles of Narnia* and J. R. R. Tolkien in *The Lord of the Rings* shows that the world of 'faerie' is no dead world. The eight- to fourteen-year-olds who are never invited to enter it are, quite literally, deprived children.

Significances and values

The inherent greatness of myth and fairy tale is a poetic greatness. The best stories are like extended lyrical images of unchanging human predicaments and strong, unchanging hopes and fears, loves and hatreds. Very diverse particular references have been attributed to these images by critics, according to training, or temperamental bias, or the fashions of the age in which they lived. In the nineteenth century philologists and folklorists saw them as pre-scientific, primitive descriptions of natural phenomena, of sunrise and sunset, or spring and winter: they supposed that the thunder gods Zeus and Odin were created by men because they did not understand the physical causes of thunder. In this century Freud has seen Zeus and Odin as terrible father figures, who represent sexual jealousies and antagonism between parents and children. Another kind of psychological explanation is given by Jung, for whom myths embody 'race memories' and represent conflicts not between father and son, but between *persona* and *anima* in one human being. Two anthropological theories have left their mark on modern criticism. Jessie Weston sees mythological stories as embroideries upon the actions performed in primitive fertility rituals; Robert Graves sees them as poetic records of the ritual marriage and slaughter of a sacred king, and of traceable historical events, conquests of matriarchal societies by patriarchal invaders, and the subjection of reigning priestesses to invading kings. Even before paganism was extinct, the fathers of the early Christian Church had seen a meaning in its images, interpreting them as Gentile prophecies of the truths of Christianity, and so preparing for the elaborate Christian allegorical readings which were worked out by mediaeval commentators. Hades and Niflheim, it seems, may 'mean' winter, or the womb, or sexual experience, or the dark side of man's soul, or infertility, or foreign conquest, or spiritual torment, or supernatural powers of evil. The testimony of all these witnesses seems to lead only to a paradox: none of them are right separately, and all of them are right collectively (perhaps Jung and the Christian Fathers tell, between them, rather more of the truth than the rest). The fixed point of a myth or a fairy tale lies in its own concrete nature; not in any of the things that it suggests to different readers, and not in its conjectural origins. The human imagination that merged ritual actions into a story, and made the story grow into a particular shape, is certainly as interesting as the imagination that produced the ritual actions. A myth 'is' everything that it has been and everything that it may become; it is like the chestnut-tree vainly asked by the poet to identify itself as one part of its growth:

> O chestnut-tree, great-rooted blossomer,
> Are you the leaf, the blossom or the bole?

There are indeed some fabulous leaves and blossoms that are felt to be artificial; it seems certain that they never grew out of the bole from which the living branches grew. This certainty is aesthetic, not historical. It does not matter if the branches grew into strange curves and contortions, instead of growing straight, as long as they are unmistakeably alive now. Beautiful and evocative stories may quite well be the product of unconscious misunderstanding and deliberate alteration.

A reader who takes his eyes off the story that is in front of him, and looks for something else behind it, will eventually see nothing but the theories he would have held whether he had read the story or not. To a reader who is attending to stories as they are, and above all to a child hearing them for the first time, Hades 'means' anything and everything he knows that can be described by the words *dark, cold, misty, formless.*

The human experience brought to mind by myth and fairy tale extends beyond the situations described by psychologists and anthropologists. It is conscious as well as unconscious, and civilised as well as primitive. In the story of Odysseus is contained both the love of home and a simultaneous love and fear of adventure and the unknown. Perseus and Beowulf and Jack the Giant Killer fight with dragons and monsters, and their battles remind us of any struggle against hostile circumstance—it is a great mistake to feel sorry for the dragon, as some adult readers do if they have not been brought up on fairy tales. The tasks imposed upon Heracles and upon Elisa in *The Wild Swans* recall any test of endurance and alter our understanding of it. The Arthurian quests and the search of the gardener's sons for the Golden Bird suggest any pursuit of an unattainable treasure. Theseus and innumerable tailors' and woodcutters' sons are obscure and ambitious young men with no apparent chance of realizing their ambitions. The Loathly Lady, the Frog Prince and the prince in *Beauty and the Beast* are creatures who are both fair and foul and remind us of any people or things that awaken love and hatred at one and the same time; and it may not be accidental that the theme of the breaking of a spell that has turned fair into foul is nearly always linked with the theme of the keeping of promises. The Secondary World of myth and fairy tale is a world of fighting, of sudden reverses of fortune, of promises kept and broken, of commands obeyed and disobeyed, of wanderings and quests, of testing and judgement, gratitude and ingratitude, and light and darkness. It is clearly impressed with patterns that anyone can trace more uncertainly in his own experience of the primary world. The realistic, localized story of Mrs Hodgson-Burnett's *The Secret Garden* shows a child what it is like for one little girl, very different from himself, to feel afraid: the story of *Beowulf* shows him fear in itself.

Childhood reading of symbolic and fantastic tales contributes something irreplaceable to any later experience of literature. It is not so much a matter of recognizing the more obscure classical references in *Paradise Lost* as of accepting a whole mode of expression as both natural and serious. The realistic novel and play is, after all, a very recent part of our European inheritance. The whole world of epic, romance and allegory is open to a reader who has always taken fantasy for granted, and the way into it may be hard for one who never heard fairy tales as a child. An obvious route leads from the fairy tales of Grimm, and the *Chronicles of Narnia*, through the Northern myths and the Arthurian stories to Tolkien's *The Hobbit* and *The Lord of the Rings* and thence to *The Faerie Queene.*

There are advantages in knowing who's who and what happens in Greek and Northern myths and legends, if one is to be free to appreciate what individual writers have done with them; and because of their poetic fertility these stories have engendered countless original works of art, which give new motivation to the characters, or show new philosophical significance in the shape of the narrative, or create a new mood through the landscape against which the characters move—the 'tales twice told' without any tediousness range from Chaucer's *Troilus and Criseyde* to Wagner's *Ring* and Prokoviev's *Cinderella*. But it is much more important to be able to recognize *the kind of thing* that Wagner is doing in the *Ring*, and to realize that the plots of Shakespeare's *King Lear* and *The Winter's Tale* are by no means vestigial absurdities.

There is another door that can be opened by reading legends and fairy tales, and for some children, at the present time, there may be no other key to it. *Religio*, in one Latin sense of the word, implies a sense of the strange, the numinous, the totally Other, of what lies quite beyond human personality and cannot be found in any human relationships. This kind of 'religion' is an indestructible part of the experience of many human minds, even though the temper of a secular society does not encourage it, and the whole movement of modern theology runs counter to it. In Christian 'religious instruction' there is likely to be less and less *religio*: it may very well be in reading about a vision of the flashing-eyed Athene or the rosy-fingered Aphrodite that children first find a satisfying formulation of those queer prickings of delight, excitement and terror that they feel when they first walk by moonlight, or when it snows in May, or when, like the young Wordsworth, they have to touch a wall to make sure that it is really there. Magic is not the same as mysticism, but it may lead towards it; it is mystery 'told to the children'.

The ability to understand mythological references without using notes or a dictionary has been greatly overrated, and I would certainly put it last among the advantages of being brought up on the European tradition of myth and legend. It is not for nothing that students of English literature talk about 'classical *illusions*' when they have nothing better to say. Nevertheless something is lost from the symbolic potency of 'Was there another Troy for her to burn?' or 'Down, down I come, like glistering Phaethon', if one has to turn to the bottom of the page to discover that it was Helen who brought about the burning of Troy, or why Phaethon undertook the manage of his unruly jades. It is in the nature of a symbol to be inscrutable, to awaken overtones in the imagination, and information gathered within the last few seconds cannot awaken any overtones. It is only when the words *Helen*, *Phaethon*, *Siegfried*, *Bluebeard*, have the same untraceable imaginative history in the mind as words like *fire* and *stone* and *green*, that they can exercise their proper power. The greatest names do need to be known in this way: names like Aphrodite, Athene, Achilles, Yggdrasil, Galahad. Very few people in fact remember why Hephaestus fell from heaven 'from morn to noon, from noon to dewy eve, A summer's day', or who married Hermione, or the names of all the nine Muses. This does not matter very much, and it does not mean that the more obscure allusions are wasted upon a modern reader. If one knows most of the greater persons and places and actions, one knows the imaginative world in which the Greek and Northern gods exist. The names which are unknown or faintly remembered are enough to take one back 'far away and long ago', into Greek sunlight or Northern frost, and very often the English poet making the allusion has himself told as much of the story as one needs to know.

Children's likes and dislikes

Almost certainly J. R. R. Tolkien is right when he suggests that fairy tales became the peculiar property of the nursery by historical accident. They were not evolved for telling to children. They were folk tales, traditional stories as they developed in the unlettered classes of society, often retaining the skeleton plots of more poetic myths and legends. The uneducated nurses and servants who looked after the children of the upper and middle classes brought their stories with them. Myths about the gods, and legends about heroes, are even more obviously adult in origin, passing through the highly developed religious rituals and court cultures of the past. Schoolboys had to come across them in learning to read Latin and Greek poetry, but it was not until the nineteenth century that it occurred to any writer that there was a natural affinity between the childhood of the race and the childhood of the individual human being.

Nevertheless the accidents that gave these stories to children were happy ones. Children under eleven are eager to know what happens next, and impatient with anything that stops them from getting on with the story. They want to listen to conversations only if direct speech is the quickest and clearest method of showing what was transacted between two people as a necessary preliminary to what these two people proceeded to *do*. At about nine or ten they are beginning to be interested in character, but in a very straightforward and moral way: they see people as marked by one particular attribute, cleverness, or kindness, or strictness, or being a good shot, and they mind whether things are right or wrong. They are especially sensitive to the heroic virtue of justice, and they are beginning to notice why people are tempted to be unjust. They are not interested in the long processes of inner debate by which people make difficult decisions, and become very irritated with grown-ups who insist upon giving them not only the practical answer or information they asked for, but also all the reasons for it. They expect a story to be a good yarn, in which the action is swift and the characters are clearly and simply defined. And legends and fairy tales are just like that. Playground games show that children like catastrophes and exhibitions of speed and power, and a clear differentiation between cowboys, cops and spacemen who are good, and Indians, robbers and space monsters who are bad.

Magic has a particular attraction for eight-to-ten-year-olds, but not because it is pretty or 'innocent'. They delight, in more senses than the usual one, in seeing how far they can go. If some people are taller than others, how tall could anyone conceivably be? If some people are cleverer than others at making things, could someone alter what things are actually made of? If there are different languages which different people understand, could there be a secret language that affected things and people against their will? Such speculations carried *ad infinitum* are given concrete form in giants, and the enchantments of elves and dwarfs, and the magic of runes and spells. The 'if' kind of question always requires consistency in the answer, and children of this age are often fascinated by consistency for its own sake, liking patterns because they are patterns, and working out for themselves intricate maps of imaginary islands and imaginary towns. The whole visual world of the Greek myths (or the Northern myths, or the Arthurian romances) satisfies this appetite imaginatively, because of the consistent mood, form and colouring of its landscapes. So does the detail of most mythical conceptions. If the moon were a goddess, or if a goddess were the moon, where would she move, and what creatures would draw her chariot?

One problem that has arisen quite recently, over the two last generations, may be partially resolved by the modern revival of myths and fairy tales. Realistic novelists, whether they write for children or grown-ups, usually write about what they know best themselves, and take for granted certain experiences and moral presuppositions in their readers. Some writers present a wider range of class and locality than others, and the best writers do not make the mistake of supposing that all the virtues reside in one class and all the vices in another; but there is rarely any doubt about what they know from the inside, or about the kind of people they are writing for. Dickens is not writing for people who live in Tom All Alone's, and he does not pretend that he has lived there himself. What happens, though, if one tries to read Eve Garnett's *Family from One End Street* to a class of eleven-year-olds in a British school today? Some of them come from families not unlike the one in the story; some are Jamaican immigrants living in one room; and there may also be the children of a well-to-do and modern-minded doctor, a poor and old-fashioned clergyman, and a brilliant and divorced oboist. It is impossible for this particular audience to be drawn together in listening to this particular story; either the events themselves or Eve Garnett's way of describing them will touch a raw nerve. It is difficult to be sure of her own attitude to the family she has created: sometimes she seems to take them for granted, and sometimes they seem to be 'low' characters in a comedy of manners. Contemporary comedy of manners always requires a homogene-ous audience. Children cannot be expected to share in a *joke* about the lives of people very like some of them and very unlike others. A recent fashion in secondary school English courses has encouraged the study of passages which are deliberately chosen in order to expose and emphasize the social differences between members of one school class; among fifteen-year-olds some of these passages fall flat because the humour cannot be shared.

Younger children are even more sensitive about their homes. The situations and emotions which are represented in myth and fairy tale have some counterpart in their lives however they have been brought up, and they turn into an audience that is corporate and unselfconscious.

Stories that lead to doing things are all the more attractive to children, who are active rather than passive creatures. Myths and fairy tales provide an unusually abundant choice of things to do. Largely because they are archetypal and anonymous (in quality, if not in provenance), they will stand reinterpretation in many forms without losing their character. They can be recreated by children not only in words but in drama, in mime, in dance and in painting. Action in them is not fussy, and lends itself to qualitative expression in the movements of the human body and in the shapes and colours of non-figurative painting. I have seen two ten-year-olds playing at Theseus and the Minotaur in a solitary orchard with no grown-up, as they thought, within sight or hearing.

93

SPELLS OF ENCHANTMENT

Jack Zipes

Source: Jack Zipes (ed.), *Spells of Enchantment*, New York: Viking Penguin, 1991, pp. 370–392.

It has generally been assumed that fairy tales were first created for children and are largely the domain of children. But nothing could be further from the truth.

From the very beginning, thousands of years ago, when tales were told to create communal bonds in face of the inexplicable forces of nature, to the present, when fairy tales are written and told to provide hope in a world seemingly on the brink of catastrophe, mature men and women have been the creators and cultivators of the fairy tale tradition. When introduced to fairy tales, children welcome them mainly because they nurture their great desire for change and independence. On the whole, the literary fairy tale has become an established genre within a process of Western civilization that cuts across all ages. Even though numerous critics and shamans have mystified and misinterpreted the fairy tale because of their spiritual quest for universal archetypes or their need to save the world through therapy, both the oral and the literary forms of the fairy tale are grounded in history: they emanate from specific struggles to humanize bestial and barbaric forces, which have terrorized our minds and communities in concrete ways, threatening to destroy free will and human compassion. The fairy tale sets out to conquer this concrete terror through metaphors.

Though it is difficult to determine when the first *literary* fairy tale was conceived, and also extremely difficult to define exactly what a fairy tale is, we do know that oral folk tales, which contain wondrous and marvelous elements, have existed for thousands of years and were told largely by adults for adults. Motifs from these tales, which were memorized and passed on by word of mouth, made their way into the Bible and the Greek classics such as *The Iliad* and *The Odyssey*. The early oral tales that served as the basis for the development of the literary fairy tales were closely tied to rituals, customs, and beliefs of tribes, communities, and trades. They fostered a sense of belonging and the hope that miracles involving some kind of magical transformation were possible to bring about a better world. They instructed, amused, warned, initiated, and enlightened. They opened windows to imaginative worlds inside that needed concrete expression outside, in reality. They were to be shared and exchanged, used and modified according to the needs of the tellers and the listeners.

Tales are marks that leave traces of the human struggle for immortality. Tales are human marks invested with desire. They are formed like musical compositions, except that the notes constitute words and are chosen to enunciate the speaker/writer's position in the world, including his or her dreams, needs, wishes, and experiences. The speaker/writer posits the self against language to establish identity and to test the self with and against language, and each word marks a way toward a future different from what may have been decreed, certainly different from what is being experienced in the present: words that are selected in the process of creating a tale allow the speaker/writer freedom to play with options that no one else has ever glimpsed. The marks are magical.

The fairy tale celebrates the marks as magical: marks as letters, words, sentences, signs. More than any other literary genre, the fairy tale has persisted in emphasizing transformation of the marks with spells, enchantments, disenchantments, resurrections, re-creations. During its inception, the fairy tale distinguished itself as a genre both by appropriating the oral folk tale and by expanding it, for it became gradually necessary in the modern world to adapt the oral tale to standards of literacy and make it acceptable for diffusion in the public sphere. The fairy tale is only one type of appropriation of a particular oral storytelling tradition: the wonder folk tale, often called the *Zaubermärchen* or the *conte merveilleux*. As more and more wonder tales were written down in the fifteenth, sixteenth, and seventeenth centuries, they constituted the genre of the literary fairy tale, which began establishing its own conventions, motifs, *topoi*, characters, and plots, based to a large extent on those developed in the oral tradition but altered to address a reading public formed by the aristocracy and the middle classes. Though the peasants were excluded in the formation of this literary tradition, it was their material, tone, style, and beliefs that were incorporated into the new genre.

What exactly is the oral wonder tale?

Vladmir Propp, in his now famous study, *The Morphology of the Folk Tale*, outlined thirty-one basic functions that constitute the formation of a paradigm, an archetypal story form that still is common in Europe. By functions, Propp meant the fundamental and constant components of the tale that are the acts of the character, necessary for driving the action forward.

To summarize the functions, with different emphasis:

1. The protagonist is confronted with an interdiction or prohibition, which he or she violates in some way.

2. Departing or banished, the protagonist has either been given or assumes a task related to the interdiction or prohibition. The task is assigned, and it is a sign. That is, the protagonist's character will be marked by the task that is his or her sign.

3. There is an encounter with: (a) a villain; (b) a mysterious individual or creature, who gives the protagonist gifts; (c) three different animals or creatures, who are helped by the protagonist and promise to repay him or her; or (d) three animals or creatures who offer gifts to help the protagonist, who is in trouble. The gifts are often magical agents, which bring about miraculous change.

4. The endowed protagonist is tested and moves on to battle and conquer the villain or inimical forces.

5. There is a peripety or sudden fall in the protagonist's fortunes, which is generally only a temporary setback. A wonder or miracle is needed to reverse the wheel of fortune.

6. The protagonist makes use of endowed gifts (and this includes the magical agents and cunning) to achieve his or her goal. The result is: (a) three battles with the villain; (b) three impossible tasks that are nevertheless made possible; or (c) the breaking of a magic spell.

7. The villain is punished or the inimical forces are vanquished.

8. The success of the protagonist usually leads to (a) marriage; (b) the acquisition of money; (c) survival and wisdom; or (d) any combination of the first three.

Rarely do wonder tales end unhappily. They triumph over death. The tale begins with "Once upon a time" or "Once there was" and never really ends when it ends. The ending is actually the beginning. The once upon a time is not a past designation but futuristic: the timelessness of the tale and its lack of geographical specificity endow it with utopian connotations – "utopia" in its original meaning designated "no place," a place that no one has ever envisaged. We form and keep the utopian kernel of the tale safe in our imaginations with hope.

The significance of the paradigmatic functions of the wonder tale is that they facilitate recall for teller and listeners. They enable us to store, fit our experiences and desires, owing to the easily identifiable characters who are associated with particular assignments and settings. For instance, we have the simpleton, who turns out to be remarkably cunning; the third and youngest son, who is oppressed by his brothers and/or father; the beautiful but maltreated youngest daughter; the discharged soldier, who has been exploited by his superiors; the shrew who needs taming; the evil witch; the kind elves; the cannibalistic ogre; the clumsy, stupid giant; terrifying beasts like dragons, lions, wild boars; kind animals like ants, birds, deer, bees, ducks, fish; the clever tailor; the evil and jealous stepmother; the clever peasant; the powerhungry and unjust king; treacherous nixies; the beast bridegroom. There are haunted castles; enchanted forests; mysterious huts in woods; glass mountains; dark, dangerous caves; underground kingdoms. There are seven-league boots, which enable the protagonist to move faster than jet planes; capes that make a person invisible; magic wands, which can perform extraordinary feats of transformation; animals that produce gold; tables that provide all the delicious and sumptuous food you can eat; musical instruments with enormous captivating powers; swords and clubs capable of conquering anyone or anything; lakes, ponds, and seas that are difficult to cross and serve as the home for supernatural creatures.

The characters, settings, and motifs are combined and varied according to specific functions to induce wonder. It is this sense of wonder that distinguished the wonder tales from other oral tales as the legend, the fable, the anecdote, and the myth; it is clearly the sense of wonder that distinguishes the *literary* fairy tale from the moral story, novella, sentimental tale, and other modern short literary genres. Wonder causes astonishment, and as manifested in a marvelous object or phenomenon, it is often regarded as a supernatural occurrence and can be an omen or a portent. It gives rise to admiration, fear, awe, and reverence. The *Oxford Universal Dictionary* states that wonder is "the emotion excited by the perception of something novel and unexpected, or inexplicable; astonishment mingled with perplexity or bewildered curiosity." In the oral wonder tale, we are to wonder about the workings of the universe, where anything can happen at any time, and these happy or fortuitous events are never to be explained. Nor do the characters demand an explanation – they are opportunistic, are encouraged to be so, and if they do not take advantage of the opportunity that will benefit them in their relations with others, they are either dumb or mean-spirited. The tales seek to awaken our regard for the miraculous condition of life and to evoke in a religious sense profound feelings of awe and respect for life as a miraculous process which can be altered and changed to compensate for the lack of power, wealth and pleasure that is most people's lot. Lack, deprivation, prohibition, and interdiction motivate people to look for signs of fulfillment and emancipation. In the wonder tales, those who are naive and simple are able to succeed because they are untainted and can recognize the wondrous signs. They have retained their belief in the miraculous condition of nature, revere nature in all its aspects. They have not been spoiled by conventionalism, power, or rationalism. In contrast to the humble characters, the villains are those who use words intentionally to exploit, control, trans-fix, incarcerate, and destroy for their benefit. They have no respect or consideration for nature and other human beings, and they actually seek to abuse magic by preventing change and causing everything to be transfixed according to their interests. Enchantment equals petrification. Breaking the spell equals emancipation. The wondrous protagonist wants to keep the process of natural change flowing and indicates possibilities for overcoming the obstacles that prevent other characters or creatures from living in a peaceful and pleasurable way. The focus on wonder in the oral folk tale

216

does not mean that all wonder tales and, later, the literary fairy tales served and serve an emancipatory purpose. The nature and meaning of folk tales have depended on the stage of development of a tribe, community or society. Oral tales have served to stabilize, conserve, or challenge the common beliefs, laws, values, and norms of a group. The ideology expressed in wonder tales always stemmed from the position that the narrator assumed with regard to the developments in his or her community, and the narrative plot and changes made in a tale depended on the sense of wonder or awe that the narrator wanted to evoke. In other words, the sense of wonder in the tale and the intended emotion sought by the narrator are ideological.

Since these wonder tales have been with us for thousands of years and have undergone so many different changes in the oral tradition, it is difficult to determine the ideological intention of the narrator, and when we disregard the narrator's intention, it is often difficult to reconstruct (and/or deconstruct) the ideological meaning of a tale. In the last analysis, even if we cannot establish whether a wonder tale is ideologically conservative, sexist, progressive, emancipatory, etc., it is the celebration of wonder that constitutes its major appeal. No matter what the plot may be, this type of tale calls forth our capacity as readers and potential transmitters of its signs and meaning to wonder. We do not want to know that exact resolution, the "happily ever after," of a tale – that is, what it is actually like. We do not want to name God, gods, goddesses, or fairies, who will forever remain mysterious and omnipotent. We do not want to form graven images. We do not want utopia designated for us. We want to remain curious, startled, provoked, mystified and uplifted. We want to glare, gaze, gawk, behold, and stare. We want to be given opportunities to change, and ultimately we want to be told that we can become kings and queens, or lords of our destinies. We remember wonder tales and fairy tales to keep our sense of wonderment alive and to nurture our hope that we can seize possibilities and opportunities to transform ourselves and our worlds.

Ultimately, the definition of both the wonder tale and the fairy tale which derives from it, depends on the manner in which a narrator/author arranges known functions of a tale aesthetically and ideologically to induce wonder and then transmits the tale as a whole according to customary usage of a society in a given historical period. The first stage for the literary fairy tale involved a kind of class and perhaps even gender appropriation. The voices of the nonliterate tellers were submerged, and since women in most cases were not allowed to be scribes, the tales were scripted according to male dictates or fantasies, even though they may have been told by women. Put crudely, it could be said that the literary appropriation of the oral wonder tales served the hegemonic interests of males within the upper classes of particular communities and societies, and to a great extent this is true. However, such a statement must be qualified, for the writing down of the tales also preserved a great deal of the value system of those deprived of power. And the more the literary fairy tale was cultivated and developed, the more it became individualized and varied by intellectuals and artists, who often sympathized with those society marginalized or were marginalized themselves. The literary fairy tale allowed for new possibilities of subversion in the written word and in print, and therefore it was always looked upon with misgivings by the governing authorities in the civilization process.

During early Christianity, there were not many signs that the oral folk tales would develop and flourish as a major literary genre in the West, and there were obvious reasons for this lack: most people were nonliterate and shared strong oral cultural traditions; the tales had not been changed sufficiently to serve the tastes and interests of the ruling classes; Latin was the dominant intellectual and literary language until the late Middle Ages, when the vernacular languages gradually formed general standards of grammar and orthography for communication; the technology of printing did not make much progress until the fifteenth century, so that the distribution of literary works was limited. Consequently it is not surprising that the first appearance of a major literary fairy tale, Apuleius's "Cupid and Psyche," was in Latin and came in the second century. Moreover, it was included in a book, *The Golden Ass*, that dealt with metamorphoses, perhaps the key theme of the fairy tale up to the present. However, whereas many oral wonder tales had been concerned with the humanization of natural forces, the literary fairy tale, beginning with "Cupid and Psyche," shifted the emphasis more toward the civilization of the protagonist, who must learn to respect particular codes and laws to become accepted in society and/or united to reproduce and continue the progress of the world toward perfect happiness.

At first this new literary fairy tale could not stand by itself – that is it did not have a receptive audience and had to be included within a frame story or in a collection of instructive and amusing stories and anecdotes. Therefore, up to the fifteenth century, the only other evidence we have of complete fairy tales is within such manuscripts as the *Gesta Romanorum* (c. 1300) or in sermons delivered by priests. Tales like "Of Feminine Subtlety" were generally used to provide instruction for the education of young Christian boys and had a strong moralistic strain. In addition, like "Cupid and Psyche," the early Latin fairy tales were largely addressed to the male sex and focused on their acquisition of moral values and ethics that would serve them in their positions of power in society.

It was not until the publication of Giovanni Straparola's *Le piacevoli notti* (*The Delectable Nights*) in 1550–53 that fairy tales were first published in the vernacular and for a mixed audience of (upper-class) men and women. Straparola brings together a group of aristocrats who flee Milan for political reasons and decide to tell tales to amuse one another during their exile. The frame narrative is set up to include erotic anecdotes, fables, and fairy tales like "The Pig Prince," and it is modeled after Boccaccio's *Decameron*.

But since Boccaccio did not include fairy tales in his collection, Straparola can be considered the first writer in Europe to have published fairy tales in the vernacular for an educated audience. His tales did not achieve the popularity of Boccaccio's collection, yet they were reprinted several times in Italian during the next few centuries, and by the nineteenth century they were translated into French, German, and English.

There is no direct evidence whether Straparola influenced Giambattista Basile, whose *Lo Cunto de li Cunti* (*The Story of Stories*), also known as *The Pentameron*, was published posthumously in 1634. Basile, who wrote in Neapolitan dialect, was the first to use an old folktale motif about laughter to frame an entire collection. His book of fifty fairy tales begins with a story about a princess named Zoza, who cannot laugh, no matter what her father, the king of Vallepelosa, does to try to assuage her melancholy. Finally, the king orders a fountain of oil erected before the palace gate so that people will skip and jump to avoid being soiled. The king hopes that their antics will overcome his daughter's melancholy. Indeed, the princess does laugh, but at the wrong person, an old witch of a woman, who places a curse on her and declares that if Zoza is ever to marry, she must wed Taddeo, a bewitched sleeping prince, whom only she can wake and save with her tears. With the help and advice of three fairies, Zoza succeeds in weeping a sufficient amount of tears, but she then falls asleep before she can achieve the rescue of Taddeo. In the meantime, a malicious slave steals Zoza's vessel of tears and claims the honor of liberating Taddeo, who marries her. Yet this does not deter Zoza, who rents a fine house opposite Taddeo's palace and manages through her beauty to attract his attention. The slave, who is pregnant, learns about this and threatens to kill her unborn child if Taddeo does not obey her every whim. Zoza responds by enticing the slave with three gifts she had received from the fairies. The third of these is a doll that causes the slave to be addicted to fairy tales, and she forces Taddeo to gather storytellers, who will amuse her during the final ten days of her pregnancy. So Taddeo gathers a group of ten motley women, who tell five fairy tales a day until Zoza concludes the sessions with her own tale, which exposes the slave's theft and brings the frame story to its conclusion. As a result, Taddeo has the pregnant slave put to death and takes Zoza for his new wife.

Basile was familiar with the customs and behavior of the Neapolitans and had also traveled widely in Italy and served at different courts. Therefore, he was able to include in his fairy tales a wealth of folklore, anecdotes, and events that celebrate miraculous changes and communion. A good example is "The Merchant's Two Sons," which has many different folk and literary versions. As in the frame narrative, the humane ties between people based on compassion and love can be solidified only if the protagonists recognize what and where evil is. The fairy tale involves arousing the protagonists and sharpening their perception of what is occurring so that they can make or bring about changes and master their own destinies. Thus the narrative structure is conceived so that the listener will learn to distinguish between destructive and beneficial forces, for the art of seeing and intuiting is nurtured by the fairy tale.

It is not by chance that in Europe the literary fairy tale flourished in Italy first. During the fifteenth and sixteenth centuries, the Italian cities and duchies had prospered by developing great commercial centers, and the literacy rate had grown immensely. Cultural activity at the courts and in the city-states was high, and there was a great deal of foreign influence on storytelling, as well as strong native oral traditions among the people. Although it cannot be fully documented, it is highly likely that the Italian literary fairy tales were gradually spread in print and by word of mouth throughout Europe. Interestingly, England, also a powerful maritime country, was the other nation that began cultivating a literary fairy tale tradition. There are fairy tale elements in Chaucer's *The Canterbury Tales* (c. 1386–1400), in Spenser's *The Faerie Queen* (1590–96), and, of course, in many of Shakespeare's plays, such as *King Lear, A Midsummer Night's Dream, The Taming of the Shrew*, and *The Tempest*, all written between 1590 and 1611. However, owing to the Puritan hostility toward amusement during the seventeenth century, the fairy tale as a genre was not able to flourish in England. France offered more propitious conditions, and the genre bloomed in full force there toward the end of the ancien régime, from 1600 to 1714.

Many factors account for the rise and spread of the fairy tale in France at this time. First of all, France had become the most powerful country in Europe, and French, considered the most cultivated of languages, was used at most courts throughout Europe. Second, the evolution of printing favored experimentation with different kinds of literature. Third, there was great cultural creativity and innovation in France. Finally, about the middle of the seventeenth century, the fairy tale gradually became more accepted at literary salons and at the court, particularly in theatrical form. Fairy tale recitations and games were devised, generally by women in their salons, and these led to the publication of the tales during the 1690s. Perhaps the most prodigious (and most prolific) of the French fairy tale writers was Marie-Catherine D'Aulnoy, whose first tale, "The Island of Happiness," was embedded in her novel *L'Histoire d'Hippolyte* (1690). It was not until she had established a popular literary salon, in which fairy tales were regularly presented, that she herself published four volumes of fairy tales, between 1696 and 1698. Though Charles Perrault is generally considered to be the most significant French writer of fairy tales of this period, Mme D'Aulnoy was undoubtedly more typical and more a catalyst for other writers. Her long and rambling narratives focus on the question of *tendresse* – true and natural feelings between a man and a woman, whose nobility will depend on their manners and the ways they uphold standards of civility in defending their love. "Green Serpent" exemplifies Mme D'Aulnoy's concerns and reflects the influence of Apuleius's "Cupid and Psyche" and her familiarity with the Italian tradition of fairy tales, not to mention French folklore. In turn, her fairy tales set the stage for the works of Mlle L'Héritier, whose "Ricdin-Ricdon" (1696) is a remarkable courtly interpretation of "Rumpelstiltskin," and Mlle de La Force, whose "Parslinette" (1697) is a fascinating version of "Rapunzel." Of course, the writer whose name has become practically synonymous with the term *conte de fée* is Charles Perrault, who wrote two verse tales, "The Foolish Wishes" (1693) and "Donkey Skin" (1694), and then published the famous prose renditions of "Cinderella," "Little Red Riding Hood," "Sleeping Beauty," "Blue Beard," "Tom Thumb," "Riquet with the Tuft," and "The Fairies" in *Histoires ou contes du temps passé* (1697). Perrault frequented the literary salons in Paris, and he purposely sought to establish the literary fairy tale as an innovative genre which exemplified the modern sensibility that was coming into its own and was to be equated with the greatness of French *civilité*. Not all the French writers of this period intended to celebrate the spendor of the ancien régime, but they all were concerned with questions of manners, norms, and mores in their tales and sought to illustrate correct behavior and what constituted noble feelings. Therefore, the "mode" of writing fairy tales was concentrated within a feudal sphere and led to what could be called the institutionalization of the genre, for after this point – that is, after the appearance of *The Thousand and One Nights* (1704–17) in twelve volumes, translated and adapted into French by Antoine Galland – the literary fairy tale became an acceptable social symbolic form through which conventionalized motifs, characters, and plots were selected, composed, arranged, and rearranged to comment on the civilizing process and to keep alive the possibility of miraculous change and a sense of wonderment.

The very name of the genre itself – fairy tale – originated during this time, for the French writers coined the term *conte de fée* during the seventeenth century, and it has stuck to the genre in Europe and North America ever since. This "imprint" is important, because it reveals something crucial about the fairy tale that has remained part of its nature to the present. The early writers of fairy tales placed the power of metamorphosis in the hands of women – the redoubtable fairies. In addition, this miraculous power was not associated with a particular religion or mythology, through which the world was to be explained. It was a secular mysterious power of compassion that could not be explained, and it derived from the creative imagination of the writer. Anyone could call upon the fairies for help, and it is clear that the gifted French women writers of the seventeenth century preferred to address themselves to a fairy and to have a fairy resolve the conflicts in their tales rather than the Church, with its male-dominated hierarchy. After all, it was the Church that had eliminated hundreds of thousands of so-called female witches during the previous two centuries in an effort to curb heretical and nonconformist beliefs. However, those "pagan" notions survived in the tradition of the oral wonder tale and surfaced in published form in France when it became safe to introduce in a symbolical code supernatural powers and creatures other than those officially sanctioned by the Christian code. In short, there was something subversive about the institutionalization of the fairy tale in France during the 1690s, for it enabled writers to create a dialogue about norms, manners, and power that evaded court censorship and freed the fantasy of the writers and readers, while at the same time paying tribute to the French code of *civilité* and the majesty of the aristocracy. Once certain discursive paradigms and conventions were established, a writer could demonstrate his or her "genius" by rearranging, expanding, deepening, and playing with the known functions of a genre that, by 1715, had already formed a type of canon, which consisted not only of the great classical tales – "Cinderella," "Sleeping Beauty," "Rapunzel," "Rumpelstiltskin" "Puss in Boots," "Little Red Riding Hood," "Beauty, and the Beast," "Bluebeard," "The Golden Dwarf," "The Blue Bird," and "The White Cat" – but also the mammoth collection *The Arabian Nights*.

Galland's project of translating the Arabic tales from original manuscripts, which stemmed from the fourteenth century and were based on an oral tradition, was important for various reasons: his translation was not literal and he introduced many changes influenced by French culture into his adaptations; eight of the tales, among them "Prince Ahmed and the Fairy Pari-Banou," were obtained from a Maconite scholar named Youhenna Diab, living at that time in Paris, and were in part Galland's literary re-creations; the exotic setting and nature of these Oriental tales attracted not only French but numerous European readers, so that Galland's work stimulated the translation of other Arabic writings, such as *The Adventures of Abdalah, Son of Anif* (1712–14), by the abbot Jean-Paul Bignon, as well as hundreds of translations from the French into English, Italian, German, Spanish, etc.

The infusion of the Oriental tales into the French literary tradition enriched and broadened the paradigmatic options for Western writers during the course of the eighteenth century, and it became a favorite device (and still is) to deploy the action of a tale to the Orient while discussing sensitive issues of norms and power close to home. Aside from the impact of the Arabic and Persian tales on Western writers through translations, another development was crucial for the institutionalization of the fairy tale in the eighteenth century. Soon after the publication of the tales by D'Aulnoy, Perrault, L'Héritier, Galland, and others, they were reprinted in a series of chapbooks called the *Bibliothèque Bleue*, and these inexpensive volumes were distributed by peddlers called *colporteurs* to the lower classes throughout France and Central Europe. The fairy tales were often abridged; the language was simplified; and there were multiple versions, which were read to children and nonliterates. Many tales were appropriated by oral storytellers, so that the literary tradition became a source for an oral tradition.

The increased popularity of the literary fairy tale as chapbook led to the cultivation of the literary fairy tale for children. Already during the 1690s, Fénelon, the important theologian and archbishop of Cambrai, who was in charge of the dauphin's education, had written several didactic fairy tales as an experiment to make the prince's lessons more enjoyable. However, they were not published, as they were considered insufficiently proper and useful for the grooming of children from the upper classes. They were first printed in 1730, after Fénelon's death, and thereafter it became more acceptable to write and publish fairy tales for children just so long as they indoctrinated gender-specific roles and class codes. The most notable example here, aside from Fénelon's tales, is the voluminous work of Mme Leprince de Beaumont, whose *Magasin des Enfants* (1743) included "Beauty and the Beast," "Prince Chéri," and other overtly moralistic tales for children. Mme de Beaumont used a frame story in which a governess engages several young girls between six and ten in discussions about morals, manners, ethics, and gender roles, which lead her to tell didactic stories to illustrate her points. The method was based on her work as a governess in England, and the frame was adaptable to institutionalizing a type of storytelling in homes of the upper classes. It was only a part of the civilizing process that storytelling developed within the aristocratic and bourgeois homes, in the seventeenth and eighteenth centuries through governesses and nannies, and later in the eighteenth and nineteenth centuries through mothers, who told bedtime stories.

As the literary fairy tale spread in France to every age group and every social class, it began to serve different functions, depending on the writer's interests. It represented the glory and ideology of the French aristocracy. It provided a symbolic critique, with utopian connotations, of the aristocratic hierarchy, largely within the aristocracy itself and from the female viewpoint. It introduced the norms and values of the bourgeois civilizing process as more reasonable and egalitarian than the feudal code. As a *divertissement* for the aristocracy and bourgeoisie, the fairy tale diverted the attention of listeners/readers from the serious sociopolitical problems of the times, compensating for the deprivations that the upper classes perceived themselves to be suffering. There was also an element of self-parody, revealing the ridiculous notions in previous fairy tales and representing another aspect of court society to itself; such parodies can be seen in Jacques Cazotte's "A Thousand and One Follies" (1746), Jean-Jacques Rousseau's "The Queen Fantasque" (1758), and Voltaire's "The White Bull" (1774). Finally, fairy tales with clear didactic and moral lessons were approved as reading matter to serve as a subtle, more pleasurable means of initiating children into the class rituals and customs that reinforced the status quo.

The climax of the French institutionalization of the fairy tale was the publication, between 1785 and 1789, of Charles Mayer's forty-one-volume *Cabinet des Fées*, which collected most of the important French tales written during the previous hundred years. Thereafter, most writers, whether they wrote for adults or children, consciously held a dialogue with a fairy tale discourse that had become firmly established in the Western intellectual tradition. For instance, the French fairy tale, which, we must remember, now included *The Arabian Nights*, had a profound influence on the German classicists and the Romantics, and the development in Germany provided the continuity for the institution of the genre in the West as a whole. Like the French authors, German middle-class writers like Johann Karl August Musäus, in his collection *Volksmärchen de Deutschen* (1782–86), which included "Libussa," began employing the fairy tale to celebrate German customs. Musaüs combined elements of German folklore and the French fairy tale in a language clearly addressed to educated Germans. At the same time, Christopher Martin Wieland translated and adapted numerous tales from the *Cabinet des Fées* in *Dschinnistan* (1786–89). "The Philosophers' Stone" is his own creation but reveals how he, too, consciously used the fairy tale to portray the decadence of German feudal society and introduced Oriental motifs to enhance the tale's exoticism and to conceal his critique of his own society. Numerous French fairy tales also became known in Germany by the turn of the century through the popular *Blaue Bibliothek* series and other translations. In fact, some, like "Sleeping Beauty," "Cinderella," and "Little Red Riding Hood," even worked their way into the brothers Grimm collection of the *Kinder und Hausmärchen* (*Children's and Household Tales*, 1812–15), which were considered to be genuinely German. Romantic writers such as Wilhelm Heinrich Wackenroder, Ludwig Tieck, Novalis, Joseph von Eichendorff, Clemens Brentano, Adalbert von Chamisso, Friedrich de La Motte-Fouqué, and E. T A. Hoffmann wrote extraordinary tales that revealed a major shift in the function of the genre: the fairy tale no longer represented the dominant aristocratic ideology. Rather it was written as a critique of the worst aspects of the Enlightenment and absolutism. This viewpoint was clearly expressed in Wolfgang Goethe's classical narrative simply entitled "The Fairy Tale" (1795), as though it were the fairy tale to end all fairy tales. Goethe optimistically envisioned a successful rebirth of a rejuvenated monarchy, which enjoyed the support of all social classes, in his answer to the chaos and destruction of the French Revolution. In contrast, the Romantics were generally more skeptical about the prospects for individual autonomy, the reform of decadent institutions, and a democratic public sphere in a Germany divided by the selfish interests of petty tyrants and the Napoleonic Wars. Very few of the German Romantic tales end on a happy note. The protagonists either go insane or die. The evil forces assume a social hue, for the witches and villains no longer are allegorical representatives of evil in the Christian tradition but are symbolically associated with the philistine bourgeois society or the decadent aristocracy. Nor was the purpose of the Romantic fairy tale to amuse in the traditional sense of *divertissement*. Instead, it sought to engage the reader in a serious discourse about art, philosophy, education, and love. It is not by chance that the German term for the literary fairy tale is *Kunstmärchen* (art tale), for in the Romantic narratives, the utopian impulse for a better future was often carried on by an artist or a creative protagonist, and his fate indicated to what extent the civilizing process in Germany inhibited or nurtured the creative and independent development of the citizens.

While the function of the fairy tale for adults underwent a major shift – and this was clear in other countries as well – that made it an appropriate means to maintain a dialogue about social and political issues within the bourgeois public sphere, the fairy tale for children remained suspect until the 1820s. Although various collections were published for children in the latter part of the eighteenth century and at the turn of the century, along with individual chapbooks containing "Cinderella," "Jack the Giant Killer," "Beauty and the Beast," Little Red Riding Hood," and "Sleeping Beauty," they were not regarded as the prime reading material for children. Nor were they considered to be "healthy" for the development of children's minds. For the most part, church leaders and educators favored other genres of stories, realistic, sentimental, didactic, which were intended to demonstrate what good manners and morals were. Even the brothers Grimm, in particular Wilhelm, began in 1819 to revise their collected tales, targeting them more for children than they had done in the beginning and cleansing their narratives of erotic, cruel, or bawdy passages. However, the fantastic and wondrous elements were retained, so that the stories were not at first fully accepted by the bourgeois reading public, which only began changing its attitude toward the fairy tale for children during the course of the 1820s and 1830s throughout Europe. It was signaled in Germany by the publication of Wilhelm Hauff's *Märchen Almanach* (1826) and in England by Edward Taylor's translation of the Grimms' *Kinder und Hausmärchen*, under the title *German Popular Stories* (1823), with illustrations by the famous George Cruikshank. The more tolerant acceptance of the literary fairy tale for children may be attributed to the realization on the part of educators and parents, probably owing to their own reading experiences, that fantasy literature and amusement would not necessarily destroy or pervert childrens' minds. Whether children were of the middle classes and attended school, or were of the lower classes and worked on the farm or in a factory, they needed a recreation period – the time and space to re-create themselves without having morals and ethics imposed on them, without having the feeling that their reading or listening had to involve indoctrination.

Significantly, it was from 1830 to 1900, during the rise of the middle classes, that the fairy tale came into its own for children. It was exactly during this time – from 1835 onward, to be precise – that Hans Christian Andersen, greatly influenced by the German Romantic writers and the Grimms, began publishing his tales, which became extremely popular throughout Europe and America. Andersen combined humor, Christian sentiments, and fantastic plots to form tales that at once amused and instructed both young and older readers. More than any writer of the nineteenth century, he fully developed what Perrault had begun: writing tales, such as "The Red Shoes," that could be readily grasped by children and adults alike but with a different understanding. Some of his narratives, like "The Shadow," were clearly intended for adults alone, and it is a good example of his use of the *doppelgänger* motif, developed by E. T. A. Hoffmann, and his exploration of paranoia within the fairy tale genre to express his individual and very peculiar fears of the diminished possibilities for autonomy in European society and the growing alienation of people from themselves.

In fact, the flowering of the fairy tale in Europe and America during the latter half of the nineteenth century has a great deal to do with alienation. As daily life became more structured, work more rationalized, and institutions more bureaucratic, there was little space left for daydreaming and the imagination. It was the fairy tale that provided room for amusement, nonsense, and recreation. This does not mean that it abandoned its more traditional role in the civilizing process as agent of socialization. For instance, up until the 1850s, the majority of fairy tale writers for children, including Catherine Sinclair, George Cruikshank, and Alfred Crowquill in England, Collodi in Italy, Comtesse Sophie de Ségur in France, and Ludwig Bechstein in Germany, emphasized lessons to be learned, in keeping with the principles of the Protestant ethic – industriousness, honesty, cleanliness, diligence, virtuousness – and male supremacy. However, just as the "conventional" fairy tale for adults had become subverted at the end of the eighteenth century, there was a major movement to write parodies of fairy tales, which were intended for both children and adults. In other words, the classical tales were turned upside down and inside out to question the value system upheld by the dominant socialization process and to keep wonder, curiosity, and creativity alive. By the 1860s, it was clear that numerous writers were using the fairy tale to subvert the formal structure of the canonized tales as well as the governing forces in their societies that restricted free expression of ideas. Such different authors as William Makepeace Thackeray ("Bluebeard's Ghost," 1843), Nathaniel Hawthorne ("Feathertop," 1846), Theodor Storm ("Hinzelmeier," 1857), Gottfried Keller ("Spiegel the Cat," 1856), George MacDonald ("The Day Boy and the Night Girl," 1879), Mary De Morgan ("The Three Clever Kings," 1888), Oscar Wilde ("The Fisherman and His Soul," 1891), and Hugo von Hofmannsthal ("The Tale of the 672nd Night," 1895) were concerned with exploring the potential of the fairy tale to reform both the prescribed way it had become cultivated and the stereotypes and prejudices in regard to gender and social roles that it propagated. The best example of the type of subversion attempted during the latter part of the nineteenth century is Lewis Carroll's *Alice in Wonderland* (1865), which has had a major influence on the fairy tale genre to this day.

226

Although many of the fairy tales were ironical or ended on a tragic note, they still subscribed to the utopian notion of the transformation of humans – that is, the redemption of the human qualities and the overcoming of bestial drives. In America, for instance, Frank Stockton, who could be considered the "pioneer" writer of the fairy tale in America, and Howard Pyle, one of the finest writer-illustrators of fairy tales, touch upon the theme of redemption in their tales "The Griffin and the Minor Canon" (1885) and "Where to Lay the Blame" (1895). But the most notable American fairy tale of the nineteenth century was L. Frank Baum's *The Wizard of Oz* (1900), which depicts Dorothy's great desire and need to break out of Kansas and determine her own destiny, a theme that Baum also explored in "The Queen of Quok" (*American Fairy Tales*, 1901).

By the beginning of the twentieth century, the fairy tale had become fully institutionalized in Europe and America, and its functions had shifted and expanded. The institutionalization of a genre means that a specific process of production, distribution, and reception has become regularized within the public sphere of a society and plays a role in forming and maintaining the cultural heritage of that society. Without such institutionalization in advanced industrialized and technological countries, the genre would perish, and thus the genre itself becomes a kind of self-perpetuating institute involved in the socialization and acculturation of readers. Thus it is the interaction of writer/publisher/audience within a given society that makes for the definition of the genre in any given epoch. The aesthetics of each fairy tale will depend on how and why an individual writer wants to intervene in the discourse of the genre as institution.

By the beginning of the twentieth century, the fairy tale as institution had expanded to include drama, poetry, ballet, music, and opera. In fact, one could perhaps assert that the pageants at the various European courts in the sixteenth and seventeenth centuries, especially the court of Louis XIV, had influenced and helped further the development of the literary fairy tale. Certainly, after Mozart's *The Magic Flute* (1791), fairy tale themes became abundant in the musical world of Europe in the nineteenth century, as can be seen in E. T. A. Hoffmann's own *Undine* (1814), Robert Schumann's *Kreisleriana* (1835–40), Léo Delibes's *Coppélia* (1870), Tchaikovsky's *Sleeping Beauty* (1889) and *The Nutcracker* (1892), Engelbert Humperdinck's *Hänsel and Gretel* (1893), and Jacques Offenbach's *The Tales of Hoffmann* (1881). Again, the manner in which the fairy tale incorporated other art forms reveals the vital role adults have played in maintaining the genre. Never has the fairy tale lost its appeal to adults, and the fairy tale for adults or mixed audiences underwent highly significant changes in the twentieth century.

During the first half of the century, the major shift in the function of the literary tale involved greater and more explicit politicization. In France, Apollinaire, who wrote "Cinderella Continued" (1919), joined with a group of experimental writers to publish their fairy tales in *La Baïonette* as commentary of the ravages of World War I. Hermann Hesse, who had written "The Forest Dweller" (1917–18) to criticize the conformity of his times, published "Strange News from Another Planet" in 1919 to put forward his pacifist views, and Thomas Mann made a major contribution to the fairy tale novel with *The Magic Mountain* (1924), which is filled with political debates about nationalism and democracy. Moreover, there was a wave of innovative and expressionistic fairy tales in Germany written by Edwin Hoernle, Hermynia zur Mühlen, Mynona, Franz Hessel, Kurt Schwitters, Oskar Maria Graf, Bertolt Brecht, Alfred Döblin, and others, which were politically tendentious. In England, the experimentation was not as great. Nevertheless, a volume entitled *The Fairies Return, Or, New Tales for Old* appeared in 1934, and it contained tales with unusual social commentaries by A. E. Coppard, Lord Dunsany, Eric Linklater, Helen Simpson, E. O. Somerville, Christina Stead, and G. B. Stern. Of course, after the Nazi rise to power and during the Spanish Civil War, the fairy tale became more and more the means to convey political sentiments. In Germany, the fairy tale was interpreted and produced according to Nazi ideology, and there are numerous examples of *völkisch* and Fascist fairy tale products. In turn, they brought out a response of writers opposed to Nazism, such as the American H. I. Phillips in "Little Red Riding Hood as a Dictator Would Tell It" (1940). Germany offers an extreme case of how the fairy tale became politicized or used for political purposes. But this extreme case does illustrate a general trend in the political intonation of fairy tales, which continued into the 1940s and 1950s. For example. J. R. R. Tolkien's *The Hobbit* (1937) was written with World War I in mind and with the intention of warning against a second world war. James Thurber's "The Girl and the Wolf" (1939) focused on power and violation. Georg Kaiser's "The Fairy Tale of the King" (1943) reflected upon dictatorship. Erich Kästner's "The Fairy Tale About Reason" (1948) projected the possibility of world peace. Ingeborg Bachmann's "The Smile of the Sphinx" (1949) recalled the terror of the Holocaust.

Following World War II, the fairy tale set out once again to combat terror, but this time the terror concerned not the inhibitions of the civilizing process, rationalization and alienation, but the demented and perverse forms of civilization that had in part caused atrocities and threatened to bring the world to the brink of catastrophe. Confronted with such a prospect at the onset of the Cold War, with other wars to follow, writers like Henri Pourrat and Italo Calvino sought to preserve spiritual and communal values of the oral wonder tales in revised versions, while numerous other writers drastically altered the fairy tale to question whether the utopian impulse could be kept alive and whether our sense of wonderment could be maintained. If so, then the fairy tale had to deal with perversity and what Hannah Arendt called the "banality of evil." Writers like Philip K. Dick ("The King of the Elves," 1953), Naomi Mitchison ("Five Men and a Swan,"

1957), Sylvia Townsend Warner ("Bluebeard's Daughter," 1960), Christoph Meckel ("The Crow," 1962), Stanislaw Lem ("Prince Ferrix and the Princess Crystal," 1967), and Robert Coover ("The Dead Queen," 1973) provoke readers not by playing with their expectations but by disturbing expectations. To a certain extent, they know that most of their readers have been "Disneyized" – that is, subjected to the saccharine sexist and illusionary stereotypes of the Disney culture industry – and therefore they have felt free to explode the illusion that happy ends are possible in real worlds that are held together by the deceit of advertising and government. Especially since the 1970s, the fairy tale for adults has become more aggressive, aesthetically more complex and sophisticated, and more insistent on *not* distracting readers by helping them focus on key social problems and issues in their respective societies. This standpoint is especially apparent in the works of Janosch, Günter Kunert, Michael Ende, Michel Tournier, Donald Barthelme, Michael de Larrabeiti, and Peter Redgrove. Perhaps the major social critique carried by the fairy tale can be seen in the restructuring and reformation by feminists of the fairy tale genre itself. The result has been a remarkable production of nonsexist fairy tales for children and adults as well as theoretical works that have explored the implications of gender roles in fairy tales. Not only have individual authors such as Anne Sexton, Angela Carter, Jane Yolen, Tanith Lee, Rosemarie Künzler, Jay Williams, and Robin McKinley created highly innovative tales that reverse and question traditional sex roles, but there have been collective enterprises in Italy, England, Ireland, and the United States that have reacted critically to the standard canon representing catatonic females flat on their backs waiting to be brought to life by charming princes.

Of course, there are numerous fairy tale works for adults that are blissfully serene and depict intact worlds that need no changing. Or there are placid revisions and patchwork reproductions of classical fairy tales meant to provide amusement and/or *divertissement*. For instance, there has been a great commercialization of the fairy tale since the 1950s. In all forms and shapes, the classical fairy tales continue to be money-makers and thrive on basic sexist messages and conservative notions of social behavior. While the production of classical fairy tale books continues to be a profitable enterprise – and publishers are often indiscriminate as long as the fairy tales are like money in the bank and produce a healthy interest – even more money is generated through fairy tale films, plays, telecasts, and videos. *Faerie Tale Theatre*, a television and video product created by Shelley Duvall, is a case in point.

The theatrical and cinematic use of the fairy tale is extremely significant since Western society has become more oriented toward viewing fairy tale films, plays, and pictures rather than reading them. Here, two fairy tale productions might serve to illustrate a shift in function that is still in process. The 1987 Broadway musical *Into the Woods*, an amusing and trite collage, is typical of one aspect of the shift. It plays eclectically with all sorts of fairy tale motifs and characters in a conventional Broadway musical manner, only to arrive at a stale happy end to "divert" audiences from thinking creatively about their lives. If it is true that the fairy tale in the seventeenth century was bound by the rules and regulations of court society and that it largely served to represent court society to itself and glorify the aristocracy, and if it is true that social and political development in the nineteenth century set art free so that the fairy tale as a genre became autonomous on the free market and in the public sphere, then it appears that there is a return, at least in the theatre, television, and cinema, to the representative function of the fairy tale. Of course, this time the society that is being represented to itself as glorious is the capitalist consumer society. In addition, the fairy tale implicitly and explicitly reflects the state's endeavors to reconcile divergent forces, to pacify malcontents, to show how there are basically good elements within the bourgeois elite groups vying for control of American society. These agents (often understood as heroes) are portrayed as seeking the happiness of *all* groups, especially the disenfranchised, who create the drama in real life and in the fairy tale productions.

The 1987–89 television series *Beauty and the Beast* is a good example of how the fairy tale as representation (and legitimation) of elite bourgeois interests functions. No matter which thirty-minute episode a viewer watched, the basic plot of the television adaptation of the classic tale followed the same lines: the young woman, Catherine, who is from the upper classes, devotes her talents to serving as a legal defender of the oppressed; and the Beast, Vincent, represents the homeless and the outcasts in America, forced to live underground. These two continually unite, because of some elective affinity, to oppose crime and corruption and clear the way for the moral forces to triumph in America. Though the different episodes do expose the crimes of the upper as well as the lower classes, the basic message is that there can be a reconciliation between beauty and beast, and we can live in a welfare state without friction.

Despite the tendency of the film and television industry to use the fairy tale to induce a sense of happy end and ideological consent and to mute its subversive potential for the benefit of those social groups controlling power in the public sphere, the fairy tale as institution cannot be defined one-dimensionally or totally administered by its most visible producers in the mass media and publishing. The readers, viewers, and writers of fairy tales constitute its broadest meaning, perhaps not in the old communal way but in an individualized way that allows for free expression and subversion of norms that are hypocritically upheld and serve to oppress people. A good case in point is Salman Rushdie's inventive fairy tale novel *Haroun and the Sea of Stories* (1990), which concerns a young boy's quest to save his father's storytelling gifts, which are ultimately employed to undermine oppression in the country of Alifbay, so ruinously sad that it had forgotten its name. Rushdie's fairy tale allows him to diagnose the sickness of the country by symbolically naming names. Himself suffering oppression, he has written a fairy tale in which he urges readers to question authoritarianism and to become inventive, daring, and cunning. He wants to leave his mark in society during troubled times, providing hope for solutions without supplying definitive answers.

This is the ultimate paradox of the literary fairy tale: it marks reality without leaving a trace of how it creates the wondrous effects. There is no doubt that the fairy tale has become totally institutionalized in Western society, part of the public sphere, with its own specific code and forms through which we communicate about social and psychic phenomena. We initiate children and expect them to learn the fairy tale code as part of our responsibility in the civilizing process. This code has its key words and keynotes, but it is not static. As in the oral tradition, its original impulse of hope for better lives has not vanished in the literary tradition, although many of the signs have been manipulated in the name of male authoritarian forces. As long as the fairy tale continues to awaken our wonderment and enable us to project worlds counter to our present society, it will serve a meaningful social and aesthetic function, not just for compensation but for revelation: for the worlds portrayed by the best of our fairy tales are like magic spells of enchantment that actually free us. Instead of petrifying our minds, fairy tales arouse our imagination and compel us to realize how we can fight terror and cunningly insert ourselves into our daily struggles and turn the course of the world's events in our favor.

94

REWRITTEN BY ADULTS

The inscription of children's literature

Maria Tatar

Source: *Off With Their Heads! Fairy Tales and the Culture of Childhood*, Princeton: Princeton University Press, 1992, pp. 3–21, 241–244.

> *Follow children learning their fables; and you will see that when they are in a position to apply them, they almost always do so in a way opposite to the author's intention, and that instead of looking within themselves for the shortcoming that one wants to cure or prevent, they tend to like the vice with which one takes advantage of others' shortcomings.*
>
> Rousseau, *Emile*

When folktales retreated from workrooms and parlors to take up residence in the nursery, something was lost in the move. The tales may not have forfeited their hold on the imagination of young and old alike, but they did lose many of the elements that accounted for their appeal to adults *qua* adults, rather than as parents, guardians, or teachers. "Little Red Riding Hood," as we shall see, started out as a ribald story with a heroine who spends a good part of the narrative undressing while provocatively asking the wolf what to do with her bodice, her petticoat, and her stockings, and who then tricks the wolf into freeing her by asking if she can go outdoors to relieve herself. It is not difficult to imagine what a skilled raconteur could do with this story to enliven the hours spent husking corn or mending tools. But in the hands of those who turned traditional tales into literary texts, the story of Red Riding Hood came to be oriented toward a new audience and transformed into a solemn cautionary tale warning children about the perils of disobeying mother's instructions. "The Frog King," a story rich in opportunities for risqué humor, was similarly recast to produce a tale designed to issue stern lessons about the importance of keeping promises— even when it means sharing your bed with an amorous frog. The twins born to Rapunzel materialize in magical fashion when they appear between the covers of books for children—not once are they connected with the heroine's daily romps with the prince in her isolated tower.

Those who recorded folktales for a posterity that included children as well as adults often took the path of least resistance and turned a deaf ear to stories that showed priests hightailing it when husbands returned home unexpectedly or that described worldly men helping naive young women "put the devil into hell." With some imagination and ingenuity, it was also not that difficult to alter a few details in a tale to make it acceptable—if not necessarily appealing—children's fare. In the oldest versions of "The Three Gifts," a boy wishes for a bow that will hit its every target and a pipe that will force people to dance. He also asks that whenever his stepmother glares at him, "her bum might then let go, and crack like roaring thunder." Later versions of the story show us the boy wishing for a bow, a pipe, and the ability to make everyone do as he commands.[1]

Every collector, of course, had a different bias. The Frenchman Henri Pourrat, for example, let scatalogical episodes slip into his multivolumed anthology of folktales but excised anything that smacked of anticlerical sentiment or sacrilegious conduct. In his story "The Stupid Wife," a woman hiding in a tree with her husband cannot restrain herself and defecates. The substance lands in a pot of soup being cooked by bandits, who chant "Bubble, bubble, rich and brown, / God's own fat is tumbling down." Pourrat had the "delicacy" to change "God's own grace" ("la grâce de Dieu") into "God's own fat" ("la graisse de Dieu").[2] Yet Pourrat's practice in this particular tale represents something of a deviation from the norm, in part because he was less intent on writing for children than on preserving rustic customs. In general, the closer we move toward the nineteenth century, the lower the tolerance of collectors for virtually anything that touches on bodily functions.

Scholars have produced abundant evidence to show that folk raconteurs took advantage of opportunities to blend generous doses of earthy humor into their plots and season them with sexual intrigue. The liberties they took by the fireside were almost always eliminated once the stories reached print and moved into the realm of "official" culture. As Bakhtin has taught us, the grotesque realism of folk culture produced a boundless world of carnival humor that stood in a contestatory relationship to the official ecclesiastical and feudal order. Bodily functions were celebrated in both their degrading and reproductive aspects—the material triumphed over the spiritual as the source of life. "Grotesque realism . . . is the fruitful earth and the womb. It is always conceiving," Bakhtin asserts.[3] Laughter becomes a subversive power, undermining the stable truths of official culture and producing an irreverently playful world of change and renewal. As folktales became divested of their humorous elements, they also lost their subversive edge and became assimilated into the official canon of children's literature, which had always been more interested in producing docile minds than playful bodies.

Thanks to the efforts of certain folklorists (many of whom were considered uncomfortably close to the lunatic fringe in their own day and age), we possess unbowdlerized versions of some popular tales. Alexander Afanasev, the Russian counterpart to the brothers Grimm, had to print the bawdy tales he had collected at his own expense, in the city of Geneva, "without fanfare, in a place far from the cataclysmic events of the world, a place that the sacrilegious hand of the censor has not yet violated."[4] Even in the recent past, folklorists have felt obliged to keep their anthologies clean and to file away any "dirty" stories they may have heard from raconteurs. The American folklorist Vance Randolph, for example, published numerous collections of Ozark folktales in the 1950s, but the off-color tales he recorded were quietly deposited in the Library of Congress and in the Kinsey Institute for Sex Research at Indiana University and did not reach print until some twenty years later under the title *Pissing in the Snow and Other Ozark Folktales*.[5]

When it came to violence, the collectors of folktales put a different strategy into operation. Instead of disguising it or blotting it out, they preserved and often intensified it, though usually only when scenes of physical suffering or mental torment could be invested with a higher moral purpose. Since many classic fairy tales for children move along the path from victimization to retaliation, there was always ample opportunity to dilate on a person's misfortune. The example of the Grimms' "Cinderella" illustrates the attentive detail lavished on a heroine's trials and tribulations:

> [The stepsisters] expected her to work hard there from morning till night. She had to get up before dawn, carry the water into the house, make the fire, cook, and wash. Besides this, her sisters did everything imaginable to cause her grief and make her look ridiculous. For instance, they poured peas and lentils into the hearth ashes so she had to sit there and pick them out. In the evening, when she was exhausted from working, they took away her bed, and she had to lie next to the hearth in the ashes. This is why she always looked so dusty and dirty and why they all called her Cinderella.[6]

The Grimms were astute enough to know that a fairy-tale character obliged to do any housework at all—let alone all of it—has the immediate sympathy of most children. To turn a heroine into a tragic martyr often required little more than putting a broom into her hands.

The punishment of villains rarely called for restraint: most nineteenth-century anthologies of folktales paint remarkably vivid scenes of torture and execution. In some instances, violence was even added to stories. In the Grimms' first printed version of "Cinderella," for example, the stepmother and stepsisters are "horrified" and "turn pale" when they witness the heroine's good fortune.[7] By the time of the second edition, when Wilhelm

Grimm was well aware that the collection had become a big hit with children, pigeons peck out the eyes of the stepsisters and they are "punished with blindness for the rest of their lives [for] their wickedness and malice." American versions of the tale were rarely so violent, in part because they were usually based on Perrault's version of "Cinderella," which showed the heroine ("as good as she was beautiful") setting aside apartments in her palace for her sisters and marrying them to "two gentlemen of high rank about the Court."[8] But Perrault's ending was the exception rather than the rule: other printed versions of "Cinderella" (including French ones) show the stepsisters and their mother enduring agonizing mental or physical pain. From Basile's stepsisters, who creep home to their mother "livid with envy and unable to bear the torment of their breaking hearts," through French stepsisters who are turned to stone or get jaundice and die, to Portuguese stepsisters who are put to death, we can get a rough idea of the full palette of punishments reserved for Cinderella's rivals.[9] As the old wives who tell the tales collected in Basile's *Pentamerone* observe, the stepsisters always get off too easy, for "no punishment or disaster can be too great for the deserts of pride and envy."

Why this strong moral indignation? If we look at the frame tale for Basile's *Pentamerone*, we discover that "The Cat Cinderella" is, like the other stories in the collection, "one of those tales that old women tell to amuse children."[10] We know, then, that in seventeenth-century Italy, folktales were already oriented toward children, though Basile's collection was produced with an adult audience in mind. The judgmental posture of the narrator derives, to some extent, from the need to provide a moral backbone to what otherwise might be perceived as an utterly frivolous tale. Unfortunately, not only stories like "Cinderella" (with its victimization/retaliation pattern) become grist for the mill of those who felt a relentless need to teach children lessons. "Little Red Riding Hood," which began with a prohibition followed by the heroine's violation of it, played right into the hands of those who were eager to find morals and send messages. In it, however, as in its folkloric cousins, the *heroine* (not her oppressors) meets with a violent end—only in a few versions (like the Grimms') is she rescued from the belly of the wolf. This cautionary tale makes an example of its protagonist, the very figure with which children identify, rather than of its adult villain, and thus becomes a true horror story.

Folktales began to reach print at just the point when a real commercial market was developing for children's literature. Ever adaptable, they could easily be harnessed into service as stories for children so long as a few key changes were made—changes that divested the tales of their earthy humor, burlesque twists, and bawdy turns of phrase to make room for moral instruction and spiritual guidance. Those who produced the great anthologies of folktales and fairy tales had an ever watchful eye on the models generated by the authors of children's books.

From its inception, children's literature had in it an unusually cruel and coercive streak—one which produced books that relied on brutal intimidation to frighten children into complying with parental demands. This intimidation manifested itself in two very different forms, but both made examples of children. First, there were countless cautionary tales that managed to kill off their protagonists or make their lives perpetually miserable for acts of disobedience. Then there were stories about exemplary behavior which, nonetheless, had a strange way of also ending at the deathbeds of their protagonists.

Since cautionary tales and exemplary stories were the two principal models available for producers of children's fiction and biography, they exercised a powerful influence on writers who were (sometimes intentionally, sometimes unwittingly) turning folktales into stories for children. Although transforming a folktale into a cautionary tale or exemplary story may seem like a futile exercise producing nothing more than tales graceless and contrived in their effect, the opposite, in fact, holds true. What is astonishing is the ease with which folktales could be transplanted into the flinty soil of what was once considered suitable reading matter for children.

Since the cautionary tale and the exemplary story played so instrumental a role in the revision of folktales, we need to take a short detour to explore their form and function. Let us begin with the cautionary tale, a genre that flourished in the harsh climate of nineteenth-century childrearing practices. Here we find Heinrich Hoffmann's Pauline, who plays with matches in the German children's classic *Struwwelpeter*, goes up in flames, and perishes. While she is reaching for the matches and lighting them, her cats chant warnings: "Your father has forbidden it. . . . Your mother has forbidden it."[11] Pauline's fate does not deviate sharply from that of her German antecedents and their French and British counterparts, who all suffer dreadful consequences for their lapses. When a young procrastinator tries to learn her lessons on the way to school, the British Miss Kilner lets her trip, fall on her face, and run home with blood pouring over her. "I am sorry you are hurt, still I do really think you deserve to be so for your own indolence and folly," the girl's mother announces with more than a touch of satisfaction.[12] Karl August Engelhardt recounts the story of a boy who, with no malice aforethought, pulls a caper whose consequences are spun out so broadly that they include the loss of the family home and the death of the boy's parents.[13] One false step, these tales imply, and you will perish or, better yet, suffer a thousand deaths as you watch your home put on the auction block, your father go blind, your mother die of grief, and your siblings land in the poorhouse.

Just what is this false step? Pauline's cats proclaim that the deeper cause of the girl's death lies in disobedience. The boy who mistakes arsenic for sugar and dies from eating it in countless children's stories and poems deserves his fate not because of his gluttony, but because he has disobeyed parental commands. "The little Fish that would not do as it was bid," in Ann and Jane Taylor's *Rhymes for the Nursery* (1835), makes the following speech before expiring on a fisherman's hook: "Dear mother, had I minded you, I need not now have died."[14] The cardinal sin of youth is disobedience, and it is a sin that habitually demands the death penalty. What is particularly odd about these stories is that the pedagogical program of each tale clashes so starkly with the tale's content: survival and good fortune are promoted through images of death and disaster.

The titles of eighteenth- and nineteenth-century bestsellers for children are telling: *A Tale of Warning, or, The Victims of Indolence*; *The Good-Natured Little Boy and the Ill-Natured Little Boy*; *Meddlesome Mattie*; *Dangerous Sports, a Tale Addressed to Children Warning them against Wanton, Careless, or Mischievous Exposure to Situations from which Alarming Injuries so often Proceed*; and *The Adventures of a Whipping-Top. Illustrated with Stories of many Bad Boys, who themselves deserve whipping, and of some Good Boys, who deserve Plum-Cakes*. The wave of moralism that swept through children's fiction to produce tales of the "awful-warning" school also encroached on other areas of childhood culture. In *Rhymes and Pictures for the Nursery and School. By a Lady*, we hear of a little girl who insists on eating forbidden fruit:

> They went on a little, but Anna complain'd
> Of pain in her stomach and head,
> And very soon follow'd most terrible pains,
> She shriek'd out with anguish and dread. . . .
> She died from not doing what Ma had desired,
> And eating the fruit of the wood.

The year 1810 witnessed the issue of the British *New Game of Virtue Rewarded and Vice Punished*, whose game board was covered with such attractive scenes and figures as "The Stocks," "The House of Correction," "Faith," and "Prudence."[15] The popular American children's game *Chutes and Ladders*, in which game pieces landing on pictures of children eating candy, reaching for a cookie, or drawing with crayons on a wall must slide away from the goal down a chute, while game pieces landing on pictures of children mowing the lawn, sweeping the floor, or baking a cake may advance up a ladder, probably evolved from its British equivalent. There too a child is to learn "the rewards of good deeds and the consequences of naughty ones."[16]

All these tales, rhymes, and games operate with a minimal narrative unit that consists of a pattern basic also to folktale plots (prohibition/violation/punishment). We can see this syntagmatic unit at work in "Sleeping Beauty," where the heroine must not touch a spindle. When she violates the (unspoken) prohibition, the penalty consists of a deathlike sleep that lasts a hundred years. Unlike the naughty children of cautionary tales, however, Sleeping Beauty never willfully defies an order—in fact, she does nothing at all to merit the punishment visited on her. There is no moral dimension whatever to her action. This could easily be changed, and often was changed, once fairy tales were appropriated by the purveyors of children's literature. Sleeping Beauty usually remained morally unimpeachable, though one recent American version turns her into a girl who, like Bluebeard's wife, succumbs to the temptation of taking a key and opening the door to a forbidden chamber—one that houses a spinning wheel. On the other hand, Sleeping Beauty's folkloric sisters (among others, Little Red Riding Hood, the princess in "The Frog Prince," and the heroine of "King Thrushbeard") nearly all became models of bad breeding. By the middle of the nineteenth century, they had become morally reprehensible in one way or another and in some sense responsible for their fates.

Defenders of fairy tales often fall into the trap of elevating these stories into repositories of higher truths and moralities. Fairy tales, we have been taught to believe, offer comfort to children, for in them we find a moral corrective to everyday life, a world in which the good are consistently rewarded and the evil are just as consistently punished.[17] In reality, the picture is quite different. Although fairy tales often celebrate such virtues as compassion and humility and show the rewards of good behavior, they also openly advocate lying, cheating, and stealing. The heroes and heroines (who are not necessarily either "good" or virtuous") get all the rewards while the villains (who are not always "evil" or "sinful") are dispossessed and tortured. Think of the miller's daughter in "Rumpelstiltskin," who marries a king and lives happily ever after even though she fails to keep up her end of the bargain struck with the "villain" of the tale's title. Rumpelstiltskin, by contrast, fulfills all the terms of his contract but perishes because he is moved by the queen's tears and agrees to build an escape clause into the contract.

The moral depravity of fairy-tale heroes and heroines did not escape the attention of those who had an audience of children in mind as they prepared volumes of fairy tales for publication. In order to please "every tender mother, and every gentle tutor," Benjamin Tabart had to make sweeping changes in traditional tales to produce his *Popular Fairy Tales; or, a Lilliputian Library*. His Jack, for example, does not rob the giant of his rightful possessions—he simply reclaims (as we learn in a lengthy digression) what the giant had previously stolen from his father.[18]

Once fairy tales entered the realm of children's literature, they took on a protective didactic coloring that has been virtually impossible to remove. Rather than toning down scenes of violence for children's stories, recorders and collectors often added moral lessons that, in their eyes, gave them license to emphasize or even exaggerate descriptions of punishment and death. At the same time, authors of conventional cautionary tales were learning some lessons of their own from didactic fairy tales, enlivening their often dreary depictions of virtue rewarded and vice punished by dwelling on the naughty, corrupt, and evil deeds of children and by borrowing surreal elements from folktales to add spine-chilling effects. The result occasionally added up to gratuitous cruelty, as in the case of Mrs. W. K. Clifford's *Anyhow Stories* (1882), in which a "wild woman" tempts two small children to engage in ever more naughty deeds until finally their mother can bear it no longer and turns over her children and her home to a woman with glass eyes and a wooden tail. The children flee into the woods. "They are there still, my children," Mrs. Clifford solemnly concludes. "Now and then ... [they] creep up near to the home in which they once were so happy, and with beating hearts they watch and listen; sometimes a blinding flash comes through the window, and they know it is the light from the new mother's glass eyes, or they hear a strange muffled noise, and they know it is the sound of the wooden tail as she drags it along the floor."[19] This story, which plays on children's deepest fears about maternal abandonment, stands as the most extreme example of what could happen when an author combined naturalistic descriptions of children's behavior with surreal incarnations of punishing parents.

The anonymous author of a collection of cautionary stories entitled *Tales Uniting Instruction with Amusement consisting of the Dangers of the Streets; and Throwing Squibs* must have had a strange notion of "amusement." The readers of this volume are treated to the contrast between wellbred Edward Manly, who is always careful to watch his step, and mischievous George, who walks out into the street, is run over by a wagon, and ends up on the operating table: "The surgeon took out his instruments, cut the flesh all round with a sharp knife, cut through the bone with a saw, and thus poor George's leg was taken completely off." Then there is Tom, who throws squibs and ends up killing his father and hurting himself: "He often bitterly laments his ill-conduct, and wishes he had followed his poor father's good advice. If he had done so, he might now have been at a genteel boarding school with both his eyes safe, instead of being a chimney sweeper, and blind of one eye."[20] The stories were probably meant to amuse in the sense of "divert," yet they inadvertently produce a comic effect. When a punishment is so disproportionate to the crime, as in these cases, there is something ludicrous about the solemnity of the narrator's pronouncements.

Tales Uniting Instruction with Amusement can help us understand just why it was that cautionary tales were probably less distasteful to children than one might suspect. The gory accidents that children meet up with when they are careless or disobedient may have been meant to repel children, but the fact is that they could also prove a source of unending fascination. What child is not mesmerized by the sight of the burning dresses, lopped-off thumbs, and tormented animals in Hoffmann's *Struwwelpeter*, a book whose appeal can be traced not just to the need of parents to coerce their children into docile behavior, but also to the desire of children to hear stories as sensational in their own way as the ones once told around the fireside. In many cases, the more carried away adult writers of cautionary tales were in their descriptions of tortures and mutilations, the more attractive the tales proved for children.

At times it seems as if some authors deliberately sabotaged the didactic aim of their stories. Mrs. Bell in Kilner's *Village School* is described as "a very good woman," a "valuable member of society," and "much beloved." Here is how she punishes one of the many "naughty" children at her school:

> She took off his coat, and beat him very much with a cane she kept on purpose to beat naughty children. She then tied his hands behind him, and his legs together, and assured him he should not go home that night; but that, when school was over, she would shut him up in some closet, where he might be safe, and not do any more mischief. (9)

It is easy enough to imagine that Mrs. Bell's death in a fire while she is concurrently nursing a sick woman and making a shirt for a neighbor whose wife is also ill is something of a relief for both author and readers. Mrs. Kilner seems almost too eager to describe the demise of her heroine, whose "flesh was so entirely consumed as to make it impossible to distinguish Mrs. Bell from the poor woman she had charitably assisted" (88). Yet when we read the sanctimonious tribute to Mrs. Bell and find that her story culminates in yet another lesson—this time "to be extremely cautious not to leave candles burning near linen"—it is hard to imagine that Mrs. Kilner's aim was parody. This would not, however, prevent young readers of *The Village School* from getting some grim satisfaction out of Mrs. Bell's death.

Exemplary stories could be just as unsparing as cautionary tales in describing scenes of suffering—in some ways they seem even crueler than stories in which boys perish because they have pulled the wings off a fly. That these stories dominated the children's book market for some time becomes clear from an observation made in the 1830s by Catherine Sinclair, when a friend residing in the country asked her to select some books for her children. On surveying what was available, it surprised Sinclair that "a large proportion of the volumes recommended had frontispieces to represent a death-bed surrounded by the clergyman, the physician, and the afflicted relatives of a dying Christian, the memoirs of children *especially*, which I examined, were almost invariably terminated by an early death."[21] The most notorious example of a book that celebrated the deaths of "good" children was James Janeway's *A Token for Children: Being an Account of the Conversion, Holy and Exemplary Lives, and Joyful Deaths of Several Young Children* (1671–72). Janeway is dead set against allowing children to enjoy themselves in this world. Pleasure and joy are reserved exclusively for dead children, or, at best, for those in their death throes. "How do you spend your time?" he asks his audience with calculated artlessness. "Is it in play and idleness, and with wicked children? . . . Do you dare to idle and play upon the Lord's day?"[22] We do not have to read far into the volume to discover the fatal consequences of idleness, but Janeway does not give us, as might be expected, death scenes of wanton young sinners. The sweet children whose deaths he documents "feared God, and were dutiful to their parents." Now that they are in heaven, they see "glorious things, and have nothing but joy and pleasure." For those children who are not yet fortunate enough to experience the "ecstasy of joy and holy triumph" that the four-year-old Mary A. felt on her deathbed, Janeway recommends a combination of "secret prayer" and weeping, with occasional pauses for quoting of scripture, expressions of gratitude for parental prohibitions, and readings in his own book, whose richness, he asserts, will not be exhausted even after a hundred readings.

The case history of young John Sudlow has Janeway's characteristic touch: a dreary, sanctimonious style combined with a hagiographic tone that wears thin even on a first reading. The death of John's brother inspires the boy "to avoid whatsoever might displease God." His interest in scripture becomes so intense that "when neighbors' children would come and call him out, and try to entice him to go with them, he would by no means be persuaded . . . if he had any hope that any pious person would come to his father's house" (44–45). His temper is so "sweet" that he is always "dutiful" to his parents and careful not to "displease" them. Compassion for his brothers and sisters runs so deep that he begs his parents to take better care of the souls of these siblings "lest they should go on in a sinful Christless state, prove their sorrow and shame, go to hell when they died, and be ruined forever" (46). Struck down by the plague, this model child remains steadfast in his faith even when the local minister consoles him on his deathbed by asking him whether he is afraid to die and reminding him that he is a sinner who cannot expect salvation.

The London Bills of Mortality reveal that in the period shortly following the publication of Janeway's *Token for Children*, the mortality rate of children age five and under could run as high as 66 percent.[23] Thus when Janeway asked, in the "directions for children" accompanying his volume: "Did you never hear of a little child that died?" he could count on "yes" as an answer. "If other children die," Janeway hastened to add, "why may not you be sick and die! and what will you do then, if you should have no grace in your heart, but are like other naughty children?" (94). Given the visible presence of death in the daily lives of most children growing up in the premodern era and the nineteenth century, the specter of an early death could be raised in a highly effective way by those who chose to use it in their childrearing practices.[24]

Janeway's sensationalizing dramas of children's victories over sin may, like cautionary tales, have ended in the cemetery, but they prospered with the reading public. One critic has likened the appeal of these spiritual biographies to that of romances and fairy tales, for in them sin figures as an ogre or monster against which the child struggles to emerge victorious.[25] Yet while folktales could easily absorb the ethos of the cautionary tale and transform themselves into miniature moral dramas, they proved more resistant to the spirituality of the exemplary story; accounts of pious children lacked the element of transgressive action required to generate fairy-tale conflicts. Still, one should not underestimate the attractiveness of the genre for children. P. L. Travers (author of *Mary Poppins*), for example, writes about her "great affection" as a child for a book called *Twelve Deathbed Scenes*.[26]

As we shall see, there are a number of tales that glorify the sufferings of their protagonists and celebrate the afterlife, among them a story whose most popular incarnation is found in Hans Christian Andersen's "Little Match Girl." *Dear Mili*, a tale by Wilhelm Grimm recently published with great fanfare in this country, is similarly oriented toward death, with a heroine who loses her life during a time of war and is translated into a higher sphere, where she lives with St. Joseph and plays with her guardian angel.

A culture with a high mortality rate will understandably reach for Janeway, Andersen, or Grimm in order to prepare children for death by offering the consolation of spiritual salvation. It is, after all, not easy for anyone to answer the concerns raised by a child in Lucy Cameron's *History of Margaret Whyte, or, The Life and Death of a Good Child* (1837): "'How can we tell that we shall ever live to grow up? Many children die much younger than either of us; and if we do not think of preparing for death, what will become of us?'"[27] Even Janeway seems quite tame by comparison with some of the sermons preached to British children in the early part of the nineteenth century. Here is an excerpt from one delivered by the grim Reverend Carus Wilson, author of a juvenile magazine called —in all seriousness—*The Children's Friend*:

> My dear children, the hooping [sic] cough is spreading fast; several little ones have died of it. Day after day I hear the bell tolling, and one little child after another has been buried here; and as I walk out into the villages, and the lanes, and go into schools, I see your little faces swelled, and hear you coughing; but I am pained to think how few of you would be found ready were you called to die of it. Let me beg of you, dears, to try to think about death; say to yourselves, "perhaps I may soon die, and then where will my soul go? will it go to heaven, or will it be cast down into hell, where there will be weeping, and wailing and gnashing of teeth?"[28]

There is no escaping the fact that tales like "The Little Match Girl" and *Dear Mili* use death in much the same way as do sermons like these. The goodness, obedience, and piety of the match girl and Mili secure them a place in heaven; implicitly, we know that their fate would be quite different were they to lack those qualities. It is thus more than odd that a text like *Dear Mili*, which is so firmly anchored in the cultural realities of its time, should be resurrected and hailed as a children's tale that speaks "so directly to the concerns of our time [1988] that it seems extraordinary to have it appear now."[29]

Collectors of folktales nearly always stand in awe of the stories they record. The Grimms never tired of declaring that the tales in their collection captured the authentic voice of the folk in all its purity and artless simplicity. The poetry of the people was also the poetry of nature, unsullied by the corrupting influences of culture and civilization. Yet at the same time, the Grimms called their book an "educational manual." Folktales were never meant to convey lessons, they proclaimed in the introduction to the *Nursery and Household Tales*, "but a moral grows out of them, just as good fruit develops from healthy blossoms without help from man."[30] In a sense, the Grimms were trying to have their cake and eat it too: They had a need to enshrine these tales as "natural" stories untainted by the hand of man, yet at the same time they felt compelled to stress their "civilizing" qualities. Unable to escape the influence of Rousseau, yet also children of the Enlightenment who would have applauded the view that "everything, animate or inanimate, may . . . be made subservient to moral instruction," they found themselves caught in a contradiction that characterized much of post-Enlightenment thinking about folktales.[31]

The myth of folktales as sacred, "natural" texts was deftly propagated by Charles Dickens, who brought to the literature of childhood the same devout reverence that he accorded children. Dickens, like the Grimms, hailed the "simplicity," "purity," and "innocent extravagance" of fairy tales, but he also praised the tales as powerful instruments of socialization: "It would be hard to estimate the amount of gentleness and mercy that has made its way among us through these slight channels. Forebearance, courtesy, consideration for the poor and aged, kind treatment of animals, the love of nature, abhorrence of tyranny and brute force—many such good things have been first nourished in the child's heart by this powerful aid."[32]

Dickens' paean to fairy tales was part of a crusade against the efforts of George Cruikshank, his illustrator and erstwhile friend, to produce a new breed of fairy tales. Passions ran high when the two quarreled over the issue. Cruikshank, in response to Dickens' attack on his versions of "Cinderella," "Hop-o'-my-Thumb," "Puss in Boots," and "The History of Jack & the Bean-Stalk," correctly pointed out that there was much in fairy tales that was not suitable for children. In the preface to his "Cinderella," he told readers that he had pored over several versions of the tale and found "*some* vulgarity, mixed up with so much that was useless and unfit for children, that I was obliged . . . to re-write the whole story."[33] Cruikshank could not resist the temptation to introduce "a few *Temperance Truths*" in his rewriting. When Cinderella is to be wed, for example, the father of the Prince orders "fountains of wine" to be set up in the courtyards of the palace and in the streets. Cinderella's godmother is appalled by these plans and reminds the monarch that these fountains of wine will foment "quarrels, brutal fights, and violent death." The King's belief that moderation in drink will avert violence is challenged by the godmother, who sanctimoniously states that "the history of the use of strong drink . . . is marked on every page by *excess, which follows, as a matter of course, from the very nature of their composition*, and . . . always accompanied by ill-health, misery, and crime" (25). The King is converted and orders all the beer, wine, and spirits in the kingdom collected for a "great bonfire" on the night of the wedding. After reading Cruikshank's "Cinderella," Dickens' words about the "intrusion of a Whole Hog of unwieldy dimension into the fairy flower garden" seem remarkably apt.[34]

Cruikshank, however, did not limit himself to "*Temperance Truths.*" In "The History of Jack & the Bean-Stalk," he rambled on about the evils of "idleness and ignorance" and introduced a fairy who tells a reformed Jack: "I have long wished to employ you in a difficult and important matter, but I could not trust you whilst you were so careless and idly disposed; but now, that you have this day shaken off that slothful habit, and have determined to be active, diligent, and trustworthy, I no longer hesitate."[35] In "Hop-o'-my-Thumb," the hero and his brothers learn to wash themselves in "cold water (which they did winter and summer, because it is most refreshing and healthy to do so)" and to "go to bed early, which they all did, like good children, without any grumbling or crying."[36] Cruikshank's passionate drive to correct the moral vision of fairy tales is nowhere harder at work than in his remarks about Cinderella's stepmother. To preserve the sanctity of motherhood, including stepmotherhood, he represents the villain of the piece as an anomalous case. "It is the nature of woman to have children," he pontificates, "because the Almighty has appointed her to bring them up; and when little boys and girls are placed at an early age under the charge of a stepmother, it is very rarely that they feel the loss of their own mother: but there are exceptions, and it was so, unfortunately, in this case; for Cinderella's mother-in-law [*sic*] was proud, selfish, and extravagant, and these bad qualities led her to be unjust and cruel."[37]

Cruikshank's reinterpretations of fairy tales may have been more heavy-handed than those of most other authors and collectors, but they dramatically illustrate the way in which the ethos of the collector/editor/rewriter penetrates the moral universe of a fairy tale, even of those tales that escaped a merger with the cautionary tale or exemplary story. "Cinderella," for example, in telling of a child persecuted by her stepmother and siblings and of how the child gets back at them, was probably never really designed to illustrate the rewards of good behavior. Still, as we have seen in the case of Cruikshank's rewriting, this story of a girl's victimization and retaliation left plenty of room for moral glosses on whatever virtue or vice happened to preoccupy its recorder.

All printed fairy tales are colored by the facts of the time and place in which they were recorded. For this reason, it is especially odd that we continue to read to our children—often without the slightest degree of critical reflection—unrevised versions of stories that are imbued with the values of a different time and place. Collections like those of Charles Perrault, the brothers Grimm, and Joseph Jacobs are documents from the past, "old-time" fairy tales which, according to the author of *The Wonderful Wizard of Oz*, should now be "classed as 'historical' in the children's library." For L. Frank Baum, the time had come for "a series of newer 'wonder tales' in which the stereotyped genie, dwarf and fairy are eliminated, together with all the horrible and bloodcurdling incidents devised by their authors to point a fearsome moral to each tale."[38] We would be well advised, as Rudolf Schenda has proposed, not only to provide the old-time fairy-tale collections with prefaces about the genesis of the tales and notes about the cultural milieu in which they flourished, but, even more importantly, to think twice before reading certain stories from the collections to children.[39]

Schenda's suggestion, however sound, does not take into account a parent's unwillingness to purchase storybooks with a scholarly apparatus, let alone a publisher's horror at the thought of printing such a volume. But how, then, do we avoid throwing the baby out with the bathwater? How do we preserve the fairy-tale canon even as we divest it of the "wisdom" of another age, of cultural constructs that are irrelevant or inappropriate for the child to whom the tale is read? One obvious answer is to rewrite the stories so that they are closer to our own time and place. But such projects do not necessarily succeed in producing "better" texts—they may end by reflecting the values of one class, ethnic group, or other social segment of our own culture, but that segment may not have much appeal for those living in a culture characterized by ideological pluralism.

Rewriting is often just as likely to produce an unsatisfying text as it is to produce an improved version of the story. Consider the example of the recently issued *Princess and the Frog*, which is a self-described adaptation of "'The Frog King and Iron Heinrich' by the Brothers Grimm."[40] This rewriting does not by any means eliminate the father's intervention and his declaration that the princess must keep her promise and let a frog climb into her bed. "Go and let the frog in," the father insists. "You have made a promise and you must keep it." This new version of an old tale gives us a dutiful daughter who obeys her father, then goes along with the frog's request to let him sleep on her pillow. Instead of a princess who—in a gesture appropriately charged with fear and frustration—dashes the importunate frog against the wall, we have a girl who falls asleep three times with the frog in her bed and finally awakens, on the third morning, to find a prince. The adapter is careful, however, to position the frog on the princess's pillow, just as she replaces the girl's feelings of disgust and anger with tolerance toward her amphibian suitor. (The countless cartoons and jokes based on this story have, incidentally, almost all rewritten the scene of disenchantment: the frog is transformed by a kiss rather than by an act of violence.[41])

In prefatory remarks to "Princess Furball," a modern version of the Grimms' "Allerleirauh," the American adapter makes a point of acknowledging that she has rewritten the story and erased the theme of incest in it, yet she also asserts that she has remained faithful to the "psychological truth" of earlier tellings.[42] Trying to assess the impact of the Grimms' version of the tale and to compare it with the effect of the rewritten version is a task that must be left to the child psychologists. But the examples of the "Frog King" and "Princess Furball" remind us how a story that has been brought "up-to-date" does not necessarily give us an interpretation that is more pedagogically sound or psychologically true.

Fairy tales are not written in granite. My own experience has shown that we continue to rewrite the tales as we reread them, even though the words on the page remain the same. But it is important to remember that what we produce in our retellings and rereadings discloses more about an adult agenda for children than about what children want to hear. Thus fairy tales may not offer much insight into the minds of children, but they often document our shifting attitudes toward the child and chart our notions about childrearing in a remarkable way. It is these discursive practices, as they are embedded in children's literature, that invite reflection as we read to a child or when we put a book into a child's hands.

Maurice Sendak once stated that, as a former child, he felt fully entitled and empowered to write children's stories. In a sense, these same credentials allow all of us to retell fairy tales to our children, even if we may never be able to get the cultural script quite right. Yet while there is a child in every adult, not every adult has the power to reach that child and to engage in empathetic identification with its former self. But as Rousseau reminds us, a child's natural gift for subversion, for moving against every author's intentions, can rescue even the most solemn or dim-witted rendition of a tale and turn it into an amusing diversion, especially when it comes at the expense of its adult authors.

Notes

1 The early version is cited by Samuel F. Pickering, Jr., *John Locke and Children's Books in Eighteenth-Century England* (Knoxville: Univ. of Tennessee Press, 1981), p. 107.

2 "The Stupid Wife," in *French Folktales*, comp. Henri Pourrat, trans. Royall Tyler (New York: Pantheon, 1989), pp. 304–11. See also Tyler's "Introduction,"

p. xxiv. Jack Zipes situates Pourrat's work in the context of other collections in "Henri Pourrat and the Tradition of Perrault and the Brothers Grimm," in *The Brothers Grimm: From Enchanted Forests to the Modern World* (New York: Routledge, Chapman and Hall, 1988), pp. 96–109.

3 Mikhail Bakhtin, *Rabelais and His World*, trans. Helene Iswolsky (Cambridge: MIT Press, 1968), p. 21.

4 Cited by G. Legman, "Toward a Motif-Index of Erotic Humor," *Journal of American Folklore* 75 (1962): 227–48.

5 Even the index of tale types (a volume that classifies all folktale types according to thematic categories) suppresses a plot synopsis and gives only a tale title if a plot is obscene (e.g. AT 1110* Hans Shows the Devil How Men Are Made [Obscene]). See Antti Aarne, *The Types of the Folktale: A Classification and Bibliography*, trans. and enlarged by Stith Thompson (Helsinki: Academia Scientiarum Fennica, 1981), p. 359. In the *Motif-Index of Folk-Literature*, Thompson reserved numbers X700–799 for "Humor Concerning Sex." "Thousands of obscene motifs in which there is no point except the obscenity itself might logically come at this point, but they are entirely beyond the scope of the present work," Thompson observed. "They form a literature to themselves, with its own periodicals and collections." Oddly enough, Thompson was unable to recognize that the "obscene stories" were not separated out from folk stories until the end of the eighteenth century, when collectors either censored or suppressed them. In view of the general reticence of folklorists to publish bawdy materials, it took some courage for Friedrich S. Krauss to edit the *Anthropophyteia* (1904–1913), a journal published in Leipzig and devoted to preserving tales deemed unfit for print by most scholars. Vance Randolph published only a fraction of the bawdy material at his disposal in *Pissing in the Snow and Other Ozark Folktales* (Urbana: Univ. of Illinois Press, 1976). On the bawdy, obscene, and scatalogical in folklore, see Herbert Halpert, "Folklore and Obscenity: Definitions and Problems," *Journal of American Folklore* 75 (1962): 190–94.

6 "Cinderella," in *The Complete Fairy Tales of the Brothers Grimm*, trans. Jack Zipes (Toronto: Bantam, 1987), pp. 86–92.

7 "Aschenputtel," in *Kinder- und Hausmärchen. Gesammelt durch die Brüder Grimm*, ed. Heinz Rölleke (Göttingen: Vandenhoeck & Ruprecht, 1986), vol. 1, p. 101.

8 "Cinderella," in *Perrault's Complete Fairy Tales*, trans. A. E. Johnson *et al.* (New York: Dodd, Mead, 1961), pp. 58–70.

9 "The Cat Cinderella," in *The Pentamerone of Giambattista Basile*, trans. Benedetto Croce, ed. N. M. Penzer (London: John Lane, 1932), vol. 1, pp. 56–63. The French "Cinderella" stories to which I refer appear in *Folktales of France*, ed. Geneviève Massignon, trans. Jacqueline Hyland (Chicago: Univ. of Chicago Press, 1968), pp. 147–49, and in *French Folktales*, comp. Henri Pourrat, pp. 7–14. The Portuguese tale, "The Hearth-Cat," appears in *One Hundred Favorite Folktales*, ed. Stith Thompson (Bloomington: Indiana Univ. Press, 1968), pp. 176–79.

10 Basile, *The Pentamerone*, 1:9.

11 Heinrich Hoffmann, *Der Struwwelpeter* (Volksausgabe), (N.p.: n.p., n.d.).

12 The quotation comes from Dorothy Kilner's *The Village School; A Collection of Entertaining Histories, for the Instruction and Amusement of All Good Children* (London: John Harris, 1831), p. 75. The book originally appeared in 1828.

13 Karl August Engelhardt, "Die gefrornen Fensterscheiben" (1812), in *Kinderschaukel: Ein Lesebuch zur Geschichte der Kindheit in Deutschland, 1756–1860*, ed. Marie-Luise Könneker (Darmstadt: Luchterhand, 1976), vol. 1, pp. 145–51. A similar "disaster tale" is narrated by Mary Ann Kilner in *William Sedley: or,*

The Evil Day Deferred (London: n.p., 1783). There the hard-working Mr. and Mrs. Active are ruined by their "perverse and disobedient" daughters. See Pickering, *John Locke and Children's Books*, p. 181.

14 The poem is printed in *Masterworks of Children's Literature* (New York: Chelsea House, 1984), p. 250.

15 The poem is cited by F. J. Harvey Darton, *Children's Books in England: Five Centuries of Social Life* (Cambridge: Cambridge Univ. Press, 1932), p. 193. He also discusses the *New Game of Virtue Rewarded and Vice Punished* produced in 1810 (p. 153).

16 *Chutes and Ladders*, Milton Bradley Co., 1979.

17 This view was developed in its fullest form by André Jolles, *Einfache Formen* (Halle: Max Niemeyer, 1929), then modified by Max Lüthi, *The European Folk-tale: Form and Nature*, trans. John D. Niles (Philadelphia: Institute for the Study of Human Issues, 1982). It is resurrected in Claude Brémond's "Les Bons récompensées et les méchants punis," in *Sémiotique narrative et textuelle*, ed. Claude Chabrol (Paris: Larousse, 1973), pp. 96–121. Volker Klotz, by contrast, has emphasized that folktales move in the direction of establishing a formal rather than a moral balance; harmony rather than justice is the driving force behind the narrated events. See his "Weltordnung im Märchen," *Neue Rundschau* 81 (1970): 73–91.

18 Tabart's version appears as "The History of Jack and the Bean-Stalk," in *The Classic Fairy Tales*, comp. Iona Opie and Peter Opie (New York: Oxford Univ. Press, 1974), pp. 211–26.

19 Lucy Lane Clifford, *Anyhow Stories, Moral and Otherwise* (London: Macmillan, 1882), p. 47.

20 Cited by Gillian Avery, *Nineteenth-Century Children: Heroes and Heroines in English Children's Stories, 1780–1900* (London: Hodder and Stoughton, 1965), p. 213.

21 Avery, *Nineteenth-Century Children*, p. 212.

22 Janeway's questions and comments come from his concluding "Address Containing Directions to Children's in *A Token for Children: Being an Account of the Conversion, Holy and Exemplary Lives, and Joyful Deaths of Several Young Children* (London: Francis Westley, 1825), p. 92. Page numbers refer to this edition.

23 David Grylls, *Guardians and Angels: Parents and Children in Nineteenth-Century Literature* (London: Faber and Faber, 1978), p. 41.

24 On the role of death in children's tales, see especially Dieter Richter, *Das fremde Kind: Zur Entstehung der Kindheitsbilder des bürgerlichen Zeitalters* (Frankfurt a.M.: Fischer, 1987), pp. 81–87.

25 Pickering, *John Locke and Children's Books*, pp. 141–42.

26 P. L. Travers, "On Not Writing for Children," *Children's Literature* 4 (1975): 19.

27 Avery, *Nineteenth-Century Children*, p. 214.

28 Avery, *Nineteenth-Century Children*, p. 215.

29 *Kirkus Children's and Young-Adult Edition*, 15 Sept. 1988, p. 1403.

30 "Preface to Volume I of the First Edition of the Grimms' *Nursery and Household Tales*," in Tatar, *The Hard Facts of the Grimms' Fairy Tales*, pp. 207–8.

31 The quotation is from an 1803 review in the *Guardian of Education* and is cited by Pickering in *John Locke and Children's Books*, p. 96.

32 Charles Dickens, "Frauds on the Fairies," in *Household Words: A Weekly Journal* (New York: McElrath and Barker, 1854), pp. 97–100.

33 *Cinderella and the Glass Slipper*, ed. and illus. George Cruikshank (London: David Bogue, 1853). On the controversy between the writer and illustrator,

see Harry Stone, "Dickens, Cruikshank, and Fairy Tales," *Princeton University Library Chronicle* 35 (1973–74): pp. 212–47.

34 Dickens, "Frauds on the Fairies," pp. 97–100.

35 *The History of Jack & the Bean-Stalk*, ed. and illus. George Cruikshank (London: David Bogue, 1854), p. 10.

36 *Hop-o'-my-Thumb and the Seven-League Boots*, ed. and illus. George Cruik-shank (London: David Bogue, 1853), pp. 5–6.

37 *Cinderella and the Glass Slipper*, ed. Cruikshank, p. 6.

38 L. Frank Baum, introduction to *The Wonderful Wizard of Oz* (New York: Dover, 1960), n.p.

39 Rudolf Schenda, "Märchen erzählen – Märchen verbreiten: Wandel in den Mitteilungsformen einer populären Gattung," in *Über Märchen für Kinder von heute: Essays zu ihrem Wandel und ihrer Funktion*, ed. Klaus Doderer (Weinheim: Beltz, 1983), pp. 25–43.

40 Rachel Isadora, *The Princess and the Frog* (New York: Greenwillow Books, 1989).

41 Wolfgang Mieder, "Modern Auglo-American Variants of the Frog Prince (AaTh 440)," *New York Folklore* 6 (1980): 111–35, and Lutz Röhrich, *Wage es, den Frosch zu küssen! Das Grimmschen Märchen Nunmer Eins in seinen Wandlungen* (Köln: Diederichs, 1987) both contain a multitude of examples.

42 *Princess Furball*, retold by Charlotte Huck, illus. Anita Lobel (New York: Greenwillow Books, 1989).

95

PRE-TEXTS, METANARRATIVES, AND THE WESTERN METAETHIC

John Stephens and Robyn McCallum

Source: *Retelling Stories, Framing Culture: Traditional Story and Metanarratives in Children's Literature*, New York: Garland, 1998, pp. 3–23.

> *As the cauldron bubbled, an eldritch voice shrieked: "When shall we three meet again?"*
>
> *There was a pause.*
>
> *Finally another voice said, in far more ordinary tones: "Well, I can do next Tuesday."*
>
> —Terry Pratchett, *Wyrd Sisters*

When compared with general literature, the literature produced for children contains a much larger proportion of retold stories. In part this is because some domains of retellings, especially folk and fairy tale, have long been considered more appropriate to child culture than to adult culture, but this relegation is not entirely because such materials might seem ingenuous and accessible to children. Rather, retold stories have important cultural functions. Under the guise of offering children access to strange and exciting worlds removed from everyday experiences, they serve to initiate children into aspects of a social heritage, transmitting many of a culture's central values and assumptions and a body of shared allusions and experiences. The existential concerns of a society find concrete images and symbolic forms in traditional stories of many kinds, offering a cultural inheritance subject to social conditioning and modification through the interaction of various retellings. Although the notional significance of a story is thus potentially infinitely intertextual, subject to every retelling and every significance that has ever accrued to it, it is also arguable that the processes of retelling are overwhelmingly subject to a limited number of conservative metanarratives— that is, the implicit and usually invisible ideologies, systems, and assumptions which operate globally in a society to order knowledge and experience. The major narrative domains which involve retold stories all, in the main, have the function of maintaining conformity to socially determined and approved patterns of behavior, which they do by offering positive role models, proscribing undesirable behavior, and affirming the culture's ideologies, systems, and institutions.

The ideological effect of a retold text is generated from a three-way relationship between the already-given story, the metanarrative(s) which constitute its top-down framing, and its bottom-up discoursal processes. Obviously enough, to be a retelling a text must exist in relationship to some kind of source, which we will refer to as the "pre-text," though it is perhaps only a minority of cases in which this source is fixable as a single work by an identifiable author. Even when this is so, few retellings are simple replications, even when they appear to reproduce the story and point of view of the source. In such cases, the purpose is generally cultural reproduction, in the sense of transmitting desired knowledge about society and the self, modes of learning, and forms of authority. The most overt example [. . .] is the plays of Shakespeare [. . .], but that example shows two things: because retellings do not, and cannot, also reproduce the discoursal mode of the source, they cannot *replicate* its significances, and always impose their own cultural presuppositions in the process of retelling; and second, even the most revered cultural icon can be subjected to mocking or antagonistic retellings. The resulting version is then not so much a retelling as a *re-version*, a narrative which has taken apart its pre-texts and reassembled them as a version which is a new textual and ideological configuration.

Reversions are frequent in a second common circumstance of retelling, when narratives emerge within a network of story versions for which there is no identifiable "first telling" or else the latest version is based on intermediate forms. A familiar fairy tale such as *Cinderella* may derive from Perrault's version, or the Disney film, or British pantomime tradition, but is more apt to borrow freely from amongst these and from versions of them circulating orally. Even where there is a strong pre-text such as Perrault, retellers are most likely to use intermediate versions—to produce a retelling of a retelling. Similarly, Robert Leeson's (1994) retelling of selected "Robin Hood" stories is unusual in its story area because it is based mainly on the oldest extant source for much of the legend, *A Gest of Robyn Hode*, which probably dates from the early fifteenth century (Dobson and Taylor, 1989, p. 74). Leeson's expressed motive in seeking pre-texts without the accretions of the last hundred years is to allow the legend's innate "message" to speak for itself: that is, "that truth, justice and courtesy should be defended, if need be *against* the law" (p. 96). Even this retelling, however, is influenced by motifs that entered with Howard Pyle's *The Merry Adventures of Robin Hood* (1883), and a famous episode such as the contest for the silver arrow (Leeson, pp. 72–77) departs from the stated pre-text in story detail, structure, and character motivation. In other words, the "message" of the story has to be reproduced by substantial intervention. At another extreme lies Tony Robinson's spoof of this story as "Robert the Incredible Chicken" in his television series *Maid Marian and her Merry Men* (1988–89). Robinson can and does assume that his audience is familiar with some specific details—especially that Robin goes to the contest in disguise—which were introduced by Pyle but have long been generally considered intrinsic to the story and disseminated throughout retellings.[1] The assumption enables the effects of incongruity to be heightened as the production drastically transforms the mode and tenor of the story by drawing on pantomime, ironic farce, and feminist reversal (Knight, 1994, p. 241).

A still looser form of pre-textual context is genre. Here a particular narrative has its relationship not so much with a recognizable story but with a range of generic features.[2] In including such narratives, we are aware that we push the notion of retold story or reversion to its limit, and many readers will prefer to consider these narratives as standing in intertextual relationships to genres (as expounded in, say, Northrop Frye's *Anatomy of Criticism*). We do, however, see some point in including them here as part of a distinguishable cline beginning with replication and moving away towards more diffuse or merely allusive reversions. We argue, for example, that a moral story consciously mapped onto a Bible story is in effect a reversion; that *The Lion King* is a reversion of the pattern of a hero's life, rather than a generically identifiable narrative; that certain modern novels about female heroes are reversions which invert that pattern; and that a motif invented after but not based on *The Arabian Nights*—the "setting the genie free" motif—generates multiple reversions (as well as being exported back into reversions of the *Aladdin* story). To a great extent, such reversions are constituted by motifs; by narrative structures isomorphic with those visible in generic pre-texts; and/or by a shared habitus—that is, a conjunction of physical and social spaces where sociality is organized by social distances and hierarchies, and where a system of schemata (that is, social codes) organizes action and practice, and thought and perception (see Bourdieu, 1986, chapter 3; 1990, chapter 8). Feudal castles and the tents of desert tribes in Tamora Pierce's *Song of the Lioness* sword-and-sorcery tetralogy are clear examples of such a functioning of habitus.

Metanarrative and metaethic

The pre-texts for a retelling, then, are known, or already given, "stories," however precisely or indeterminately evoked. The principal domains in children's literature include biblical literature and related religious stories; myths; hero stories; medieval and quasi-medieval romance; stories about Robin Hood, which constitute a large and distinctive domain; folktales and fairy tales; oriental stories, usually linked with *The Arabian Nights*; and modern classics. Two central aspects about such traditional materials are that they come with predetermined horizons of expectation and with their values and ideas about the world already legitimized. In other words, they are always already shaped by some kind of metanarrative, and their status makes them a good site on which to impose metanarratives expressing social values and attitudes prevailing in the time and place of the retelling. As we said above, a metanarrative is a global or totalizing cultural narrative schema which orders and explains knowledge and experience. A simple illustration is offered by Leeson's summary of the message of Robin Hood stories which we cited earlier. The statement that "truth, justice and courtesy should be defended, if need be *against* the law" is presented as if it expresses self-evident propositions. It only does this, however, because it is enabled to do so by evolved cultural assumptions which furnish the statement's metanarratives: in all stories, in Western cultures at least, where truth and justice are an issue, the metanarrative which informs and shapes the outcomes of particular stories furnishes the assumption that they will—or morally should—prevail. Moreover, truth and justice are transcendent significations which occupy positions in a moral and intellectual hierarchy above attempts to codify them specifically as law; truth and justice are absolute values, whereas law is contingent and relative. An interesting place is then occupied in this larger schema by "courtesy," since its interlinking with the other terms offers the presumption that it, too, is the outworking of a metanarrative; people whose behavior is prompted and guided by intersubjective relationships, by consideration for others, and by selfmodesty, represent an exemplary ideal in culture. Key words which have been used to express such a concept, apart from *courtesy* itself,[3] are *civility* and *piety* (that is, in the old *Oxford English Dictionary* definition as "faithfulness to the duties naturally owed to parents and relatives, superiors, etc.; dutifulness"). Leeson's statement, then, comes charged with an enormous weight of culturally determined beliefs and assumptions which not only function as ideological presuppositions but also have a presence as narrative forms. When a particular exemplification replicates the metanarratival shape, the outcome is socially and emotionally satisfying and confirms the metanarrative; if the shape is not replicated, the outcome is recognized as "tragic." In other words, metanarratives both supply the structure for individual narratives and the criteria for perception and appreciation by which sense is made of that structure. This is why ideas about the social world can seem self-evident.

Our argument [. . .] is that the retelling of traditional stories for young audiences takes place within the frame of such metanarratives. They do not function randomly, however, but as a large interlocked set, which implies the existence of a less readily definable meta-metanarrative, so to speak, operating at a still more abstract level. This is what determines that a particular narration has value because it offers a patterned and shapely narrative structure, expresses significant and universal human experiences, interlinks "truth" and cultural heritage, and rests moral judgments within an ethical dimension. We are going to refer to this as the "Western metaethic," which is not a pretty phrase but is definitely preferable to meta-metanarrative. We think it is important to remember that this metaethic has been evolved within European-based or derived cultures; so, "Western" always has the effect of a reminder that, despite any implicit or overt assumptions to the contrary, the metaethic expresses a culture-specific idea of transcendence and not a universal. Because of this, there are some domains of retold story we have deliberately excluded from our discussions because the metaethic will always be imposed from outside, and we have decided that such retellings lie outside the scope of our present enquiry. One such domain is narratives which appropriate the beliefs and stories of indigenous peoples within the post-colonial societies of North America, Australia, New Zealand, and so on. We think such retellings are of a drastically different order, even when not extremely insensitive to the metanarratives of another culture, and would really require a book in themselves (see the discussion of some of the problems in Nodelman, 1996, pp. 264–267). Second, stories retold from other cultures involve not just questions of trampling on religious beliefs in quest of some vague intercultural understanding, important as this consideration may be, but also involve misapprehension and misapplication of metanarratives, as will happen with stories borrowed from, say, Chinese cultures. Regardless of whether or not retellers are equipped with appropriate cultural knowledge, such as the metanarratives generated by Confucianism or by the centrality of the family in a Chinese habitus, it is practically certain that the majority of audiences will have little alternative but to misread by contextualizing such stories within the Western metaethic, even if, as Nodelman suggests, audiences are provided with some of the distinctive qualities and conventions of these stories (p. 267). Because metanarratives are invisible and self-evident and Western audiences assume their metaethic is naturally universal, it is very difficult to resist Westernizing a story at the stages both of production and reception.

The Western metaethic is perhaps no more clearly evident than in notions about canons. For some time now theorists of mainstream literature have been actively engaged in defining the literary canon—"a body of texts larger than the sum of its members, a grand cultural narrative" (Gorak, 1991, p. 259)—in order to dismantle it. Gorak's "grand cultural narrative" points in the same direction as our "metaethic," and the postmodern world is skeptical of metanarratives, as everybody knows—everybody, that is, except most of the people who retell traditional stories for children. Theorists and practitioners of children's literature are generally still quite active in the construction of a canon of children's literary texts, an enterprise that can be seen quite clearly in the Children's Literature Association's publication of the *Touchstones* volumes (1985–87). These volumes, subtitled "Reflections on the Best in Children's Literature," seek to identify those "classic" texts, or "touchstones," written for children: "book[s] beside which we may place other children's books in order to make judgments about their excellence" (Nodelman, 1985, p. 2). Canonization does have a pragmatic function, in that it enables definition of the parameters of children's literature as a genre, what that genre consists of, what matters in it, and "what needs to be discussed and studied and understood" (Nodelman, p. 6). Such an enterprise is only ostensibly informed by notions of literary excellence, however. Instead it is largely driven by ideologies—ideologies which inform the decisions made by the culture about "what matters" in children's literature, including decisions as to the criterion of literary merit. As Nodelman contends, a list of "classic texts," such as the *Touchstones* volumes provide, is not prescriptive in so far as it simply "describes communal values" (p. 11), but, to continue Nodelman's line of argument, it is precisely those values, or ideologies, which implicitly prescribe the parameters of the literature. As Nodelman suggests, these values can be discussed, explored, explained, and disagreed with, and thus the *Touchstones* enterprise seeks to "open a dialogue," to show that "far from being sacrosanct and unquestionable, [the 'classic' texts] do indeed offer much to think about, much to disagree about" (p. 11). The practice of retelling and rewriting classics for children is part of this dialogue. Reversions disclose the ideologies and metanarratives driving those classic texts because they both legitimize and open to question their "classic" pretexts. They affirm the status of such classic texts, while at the same time entering into a dialogue and calling into question the ideologies informing both the texts and, by implication, the ideological basis of the canonical enterprise. So while what we are arguing here about the retelling of traditional stories may seem intellectually and culturally oppressive, there are always possibilities for resistance, contestation, and change. This occurs on two fronts: by the introduction of new or rival metanarratives, which effectively dispute the grounding metaethic, and in actual textual processes, the bottom-up production of narrative discourses.

The relationships between a retelling and its pre-text(s) are, in the main, dominated by metanarratives which are androcentric, ethnocentric, and class-centric, so the purposes of inducting audiences into the social, ethical, and aesthetic values of the producing culture are colored by those particular alignments. Any retelling is oriented towards those metanarratives and their informing metaethic in stances which are usually legitimizing, but may develop interrogative positions. The pre-text is always bearer of some historically inscribed ideological significances, but does not invariably fix ideological significance. Rather, it functions as a site on which metanarratival and textual processes interact, either to reproduce or contest significance. Because both of these are subject to change between one historical moment and another, any particular retelling becomes, at least potentially, a new negotiation between the already given and the new. When new metanarratives are acutely incompatible with the older metanarratives that have shaped a given story, the outcome can be a moment of cultural crisis. For example, the modern women's movement, and feminist social and critical analysis in particular, has produced a bundle of metanarratives so incompatible with the metanarratives which have informed many traditional stories in the past that if feminist metanarratives become socially dominant—and hence implicit and invisible—many traditional stories will be rendered unreadable and beyond recuperation.

A domain where we see this already happening is classical mythology, where inherent metanarratives are more persistent than in any other domain of retellings. It is not hard to argue that the metanarratives which informed classical mythology until well into the modern era were grounded in social assumptions which were masculinist, misogynistic, socially elitist, imperialistic, and often militaristic and violent. Thus Barbara G. Walker's *Feminist Fairy Tales* (1996), a collection of New Age, goddess-focused feminist stories and reversions, quite systematically addresses and overthrows these assumptions in most traditional story types we are concerned with here. Walker's collection does not, however, attempt to rework any of the better-known classical myths, and where she does deal with classical motifs she reshapes them into a female-centered archetype by blending them with other mythological systems. The effect is to represent classical mythology as a derivative and redundant corruption of the archetype. Read from a more traditional perspective, the reversals of roles and the transformations of ideology and outcomes in these stories seem very heavy-handed, though that does have the useful function of highlighting how an equivalent heavy-handedness has become invisible in the widely known myths.

In general, adults whose retellings reproduce stories from classical mythology, or who write about these retellings, are still apt to assert those metanarratives developed historically within education systems and a hegemonic social class; that is, that classical myths (among other functions) embody "timeless and universal" significances and are an indispensable part of Western cultural heritage, that they are metaphorical expressions of spiritual insights, and that they address archetypal aspects of the human psyche. If, in the face of such assumptions, myth is read from a feminist and/or cultural materialist position—that is, from an ideological stance which begins in rejecting the basis of the positions outlined—then myth may well be unrecuperable as part of children's experience of culture. As far as children's texts go, it remains a domain from which a substantial body of feminist rewriting is significantly absent. [. . .]

Retellings and register

As we suggested above, metanarratives can be subject to modification, as well as reproduction, within actual textual processes. A key component of these processes is the *register* which a reteller selects as the ground for her or his discourse. As the narrative genres and informing metanarratives of traditional stories are produced textually, authors select from amongst three registers, which we will refer to as *hieratic*, *epic* (for want of a better term), and *demotic*. Any particular domain of retold story may be characterized by a predominant preference amongst the three registers. Categorization is not necessarily fixed or stable, because texts from different domains share many structures and features, but it is nevertheless useful in pointing to some domain-specific qualities. We are using *register* here in the common sense of a variety of language defined according to situation of use. Linguistic choices constituting a register are determined by three elements. First, by *field*, or the subject matter or situation which grounds the story: examples are creation-myth; an encounter between a mortal and a divinity; a hero's battle with an evil adversary; an encounter with a magic-worker; a quest in folktale; and so on. Second, by *tenor*, or the relationships between participants in situations: examples are social hierarchies; gender relationships; conversational exchanges between the hero of a story and another participant, such as a god, a dragon, a wizard, a victim-in-distress, and the like. Third, by *modality*, or the interpersonal function of register which expresses relationships between textual "voices" and audience: in particular, varieties of omniscient ("third-person") narration (expository, factual, or didactic mode, emotive mode, and so on); and zero, limited, or extensive character focalization (and which may involve single or multiple characters).

Hieratic register is apt to be figurative, especially metaphorical or allegorical, and implicitly grounded in transcendent significances which are usually too abstract to be articulated in children's literature. It proceeds by representation of concrete events and incidents, and will often directly assert some aspects in which these are temporal expressions of a transcendent and eternal order "above." Its usual domain is thus religious or mythological narratives, exemplified in our study by biblical narrative and classical mythology, and from there it is extended into modern fantasy literatures.

Epic register is exemplary, grounded in more mundane or material significances, normally set within firmly hierarchical social institutions, and therefore apt to affirm social order conservatively. Its language choices will move between everyday discourse and less usual forms, such as archaisms, or forms of overwording (that is, signifiers whose meaning is in excess of contextual requirements, or which are clearly "elevated"), and descriptive terms which are apt to occur as doublets or in clusters. The following exchange illustrates some aspects of this discourse: " 'Have you heard tell of Sir Tristram of Lyonesse?' 'Yea, noble Arthur, and him have I seen full often' " (Green, 1953, p. 133). This is not particularly complex linguistically, but no part of it is untouched by archaic vocabulary ("heard tell of; yea; *full* often") or archaic syntax ("Yea, noble Arthur; him have I seen"). The characteristic domains of epic register are heroic legend, saga, and romance, but beyond those domains it can be drawn on variously by both fantastic and realistic literatures. Reading epic register is an acquired skill, however, even if it is not particularly difficult for an able reader to acquire it; therefore the register tends to mark a discourse as high culture or minority property. As Bourdieu commented in a different context, "the possessors of a sophisticated mastery of language are more likely to be seen in a museum than those who don't have this mastery" (1990, p. 133).

Finally, demotic register, also grounded in the mundane, is apt to be metonymic and event-focused; lexical and syntactic choices are, broadly, taken from everyday discourse, though sustained dialect is a demotic form. Most retellings, in fact, have a demotic base on which hieratic and/or epic registers are raised, but in some domains demotic is the staple. It tends, however, to occur mainly in folktale and reversions of modern classics, and is of course the staple of nontraditional realist fiction, biography, and some forms of historical fiction.

The choice (and mixing) amongst hieratic, epic, and demotic registers may function normatively, but can also be used to destabilize norms; likewise, focalization (that is, origin of perception and perspective within the narrative) can be employed for either purpose, especially in determining the question of whose interests are addressed and served. So to examine how or if textual processes intervene in the production of metanarratives, the following questions might be asked: Who takes effective action? Whose actions deliver a social benefit? Who is linguistically privileged? Who focalizes? Who operates socially within intersubjective relations? and Who expresses judgments? The implications can be seen virtually at a glance in a novel such as Pratchett's *Wyrd Sisters*, a reversion of Shakespeare's *Macbeth* in which the answer to all of these questions is "the three witches."

Many retellings do not reproduce the register or register-mix of the pre-text, and the most common direction of change is toward an authoritative narrative voice aligned with a culturally ascendant language. In other words, the texts speak from a cultural center and sometimes efface elements which might be potentially disruptive. Such an effect is evident in quite diverse texts, and we will briefly illustrate it here in Arthurian romance and folktale. Linda Yeatman's "The Knight of the Kitchen" (1991, pp. 88–97) is an abbreviated retelling of the first half of Malory's "The Tale of Sir Gareth."[4] The pre-text is substantially Malory's invention, though constructed from common romance motifs: the quest; the hero as a "fair unknown" who proves to be of noble birth; the damsel in need of rescue; and the incremental series of adventures of increasing difficulty through which the hero proves himself. In form it coincides with what is perhaps the most common romance metanarrative, the hero's quest for self-definition and identity, which is achieved against the odds, and which is expressed narratively by the metonymy of a desirable marriage. The register of Malory's story shifts between epic and demotic, often doing so to achieve comic effects. This is especially evident in the conversational exchanges between Gareth and his reluctant guide, Linnet, who continually flings abuse at him and is met with studied, ironic politeness, as here:

> [Linnet]: Lat be, . . . thou bawdy kychyn knave! Sle hym nat.
> [Gareth]: Damesell, . . . your charge is to me a plesure, and at youre commaundement his lyff shall be saved. (p. 306: note that the *thou/ you* contrast is at this time a strong marker of social orientation; it alone indicates Linnet's contempt)

Much of Malory's writing in this story is very funny indeed, but its broad comic element is not reproduced in the reversion. Instead, Yeatman narrows the range of registers, presumably on the assumption that narratives derived from medieval romance are a mode of high seriousness, but also reflecting how in children's literature epic register is both exemplary and apt to affirm hierarchical social order. Thus the above exchange becomes:

> "No, stop, you kitchen knave. Spare this man's life," Linnet called out. So Gareth stopped his sword in mid air, and said to the knight in green . . .

That is, the strong contrast in register between Malory's speakers has been smoothed over by rendering Linnet's command in more polite language and replacing Gareth's reply with a narrated epic cliché.

Second, the English folktale "Tom Tit Tot" (Briggs, 1970, pp. 535–539), a variant of the "Rumpelstiltskin" tale type, was first published in the *Ipswich Journal* 15 (1878), the contributor, Mrs. Thomas, "having heard it as a girl from her old West Suffolk nurse" (cited in Crossley-Holland, 1987, p. 370). Like so many folktales it thus enters recorded folk literature simultaneously authenticated as demotic discourse and mediated through literary collecting. It is valued for its local Suffolk flavor (Crossley-Holland, ibid.; Carter, 1991, p. 238). In the "original" demotic text there is little differentiation between the language of narrator and of characters, with the narrative language containing many nonstandard idioms and forms, both grammatical and syntactic. The version of this tale most usually printed is that of Jacobs's *English Fairy Tales*, in which the Suffolk dialect was reduced. In his reversion of Thomas in *British Folk Tales*, Crossley-Holland seeks to preserve the local flavor in the dialogue, where he makes few changes to his pre-text, but reworks the narrative components so they conform more both to standard English and to literary narrative. The Thomas text begins as follows:

> Well, once upon a time there was a woman, and she baked five pies. And when they come out of the oven, they were that overbaked the crust were too hard to eat. So she says to her darter:

"Maw'r ['girl; daughter']," says she, "put you them there pies on the shelf an' leave 'em there a little, an' they'll come agin." She meant, you know, the crust 'ud get soft.

But the gal she says to herself, "Well, if they'll come agin, I'll ate 'em now." And she set to work and ate 'em all, first and last.

(Briggs, p. 535)

This narrative is event-focused, moving straight into the story without offering any information about the characters or setting, and offering little motivation for incidents. It is up to the audience to infer from the wordplay that the girl is not clever, and from her actions that she is prone to gluttony, details which will prove central to the unfolding situation. In contrast, Crossley-Holland begins in this way:

There was once a little old village where a woman lived with her giddy daughter. The daughter was just sixteen, and sweet as honey-suckle.

One fine morning, the woman made five meat pies and put them in the oven. But then a neighbor called round and they were soon so busy with snippets of gossip that the woman completely forgot about the pies. By the time she took them out of the oven, their crusts were almost as hard as the bark of her old oak tree.

"Daughter," she said, "you put them there pies in the larder."

"My! I'm that hungry," said the girl.

"Leave them there and they'll come again."

"Come again?"

"You know," said the woman. And she hurried out into the warm wind and her waiting neighbor.

"Well!" said the girl. "If they'll come again, I'll eat these now." And so she went back to the larder and picked up the pies and ate them all, first and last.

(p. 47)

In the shift from (at least putative) oral to literary folktale, Crossley-Holland has almost doubled the length of this sequence (164 words compared to 95) by introducing spatio-temporal settings and descriptive epithets ("giddy daughter," "meat pies"), and a causal explanation for the hardness of the pie crusts. An audience must now make the simple inference that the pies would be difficult to eat and the much more complex inference that the girl has misunderstood the meaning of "come again." The reshaping of the narrative to mark the girl as giddy and nubile and the mother as domestically negligent foregrounds the tale's underlying folktale schema, the subjecting of a beautiful female character to an unperformable test of her domestic competence. This happens, though, by allowing the comedy

260

of the opening to be carried by the stock antifeminist joke about women's gossip rather than by the "come again" wordplay.

In general, Crossley-Holland's retelling is beautifully crafted and a delight to read. It does not introduce drastic changes, and follows the Thomas version quite closely after the opening movement. But, as with the Jacobs version, the strategy of differentiating the language of narrative and dialogue has substantial implications. It means that a center-periphery perspective is constructed whereby the folktale characters and their world, viewed from the normative center of standard English and literary narrative, become peripheral, other, representatives of an exotic culture mediated to readers through the "standard" narrative components.

Metanarratives and ideology

We argued above that metanarratives determine interpretive strategies as well as strategies for text production. In this regard, it is essential to recognize that children's literature has been, and remains, a crucial repository of humanist ideology. While the humanist tradition pervades, and indeed grounds, children's literature in general, it manifests itself most apparently in those kinds of text which are, in some sense, a reversion of a known story. Further, to a great extent children's literature attempts in this way to cultivate ethical and cultural values which would function as a replacement for or surrogate of older forms of socially inscribed transcendent meaning, especially religion. The extent to which this is embraced by retellers of traditional stories is reflected in the almost immeasurable influence exerted over the field by the writings of Joseph Campbell, especially his *The Hero with a Thousand Faces*. The appeal of Campbell is not just because his account of myth points toward a universal story spanning epochs, places, and cultures, but because it is a thoroughly transcendent vision consistently expressed in a hieratic register. For example, in *The Power of Myth* this is how he defines the "one great story":

> We have come forth from the one ground of being as manifestations in the field of time. The field of time is a kind of shadow play over a timeless ground. And you play the game in the shadow field, you enact your side of the polarity with all your might. But you know that your enemy, for example, is simply the other side of what you would see as yourself if you could see from the position of the middle.
>
> (1988, pp. 54–55)

The paradoxes and the metaphoricity evoke large metanarratives dealing with temporality, binarisms of good and evil, the struggle between conflicting impulses within the human psyche, the value of transcending selfhood to achieve a visionary state, the subordination of sociality to individual heroic striving, and so on. And apart from anything it actually says, the language itself is excited and inspirational, the traces of archaic expression implying timeless and arcane wisdom. In actual practice, retellings for young readers don't reproduce these effects, but merely operate under their assumptions, looking for strategies to direct readers from story to its significance. A primary model is still found in biblical literature, in that the forms that can be seen in place in biblical reversions and their spin-offs are replicated in other contexts which make use of traditional literature.

As an example of how a retold story produces an ideological effect, though not in this case humanistic, we will examine a brief retelling of a Bible story. As Northrop Frye points out (1982, p. 7), hieratic language such as that of the Bible is "the culturally ascendant language, a language that, at the time or later, is accorded a special authority by its society." Beyond language itself, of course, Bible narratives long occupied a comparable status, functioning, implicitly if not explicitly, as normative models both for narrative structures and outcomes and for moral and ethical structures and outcomes. Such a status is still claimed for biblical reversions, as when McLean (1990, p. 6) introduces her collection by asserting that "The Bible has been called 'the greatest book in the world'. It certainly is, for its stories are more stirring and dramatic than any tale ever conceived by a storyteller." This rather simple-minded assertion of the primacy of truth over fiction (implicit in the opposition between "story" and "tale"), on the basis that true stories are innately "more stirring and dramatic" than invented ones, evades the question of signification. The greatness, at this prefatory moment, lies in the narrative power of the stories rather than in their exemplary possibilities or in any claim for spiritual or moral insight or edification, though the unstated significance is presumably the raison d'être of the volume. A key assumption about retold stories is that they are invested with the equivalent of *truth* as implied here; that is, their capacity to be retold over centuries suggests their unique value as stories in themselves, but also implies that they continue because they are bearers of transcendent meanings. But Bible story is also unique in that it operates under the further premise that its narrative outcomes derive from an irrefutable divine authority. Further, modern Bible retellings also often serve the same purpose of conserving cultural and literary tradition we mentioned earlier in relation to myth.

The reversion we have chosen to comment on is "Naaman's Little Maid," from David Kyles's *Classic Bible Stories for Children* (1987, pp. 117–120). The episode, from *2 Kings 5*, is a miracle story which is part of the saga of Elisha but, as the titling indicates, a minor character, an enslaved Israeli child, has been moved into a frame position. In *2 Kings 5*:3 her role is to say to her mistress, "Would God my lord [Naaman] were with the prophet that is in Samaria! for he would recover him of his leprosy." At this point the biblical account says that someone reported her words to Naaman and his

King sent him with a letter to the King of Israel, ordering him to cure Naaman. The cure is effected when Elisha instructs Naaman to bathe seven times in the River Jordan, and Naaman thus comes to recognize the preeminence of the Hebrew God. Kyles expands this account by inferring absent details: for example, why Naaman's wife didn't pass on the information, and how the King learned of it. Subsequently, he explains that when Naaman sought advance forgiveness because his bond to his king would compel him to acknowledge his king's god, Elisha's response—"Go in peace"—was not a sanctioning of such an action; rather, "He probably would have been better pleased if Naaman had shown more courage in the matter of following the only true God" (p. 120). Finally, Kyles omits the last third of the episode (verses 20–27), which tells of the sin of Gehazi, Naaman's servant, in seeking to profit from Naaman's healing and his own contracting of leprosy as punishment. Instead, he reintroduces the "nameless" little maid, commenting, "Her story has thrilled boys and girls in all ages since, and all over the world: how, instead of moaning about her sad lot, she looked upon herself as a missionary, carrying the message of the true faith to a foreign land" (p. 120). This conclusion is part of the process whereby the whole story has been more or less implicitly transformed by the imposition of a Christian evangelical schema. Two crucial components of this schema are that the weak and marginalized are instrumental in converting the powerful, and that proselytizing in foreign lands is, of course, an unchallengeable institution (the schema precludes the possibility that it might actually be a form of cultural imperialism). The assertion of a boundless temporal and spatial vista in which her story "has thrilled boys and girls" implicates the audience with that schema, building in the desired emotional and religious responses: to be "thrilled," and to bear witness to "the message of the true faith" wherever one happens to be. In *2 Kings* 5:3 the intention of the girl's utterance is uninterpreted; it becomes meaningful in the reversion because the evangelical schema offers particular default values which imbue it with meaning. It is only when interpreted that the girl's story might even be noticed, let alone responded to as "thrilling." Finally, the schema underlines the transcendent significance of the dramatic, but unexplicated, details of the narrative: the affirmation of divine providence and power; the miraculous healing; the bathing in the Jordan as a type of baptism. In terms of the schema that is operating here, the problem of Naaman's dual worship must be addressed because it deviates from the implicit assumption that physical healing should unequivocally figure spiritual healing.

"Naaman's Little Maid" is a very obvious example of how a retelling can be filtered through a common metanarrative, right down to the use of demotic register for the language of comment and instruction. What happens in this telling is, nevertheless, paradigmatic of how metanarratives operate in other domains of retold stories. In Bible story we expect it. Of the substantial body of secondary literature dealing with reversions in children's literature, only that relating to fairy tale can be said to be self-consciously grounded in an awareness that neither literary representations nor critical perspectives are objective and value-free. When values are identified in children's books, and when they are commended, they are usually presented as *natural* human values which reflect the world as it is. On the contrary, retellers and their commentators are both engaged in producing interpretations of the world, and, in some cases, in attempts to change it by changing the consciousness of readers and their attitudes toward pre-existing narratives and concepts. The crucial strategy which interprets narrated experience for readers is the representation or construction of subjectivity. What is seldom acknowledged—because it is natural, an invisible assumption of the metaethic which gives significance to works of children's literature and informs most of the literature about them—is that the values, attitudes, and conceptualization of individual subjectivity which inform the literature are firmly grounded in the Western humanist tradition.

Humanism as the ground of the Western metaethic

The concepts comprising the metaethic on which the production and reception of children's literature seem to depend clearly originate in a humanist/historicist paradigm. Literary humanism promotes tradition and the conserving of culture; imagination and its cultivation; separation of literary texts from other forms of human activity (politics, for example, or ideology), while valuing altruistically intersubjective social and personal relationships; and the organic unity of texts shaped towards teleological outcomes. The interpretive metanarrative which underlies this bundle of ideas is widely naturalized in interpretive discourses and hence generally unarticulated. For example, in 1968 Penelope Lively, author of many children's books, published a trenchant assault on C. S. Lewis's "Narnia" series. This was an attack by a humanist novelist on a body of texts she considered to be anti-humanist, though the attack was not couched in those terms. Lively's criticisms were based on two arguments: that in writing his didactic Christian apologia Lewis condescended to children, writing at them rather than for them, and that his moral—depending on a "theology of a world in which Good and Evil are locked in an eternal struggle which can only be resolved by violence" (1968, p. 128)—was "distasteful and alarming" (p. 127). In other words, Lewis offends against two liberal humanist tenets: the first textual (the outcome is imposed on the narrative process, rather than being an organic outgrowth); and the second intellectual (the texts are determinist and authoritarian, and Lewis offends against humanist principles through his espousal of violence, his theological reductionism, his approval of hierarchy and caste systems, his implicit racism, and his religious intolerance).

264

Further, humanism's two most important and constant characteristics are first, that it focuses on human beings and starts from human experience—all beliefs, values, and knowledge are derived by human minds from human experience; and second, that individual human beings have a value themselves, grounded in the power to communicate, and in the power to observe themselves, to speculate, imagine, and reason. These powers enable freedom of choice and will, innovation, and the possibility of improving the self and the human lot. Two things necessary for this are individual freedom and cultivation of a young person's humanness. This complex of ideas drives Lively's textual objections to Lewis, in that the child characters are "never more than cardboard figures" and display neither convincing child language nor any possibilities of character development (p. 127); and their adventures lack urgency because subordinated to the interventions of Aslan and the presentation of the Christian message behind the stories. A humanist expectation is that awareness needs to be evoked through a rounded development of personality and of a character's abilities and talents, derived by human minds from human experience, a possibility not open to Lewis's characters. Further, the characters' lack of agency or focalization contributes to a failure to construct an interrelation of parts and whole which might lead to a narratively convincing teleology.

A revealing contrast to Lively's discussion of Lewis is Peter Abbs's discussion of Lively, significantly titled "Penelope Lively, Children's Fiction and the Failure of Adult Culture" (1975). No overt reference is made to humanist thought in this paper, which proves to be a good illustration of how in such critical discourse the interpretive metanarratives have become naturalized and invisible. In setting a humanist conception of culture against what he sees as the disorder and shallowness of postmodern society, Abbs gives overt expression to a position which widely pervades the discourse of and about children's literature. Thus in the one camp stands humanistic children's literature, which, offering an "alert and imaginative response to our age" (p. 119), presents transcendent truths, images of integration and transformation, and teleological structures; and in the other camp, the "diseases" of impoverished mass culture (actually postmodernism): pop art, mass-produced shapes and rhythms, unstructured sensation, and a failure of ethics or values. What Abbs seems to be expressing is despair at how postmodern discourses—with their fixation on surface detail, resistance to depth, and metafictive absorption in textuality for its own sake—apparently preclude the possibility of a humanist representation of reality with a capacity simultaneously to express and transcend contemporary culture. Lively's children's fiction certainly offers powerful ammunition to this argument, excelling as it does through her concern for the relationship between past and present and in her consummate skill in using a sense of historical continuity to map the growth of a character's individual subjectivity. *The Driftway*, for example, constructed as a framed set of retold stories, illustrates this exquisitely.

A humanist educational program proposed by Bullock (1985, pp. 186–187) focused on the themes of conscience, conflicts of loyalty, rebellion and authority, the ambivalence of feelings, the search for identity, the power of art and myth, and passions and compassion. Moreover, as might conventionally be expected in a humanist stance, Bullock sees value not just in any results such a program might produce, but in the activity itself, "engaging the imagination and the emotions in the penetration of other people's worlds and ideas . . . fostering the emotional, subjective side of human nature" (p. 187). This complex of themes, aspirations, and values, which is such a precise description of the dominant processes in retelling stories, is also the ground on which oppositional contemporary thinkers have sought to assail and overthrow humanism's cultural hegemony.

The controversies about the sway of humanism over intellectual life and artistic production in the twentieth century are too large and complex to explore here, but we do want just to glance at some aspects which are of special interest to the production of retold stories for child readers. The focal issues of contention are the necessarily abstract notions of the self and the related concept of the subject. Since neither selfhood nor subjectivity is a demonstrable entity or state, they always remain a hypothesis about being, but once hypothesized occupy a central position in the humanist tradition. The humanist subject pivots on the further notion of "agency," which Paul Smith defines as "a form of subjectivity where, by virtue of the contradictions and disturbances in and among subject-positions, the possibility (indeed, the actuality) of resistance to ideological pressure is allowed for (even though that resistance too must be produced in an ideological context)" (1988, p. xxxv). Thus, although it is posited on the notion of a self which is essential, the subject which manifests itself implies a multiplicity of being. This is an important issue because humanist ideology is often rightly accused of falsely or naively constructing a unified subject as a romantic unitary self capable of action outside ideological systems, and such a notion of the self pervades children's literature. At the other extreme, characteristically associated with the thought of Althusser, is the conceptualization of the subject as an inscribed function of discursive and institutional structures and, incapable of agency, thereby inserted into social formations. Neither of these extremes had retained much intellectual currency by the 1990s, but only the former has ever been widely exhibited in stories retold for children—and, it should be added, usually quite anachronistically. We now seem to be in a climate in which the "death of the subject," a possibility widely proposed in the 1970s and 1980s, is becoming constituted as a particular historical moment, with something like Smith's account of subjectivity-as-agency emerging as the present orthodoxy. Agnes Heller's description of the subject as "the idiosyncracy of the interpretation of human world-experience and self-experience under the condition of modernity" (1992, p. 283) precisely fits the discovery of agency in Lively's *The Driftway,* and would seem to be good news for mainstream children's literature. It would be a pity, though, if current intellectual developments enabled a foreclosure on any challenge to the continuation of the status quo before it has been substantially exposed to such a challenge.[5]

The modernist view of being, presenting an image of human experience produced without any universal referent or uncontestable code of values, proposed that consciousness was fragmentary, experience ambiguous, and truth relative, and that human lives and social relationships were driven by nonrational impulses. This view of existence has generally proved anathema to children's literature, its scant appearances virtually being confined to young adult literature. The result of this situation is that no attempt has been made to interrogate the basis of retellings, or their underlying assumptions about transhistorical meaning, the existence of "truth," or the efficacy of role models. Hence important questions are not asked— questions about how we are to produce and consume literary reversions —since the representation of significant heroic figures as role models, allegories, or precursors is a common point at which metanarratival significances are expressed in children's literature.

The literary and cultural formations re-presented in retold stories are often apparent bearers of clear attitudes to such things as power (political, social, and personal), hierarchy, gender, class, and race. If the function of a canon is to construct, preserve, and perpetuate particular forms of cultural knowledge, then in their assumptions and reassertions of canonicity retold stories are deeply implicated in this process. The effect of a canon is to mediate the ways ideas are transformed as they pass from one historical-ideological situation to another, in a myriad number of transformations. An analysis of the process would thus need to consider not just the represented content of a text, which may be transmitted virtually unchanged, but also the modes of representation and then, crucially, any critiques of that representation or others like it. Texts enter (or leave) a canon by means of the discourse which surrounds them; in effect, Lively's paper sought to displace Lewis from a central position in the canon, whereas Abbs's presented a case for Lively's admission. This suggests an institutionalized process which interlocks content, mode, and critique, and in part this is so, though its processes are probably not quite that well-contained. It is possible to argue, however, that while the Lewis-Lively opposition appears to represent a state of healthy difference and debate, that opposition functions within a very narrow and elitist cultural band. It offers a small example of how over time a hierarchy of ideas is modified, but a harsher view would be that what is really at stake is whether the "tradition" to be disseminated through childhood reading, libraries, and educative systems is to be grounded in conservative Christianity or liberal humanism. For someone who subscribes to neither, but prefers to argue that literary canons function to uphold ideological, national, gender, and class hegemonies, the effect would be the same. In such a context, the retelling of old stories requires careful scrutiny. In all of the domains of reversion we are concerned with here there is a high probability that replication of an old content and mode of representation may result in the further replication of, for example, old masculinist and antifeminist metanarratives. At the same time, retold stories have the potential to disclose how old stories suppress the invisible, the untold, and the unspoken. Such a potential will be realized through changing the modes of representation as well as, and more than, changing the content: by careful attention to point of view; by focalization strategies, since agency cannot be manifested by characters who do not focalize; and by textual self-reflexiveness or other strategies which remind readers not only of how they read the text but of how they read the world.

[. . .]

Notes

1 For much of the audience, the most likely pre-text would be the slightly earlier television version, *Robin of Sherwood* (1984).

2 Throughout this book we have followed Mary Gerhart's use of *genric* instead of the more usual *generic*. We accept her argument that *genric* emphasizes "the functions of the concept of genre in interpretation," whereas *generic* "has come to connote aspects such as non-specificity and common variety" (1992, p. 228, n. 7).

3 *Courtesy* is especially semantically charged when associated with a "medieval" text, in that it is a preeminent value in medieval romances. A bundle of linked terms equivalent to those we give here can be found, for example, attributed to the ideal knight in *Sir Gawain and the Green Knight*, lines 652–654, where *cortaysye* is joined by *fraunchyse* "generosity," *felawschyp* "love of fellow men," *clannes* "purity, chastity," and *pité* "compassionateness."

Leeson's metanarrative also coincides in interesting ways with the humanist/ realist metanarrative articulated by the narrator of George Eliot's *Adam Bede*:

> There are few prophets in the world; few sublimely beautiful women; few heroes. I can't afford to give all my love and reverence to such rarities: I want a great deal of those feelings for my everyday fellowmen, especially for the few in the foreground of the great multitude, whose faces I know, whose hands I touch, for whom I have to make way with kindly courtesy.
>
> (Harmondsworth: Penguin Books, 1980, pp. 224–225)

4 See Eugene Vinaver, ed. *The Works of Sir Thomas Malory* (1967, Vol. I, pp. 293–363). Yeatman's reversion covers the material on pages 293–326. The second half of Malory's narrative, which Yeatman summarizes in four lines, deals with events leading up to the marriage of Gareth and Lyonesse. It is misleading, however, to suggest that Yeatman's relation to Malory is unmediated: an examination of the language and the processes of inclusion and omission in Roger Lancelyn Green's version (1953, pp. 117–131) suggests that this has also served as a pre-text, though there are also some substantial differences. We will say more about the pervasive influence of Green in chapter 5, below.

5 Once again, the notable exception is the critical discourse centering on fairy tale, where writers have been able to demonstrate the extent to which ideas and individual actions are both socially produced.

References

Primary sources

Briggs, Katherine M., *A Dictionary of British Folk Tales in the English Language*. London: Routledge, 1970.

Carter, Angela, *The Virago Book of Fairy Tales*. London: Virago Press, 1991.

Crossley-Holland, Kevin, *British Folk Tales*, London and New York: Orchard Books, 1987.

Dobson, R. B., and Taylor, J. (eds), *Rymes of Robin Hood*, London: William Heinemann, 1976.

Green, Roger Lancelyn, *King Arthur and his Knights of the Round Table*, Harmondsworth: Puffin, 1953.

Kyles, David, *Classic Bible Stories for Children*, London: The Warwick Press, 1987.

Leeson, Robert, *The Story of Robin Hood*, London: Kingfisher, 1974.

McLean, Katherine, *Old Testament Bible Stories*, Manchester: Clivedon Press, 1990.

Pratchett, Terry, *Wyrd Sisters*, London: Gollancz, 1988.

Pyle, Howard, *The Merry Adventures of Robin Hood*, New York: Junior Deluxe Editions, n.d. (1883).

Walker, Barbara G., *Feminist Fairy Tales*, Sydney: Bantam Books, 1996.

Yeatman, Linda, *King Arthur and the Knights of the Round Table*, London.

Secondary sources

Abbs, Peter, "Penelope Lively, Children's Fiction and the Failure of Adult Culture", *Children's Literature in Education* 18 (1975): 118–124.

Bourdieu, Pierre, *Distinction: A Social Critque of the Judgement of Taste*, Richard Nice (trans.), London and New York: Routledge and Kegan Paul, 1986.

—— *In Other Words: Essays Towards a Reflexive Sociology*, Matthew Adamson (trans.), Cambridge: Polity Press, 1990.

Bullock, Alan, *The Humanist Tradition in the West*, New York: W. W. Norton and Company, 1985.

Campbell, Joseph, *The Hero With a Thousand Faces*. 2nd edn, Princeton: Princeton University Press, 1968.

—— (with Bill Moyers), *The Power of Myth*, New York: Doubleday, 1988.

Frye, Norhrop, *The Anatomy of Criticism: Four Essays*, Princeton: Princeton University Press.

—— *The Great Code: The Bible and Literature*, London: Routledge and Kegan Paul, 1982 (Ark Edition, 1983).

Gerhart, Mary, *Genre Choices, Gender Questions*, Norman: University of Oklahoma Press, 1992.

Gorak, Jan, *The Making of the Modern Canon*, London: Athlone, 1991.

Heller, Agnes, "Death of the Subject?", in George Levine (ed.), *Construction of the Self*, New Brunswick, NJ: Rutgers University Press, 1992, pp. 269–284.

Knight, Stephen, *Robin Hood: A Complete Study of the English Outlaw*, Oxford: Blackwell, 1994.

Lively, Penelope, "Wrath of God: An Opinion of the 'Narnia' Books", *Use of English* 20 (1968): 126–129.

Nodelman, Perry, *The Pleasures of Children's Literature*, 2nd edn, New York: Longman, 1996.

—— (ed.), *Touchstones: Reflections on the Best in Children's Literature*, Vol. I, West Lafayette, IN: Children's Literature Association Publishers, 1985.

Smith, Paul, *Discerning the Subject*, Minneapolis: University of Minnesota Press, 1988.

96

DID THEY LIVE
HAPPILY EVER AFTER?

Rewriting fairy tales for a
contemporary audience

Laura Tosi

Source: *Hearts of Lightness: The Magic of Children's Literature*, Venice: Cafoscarina, 2001, pp. 101–124.

A long time ago, people used to tell magical stories of wonder and enchantment. Those stories were called Fairy Tales.

   Those stories are not in this book. The stories in this book are almost Fairy Tales. But not quite. The stories in this book are Fairly Stupid Tales. [. . .] In fact, you should definitely go read the stories now, because the rest of this introduction just goes on and on and doesn't really say anything. [. . .] So stop now. I mean it. Quit reading. Turn the page. If you read this last sentence, it won't tell you anything.

(Scieszka 1992)

We have obviously travelled a long way from the familiar "Once upon a time" opening: a promiscuous anarchic genre which digests high and low elements, the fairy tale has undergone a process of textual and social alteration in the course of the centuries[1].

   The fairy tale, relying on various forms of cultural transmission and ever-changing ideological configuration for its very existence, has pride of place in the system of children's literature. Like many children's genres, it is characterized by a much higher degree of intertextuality than general literature. The term "intertextuality", still relatively recent, may not yet have reached a definitive formulation (see Kristeva 1970; Genette 1982; Worton 1990; Clayton and Rothstein 1991. Among Italian contributors see Polacco 1998 and Bernardelli 2000), but in its extended sense, it is an essential term, defining the intersection of texts or cultural and ideological discourses (see Segre 1984) within the literature system: as Stephens (1992) has put it succinctly: "intertextuality is concerned with how meaning is produced at points of interaction" (16). No text exists in isolation from other texts or from social and historical contexts (see Lotman 1980). The initiating and socializing function of children's literature, concerned, among other things, with transmitting the cultural inheritance of values, experiences, and prohibitions, makes it necessary to address an audience whose decoding must rely on the reader's recognition of familiar genres and narratives – hence the value of retelling as a strategy to activate the implied child reader's often partial competency and this reader's aesthetic pleasure of recognition and appreciation. Fairy tales in particular – possibly the first examples of poetic form we confront in life – as part of contemporary (even consumer's) culture, are constantly refashioned, restructured, defamiliarized in modern times, so that they resemble, as Marina Warner says,

> [. . .] an archeological site that has been plundered by tomb robbers, who have turned the strata upside down and inside out and thrown it all back again in any old order. Evidence of conditions from past social and economic arrangements co-exist in the tale with the narrator's innovations: Angela Carter's Beauty is lost to the Beast at cards, a modern variation on the ancient memory, locked into the plot of Beauty and the Beast, that daughters were given in marriage by their fathers without being consulted on the matter.
>
> (Warner 1994: XIX)

The scholar and common reader alike need a high threshold for tolerance as far as reinterpretation is concerned since even a hasty overview of the rise of the literary fairy tale in Europe reveals further evidence of its hybridity and intertextual nature. As we are often reminded, the fairy tale was not even a genre meant primarily for children. By incorporating oral traditions into a highly literary and aristocratic discourse, the fairy tale dictated and celebrated the standards of *civilité* in the French salons of the seventeenth century (in Italy a century earlier literary fairy tales circulated in the vernacular for an educated audience of upper-class men and women). As Zipes (1983) has written, challenging the assumption that the best fairy tales are universal and timeless:

> The shape of the fairy tale discourse, of the configuration within the tales, was molded and bound by the European civilizing process which was undergoing profound changes in the sixteenth, seven-

teenth and eighteenth centuries. The profundity of the literary fairy tale for children, its magic, its appeal, is marked by these changes, for it is one of the cornerstones of our bourgeois heritage. As such, it both revolutionized the institution of literature at that time while abiding by its rules.

(10, and see Zipes 1999)

Literary appropriation of oral folk tales also characterizes the Grimms' enterprise of collecting traditional folk tales of German origin (see Kamenetsky 1992), which, in translation, had a powerful influence on further developments of the genre. One of the most common misconceptions about the brothers Grimm's method regards their informants: far from being illiterate peasants, as has often been claimed, the Grimms' storytellers belonged to a cultivated middle class which might have been familiar with written, literary versions of folk tales. Any scholar who handles fairy tales (as the Grimms were perfectly aware) must necessarily abandon the idea of a faithful, "original" tale (for example, the myth of an "Ur-Little Red Riding Hood") and take the plunge in the wide sea of folklore variants in different countries or centuries, with diverse historical perspectives and ideological conformations. In our own time, the younger generation is probably best acquainted with the Disney versions of *Snow White* and *Cinderella*, only loosely based on the Perrault and Grimms' plots and characterization, with much simplification and reinforcement of stereotypes of female passivity (see Zipes 1979 and Stone 1975). The wholesale exploitation of fairy-tale and folklore material by the mass media has only recently been studied by critics, and provides one of the latest additions to the abundant and heterogeneous body of criticism on the fairy tale.

As a transitional genre, intended for children and adults alike, the fairy tale has been made the object of several critical approaches. These range from the anthropological (for example, in studies of comparative mythologies and recurrent and cross-cultural folktale themes) to the psychoanalytic, of which Bettelheim's (1977) interpretation of the Grimms' tales as significant instruments in helping the process of maturation in a child is probably the best-known, to the formalistic and structuralist methods of classifying folktales in catalogues, or examining individual structural components as functions (see Propp 1928/1968 and Bremond 1977). When we analyze folk or fairy tales from the vantage point of children's literature, then, it is inevitable that we should use an integrated cross-cultural, interdisciplinary approach. In the last few decades, Jack Zipes has focussed critical attention on the social function of fairy tales, thus providing the basis for an ideological critique of dominant cultural patterns in fairy tales, previously perceived as natural, but "Which appear to have been preserved because they reinforce male hegemony in the civilization process" (Zipes 1986: 9).

Many contemporary rewritings of fairy tales tend to challenge the conservative norms of social behaviour and the implications of gender roles in fairy tales. Feminist critics and writers have collaborated in the critical exposure of fairy tales as narratives voicing, in the main, patriarchal values, both by providing critical readings which investigate the social construction of gender, and by rewriting traditional fairy tales in order to produce non-sexist adult and children's versions.

However, the compulsion to retell or rewrite fairy tales in order to subvert historically inscribed ideological meanings should not be considered exclusively a contemporary practice. One only needs to recall the extraordinary flowering of the fairy tale in Victorian England, a flowering which succeeded the well-documented English resistance to fairy tales in the eighteenth century, born out of a combination of Puritan disapproval and a rationalist distrust of the imagination. Fairy tales, as carriers of reformist ideas and social criticism, not only provided Dickens and Wilde, for example, with a symbolic and imaginative form for their protest against the growing alienation of an increasingly industrialized society, they also questioned stereotypical gender roles and patterns (Zipes 1987 and 1999). Tales like Mac Donald's *The Light Princess* (1893), a parody of "Sleeping Beauty", or Mary de Morgan's *A Toy Princess* (1877), the story of an unconventional princess who is is rejected by her Court in favour of a more docile toy replica, anticipate feminist issues and concerns in their depiction of strong heroines who refuse to conform to the passive female ideal of the age. In Edith Nesbit's *The Last of the Dragons* (1925/1975), for example, the traditional pattern of "prince rescues princess" is satirically reversed. Though familiar with endless tales where princesses, tied to a pole, patiently wait for a prince to rescue them from the dragon ("such tales are always told in royal nurseries at twilight, so the Princess knew what she had to expect"), the heroine objects to this:

> "All the princes I know are such very silly little boys," she told her father. "Why must I be rescued by a prince?"
> "It's always done, my dear," said the King, taking his crown off and putting it on the grass, for they were alone in the garden, and even kings must unbend sometimes. [...]
> "Father, darling, couldn't we tie up one of the silly little princes for the dragon to look at – and then I could go and kill the dragon and rescue the prince? I fence much better than any of the princes we know."
> "What an unladylike idea!" said the King, and put his crown on again, for he saw the Prime Minister coming with a basket of new-laid bills for him to sign.
> "Dismiss the thought, my child. I rescued your mother from a dragon, and you don't want to set yourself up above her, I should hope?"
> "But this is the last dragon. It is different from all other dragons." (10)

In the end the strong, fencing princess and the pale weak prince "with a head full of mathematics and philosophy" (10) come to an agreement ("he could refuse her nothing". 12) about the way to handle the dragon, who is easily tamed by the princess and becomes a valuable asset to the court as a sort of scaly aeroplane employed to fly children around the kingdom or to the seaside in summer.

The impact of these protofeminist precedents in fairy-tale tradition should not be underestimated: Jay Williams's "The Practical Princess" and "Petronella" (1978) follow a very similar pattern in their depiction of a brave and assertive princess. Williams's ideal audience includes teenagers and adults; in the second half of the twentieth century the fairy tale, once again crossing the boundary between children's and adult literature, was appropriated by postmodernist and feminist writers like Angela Carter, Anne Sexton and Margaret Atwood, as a powerful discourse for the representation of gender (see Bacchilega 1997). Fairy tales have also served as structuring devices for both canonical novels (see the *Cinderella* and the *Beauty and the Beast* subtexts in *Jane Eyre*) and for popular romance. Rewritings both for children and adults assume the reader's knowledge of the original tales, thus encouraging the reader to take note of the formal changes which have led to an ideological reorientation of the tales.

In this essay I intend to give a survey (albeit incomplete and partial, given the ever-growing number of fairy-tale adaptations in the English language) of rewriting practices and techniques, although, as mentioned earlier, it is impossible to trace an archetypal "first telling" or version of a particular fairy tale, nor can the critic expect to fix a fairy tale "hypotext". Genette (1982) in his *Palimpsestes*, defines a hypertextual relationship as "toute relation unissant un texte B (que j'appellerai *hypertexte*) à un texte antérieur A (que j'appellerai, bien sûr, *hypotexte*) sur lequel il se greffe d'une manière qui n'est pas celle du commentaire" (11–12). With reference to fairy tales, Genette's concept of the hypotext as a single and identifiable entity needs to be enlarged and renamed as "hypotextual class", which would include all those versions of a single fairy tale that have combined to create the reader's cultural and diegetic construct of that traditional tale in the canon (the hypotextual class of the *Cinderella* tales, for example). Ironically, the constant restructuring and rewriting of fairy tales' hypotextual classes, in order to adapt them to the new social and moral requirements of contemporary audiences, has had the effect of preserving and encoding traditional fairy tales within the canon so that they are still widely read, alongside more challenging and subversive versions (see Tatar 1992).

In an attempt to classify different practices of fairy-tale adaptations, so as to make this abundant and heterogeneous material easier to analyse, I have chosen to discuss three types of fairy-tale rewritings which I have called: a) "morally correct" rewritings; b) post-modernist/metafictional rewritings; c) feminist rewritings. There are several overlappings in the three groups:

many adaptations could be grouped indifferently under more than one category as to their ideological orientation and often share formal changes (changes of setting, place and time, focalization – Genette's "transpositions diégétiques", 341). In the first group, however, I shall discuss primarily rewritings which aim at exposing the presence of an ambiguous morality or a moral gap in the hypotextual class, by superimposing a new ethics of justice and human compassion on traditional tales which reward, for example, acquisitive behaviour. The second group includes tales which emphasise their fictional and conventional status, which leads to a more or less good-natured critique of ideological assumptions about the culture of the child. The third group is probably the most widely studied, and includes fairy-tale adaptations which, by breaking established diegetic patterns, like "Princess marries prince", subvert accepted notions of female cultural identity.

Discussions about the ethics or justice of traditional fairy tales are not a recent phenomenon: one only needs to think of the political-ideological appropriation of the Grimms' tales in the Nazi era (Kamenetsky 1992).

Even to the naive reader it is painfully (or enjoyably) clear that the youngest brother often gets his fortune by chance rather than merit, that valiant little tailors are rewarded for deceit, and that the Giant's seven daughters do not really deserve to die at their father's hand. Many scholarly explanations of fairy or folk-tale ethics have been provided, from the analysis of the Grimms' own moral outlook to the discussion of the peculiar kind of knowledge about life fairy tales were meant to instil: the value of resourcefulness and risk-taking rather than of traditional morality, and the importance of perseverance. Contemporary retellings have challenged the value system of some traditional fairy tales, which, contrary to popular belief, do not always reward good characters and punish evil ones.

This redressing of the moral balance can be effected by means of a change in the narrating voice and the point of view. In the traditional story "Jack and the Beanstalk", the young boy Jack comes into possession of magic beans which allow him to climb a beanstalk and reach the giant's house. He is fed by the giant's wife who takes pity on the starved boy each time he visits their house. As we all remember, Jack first steals the giant's gold, then the magic hen who lays golden eggs, and ultimately the giant's golden harp[2]. By chopping away at the beanstalk on his way home so that the giant falls to the ground on his head, Jack secures for his mother and himself a wealthy future, with the giant's gold, hen and harp.

Alvin Granowsky's *Giants Have Feelings, Too* (1996) exposes the ambiguous morality of the tale, which sets greed as the rewarded virtue, by having the giant's wife retell the story:

> I am sure that the rest of you people living down below are very nice. But that boy, Jack, is something else. After I was so kind to him, he stole from us, and he hurt my husband. All because we are

giants! That's no reason to take our treasures or to make my husband fall on his head. See what you think (3).

The giant couple is reframed as good-natured and middle class, with grown-up children, with savings which are a necessity for their old age, and with an innocent love of food, Mrs Giant being apparently an exceptional cook:

> Then Herbert came in singing "Fe! Fi! Fo! Fum! My wife's cooking is Yum! Yum! Yum! Be it baked or be it fried, we finish each meal with her tasty pies! (13)

The reaction to Jack's treachery is a common sense open-hearted discussion between husband and wife:

> "Oh, dear," Herbert said. "We can only hope that the boy's mother will find out what he has done. Surely, she will make him return our things. Maybe she will even return them herself."
> "You're right, Herbert," I said. "When his mother brings back our gold and our hen, I'll be here to thank her" (18).

Jack, as we all know, only comes back to collect the giant's last treasure, the golden harp:

> "Stop! You're stealing!" Herbert yelled as he ran after Jack. "Don't you know it's wrong to steal?" (22).

The moral at the end of the tale turns into a direct appeal to the reader for sympathy:

> He had no right to take what was ours or to hurt my husband. Giants have feelings, you know. You wouldn't hurt a giant's feelings, would you? (25)

One interesting aspect of this retelling is that both stories are contained in the same book with a "flip me over" system so that the reader can access both versions of the story at the same time (the series is called "Another Point of View") and question, rather than take passively for granted, Jack's real motives for his actions.

Garowsky's adaptations seem very serious when compared with Dahl's inventive and highly irreverent retellings in *Revolting Rhymes* (1982/1984) and *Rhyme Stew* (1989). His version of the story of *Goldilocks and the Three Bears*, in *Revolting Rhymes*, addresses the issue of Goldilock's infraction of the basic rules of polite behaviour (i.e. entering a home without an invitation, touching other people's things, breaking an item of furniture in someone else's house) which parental figures teach children in order to ease their assimilation into the adult community. The socializing and cautionary function of fairy tales is generally dependent on the transmission of a code of social behaviour and norms from an older voice of experience to a younger audience badly in need of moral and social guidance.

Goldilocks is called in the course of the story "little toad", "little louse", "a delinquent little tot", "a brazen little crook", graphic and comic expressions which, rather than celebrating the cuteness of the little blonde girl, convey adult horror at the misbehaved unrestrained child's invasion of one's personal space. One interesting aspect of this retelling is that Dahl is clearly playing with the figure of his ideal reader – not so much the house-proud bourgeois wife who takes pride in "one small children's dining-chair, Elizabethan, very rare" smashed by Goldilocks, as the irreverent and playful reader, to whom he addresses one of his characteristic sadistic endings. In this version Big Bear advises Baby Bear to go upstairs and eat his porridge: "But as it is inside mademoiselle, you'll have to eat *her* up as well" (39).

Among the various kinds of correspondence that the Ahlbergs' *The Jolly Postman* (1986) delivers to fairy-tale characters, there is a repentant letter by Goldilocks, addressed to Mr and Mrs Bear, three Bears Cottage, the Woods, which says:

Dear Mr and Mrs Bear and Baby Bear,
I am very sorry indeed that I cam into your house and ate Baby Bears porij. Mummy says I am a bad girl. I hardly eat any porij when she cooks it she says. Daddy says he will mend the little chair.
Love from
Goldilocks

In one of the next tableaux among the several fairy-tale characters with whom Goldilocks is celebrating her birthday (a little pig, Humpty Dumpty, the magic goose etc) Baby Bear has pride of place near the little girl, who has obviously been forgiven. The Ahlbergs' ingenious toy and picture book, which relies on the reader's knowledge of other children's texts, creates an appealing context for a genial twist in the morality of the tale. It is the heroine herself, in her own tentative and childish writing, who condemns her selfish behaviour and promises to mend her ways.

Not all the protagonists of fairy tales, when allowed to speak and give their side of the story, are as convincing or trustworthy. In Scieszka's *The True Story of the Three Little Pigs* (1989) Mr Wolf's attempt to rehabilitate his good name is only partly convincing:

I'm the wolf. Alexander T. Wolf.
You can call me Al.

I don't know how this whole Big Bad Wolf thing got started, but it's all wrong.
Maybe it's because of our diet.
Hey, it's not my fault wolves eat cute little animals like bunnies and sheep and pigs. That's just the way we are. If cheeseburgers were cute, folks would probably think you were Big and Bad, too.

A contemporary audience, due to environmental awareness, might be willing to concede that wolves eat little pigs as part of the nature food chain, and not because they are intrinsically bad. My Wolf's version of the story, however, lays the blame for the destruction of the pigs' houses on the wolf's bad cold and urge to sneeze while he was innocently asking to borrow a cup of sugar for his granny's birthday cake.

Another example of a fairy-tale retelling which, by giving voice to the traditional villain of the piece, attempts to justify his/her actions is Donna Jo Napoli's *The Magic Circle* (1983), marketed to a young adult audience. This prequel, in novel form, to *Hansel and Gretel*, explains the reason for the witch's cannibalistic drive. As the "Ugly One" unfolds the story of her past as a loving mother and blessed healer, the reader learns of the circumstances which led her to be claimed and possessed by devils. The description of her death, which she willingly brings about in order to disobey the demons' order to harm the children, is a tale of liberation and purification from evil.

"A site on which metanarratival and textual processes interact, either to reproduce or contest significance" (Stephens and Mc Callum 1998: 9), the retold fairy tale on the one hand can distance itself from conventional concepts of morality, perceived as unsuitable or outmoded guidelines for the child's social and moral development, on the other it may suggest a new ethics of compassion and respect for other people's culture and possessions, even extending it, in some cases, to canonically undeserving characters[3] whose motives and actions are defamiliarized in order to be re-encoded in a new system of beliefs.

A second group of fairy tale adaptations includes self-reflexive, often explicitly postmodernist, versions, where make-believe or illusionist conventions are exposed in order to highlight the hypercodification of fairy-tale conventions. In the case of *The Stinky Cheese Man and Other Fairly Stupid Tales*, which opened the present discussion, basic literary conventions are parodied so that the young reader is invited to reflect on what constitutes a book, and the rules that are normally followed by the author, the editor, the publisher etc. In Scieszka's book, essentially postmodernist in its critical and ironic revisiting and disruption of the cultural and literary pattern of the fairy tale, the table of contents falls and squashes all the characters of the first story of the collection ("Chicken Licken"), the dedication is upside down, the "lazy narrator" at some point disappears, leaving a blank page, the little red hen is never given the opportunity to tell her story and the various narratives are constantly interrupted by arguments between the narrator and the characters:

> Now it's time for the best story in the book – my story. Because Once Upon a Time I traded our last cow for three magic beans and . . . hey, Giant. What are you doing down here? You're wrecking my whole story."
> "I DON'T LIKE THAT STORY," said the Giant.
> "YOU ALWAYS TRICK ME."
> "That's the best part," said Jack.
> "FEE FI FUM FORY I HAVE MADE MY OWN STORY."
> "Great rhyme, Giant [. . .] But there's no room for it. So why don't you climb back up the beanstalk. I'll be up in a few minutes to steal your gold and your singing harp.
> "I'LL, GRIND YOUR BONES TO MAKE MY BREAD."
> "[. . .] And there's another little thing that's been bugging me. Could you please stop talking in uppercase letters? It really messes up the page."

In such a context of textual and narrative instability a number of fairy-tale retellings are defined by parodic hyperrealism and comic dismissal of the magic and romantic element. "The Really Ugly Duckling" grows up to be just a really ugly duck instead of a beautiful swan, the frog lies to the princess about being a handsome prince under a spell ("'I was just kidding', said the frog. He jumped back into the pond and the princess wiped the frog slime off her lips. The End"), the Prince, in order to make sure of marrying the girl of his dreams, places a bowling ball under the one hundred mattresses.

"Cinderrumpelstiltskin" in Scieszka's collection furnishes an example of fairy-tale conflation, or, as the Italian educationalist and children's writer Gianni Rodari would call it, a fairy-tale salad, "una insalata di favole" (Rodari 1973/1997: 72): Cinderella, expecting the customary visit of her fairy godmother to provide her with a dress, glass slippers and a coach to go to the ball, sends Rumpelstiltskin (a character from another Grimms' tale who knows how to spin gold) away ("I am not supposed to talk to strangers", she says), consequently missing the opportunity to become rich ("Please don't cry", he said, "I can help you spin straw into gold". "I don't think that will do me much good" [. . .] If you don't have a dress, it doesn't really matter"). Scieszka's Cinderella, who obviously intends to be faithful to the traditional version, is not rewarded at the end (the ironic subtitle to the tale is "The girl who really blew it").

Fairy-tale salads, based on the comic coexistence of heterogeneous fairy-tale plots and character types, create playful conflations of traditional fairy tales which are easily recognized by the implied child reader who brings his/her knowledge of the character's familiar traits to bear on the new version. These highly intertextual and metafictional versions work within conventions, casting well-known fairy characters in different settings and story lines or, by contrast, combining two or more plots with the same protagonist. An example of the latter kind of procedure is the conflation of *Red Riding Hood* with *The Three Little Pigs*, both based on the powerful and murderous figure of the wolf. In Dahl's *Revolting Rhymes* (1982/1984) Pig number 3, who has built his house of bricks, but is made nervous by the wolf's huffing and puffing, phones Little Red Riding Hood for help. Having already shot a wolf in her own story earlier in the collection, the resourceful girl can now boast a "lovely furry wolfskin coat", but the ending has an unexpected twist, as the pig makes the mistake of trusting Miss Riding Hood. At the end of the story, not only can she boast of two wolfskin coats, "But when she goes from place to place, / She has a PIGSKIN TRAVELLING CASE" (47).

Similarly, in the already quoted Ahlbergs' Postman book, the wolf receives a letter from a law-firm representing the interests of both Little Red Riding Hood and the Three Little Pigs:

> Dear Mr Wolf
> We are writing to you on behalf of our client, Miss Riding-Hood, concerning her grandma. Miss Hood tells us that you are presently occupying her grandma's cottage and wearing her grandma's clothes without this lady's permission. [. . .] On a separate matter, we must inform you that Messrs. Three Little Pigs Ltd. are now firmly resolved to sue for damages [. . .]
> Yours sincerely,
> Harold Meeney, solicitor

Even in fairy tales which do not deviate from a recognizable story line, characters often show an unusual degree of knowledge of fairy-tale conventions and of their own fictional status. Their awareness of the conventionality of stock situations and the outcome of their expected choices may lead them to question and change the task or the role they are assigned in the story. In Jane Yolen's *Sleeping Ugly* (1997) prince Jojo, who, "being the kind of young man who read fairy tales, [. . .] knew just what to do" (49), decides to devote special consideration to the issue of kissing and thus awakening the three ladies who lie asleep in the cottage, covered in spiderwebs. The most striking woman is the beautiful, albeit cruel, princess, protagonist of many fairy tales: "But Jojo knew that kind of princess. He had three cousins just like her. Pretty on the outside. Ugly within" (59). Prince Jojo decides to let the beautiful sleeping princess lie, so that she is later used as conversation piece or coat hanger, and kisses (and marries) instead plain Jane, blessed with a kindly disposition, with whom he will attain marital bliss if not social elevation or riches.

Fairy-tale characters who are not well informed regarding fairy-tale conventions are often at a disadvantage in contemporary retellings. In Drew Lamm's *The Prog Frince. A Mixed-Up Tale* (1999) the only chance for the heroine to break the spell, as the reader discovers only at the end of the story, is to learn "The Frog Prince" and behave accordingly towards the talking frog. A sensible girl, Jane dismisses tales of the imagination as untrue:

> "Do you read fairy tales?," interrupted the frog, "like the Frog Prince?"
> "No," said Jane. "They don't make sense. And they're not true."
> "What do you dream about?" he asked.
> "I don't," said Jane.
> "What do you do?"
> "I go to school," she said, glaring at the frog.
> "Unfortunate," croaked the frog, and he leapt off Jane's hand.

Only when she is ready to sit and listen to the *The Frog Prince* and therefore begins to grow fond of the frog, does she recover her lost memory and identity as Jaylee, the prince's lover of base descent whom he had to forsake:

> Jaylee blinked. The spell was broken. In front of Jaylee stood the prince. He smiled.
> "I thought the princess had to kiss the frog," said Jaylee.
> "You're not a princess. You had to miss me."
> "Magnificent," said Jaylee. "I'd rather kiss you know, when you are not so green".

In this story the need for familiarity with fairy stories if one is to fulfil one's destiny (even if in a slightly different manner than that suggested in the canonical story) is constantly reasserted.

The comic retelling of *Snow White* in the "Happily Ever Laughter" series (Thaler 1997) has "Schmoe White and the Seven Dorfs" forming a pop group in which Schmoe will play the part of lead singer by virtue of her role in the fairy story:

> "We'll call ourselves 'Schmoe White and the Seven Dorfs,'" said Schmoe.
> "Why do you get top billing?" asked Grouchy.
> "Because if it weren't for me, you wouldn't be in this story," replied Schmoe.

Similarly, in Margaret Atwood's "Unpopular Gals" (1994), the character's self-consciousness as the narrative pivot of the folk tale emerges as the female villain is given a voice:

> The thing about those good daughters is, they're so good. Obedient and passive. Sniveling, I might add. No get-up-and-go. What would become of them if it weren't for me? Nothing, that's what. All they'd ever do is the housework, which seems to feature largely in these stories. They'd marry some peasant, have seventeen kids, and get 'A Dutiful Wife' engraved on their tombstones, if any. Big deal. [. . .] You can wipe your feet on me, twist my motives around all if you like, you can dump millstones on my head and drown me in the river, but if you can't get me out of the story. I'm the plot, babe, and don't you ever forget it.
>
> (11–12. See also Gilbert and Gubar's analysis of
> "Snow White" in *The Madwoman in the Attic* 1979: 38–39)

A strong narratorial voice (especially when it is intradiegetic) in fairy-tale adaptations (whether directed to an adult or a child reader) obviously implies that the story is a fictional construct which needs to be told (and retold) in order to exist, and relies on a number of diegetic, linguistic, as well as cultural and moral rules in order to be recognizable as such. In metafictional rewritings for children a form of detachment and the surprise following defamiliarization are encouraged, rather than emphatic alignment with the characters. Adaptations of traditional fairy tales continue to awake the child reader's sense of wonder and humour through the introduction of new narrative incidents, and highly recognizable characters who, by reflecting on their fictional status, engage in playful alliance with the child reader – the aesthetic pleasure of recognition should not be underestimated.

It is to be noted, however, that child readers do not always tolerate retellings or modifications of their favourite stories. Within contemporary retellings experiments of juxtaposing traditional fairy plot-types with unconventional patterns may serve to dramatize the child's resistance to letting go the stereotypes of the hypotextual class. The adaptation can turn into a hilarious battleground between orthodoxy and innovation, as in Storr's *Little Polly Riding Hood* (1953/1993). In this version the wolf is unable to assimilate the refashioning of the story of which he is a central character:

> "Good afternoon, Polly, "said the wolf. "Where are you going, may I ask?"
> "Certainly," said Polly. "I am going to see my grandma."
> "I thought so!" said the wolf, looking very much pleased. "I've been reading about a girl who went to visit her grandmother and it's a very good story."

"Little Red Riding Hood?" suggested Polly.

"That's it!" cried the wolf. "I read it out loud to myself as a bedtime story. I did enjoy it. The wolf eats up the grandmother, and Little Red Riding Hood. It's almost the only story where the wolf really gets anything to eat," he added sadly.

"But in my book he doesn't get Red Riding Hood," said Polly.

"Her father comes in just in time to save her."

"Oh, he doesn't in my book!" said the wolf. "I expect mine is the true story, and yours is just invented. [. . .] Where does your grandmother live, Polly Riding Hood?"

"Over the other side of town," answered Polly.

The wolf frowned.

"It ought to be 'Through the Wood,'" he said. "But perhaps town will do. How do you get there, Polly Riding Hood?"

"First I take a train and then I take a bus," said Polly.

The wolf stamped his foot.

"No, no, no, no!" he shouted. "That's all wrong. You can't say that. You've got to say, 'By the path winding through the trees,' or something like that. You can't go by trains and buses and things. It isn't fair. [. . .] it won't work, [. . .] You just can't say that!" (234–235).

The wolf's unwillingness to adapt to the new story, his blind adherence to the traditional configuration of Little Red Riding Hood, and his refusal to accept major changes in society (like modern means of transport), as well as a more active and assertive version of the tale will lead him to frustration and defeat. The wolf may thus come to embody the young reader's anxiety about unfamiliar retellings of fairy tales, which pose a threat to his/her conventional assumptions and expectations about gender roles and social behaviour.

There is no need to expatiate on the fact that, as educators and psychotherapists have demonstrated, fairy tales do influence the way children conceive the world in terms of power relations, patterns of behaviour and gender roles.

The third group of fairy-tale adaptations for children I shall be examining shortly, addresses precisely the issue of presenting a nonsexist vision of the world in fairy tales. As Zipes (1986) has remarked: "the political purpose and design of most of the tales are clear: the narratives are symbolical representations of the author's critique of the patriarchal status quo and their desire to change the current socialization process" (XI–XII). In feminist rewritings of canonical fairy tales a tendency to retell princess stories which dispense with marriage-dominated plots and the traditional equation between beauty and goodness can be detected. In both adult and children's modern revisions of princess stories, plots and patterns as well as characterization are subverted and deconstructed, in order to reshape female cultural identity into that of an independent, liberated and self-confident heroine. A new generation of smart princesses can oppose tyrannical or stereotyped role models by assuming active roles or considering alternative options for their self-definition as females: in A. Thompert's *The Clever Princess* (1977) self-fulfilment can be achieved through active involvement in ruling one's kingdom rather than by getting married.

Rewriting *Sleeping Beauty*, the tale that features the most emblematic example of female passivity, can turn into a positive attempt to acculturate women to new rewarding social roles as well as pointing out the value of overcoming ignorance and of intelligent initiative (see Lieberman 1972/1986). Katherine Paterson's *The Wide-Awake Princess* (2000) is given a very precious gift by her judicious fairy godmother, that of being wide-awake all her waking hours in a sleeping world (that is, in a world where greedy and indifferent nobles live in luxury). Throughout the story the value of seeing for oneself (the poverty and unhappiness of the people, for example), the value of being able to assess a situation, and the value of working to spread awareness, are constantly reaffirmed. Only by keeping her eyes open while mixing with the people of the kingdom can Princess Miranda form a plan to help her people, and regain her rightful place as a queen – a strikingly different model for female behaviour from that of submissive sleeping beauty waiting for a brave prince to kiss and wake her (on *Sleeping Beauty* as a literary model for female passivity see Kolbenschlag 1979).

Cultural autonomy, and a sense of compassion and sisterhood for other girls who embody more conventional prototypes of female passivity, are emphasized in Harriet Herman's *The Forest Princess* (1974), a rewriting of *Rapunzel*, where the lonely heroine is free to climb up and down the tower by a ladder. After having rescued a prince, she learns of gender differences and spends many happy hours with him. In the neutral setting of the forest they are free to exchange experiences and share the knowledge of the world. Back in the prince's court, however, rigid gender rules are assigned. What is considered praiseworthy in males (reading books, riding horses) is rejected in females, who are forbidden to read and must be suffocated in tight and uncomfortable clothes all day. When the forest princess questions the unfairness of the situation, the Prince defends the status quo:

> "There are so many people here and so many rules. Tell me, prince, why is that only boys are taught to read in your land?"
> His smile turned into a frown.
> "That is the way it has always been."
> "But you taught me to read."
> "That was in the forest. Things are different here."
> "They don't have to be different. I could teach the girls what you taught me."

The prince stood up abruptly.

"Why can't you accept things the way they are?"

As things turn out, because of her outrageous requests, the Princess is forced to leave the castle:

> But if you go to the land of the golden castle today, you will find the boys and girls playing together, reading books together, and riding horses together. For you and I both know that a fairy tale isn't a fairy tale unless everyone lives happily ever after.

The female desire to conform to a pattern of desirability that posits beauty and passivity as the virtues required for marriage is presented as a dilemma in Desy's *The Princess Who Stood On Her Own Two Feet* (1982/1986). The protagonist, in order to subscribe to the prince's patriarchal view of femininity ("haven't you ever heard that women should be seen and not heard?" 42), pretends to be struck mute, as earlier she had feigned not to be able to walk due to a riding accident (the prince seems unable to get over the fact that the princess is much taller than he is). It is through a painful experience of loss that the princess arrives at a new understanding of her self-worth, which results in her meeting a wiser, if shorter, suitor for her hand. Desy's princess story, like *The Forest Princess* and *The Wide-Awake Princess* is aimed at an audience of older children, and can therefore explore gender issues in relative depth, but even in some picture books for younger children there is an awareness of sexual stereotyping. In Mike Thaler's *Hanzel and Pretzel* (1997), for example, Pretzel is much more assertive and resourceful than the original Gretel (who, in the Grimms' story displays a worrying tendency to burst into tears at very inappropriate moments). In fact, it is a rejuvenated frightened Hanzel who constantly cries and is jokingly reassured by his cool-tempered sister:

> "Hanzel looked out through the bars and began to cry.
> "Look on the bright side," joked Pretzel.
> "At least we're not lost anymore."

The happy ending is brought about, as in the Grimms' tale, by efficient Pretzel who, after having thrown the witch into a cauldron, flies her brother home on the witch's broom without losing her sense of humour and love for puns.

Babette Cole's *Princess Smartypants* (1986/1996) and *Prince Cinders* (1993) comically reverse fairy-tale plots and culturally determined sexual stereotypes, keeping the text to a minimum and letting pictures convey most of the information regarding the characters. Princess Smartypants, for example, is pictured wearing denim dungarees, and watching horse races with her pet dragons, or brushing her pet giant crocodile with dishevelled hair like a common stable girl. It is only fair that such an informal and sporty princess should not automatically fall in love with smug Prince Swashbuckle who drives a posh sportscar, wears a multi-medalled uniform and flaunts a Clark Gable-type moustache. The end reaffirms the princess's independence and rejects the picture of the narcissistic macho man as the patronizing hero of the piece.

If we agree with the assumption that gender has a cultural character, we should not underestimate the impact of fairy-tale characters or circumstances in the formation of psycho-sexual concepts of the female or male self. The device of the change of sex in *Prince Cinders* is in itself a statement about the nature of male personality when this is culturally determined as a combination of physical strength, lack of sensitive feelings, and contempt for more vulnerable males. Prince Cinders' three hairy brothers, who belong to the same category as Prince Swashbuckle, spend their time at the palace disco with their princess girlfriends while Prince Cinders is left behind to clean up their mess: Cole's highly communicative pictures show the princes' rooms scattered with empty beer cans, football and body building magazines, and cigarette ends. Cinders' wish to be "big and hairy" like his brothers exposes the dominant cultural paradigm of masculinity (based on aggressive and insensitive behaviour) as ridiculous and old-fashioned: when the inexperienced fairy godmother, a teenage school-girl in her grey uniform and tie, performs the necessary magic, he will be turned into a big hairy monkey. After the customary happy ending with the marriage to Princess Prettypenny (who believes Cinders to have scared off the big hairy monster at midnight) the hairy brothers are suitably punished by being turned into house fairies, "and they flitted around the palace doing the housework for ever and ever".

By ridiculing stereotypical and outmoded notions of masculinity and having the fairy fulfil his desires to the letter (for in fairy tales one must really be careful what to wish for), Babette Cole's retelling ironically deconstructs a traditional paradigm of male identity, in order to stress the value of individuality and self-esteem. Even though some ambiguity as to gender roles remains, as Prince Cinders is cast in the conventional role of rescuer, this is one of the few adaptations which addresses the issue of male acculturation into traditional social roles. In retellings which challenge stereotypical sexual and social roles, fairy-tale discourse becomes emancipatory and innovative, rather than a reinforcement of patriarchal culture.

Fairy stories are "elastic": they evolve revealing a process of organic reshaping around a set of core elements in response to historical and cultural influences (see Hearne 1988). Fairy-tale hypotextual classes have survived many adaptations and will outlast many more. The central issue is that, by revitalizing canonical fairy-tale values and conventions, to which they add layers of non-conventional meanings, creative retellings liberate the imaginative and subversive potential of fairy tales in contemporary child culture.

Notes

1 By "fairy tales" I mean canonic fairy tales of Western tradition which have always been called by that name even if they do not feature fairy or fairy-tale characters. I am aware of the looseness of the term, which overlaps with very similar genres, like the folk tale, the wonder tale, legends etc.
2 In the English version of the tale, the giant is the villain of the piece. One only needs to remember his
"Fe fi fo Fum
I smell the blood of an Englishman
Be he alive of be he dead
I'll grind his bones to make my bread".
3 For example, in Robert Coover's retelling of *Snow White* for an adult audience, *The Dead Queen* (1973), the prince feels sorry for the harsh punishment which is meted out for Snow White's stepmother as he tries, in vain, to kiss her back to life.

References

Ahlberg, J. and A. (1986) *The Jolly Postman or Other People's Letters*, Harmondsworth: Penguin.

Atwood, M. (1994) *Bones and Murder*, London: Virago.

Bacchilega, C. (1997) *Postmodernist Fairy Tales. Gender and Narrative Strategies*, Philadelphia: University of Pennsylvania Press.

Bernardelli, A. (2000) *Intertestualità*, Bari: La Nuova Italia.

Bremond, C. (1977) "The Morphology of the French Fairy Tale: The Ethical Model" in Janson, H. and Segal, D. (eds.) *Patterns in Oral Literature*, Paris, The Hague: Mouton, 50–76.

Bettelheim, B. (1977) *The Uses of Enchantment. The Meaning and Importance of Fairy Tales*, New York: Random House.

Clayton, J. and Rothstein, E. (eds.) (1991) *Influence and Intertextuality in Literary History*, Madison: The University of Wisconsin Press.

Cole, B. (1986/1996) *Princess Smartypants*, Harmondsworth: Penguin.

Cole, B. (1993) *Prince Cinders*, Hayes, Middx.: Magi Publications.

Coover, R. (1973) "The Dead Queen", *Quarterly Review of Literature* XVIII, 3–4: 304–313.

Dahl, R. (1982/1984) *Revolting Rhymes*, Harmondsworth: Penguin.

Desy, J. (1982) "The Princess Who Stood On Her Own Two Feet" in Zipes, J. (ed.) (1986) *Don't Bet on the Prince: Contemporary Feminist Fairy Tales in North America and England*, New York: Routledge, 39–47.

Genette, G. (1982) *Palimpsestes. La littérature au second degré*, Paris: Éditions du Seuil.

Gilbert, S. A. and Gubar, S. (1979) *The Madwoman in the Attic. The Woman Writer and the Nineteenth-Century Imagination*, New Haven: Yale University Press.

Granowsky, A. (1996) *Giants Have Feelings, Too*, Austin: Steck-Vaughn.

Hearne, B. (1988) "Beauty and me Beast-Visions and Revisions of an Old Tale: 1950–1985", *The Lion and the Unicorn* 12,2: 74–109.

Herman, H. (1974) *The Forest Princess*, Berkeley: Rainbow Press.

Kamenetsky, C. (1992) *The Brothers Grimm & Their Critics. Folktales and the Quest for Meaning*, Athens: Ohio University Press.

Kolbenschlag, M. (1979) *Kissing Sleeping Beauty Good-bye. Breaking the Spell of Feminine Myths and Models*, S. Francisco: Harper and Row.

Kristeva, J. (1970) *Le texte du roman. Approche sémiologique d'une structure discoursive transformationelle*, The Hague, Paris: Mouton.

Lieberman, M. K. (1972) " 'Some Day My Prince Will Come': Female Acculturation through the Fairy Tale", in Zipes, J. (ed.) (1986) *Don't Bet on the Prince: Contemporary Feminist Fairy Tales in North America and England*, New York: Routledge, 185–200.

Lotman, J. (1980) *Testo e Contesto. Semiotica dell'arte e della cultura*, Roma-Bari: Laterza.

Napoli, D. J. (1993) *The Magic Circle*, Harmondsworth: Penguin.

Nesbit, E. (1925/1975) *The Last of the Dragons and Some Others*, Harmondsworth: Penguin.

Paterson, K. (2000) *The Wide-Awake Princess*, New York: Clarion Press.

Polacco, M. (1998) *Intertestualità*, Bari: Laterza.

Propp, V. (1928/1968) *Morphology of the Folktale*, Austin: Texas University Press.

Rodari, G. (1973/1997) *Grammatica della fantasia. Introduzione all'arte di inventare storie*, Torino: Einaudi.

Scieszka, J. (1989) *The True Story of the Three Little Pigs*, Harmondsworth: Penguin.

Scieszka, J. (1992) *The Stinky Cheese Man and Other Fairly Stupid Tales*, New York: Viking.

Segre, C. (1984) "Intertestualità e interdiscorsività nel romanzo e nella poesia" in *Teatro e romanzo*, Torino: Einaudi, 103–108.

Stephens, J. (1992) *Language and Ideology in Children's Fiction*, London and New York: Longman.

Stephens, J. and Mc Callum, R. (1998) *Retelling Stories, Framing Culture. Traditional Story and Metanarratives in Children's Literature*, New York and London: Garland.

Stone, K. (1975) "Things Walt Disney Never Told Us", in Farrer, C. R. (ed.) *Women and Folklore*, Austin, TX: University of Texas Press, 42–50.

Storr, K. (1955) "Little Polly Riding Hood" in Zipes, J. (ed.) (1993) *The Trials and Tribulations of Little Red Riding Hood*, New York and London: Routledge, 234–238.

Tatar, M. (1992) *Off With Their Heads. Fairy Tales and the Culture of Childhood*, Princeton: Princeton University Press.

Thaler, M. (1997) *Schmoe White and the Seven Dorfs*, New York: Scholastic.

Thaler, M. (1997) *Hanzel and Pretzel*, New York: Scholastic.

Warner, M. (1994) *From the Beast to the Blonde. On Fairy Tales and Their Tellers*, London: Chatto and Windus.

Williams, J. (1978) *The Practical Princess and Other Liberating Fairy Tales*, London: The Bodley Head.

Worton, M. and Still, J. (1990) *Intertextuality. Theories and Practices*, Manchester: Manchester University Press 1990.

Yolen, J. (1981/1997) *Sleeping Ugly*, New York: Putnam and Grosset.

Zipes (1979) "The Instrumentalization of Fantasy. Fairy Tales, the Culture Industry and Mass Media" in *Breaking the Magic Spell. Radical Theories of Folk and Fairy Tales*, Austin: University of Texas Press, 93–128.

Zipes, J. (1983) *Fairy Tales and the Art of Subversion. The Classic Genre for Children and the Process of Civilization*, New York: Routledge.

Zipes, J. (1986) *Don't Bet on the Prince: Contemporary Feminist Fairy Tales in North America and England*, New York: Routledge.

Zipes, J. (ed.) (1987) *Victorian Fairy Tales*, New York and London: Methuen.

Zipes, J. (1999) *When Dreams Come True. Classic Fairy Tales and Their Tradition*, London: Routledge.

97

FOLK MATERIALS, RE-VISIONS, AND NARRATIVE IMAGES

The intertextual games they play

Claire Malarte-Feldman

Source: *Children's Literature Association Quarterly* 28(4) (2003–2004): 210–219.

Introduction

Today's children read any number of postmodern tales that join together disparate and distorted pieces of an ageless master text made of folk materials or literary tales from a long-gone past. The foundation of those retellings is well inscribed in readers' memories and gives rise to various responses that are essentially dictated by a shared cultural heritage. Modern rewrites transform the ancient materials by progressively adding new layers in the manner of a palimpsest, to borrow from the title of Gérard Genette's seminal work. *Les Contes de Perrault* is a good example of an original text that has made room for new ones, its imprint still shining through more recent layers of narrative. "Recycled" tales (Sandra Beckett may well have coined this expression used in the title of her most recent book) grow from old roots and gain vitality in the process. Children thus receive the legacy of those retold stories, which now constitute a large part of the field of children's literature. They share this legacy with adults, who can also appreciate the intertextual play between multiple models, copies, parodies, and their representations, and the blurring of the borders between one genre of literature and another. Carole Scott comments that there is "a collaborative relationship between children and adults, for picture books empower children and adults much more equally" (101). Parodic retellings assign to both adults and children the role of textual interpreter, forging a strong bond of complicity between readers or listeners and authors or storytellers. Indeed, the multilayered nature of parodies of texts and images in contemporary children's books enables the inclusion of a "cross audience" made of adults and children, reminding us of the practice of traditional storytelling, in which adults and children, as well as peasants and nobility, were united for a moment in the sharing of tales that transcend ages and classes.

John Stephens and Robin McCallum, in their book *Retelling Stories, Framing Culture*, observe that folk materials lend themselves naturally to this phenomenon because of the uncertainty of their origins and, in some cases, the lack of a dependable "pre-text." They note also that "the process of retelling is always implicated in processes of cultural formation, of recycling frames used to make sense of culture" (ix), insisting thus that the creation and/or adaptation of new versions of an old tale still reproduce certain models of social practice and reinforce cultural beliefs and ideologies shared in the Western world. I would like to add that the "process of retelling" discussed by Stephens and McCallum involves the word, whether it is oral or written. It becomes truer and even more complex when combined with and sustained by what French author and illustrator Claude Lapointe calls "images narratives," which is in his view a more meaningful expression to refer to illustrations (13). Stephens and McCallum's "Western metaethic" is conveyed not only by layers of narrative but also in the multiple and widely differing illustrations that accompany and decode the text, providing the critic with a rich source of socio-cultural material in the form of interacting images and words and underlining the inherent social nature of intertextuality (3). Illustrators today provide as fertile a field of research as writers in that modern picture books are now a significant cultural sign in a booming market that targets an increasingly sophisticated audience. Intertextuality, with its multiple layers of cultural allusions, is just as much a force in the illustration of recycled folk materials as it is in the retelling of tales. The "narratives images" of late-twentieth- and twenty-first-century picture books allude to a variety of media from famous masterpieces of painting to comic strips, cartoons, films, and other icons of popular culture ... and they speak a thousand words!

The Three Little Javelinas, by Susan Lowell, is a southwestern example of an old palimpsest of *The Three Little Pigs*, which retells a familiar story with "a new chile flavor" (as is indicated in the book's introduction, n.p.), demonstrating the type of relationship between an anterior narrative (or hypotext) and posterior versions (or hypertexts) that Genette called "hypertextuality" (13). To accompany Lowell's hypertextual tale, the talented illustrator Jim Harris has created what could logically be called the "hyperimage" of three very hairy wild pigs.[1] These "collared peccaries" (n.p.), native to the southwestern United States, superimpose themselves on the more traditional image of three little pigs whose plump pinkness has been fixed in our cultural memory by familiar characters of children's lore such as Piglet, Wilbur, or, more recently, Babe, which makes me wonder which part exactly of those "classical" texts is fixed in today's children's minds: the character or its image? A truly familiar image is the richly framed *Mona Lisa* looking at the backs of the three hairy cowboys/pigs, which adds another intertextual level by referring directly to one of the Western world's most famous works of art. The humorous glance of *La Gioconda* tells us that, like us, she is curious to find out how the tale ends. This illustration is also representative of the increasing importance that contemporary artists accord to pictorial interrelations, as they define a new form of imagistic hypertextuality for children's picture books that echoes its verbal counter-part. "Parody is a form ready-made for both adults and children. It has a leveling force," comments Rod McGillis (114). The power of this force is grounded in a post-modern aesthetics, defined by fragmented and disparate pieces of narratives in a *bricolage* of authorless texts. Also, the humorous tone of the *Three Little Javelinas* underlines the use of pastiche and parody, as a part of the now well-known phenomenon of "cross-writing child and adult,"[2] and, as a result, child and adult are empowered to "cross-read" as well. We cannot ignore that children's literature in general has been under-going significant changes in a time when, to quote Hans-Heino Ewers, "the supply of multimedia products to private households" has increased (6). In a multimedia age that enables us to grasp the world more immedi-ately, and on an ever-larger scale, pictorial retellings define new goals for children's literature by shaping new cross-generational audiences who are more than ever subject to visual stimuli, while well versed in traditional folk narratives.[3]

Re-visions of classic tales

Recently, France has seen a remarkable production of high-quality picture books in a market that can still recognize artistic expression and original-ity. A significant number of French illustrators and authors have revisited classic tales, offering their own pictorial retellings of fairy tales and other well-known folk materials. Artists such as Georges Lemoine, Claude Lapointe, Kelek, Laurence Batigne, Jean Claverie, Béatrice Tanaka, Danielle Bour, and Alain Gauthier, among others, express their own aesthetic con-cerns about illustrations, which recontextualizes the stories they accompany and creates new types of relationships between books and their readers. These illustrators add a uniquely personal artistic dimension to old tales while often alluding to previous illustrations or to masterpieces of painting. The resulting *bricolage*, or ad hoc combination, provides a unique oppor-tunity to evaluate the impact of images on the meaning that we readers invest in classic tales. Undeniably, the most classic of fairy tales for a French reader would be Charles Perrault's *Contes et Morales du Temps passé avec des moralités*, brought out in 1697 by Barbin, a well-known publisher in the literary Paris of late seventeenth-century France. The French Academy member Perrault, a former top-ranking minister of Louis XIV's court operating at the highest levels of absolute power, himself named these tales "bagatelles,"[4] or "trifles," against the backdrop of a number of literary and political quarrels in which he was personally involved. It would undoubtedly astonish this tireless government official to learn that today, the most memorable volume in all of Charles Perrault's works is his collection of *contes de fées*, or fairy tales.

Moreover, it would be now difficult to dissociate from this text the canonical illustrations that Gustave Doré made for it. The nineteenth-century French artist created "narrative images" of Perrault's folk characters, which became "in-printed" in the cultural memory of generations of French fairy tales readers, just as the seventeenth-century academician had "institutionalized" the written versions of some of the most popular tales circulating in France during his own time. Significant historical, social, and cultural changes are thus reflected in the evolution of the iconography of picture books and addressed by their increasingly innovative aesthetics. Since Perrault's own times, when he "recycled" from ancient oral narratives whose authors may remain forever unknown, written versions of the French classic tales and corresponding illustrations have proliferated.

With the passing of time this material has acquired diverse marks of socializing intentions and cultural preoccupations. Where the "paratextual" elements of children's picture books are concerned, illustrations are clearly the most important of those "incidental signals" in and around the text.[5] Even in a culture that has traditionally favored the written over the spoken word, there is still a privileged ground where illustrations thrive. It is the *album pour enfant*, where images play a key role in facilitating communication between the child and the text, the reader and the book, establishing bridges between the words and their meaning. Ségolène Le Men reminds us that "le mot *album* évoque en latin une surface blanchie à la chaux pour servir de champ d'inscription" (146).[6] A number of contemporary French artists have elevated to pure art the status of pictures in the children's *albums*, encouraged in their efforts by a handful of publishing houses supportive of the quality and diversity of their talents. In Claude Lapointe's words, illustration is "un art contemporain à part entière" (a contemporary art in its own right, 17). French scholar Claude-Anne Parmegiani, talking about the unique relationship between the text and its illustrations, comments on "a shared perspective between publisher and artist who both agree to educate children's eyes, to lead them from the visible to the legible, from senses to meaning, from the sensitive to the intelligible" (*Les petits Français* 278). Indeed, the interplay between images in picture books helps readers become sophisticated decoders of texts that acquire added layers of meanings with each retelling. Intertextuality within the illustrations of picture books enables words and images to ricochet off one another, with the literary and visual arts interacting in different ways along the spectrum of various readers' responses.[7] By bringing children's literature into the world of art, this blend of cultural references and playful parodies is a pictorial form of cross-writing genres and generations.

Jean Claverie, for example, illustrating Perrault's *Bluebeard* makes a clear allusion to Doré's engraving of the 1861 Hetzel edition of the *Contes*. It is here important to stress that this particular edition that Le Men calls "cette particularité monumentale, dont Hetzel et Doré devaient tirer le meilleur parti dans *Les Contes de Perrault*, livre qui se rattache à plusieurs égards à l'album" (a monumental feature used to the best by Hetzel and Doré in *Les Contes de Perrault*, a book related to the album in many ways, 148) also marks the moment in France when this famous collection of literary fairy tales gained definite access to the realm of children's books. Claverie's images echo the style of Doré's, alluding to the seminal combination Perrault/Doré in a way that should not escape the eyes of many French readers. In this case, the term "echography" would fit better than "hyperimage" because, under Claverie's new graphic representation, one can still see the pale reflection and hear the faint echo of Doré's previous one, with which the contemporary artist has established a strict intertextual pictorial correlation. Now, despite the unambiguous nature of the allusion, the illustrator's viewpoint has changed. Both pictures radiate with energy and burst with movement, although directed differently: Doré relies on a descending motion, while Claverie orients his picture the opposite way, making his characters move upward on the page. Claverie shows only the boot of Bluebeard running out of the frame of the picture, as well as out of our contemporary frame of reference. Also at the center of the double-page spread, the focus has shifted from Doré's dying ogre to Claverie's surviving heroine. This is an example of how pictorial retellings of children's favorite tales, acting as facilitators between the reader, the author, and the illustrator, can rejuvenate or confront anterior texts and their previous illustrations, and add new cultural layers to their meaning, while providing new reading conditions. Claverie's simple shift of focus provides a social commentary on the changing conditions of women and young girls in modern days.

Re-visions of a folksong

Folksongs, like folktales and fables, belong to a "hypertextual genre" that Genette describes as "parodic in principle, since they assign human behavior and discourses to animals" (95). In the case of the French author Pierre Gripari's rewrites of *Il était un petit navire* (*There was Once a Small Ship*), human characteristics are assigned to an object—namely, a ship—the new hero of an age-old French *chanson populaire* (a popular song whose origins and authorship are sometimes hard to trace), which will help us look closely at the "recycling" of folk material and its reception by today's readers. Gripari rewrote *Il était un petit navire* five times, in the form of five different parodic poems: "Le navire peureux" (fearful), "Le navire paresseux" (lazy),

"Le navire zélé" (zealous), "Le navire spatial" (spatial), and "Petit navire," which, as we shall see, stands apart. Four illustrators of international reputation contributed their own graphic interpretations of Gripari's verses, juxtaposing meta-images to these parodic meta-narratives.

In composing these five poetic parodies, Gripari took advantage of the flexibility of the traditional genre, which is by essence at the limits of the oral and the written word, thus unfinished (to be continued, so to speak). The master text, introduced at the beginning of the picture book, can be summarized as follows: after five or six weeks of seafaring, food is lacking on board the ship. Sailors draw lots and the youngest in the crew is designated by fate to be eaten. The poor child calls the Virgin Mary to his aid, and soon thousands of little fish jump into the ship, saving the unfortunate boy's life.[8]

The song ends with a literal invitation to parodic rewrites: "Si cette histoire vous amuse, nous allons la recommencer" (if you like this story, we shall start it again). This is what Gripari does in his five poems, albeit with notable shifts of focus. Where the traditional song, despite its title, highlights the younger sailor's misfortunes and his miraculous rescue, Gripari's parodies revolve around the ship itself. The rhythm and rhymes, the intrinsic orality of the traditional material, are an open invitation to playful poetic and artistic creativity. The multiplicity of pictorial signifiers for each poem creates multilayered fields of possibilities for interpretation and gets the reader actively involved in the discovery process and the "décryptage" of the sign as a whole, in a sort of intellectual "jeu de piste," or treasure hunt, which is both ludic and meaningful. Here illustrations engage the written texts in a variety of creative ways, issuing a wide range of messages that reflect, as we shall see, contemporary cultural and social concerns.

Béatrice Poncelet's pictorial retelling of "le navire paresseux," a ship so lazy that it opts to spend the rest of its life at the bottom of a glass of orange juice, making bubbles, is a collage made of various media: a picture, a paper boat made out of the page of a book on which one can read the lyrics of *Il était un petit navire*, a sailor's hat on the head of a doll, a jump rope and soap bubbles, the childish representation of a pirate's flag on top of a straw (in a direct reference to and play on the French word "paille" in the expression "tirer à la courte paille," to draw lots), a cheerful picnic tablecloth—all are signs that associate the idea of childhood with the ludic function of parodic retellings.

"Petit navire" (Gripari's fifth poem), however, stands in sharp contrast to the playful mode of the first four poems, offering a serious reflection on children's absence of social status, and the abuses that too frequently follow. Its grating tone becomes increasingly biting and incisive. Gripari, in another example of cross-writing adults and children, retells this "navrante et sombre histoire" (sad and somber story) of a young sailor designated by fate to provide nourishment for his elders.

> Chaque fois que les vivres manquent
> C'est l'enfant qu'on veut manger
> Quand on tire à la courte paille
> C'est lui qui se fait égorger.
> (Every time food is in short supply,
> We want to eat the child.
> When you draw lots,
> He is the one we slaughter.)

Gripari, a passionate advocate of fantasy tales, *le roman populaire*, epic traditions, and folklore, is dictating new reading conditions. His parodic poems, along with their illustrations, intentionally clash with the folksong on which they are based, which has become a commodity to help make better sense of a hegemonic culture. As Stephens and McCallum have observed in the preface of their study of retellings, Gripari's grim conclusion, which transposes the traditional narrative into a contemporary social context, "discloses attitudes and ideologies pertaining at the cultural moment" of the retelling (ix). The cultural outcome of recycled tales is more informative and more relevant than the story that is retold, underlining in this case the primacy of hypertexts over the hypotext. Humor turns to irony, which in turn gives way to sarcasm in "Petit navire," particularly in the bitter morality of the conclusion:[9]

> La moralité de cette affaire
> Est bien facile à deviner
> C'est qu'il ne faut pas être faible,
> Et, si on l'est, faut pas l'rester!
> (The moral of this story
> Is easy to guess.
> You cannot be weak,
> And if you are, you better not stay that way!)

The four illustrations go even further than Gripari's text, displacing its focus and, once again, creating new conditions and perspectives for reading. With his illustration of Gripari's poem, Claude Lapointe captures the satirical essence of the retelling and takes it one step further, adding his own narrative elements and at the same time parodying Honoré Daumier, an enormously talented French artist and a famous political and social caricaturist of nineteenth-century France. In a convincing style reminiscent of Daumier's disillusioned gaze upon his own society at the time of Louis-Philippe's reign, and the Parisian Revolution of 1848 with which it ended, Lapointe's striking echography faithfully echoes both Gripari's text and Daumier's inescapably caustic viewpoint: "Navrés, l'étranger . . . Vous êtes désigné par le sort pour être sacrifié . . . pour la survie du Bateau . . .

vous avez dès à présent, notre Reconnaissance Eternelle..." (Sorry, stranger... You have been designated by Fate to be sacrificed... for the survival of the Ship... as of now, you have our Eternal Gratitude.)

These cynical words not only make us wonder, as has Rod McGillis, "whose voice is being parodied here?" (116). They also denounce the all too frequent abuse of power and ostracism of the young, the weak, the stranger, and all the "others." As a constituting part of the artist's illustration, those words incorporate a meta-narrative into the image itself in a complex postmodern interplay of social, cultural, linguistic, and artistic elements born from multiple places and times and inscribed on the ever-white page of the *album* and into a centuries-old palimpsest.

The case of Little Red Riding Hood

This sophisticated mode of retelling bears more than a passing resemblance to some contemporary interpretations of *Little Red Riding Hood*, the ever popular character pointedly named by Sandra Beckett "a highly effective... unmistakable... intertextual referent" (1). This tale will dem-onstrate the playful nature of intertextuality while employing creative strategies that establish readerly complicity between adults and children. In the second edition of his *Trials and Tribulations of Little Red Riding Hood*, Jack Zipes extended his study of Little Red Riding Hood and retellings up to 1990 and noted in his epilogue that "fortunately, as a result of the women's movement and continued struggles against [*sic*] sexism during the past twenty years, our eyes have been opened and made more receptive to a re-framing of Little Red Riding Hood's story" (380). And yes, this time has come! Mademoiselle Sauve-qui-peut terrifies all kinds of animals, who run as quickly as they can away from her to avoid her mischief, hence her name "Miss Run-For-Your-Life," the tireless anti-Little Red Riding Hood created by Philippe Corentin. When she arrives at her grandmother's house, a poor wolf is recovering in the bed under the tender and loving care of the old woman who found him starving and freezing in the woods. Unaware of the situation, the little girl proceeds to kick the beast out of bed, informing him that she can't be fooled because she already knows the story, and asking him whether he thinks she is as dumb as Little Red Riding Hood who could not make the difference between a wolf and an old woman. In a now familiar form of intertextual game, Corentin has reversed the charac-ters' roles and thus re-framed the message of the story. Philippe Dumas and Boris Moissard used a similar technique in the 1970's with the feisty protagonist of their retold tale, *Le petit Chaperon bleu marine* (*Little Aqua Riding Hood*), who managed to lock the wolf in a cage at the Vincennes Zoo in Paris. Retellings such as those stage a strong-willed girl who goes against the grain of Perrault's own version. In the postmodern universe of *Little Red Riding Hood* retold, the parodies of *Mademoiselle Sauve-qui-peut* or *Le petit Chaperon bleu marine*, herald postmodern liberation itself. They not only make children laugh and feel joy, they teach them that history itself may be changed and rewritten to suit them, that we don't have to settle for the same old story. These liberating tales challenge authority and convention, helping children to look critically and creatively at the world around them, to develop open minds, and to think for themselves. These humorous and optimistically emancipating rewrites make us see that the healthy changes predicted by Zipes are taking place now.

Illustrations frame the undoing of those lessons in a new landscape of social and cultural concerns, using new means of graphic expression. That is, for example, what Sarah Moon has done in the black and white photographs and montages that she made to illustrate *Le Petit Chaperon rouge*, while the publisher respected Perrault's original text of 1697. Moon has taken advantage of the relative lack of temporal markers in Perrault's tale—and ignored the few that seventeenth-century scholars would probably have identified—in order to bathe the story in a new light. The artist shifts the reader's frame of reference to the context of World War II and France's occupation by the Germans. The traditional wolf becomes an incarnation of the Nazi power during the Third Reich under the appearance of a Citroën *Traction Avant*, the black sedan favored by Gestapo officers. Little Red Riding Hood still has her hood and little basket of goodies, but the wolf she flees is a "wolf in the second degree," to borrow Genette's expression, a danger of another kind, one made explicit in the final two-page black and white photograph of a bed which has just been the scene of an act of violence. Moon's gray-black allusion to a war that today's children have not experienced conveys the same sense of vague lurking danger that one finds in Perrault's text. Her warning, like Perrault's *moralité*, that the most dangerous wolves can be found under many disguises, is a timeless one.

Today's children can thus feel a strong sense of connection with the past, from which they draw interpretive strength. When young readers recognize the pattern of the old familiar tale beneath the surface of a new story, they gain a feeling of mastery over their reading. Particularly in the case of Little Red Riding Hood, Beckett observes that the simple suggestion of the character's name "evokes a network of associations," despite the fact—she is happy to report—that Little Red Riding Hood is one of the few "classics" that Disney has not appropriated himself (1). Warja Lavater's "imagerie" of *Le Petit Chaperon Rouge*, as she calls her interpretation of *Little Red Riding Hood*, with its strictly abstract visual universe of shapes and colors, radically rejuvenates the old tale while giving the "readers" the license to create their own "text." This book consists of accordion-like pages along which the traditional story unfolds without words. It is the "reader" who supplies the text, in his or her own words—and his or her own native language —using the color code on the first page, which assigns particular meanings to a set of signs and symbols in different colors and languages (Chinese,

German, English, and French). Images become language, written text, and illustrations all in one; they are truly "narrative images." Warja Lavater belongs to both worlds of art and children's literature. Influenced by the Bauhaus movement and American paintings of the 1960s, she understands that associating codes and signs with shapes and colors can create a new language, no longer verbal but visual and pictorial. Lavater's interactive book-object, with its various possible scenarios, with its menu, options, and icons (found on the first couple of pages), is, if anything, even better suited to the twenty-first-century Western child's world of multimedia and computers than it was to the decade in which it was conceived.[10] It is no wonder that children have taken enthusiastically to this form of narrative art,[11] because they spontaneously understand Lavater's abstract but visual perception of written concepts. In her cinematic approach to the plot, Lavater engages readers in an active, artistic, and personal revision of the tale. While this graphic game is based on the artist's own codification of symbolic shapes and colors, each child can find in it a reflection of his or her relation to the world,

Conclusion

Maria Nikolajeva, reflecting on the nature of intertextuality in children's literature, comments that it bears a "both conscious and unconscious relation to a previous text" (154), as revealed by the hypertextual illustrations in picture books. Sometimes they stress visually the clash between master text and retellings, as is the case when Cinderella's glass slipper (a "hypo-image" within the Western metaethic) is contrasted with the penny loafer (a "hyper-image" in the same frame of reference) worn by no-nonsense Cinder Edna, who knows better than to wear uncomfortable dancing shoes. What Nikolajeva calls a "silent and unarticulated relationship" between different layers of text has its pictorial counterpart in the exchanges that take place between parodic illustrations of recycled folktales (154). These two clashing representations of the attribute that best defines Cinderella—the glass slipper—right on the dust jacket of the book, use a mix of open-mindedness, irreverence, playfulness, and humor to unite readers of all ages and generations in a shared laughter. The double-fold cover of *Cinder Edna* by Ellen Jackson stands as an icon of the tale as a whole, because it juxtaposes two images that summarize the two viewpoints offered by the "recycled" tale. Illustrator Kevin O'Malley has placed the humoristic synecdoche of the penny loafer in a prominent place on the front page, while the familiar glass slipper still sparkles—all alone—on the back page! Illustrating the traditional climactic scene in which Cinderella must hurriedly leave the ball on the twelfth stroke of midnight, on one page the reader sees next to each other one little glass slipper and one penny loafer (Cinder Edna, too, had to make a hasty exit, since she did not want to miss the last bus home), while on the opposite page a city bus leaves the bus stop on the wheels of the pumpkin carriage. Two models are clearly offered as possible choices for the reader in the final question on the last page of the book: "Guess who lived happily ever after?"

The answer to this question is grounded in the redefinition of social roles on the one hand, and the reinforcement of old patterns on the other. "I do not have to wait for a prince, I do not even *want* a prince" is what the reader may think. But certainly not all readers—my little friend Emily still prefers the more glamorous Cinderella, *because* of her old glamour! Also, in our day and age, for some readers, a husband who cares for the environment and the ozone layer, a companion who loves where his heart is, can put a prince to shame. The content of Perrault's carefully crafted moral lesson has disappeared, but the moral intent is still there on the page for whoever wishes to seize its recycled meaning. And, as is ironically stated in Jon Scieszka and Lane Smith's now classic *Stinky Cheese Man and Other Fairly Stupid Tales* (1992), even if the Surgeon General warns us that "these tales are fairly stupid and probably dangerous to your health," we want more, because the irreverence of those subversive retellings gives us pleasure. This upside down, topsy-turvy form of narrative, echoed in highly interactive visual images, is appealing. And with technology evolving at lightning speed, the combination of two sets of signs, the "iconic" and the "conventional" (Nikolajeva and Scott 1), fulfills the twenty-first-century reader who, more and more urgently, wants to see the word . . . and the world.

In *Shrek* by William Steig, the ugliest possible green ogre is the hero of a tale that ends, as it should, in a world that is predictably inside out. He finds "the most stunningly ugly princess on the surface of the planet," and together, they "lived horribly ever after, scaring the socks off all who fell afoul of them" (n.p.). Its recent Oscar-winning, yet loose, adaptation into an animated film achieves the goal of blending audiences, generations, genres, and narrative forms, which explains film reviewer Olivier Pélisson's prescription: "A savourer sans modération par tous les âges" (to enjoy without moderation by all ages).[12] The movie version of *Shrek* provides the ideal medium for games with a wide range of visual allusions—to other fairy tales, to other films (*Crouching Tiger, Hidden Dragon*), to other cartoonists, and to competing production studios (Dreamworks vs. Pixar/Disney). *Shrek* pays at some level an indirect homage to the art of Disney. But it is also a joyous if ferocious attack on the Disney Empire of amusement parks, singing blond heroines, cute chirpy birds (remember the bluebird who tries to sing at the top of its lungs, and . . . explodes?). However, not all the cultural allusions of this "extratextual intertextual" game are so easily recognizable, with some so deeply rooted in American culture, bereft of any French or Francophone equivalent, that they may escape the art of the best translator. "Do you know the muffin man?" Go pose this question in France and your response will be nothing but a blank stare. Nor will the gumdrop button of the tortured gingerbread man ring any bells in the French cultural memory bank. Like Claverie's Bluebeard running off the page and out of our modern perspective, those words will remain without any cultural frame of reference, giving no clue for recognition. Nevertheless, by drawing on a rich international heritage of folktales, a Western multicultural audience will appreciate Shrek's multi-mediatic character and pick up amusing references to Charles Perrault or the brothers Grimm, and artistic allusions to great painters of the Western world.

As an intrinsic part of the retellings of texts, the revisions of their illustrations transcend age, generations, and genres and literally shed a new light on the "processes of cultural formation, of recycling frames," as noted by Stephens and McCallum (xi). The tale is made of a material of great resilience and can best accommodate the blurring of lines and the mix of genres (Kareland 363). Folk materials are the privileged ground for the transgression of borders between genres and the separation of audiences, because of their blend of popular traditions that have seeped into a literate culture, and our postmodern aesthetics thrive on such a blend. From Doré to Daumier, from Moon to Lavater, from Lapointe to Claverie, all their "narrative images" push us further in a number of useful inquiries into the identities of the players in these intertextual games, as well as the kinds of voices and the genres of literature, which are being parodied. From the kitchen to the parlor, from the nursery to the library, tales and their re-visions, at their modest level, have always been around to help us "make sense of culture."

Notes

I wish to thank UNH for its generous support of my research, in particular the Director of the Center for the Humanities, the Dean of the College of Liberal Arts, and the Chair of the Department of Languages, Literatures & Cultures. I am also grateful for the invaluable comments from my dear friends and respected colleagues Professors J. Howard and R. Tzakiri.

1 Just recently, at the last ChLA conference in El Paso, Texas, I discovered a wonderful bilingual rewrite of the tale of the three pigs, *The Three Pigs. Los Tres Cerdos Nacho, Tito and Miguel* by Bobbi Salinas, who received the Tomas Rivera Mexican American Children Book Award for this wonderful retelling "for children 3–103, all colors, all sizes and all sexes."

2 See *Children's Literature* 25 (1997), a special issue devoted to this phenomenon. In their introduction, editors U.C. Knoepflmacher and Mitzi Myers consider "*Cross-Writing* and the Reconceptualizing of Children's Literary Studies." See also Beckett (1999, 2002).

3 We must (sadly) agree with Hans-Heino Ewers when he noted that "the audio-visual competence developed by children is a good precondition for deciphering more easily and quickly the complex messages offered through books. Additionally, when they start school many children acquire a considerable fund of stories and fictional worlds through multimedia. They are already familiar with the

essential features of the classics of children's literature and their childlike heroes have long since become their close companions via audio cassettes or animated cartoons" (6). The question that we face here again regards the preeminence of the *popular representation* of the character over the *literate character* itself.

4 As worded in the preface to his *Contes*, where Perrault hastened to specify that his tales "were not mere 'bagatelles,' that they contained a useful morality, and that the entertaining narrative they were hidden behind, was only chosen in order to better get them into the minds, and in a fashion that could teach and entertain at the same time" (my translation, 3).

5 Genette lists a number of "incidental signals," such as titles, prefaces, notes, warnings, illustrations, and so forth, all of which, having an implicit relation with the text, constitute its "paratext" (10).

6 "The word *album* evokes in Latin a white-washed surface which is used for inscriptions." This translation is mine, and all following translations will be mine unless otherwise indicated, and will appear parenthetically in the text of the article.

7 Jean Perrot crafted extensive and convincing analyses of the connections between masters of painting such as Carpaccio and Velasquez and contemporary illustrators of French children's books Kelek and Jean Claverie. See in particular the first part of Perrot's *Art baroque, art d'enfance*, "Ouvertures, résurgences et libérations" (19–68).

8 These are the lyrics in French: "Il était un petit navire / Il était un petit navire (bis) / Qui n'avait ja-ja-jamais navigué (bis) / Il entrepris un long voyage (bis) / Sur la mer Mé-Mé-Méditerranéenne (bis) / Au bout de cinq à six semaines, (bis) / Le lard, le pain, pain vinrent à manquer (bis) / On tira z'à la courte paille (bis) / Pour savoir qui, qui, qui serait mangé? (bis) / Le sort tomba sur le plus jeune (bis) / Le pauvre mouss', mouss', mousse sera mangé. (bis) / Il est monté sur la grand'hune(bis) / Ne voit que l'eau, l'eau, l'eau de tous côtés (bis) / O bonne mère, ma patronne (bis) / Empêchez les, les, les de me manger (bis) / Du haut du ciel sur le navire (bis) / Il voit des gros, gros, gros poissons tomber (bis) / On apporta la poêle à frire (bis) / Tout l'équipa-pa-page fut sauvé (bis) / Si cette histoire vous amuse (bis) / Nous allons la, la, la recommencer. (bis)"

9 This is not without reminding us of the equally sarcastic and adult tone of Gripari's *La Patrouille des contes*.

10 This may explain why six animation films have been made transcribing six well-known tales by Perrault and others ("Le Petit Chaperon Rouge," "Cendrillon," "Le Petit Poucet," "La Belle au Bois Dormant," "Blanche Neige," "La Fable du Hasard").

11 As shown by a number of experiments in elementary and secondary schools in France, where teachers have their students retell, rewrite, and illustrate classic fairy tales.

12 "Ages: All" is also the rating on the inside of the cover page of *The Stinky Cheese Man*. Rod McGillis used the expression as the title of his article in the volume edited by Sandra L. Beckett entitled *Transcending Boundaries*.

Works cited

Beckett, Sandra L. *De grands romanciers écrivent pour les enfants*. Montreal: Presses de l'Université de Montréal, 1997.

——, ed. *Transcending Boundaries: Writing for a Dual Audience of Children and Adults*. New York: Routledge, 1999.

——. *Recycling Red Riding Hood*. New York & London: Routledge, 2002.

Cross-Writing Child and Adult. Special Issue of *Children's Literature* 25 (1997).

Claverie, Jean. *Le Petit Chaperon rouge*. Paris: Albin Michel Jeunesse, 1994.

Corentin, Philippe. *Mademoiselle Sauve-qui-peut*. Paris: L'école des loisirs, 1996.

Dumas, Philippe, and Boris Moissard. *Contes à l'envers*. Paris: L'école des loisirs, 1977.

Dupont-Escarpit, Denise, and Claude Lapointe. *Guide des illustrateurs du livre de jeunesse français*. Paris: Salon du Livre de Jeunesse/Editions du Cercle de la Librairie, 1988.

Ewers, Hans-Heino. "Changing Functions of Children's Literature: New Book Genres and Literary Functions." *Bookbird* 38. 1 (2000): 6–11.

Genette, Gérard. *Palimpsestes: La littérature au second degré*. Paris: Editions du Seuil, 1982.

——. *Palimpsests: Literature in the Second Degree*. Trans. Channa Newman and Claude Doubinsky. Lincoln: U of Nebraska P, 1997.

Gripari, Pierre. *Il était un petit navire*. Geneva: La Joie de lire, 1988.

——. *La Patrouille du conte*. Lausanne: L'Age d'Homme, 1983.

Jackson, Ellen. *Cinder Edna*. Illus. Kevin O'Malley. New York: Lothrop, 1994.

Kareland, Lena. " 'Il y a un trou dans la réalité.' Le conte dans le roman suédois du XX siècle. Une perspective féminine." In *Tricentenaire Charles Perrault. Les grands contes du XVIIe siècle et leur fortune littéraire*. Sous la direction de Jean Perrot. Paris: In Press Editions, 1998. 355–64.

Kelek. *Contes de Perrault*. Paris: Hatier, 1986.

Lapointe, Claude. "Pour un art à part entière." *Guides des illustrateurs du livre de jeunesse français*. Paris: Salon du Livre de Jeunesse/Editions du Cercle de la Librairie, 1988. 11–19.

Lavater, Warja. *Le Petit Chaperon Rouge*. Paris: Adrien Maeght, 1965.

Le Men, Ségolène. "Le romantisme et l'invention de l'album pour enfants." *Le Livre d'enfance et de jeunesse en France*. Bordeaux: Société des Bibliophiles de Guyenne, 1994. 145–75.

Lowell, Susan. *The Three Little Javelinas*. Illus. Jim Harris. Flagstaff Northland, 1992.

McGillis, Roderick. " 'Ages: All': Readers, Texts, and Intertexts in *The Stinky Cheese Man and Other Fairly Stupid Tales*." *Transcending Boundaries: Writing for a Dual Audience of Children and Adults*. Ed. Sandra Beckett. New York: Routledge, 1999. 111–26.

Melot, Michel. *L'Illustration: Histoire d'un art*, Geneva: Albert Skira, 1984.

Nikolajeva, Maria. *Children's Literature Comes of Age: Toward a New Aesthetic*. New York and London: Garland, 1996.

——, and Carole Scott. *How Picturebooks Work*. New York and London: Garland, 2001.

Parmegiani, Claude-Anne. *Les petits Français illustrés, 1860–1940*. Paris: Editions du Cercle de la Librairie, 1989.

——. "Pourquoi les livres d'images ont cessé d'être sages." *La Revue des livres pour enfants* 163–64 (1995): 51–65.

Perrault, Charles. *Contes*. Ed. Gilbert Rouger. Paris: Garnier, 1967.

——. *Fairy Tales*. With thirty-four full-page illustrations by Gustave Doré (1867). Trans. A.E. Johnson (1921). New York: Dover, 1969.

——. *Contes*. Engravings from the first illustrated Hetzel edition, Drawings by Gustave Doré. Paris: Hachette-Grandes Oeuvres, 1978.

——. *La Barbe Bleue*. Illus. Jean Claverie. Paris: Albin Michel, 1991,

——. *Le Petit Chaperon rouge*. Illus. Sarah Moon. Paris: Grasset-Monsieur Chat, 1983.

——. *Riquet à la Houppe*. Illus. Jean Claverie. Paris: Albin Michel, 1988.

Pélisson, Olivier. http://perso.respublica.fr/fruault/cinema/shrek/shrek.htm Critiques professionnelles.

Perrot, Jean. *Art baroque, art d'enfance*. Nancy: Presses Universitaires de Nancy, 1991.

——. *Jeux et enjeux du livre d'enfance et de jeunesse*. Paris: Editions du Cercle de la Librairie, 1999.

Salinas, Bobbi. *The Three Pigs. Los Tres Cerdos Nacho, Tito and Miguel*. Spanish version by Amapola Franzen and Marcos Guerrero. Oakland, CA: Pinata, 1998.

Scieszka, Jon, and Lane Smith. *The Stinky Cheese Man and Other Fairly Stupid Tales*. New York: Viking, 1992.

Scott, Carole. "Dual Audience in Picturebooks." *Transcending Boundaries: Writing for a Dual Audience of Children and Adults*. Ed. Sandra Beckett. New York: Routledge, 1999. 99–110.

Shrek. Dir. Andrew Adamson and Vicky Jenson. Dreamworks Pictures, 2001.

Steig, William. *Shrek*, New York: Farrar, 1990.

Stephens, John, and Robyn McCallum. *Retelling Stories, Framing Culture: Traditional Story and Meta-narratives in Children's Literature*. New York: Garland, 1998.

Zipes, Jack. *The Trials and Tribulations of Little Red Riding Hood: Versions of the Tale in Socio-Cultural Context*. 2nd ed. New York: Routledge, 1993.

Part 20

THEATRE

98

POLITICAL CHILDREN'S THEATER IN THE AGE OF GLOBALIZATION

Jack Zipes

Source: *Theater* 33(2) (2003): 3–25.

Thirty years ago I went to Germany to write about Peter Stein's Schaubühne am Halleschen Ufer and other experimental theater groups sprouting in the aftermath of the 1960s student movement. While I was in Berlin, a friend told me that its most significant political theater was not really the Schaubühne, but Grips, founded by the writer Volker Ludwig. Its members, who used to perform in a left-wing cabaret for adults, had recently turned their attention to developing unusual plays for children that incorporated rock music and Brechtian dramaturgical methods. Their work overwhelmed me. And unlike the spectacular Schaubühne and many other so-called political theaters of that time, Grips continues to challenge and provoke children and adults to change their lives, if not society as a whole.

The name *Grips* means something like "common sense" and implies using one's intelligence politically to understand the world; accordingly, Volker Ludwig, Grips's director and major writer, seeks to link theater to emancipatory education. He has often remarked that Grips's plays are designed to show our condition as changeable and to reveal possibilities for social transformation and critical thinking: "Primarily this means that we want to encourage children to ask questions, to understand that criticism is their undeniable right, to enjoy creative thinking, and to gain pleasure from seeing alternatives."[1] How does the Grips ensemble, which has constantly responded to changing political conditions, bring this about? Almost all of their plays are Brechtian *Lehrstücke* (learning plays) performed in a cabaret style. The adult actors do *not* try to mimic children or to act naturalistically. On the contrary, social conditions and events are explained and demonstrated from a child's point of view. The plays do not present solutions but show possible alternatives to conditions that are oppressive or self-defeating. The plays are not ends in themselves; they do not preach the right answers, nor should they be performed this way.

Each scene tends to be a social experiment, a testing of social conditions to see if perhaps some other form of organization might allow for more freedom of movement and development. Characters represent antagonistic principles, and as they are unmasked, the social relations underlying the principles become more visible, as in *Mannomann!* (1973), an early play about male chauvinism, in which a factory worker realizes that his violent behavior is connected to his own exploitation; *Bella, Boss und Bulli* (1995), a drama about bullying, in which children grasp how their conflicts are tied to family issues; and *Melodys Ring* (2000), a musical that connects the behavior of the homeless to business corruption and unemployment. Cabaret performance has been the dominant influence on the actors and the playwrights, because it is illusion-smashing, frank, quick, and jovial, yet serious. Grips's productions and techniques can be repetitive, but more than any children's theater I know, Grips has resisted the forces of compromise and continues to demonstrate how theater can address ordinary children's daily struggles with the authorities and institutions that govern their, and our, lives.

But this essay is not about Grips, which even in Berlin is special and unique.[2] Rather, it is an attempt to grasp why we need an alternative, not just to lily-white, run-of-the-mill, middle-class children's theater but also to a youth entertainment industry whose spectacles make even the productions of middle-class children's theater seem radical at times. First I want to hark back to Walter Benjamin's essays on children's literature and culture.[3] Then I want to say a few words about the state of children's culture in the United States and how it is organized—that is, homogenized—for them. Finally I want to discuss different kinds of "unspectacular" children's theater that thrive in the nooks and crannies of public realms.

The timeless Walter Benjamin

In 1928, Walter Benjamin, who had already expressed an interest in children's literature by collecting children's books, began to do radio commentary on children's culture. The same year he wrote a curious piece entitled "Program of a Proletarian Children's Theater"—curious because Benjamin knew very little about children's theater, which nobody then took notice of—a piece that forty years later, in the late 1960s and 1970s, shaped the way West German activists approached children's culture. Benjamin wrote "Program" for the Latvian director Asja Lacis, whose work he admired and with whom he was very much in love.[4] Benjamin met Lacis on the isle of Capri in 1923. A dedicated Communist, Lacis played a short but important role in developing a unique Russian children's theater during the agitprop years of the Revolution. In 1928 she was sent to Berlin as a

Communist cultural worker to do experimental drama with young people at the Liebknecht House. Benjamin proposed to assist her by writing a theoretical framework for a new political children's theater. The result, based on their conversations, stressed spontaneity, collectivity, and autonomy in young people and focused on process, on integrating children's intuition into the work, and on raising the participants' awareness of social and economic differences.

In the 1920s, a period of cultural war in Weimar Germany, theater became a battlefield and a realm for experiments ranging from the agitprop work of Erwin Piscator to the opulent productions of Max Reinhardt. All the major parties—Social Democratic, Communist, and Nazi—formed youth groups that made theater into propaganda, a means to win the minds of children. Because this political aspect of theater was less obvious in the mainstream middle-class *Luxustheater*, which generally produced charming fairy-tale plays at Christmas and other appropriate times, Benjamin declared: "The theater of the present-day bourgeoisie is economically determined by profit. Sociologically it is, above all, an instrument of sensation in front of and behind the curtains. It is different with the proletarian children's theater. Just as the first firm grip of the Bolshevists was used to raise the red flag, so their first instinct was to organize the children. . . . From the viewpoint of the bourgeoisie, nothing is more dangerous for children than theater" (81).

Neither Benjamin's use of such terms as *bourgeois* nor his strident tone should put us off. After all, he was writing for his "comrades" and for Lacis. He was trying to make a crucial class and experiential distinction that holds true even today: theater that addresses the concerns of the majority of children—who, then as now, are poor and disadvantaged—fuses play and reality and allows children to become more conscious of how they can explore the forces that act upon them. This indeed makes theater dangerous, but not just for today's corporate and professional elite groups. Theater that prompts children to take charge of their actions is risky for all social classes. It upsets authorities and institutions. Freed to explore, children will cross all sorts of lines, often in politically incorrect ways, something even Benjamin did not grasp.

Or did he? Benjamin goes on to say that productions are not the real goal of the strenuous collective work accomplished in the children's clubs. Productions are incidental; "they come about by mistake, almost as a whim of the children. . . . More important are the tensions which are resolved in such productions. The tensions of the collective work are the educators" (81).

Such tensions between individuals and social conditions are explosive, demanding patience and comprehension on the part of the theater's adult leaders and the young people themselves. Emphasizing the status of children as independent agents, Benjamin conceived of young people, especially between the ages of six and sixteen, as supremely qualified directors. They were *erdenfern und unverfroren*—that is, they were not yet fixed and bound to earth, but were fluid and malleable. They could take ordinary situations and turn them around to reflect their own tastes and needs.

Key ideas of Benjamin's "Program" and his essays on children's culture were in direct opposition to the pedagogical principles and discipline of his period, when formal German idealism and middle-class notions of what was appropriate for children regulated youthful enthusiasm and naive susceptibility. If I summarize some of his ideas, their subversiveness will become apparent.

- All books, toys, clothes, plays, films, and other products for children are created by socialization and by the prevailing means of production and reception. Class specific even when they do not appear to be so, they were and still are used for children's "own good." Their inescapable prescriptiveness can be suspended only by children who appropriate them on their own terms and use them to create their own world, one that functions according to relatively new rules.
- From the "bourgeois" perspective, the carefully designed and censored production of children's objects greatly determines their reception. Children are to be protected from reality and are to see, read, and buy only what adults believe is good for them. In other words, children are to be raised as passive and obedient spectators and readers.
- It has always been illusory to believe in predictable, positivist social conditioning. Children are not automatons. To develop their own identities, they read and play with what has been printed, produced, manufactured, and organized not only for them but also for adults.
- Only through play can children create an environment where they can pursue their own interests, which they intuit and need to articulate in a free space.
- A "true" childhood, in which the child functions as a player, a collector, and a producer of his or her identity, is impossible in the traditional public sphere, for there a child's life is narrowly prescribed and reflects the interests of hierarchical classes.
- By developing a "proletarian" public sphere, that is, a "proletarian" children's theater, one creates the conditions for producing new plays, new books, new insights. At the heart of children's play is the re-formation of the world.

Today in the United States the old divisions between the proletariat, petite bourgeoisie, agrarian class, middle class, and upper class no longer function as cleanly as they did in Benjamin's Germany. The ideology of consumerism tends to erase or conceal differences. For anyone with sufficient money, class boundaries are easy to cross and transgress. Because the international conglomerates that produce books, toys, clothes, plays, videos, and so on seek the lowest common denominator, any boy or girl can subscribe momentarily to an illusive social group and feel wealthy, important, strong, or cool. The purpose of production is to conceal class.

Multiculturalism contributes to the concealment of class differences because it argues for inclusion in the "grand" middle class of America. But whatever is produced by America's underclasses and nonmainstream groups eventually is appropriated by the professional and corporate classes and marketed for everyone. Cultural homogenization makes it extremely difficult to demarcate a class-specific game, toy, film, or play. The discourse of the professional and corporate classes in the public sphere and in the cultural industry tends to foster a notion of one nation or one family under God, which can enjoy the fruits of American life if we all do our respective jobs and keep the economy working. Such occlusion of class differences makes it all the more important to find the differences that do exist.

For American children to have a "true childhood," in Benjamin's sense of the term, they must live and interact within both public and private spheres and be allowed to use their imaginations freely, to notice class differences, to grasp the ideology of consumerism, and to deal with imposed religions, ideologies, and pressures.[5] Accordingly, their adult leaders should not act just as observers who receive new impulses from the creative efforts and productions of the children; they should encourage and guide the children, fostering awareness of how consumerism works and how society's spectacles can conceal reality.

For the learning process to be effective, the adults must be honest with the children, and they must also learn how to learn from the children, who will appropriate everything that comes their way. As Benjamin writes in *Einbahnstraße*: "It is foolish to grumble pedantically about the production of objects appropriate for children—illustrative materials, toys, or books," because "the earth is full of the most incomparable objects that capture the attention of children who use them," especially "garbage and junk left over from building, gardening, housework, sewing, or carpentry." Using these "objects of junk" in play, they "form their world of things by themselves, a small world in the large one. One has to have an eye for the norms of this small world of things if one wants to create deliberately for children" and let oneself find a way to them (73). Now, in the age of consumerism and globalization, Benjamin's critique can help us understand how social conditions and contradictions limit our ability to let children play freely with "junk" to explore alternatives and discover their talents.

Children and children's culture today

American children have become insatiable consumers of manufactured identities that falsely promise excitement and happiness. This creates a major dilemma for children's theater: how to attract an audience while at the same time avoiding absorption into the culture industry, where it would be subjected to the forces of globalization, which turn everything into spectacle. Because the transformation of theater into spectacle diminishes the "threat" of theater to the dominant forces of power, it is important to understand the distinction between the two. In *The Society of the Spectacle*, written in the heyday of the student revolution in France, Guy Debord declared:

> By means of the spectacle the ruling order discourses endlessly upon itself in an uninterrupted monologue of self-praise. The spectacle is the self-portrait of power in the age of power's totalitarian rule over conditions of existence.... If the spectacle—understood in the limited sense of those "mass media" that are its most stultifying superficial manifestation—seems at times to be invading society in the shape of a mere *apparatus*, it should be remembered that this apparatus has nothing neutral about it, and that it answers precisely to the needs of the spectacle's internal dynamics.[6]

There are many problems with Debord's overall analysis, such as his attribution of monolithic power to the state and his conviction that we are living in a totally administered society, a viewpoint that he shared with other eminent postwar critics, including Theodor Adorno, Max Horkheimer, Herbert Marcuse, and Louis Althusser. They were not entirely wrong, but they did not give enough credit to the resilience and sheer inventiveness of human beings: we create spaces for alternative lifestyles; we find ways to undermine the abuses of power and show the spectacle for what it really is.

Still, Debord's discussion helps us grasp that the spectacle, instead of revealing society, produces and reproduces power relations that maintain and reinforce the status quo. It is a social construct that reduces us to mere spectators, thus engendering alienation. Debord argues that the more the spectator watches, "the less he lives; the more readily he recognizes his own needs in the images of need proposed by the dominant system, the less he understands his own existence and his own desires. The spectacle's externality with respect to the acting subject is demonstrated by the fact that the individual's own gestures are no longer his own, but rather those of someone else who represents them to him. The spectator feels at home nowhere, for the spectacle is everywhere."[7]

We need only think of the staging of "authentic" emotions on TV talk shows to realize how people *perform* emotions and end up looking like replicas of themselves. It is not just this deep alienation of emotions that the spectacle fosters, however. It also generates modes of behavior. Whether children actually will become what the culture industry presents as ideal is an open question. In fact, the culture industry does not care in the least what happens to children as long as they agree to consume, as long as they are disposed to become professionals who will maintain the system in some capacity. Benjamin was right when he talked about the profit motive of bourgeois theater, but he underestimated the power of the culture industry.

Children's theater as spectacle furthers the pauperization of children, if not their prostitution: material pauperization and pauperization of the mind, prostitution of the body, and prostitution of talent. Much children's theater today tries to prevent critical thinking by children even as it presents itself as moral, serious, patriotic, and God-fearing. Public spectacles are rampant, and children cannot escape their vamped-up ideologies. To be sure, they continue to play with junk, but even that won't help them form new meanings without guidance. They may become "shrubs"—wooden Howdy Doodies, funny, cute, adorable puppets who trip over their own strings. Although they are jerked constantly, they believe that they do not have strings attached to them. Shrubs are devoid of identity.

Globalization contributes to the devastation of everyone's identities, especially children's, but it does this in a very class-specific manner. In perhaps the most astute and concise analysis of globalization I have read, Zygmunt Bauman says,

> To put it in a nutshell: *rather than homogenizing the human condition, the technological annulment of temporal/spatial distances tends to polarize it.* It [globalization] emancipates certain humans from territorial constraints and renders certain community-generating meanings extraterritorial—while denuding the territory, to which other people go on being confined, of its meaning and its identity-endowing capacity. For some people it augurs an unprecedented freedom from physical obstacles and unheard-of ability to move and act from a distance. For others, it portends the impossibility of appropriating and domesticating the locality from which they have little chance of cutting themselves free in order to move elsewhere. With "distances no longer meaning anything," localities, separated by distances, also lose their meanings. This, however, augurs freedom of meaning-creation for some, but portends ascription to meaninglessness for others. Some can now move out of the locality—any locality—at will. Others watch helplessly the sole locality they inhabit moving away from under their feet.[8]

With the dissolution of public places, or public spheres, communities break down. One of the ironies of polarization is that it leaves loose bunches of people, who are no longer bound by community ties, open to homogenization and uniformity. They want to belong to some sort of meaning-producing group, be it a church, sports team, cult, choir, or fan club.

This is the paradox, I think, that evades Bauman. As he correctly remarks, globalization brings about polarization and fractures communities. Yet it also seeks to replace religious and social forms of community with a consumer ideology and to replace established forms of work and play with more organized forms that homogenize behavior and limit the development of class and political consciousness.[9] Seemingly diverse and enclosed groups that seek to form distinct identities are actually more uniform and similar than they realize; all forms of interaction revolve around the same customary practices, which make activities into commercial undertakings and children into consumers.

Here are two brief examples: organized sports and school. The pressure to conform and celebrate uniformity begins, in American sports, before children turn five. They learn to perform according to adult expectations—how to play the game, which uniforms to purchase, what to expend energy on, what to feel. Only forty years ago, children organized themselves on streets and in backyards and playgrounds and developed their own games. Now the dominant forms of sports are associated with professionalization; the child is raised, educated, and groomed to think of selling his or her body for profit at some point. If that expectation cannot be fulfilled, there are others, such as perfecting one's body so that it looks like a machine, an exercise of self-denial instead of self-expression.

The most startling transformations in schooling are connected to the encroachment of business corporations into schools and the privatization of public schools.[10] The focus used to be on children and how they might be assisted in defining their identity; now it has shifted conclusively toward adult expectations of preparing their children for careers, and state expectations of maintaining the level of functional literacy needed for business and government to preserve themselves. Except at certain schools, such as those run according to the Montessori, Reggio Emilia, and Waldorf (Rudolf Steiner) philosophies, the child is now merely the object of experimentation.

Children's theater as the unspectacular

Theater cannot avoid spectacle. Most plays for children are produced for the play's sake, not for the children's; most pander to the entertainment industry's expectations and conceal power relations in the way Debord demonstrated. Traditional plays show off talent while concealing any connection to the daily struggles of children or their attempt to grasp how art can play a role in their immediate lives. While many performances deal with social issues, they divert attention from those mediations that bind children into the corporate interests of the public sphere. A good example of this perniciousness is *A Christmas Carol*. The Guthrie Theatre in Minneapolis, for one, reproduces a version every December—not to prompt children to think about capitalism, misers, poverty, and exploitation but to exhibit grandiose stage effects and fine acting. *A Christmas Carol* is performed to ease the conscience of the rich and to celebrate philanthropy without questioning it. The producers imagine that children cannot think for themselves.

Fortunately, work in the theater can also endanger spectacle. Many forms of theater are subversive. But theater demands space for constant experimentation with the world of objects and for self-experimentation with one's body and mind. And unless children can appropriate the scripts, all plays—Broadway plays, classical dramas, adaptations of famous novels—have minimal value for their lives. To appropriate scripts, children must have the freedom of space and time to investigate the texts and see how they have been produced, received, and distributed. Any leftover signification forms the basis of the children's production.

I do not mean to dismiss the production of such traditional plays as *A Christmas Carol, Little Orphan Annie,* and *Peter Pan* in the professional children's theater or in schools. I have often been struck by the excitement and pleasure children exude when they watch a live performance. Yet they are being introduced to prescribed ways of performance. Even question-and-answer sessions after a play or a tour of the stage do not lead to self-exploration or critical examination of their environment.

Benjamin insisted that plays not be performed for children. Rather, children should develop their own plays with the guidance of adults, who are also part of the learning process. All other theatrical forms he disregarded as "bourgeois" and discounted as spectacle, although he did not use that term. This position, I think, is too narrow. No matter what children watch, they will cherish and cultivate some aspect of it in original ways. There is, however, no doubt in my mind that the most effective political theater for children demands children's physical and intellectual immersion in a project of their own conception and undertaking.

Numerous Western theatrical groups formed of adults only or a mixture of adults and children are nonetheless managing to do unusual unspectacular work that can be considered politically subversive or threatening. Grips is the kind of theater that produces plays written and performed by adults to provoke children and adults to question the political relations in their lives.

Antispectacular theater conceived and performed by adults to animate children opens up fissures in the totalizing tendencies of global capitalism. No one model of political children's theater exists, and perhaps even the term *political* fails to describe adequately some of the important experiments I have seen in the past ten years. I will use the term *political children's theater* anyway, because the political nature of their work is what sustains the focus of the young spectators, enabling them to glimpse the power relations that distort their view of the world.

Reviewing the unspectacular

What, then, is children's theater? Is it theater for the very young, aged three to ten, or for teenagers? Are some plays and performances age-specific? Should plays be censored for certain age groups? Why even make distinctions?

Aren't the best plays and performances for children productions that appeal to people of all ages?

It would take a book to answer these questions, but certainly distinctions can be made with regard to children's reception of plays. While the best work is universal, many theater groups create modes of production expressly designed for people of certain ages. Dockteatern Tittut (the Peek-a-Boo Puppet Theatre, Sweden), Mimika Theatre (England), Teater Terra (Netherlands), and the Catherine Wheels Theatre Company (Scotland) have all created plays that address very young audiences and use space and sound in unusual ways to address alienation, loneliness, and loss. The actors, directors, and designers invest care and thought in their productions. This adult investment in animating children to ponder complex existential problems is, I think, what is of value in political children's theater.

I saw two plays, *Langel and the Horse Named Blue* and *Wanna Be Wolf*, performed by the Dockteatern Tittut in Minneapolis, and what struck me was the manner in which they used puppets, dolls, and scenery to tell simple narratives with poetry, humor, and poignancy. *Langel and the Horse Named Blue* is about a boy who has a best friend named Gudmar; a blue horse comes between them, and jealousy almost ends their friendship. *Wanna Be Wolf*, based on a book by Ulf Stark, is a shadow-puppet play about a wolf with whom nobody wants to play because she is so zany and wild and a rabbit who is scared of his own shadow. They meet, exchange identities, play together, and in the end become good friends.

All the plays created and produced by Dockteatern are intended for children between the ages of two and six, and the audience is generally limited to thirty or forty spectators at most. The atmosphere of intimacy and the stage music are soothing, and the brevity of the plays (approximately thirty minutes) enables the children to relax and concentrate. The dialogue, sounds, rhymes, and songs demonstrate how language and relationships can be played with and transformed, recalling how children interact with one another in their own play. The puppets are almost like the found objects that children invent stories for. There is nothing overtly political about Dockteatern's plots or dramatic style, but the unpretentious acting is exactly the opposite of spectacle theater. The actors talk to the children before and after the performance and invite them to touch and look at the sets and puppets. These interactions show respect for the children's intelligence. There is nothing sweet about Dockteatern. The language is idiomatic, and although the characters and colors are marvelous, the problems depicted are real ones that the very young confront in their everyday lives.

The struggles of daily life also shape Mimika Theatre's production *Landscapes*, which I saw at the 2002 International Children's Festival at the Ordway Center for the Performing Arts in St. Paul. Like the Dockteatern actors, Mimika's two puppeteers limited the audience to twenty children, taking them two at a time into a dimly lit canvas tent filled with music based on sounds from nature. Once the play started, the audience was taken on a journey through a desert, a tropical rain forest, the sea, and Antarctica. The scenery kept changing, and the animals in each landscape preyed on, as well as played with, one another. There was a sense of survival of the fittest, but with the twinkle of an eye, for the smaller creatures managed to escape the predators. Here, too, the puppeteers were often visible, and after the play came to a close, they talked with the children and showed them how they worked the puppets and scenery. Although the magic of the performance was thereby dispelled, the art was passed on, and the children may later experiment in much the same way the actors themselves did.

The unselfish dedication of the actors to educating children through their experimental art always comes through in the best of the small groups I have seen, as does a persistent attempt to link the personal to the social and political. At the 2001 Ordway festival, the Dutch troupe Teater Terra performed *Swan's Down*, about a child's confrontation with death. Simon, a small boy played by a large puppet, lives with his father near the sea. The boy's mother recently drowned, but thanks to a friendship the boy develops with a mother swan, he begins to take joy in life again. When a nasty neighbor kills another swan, the boy empathizes with the mother swan and comes to terms with the loss of his own mother. Performed by three actors on a proscenium stage with no change of scenery, this play moved slowly yet had a poetic flow: the actors did not waste a gesture or word, nor did they seek to create a melodrama. Rather, the reserved, somewhat blunt acting style and the spare scenery captured a mood of loss that was gradually overcome by the puppet/boy, who shared his feelings with the young spectators without trying to overwhelm them.

The Catherine Wheels Theatre Company performed a drama entitled *Martha* at the 2002 Ordway festival. A grumpy woman of that name lives in a shack by the sea. She has tacked a sign on her shack that reads: "Don't knock. Just go away!" Most people are scared of her, and even the mailman, who tries to befriend her, is driven away. Then a stray white goose shows up at her shack and begins to pester and play with her. When the goose gets sick, Martha brings him into her home, where she nurses him back to health. They form a friendship, and Martha becomes an agreeable and joyful person. When the goose disappears overnight to join his flock, Martha realizes why the goose had to leave. She joins the mailman on an outing and appears to have overcome her loneliness. Performed by two actors, the play had no young characters, unless one considers the goose a kind of wild child. The goose was a rod puppet, and the setting was spare. Once again, the actors took a simple situation—the outcast condition of a disgruntled older woman—and turned it into a poignant drama about the possibility for change and friendship.

The didactic elements of these unspectacular dramas for the youngest spectators were not emphasized by any of the groups I have discussed.

Adult actors used metaphors and puppets to tell a simple, fantastic story as realistically as possible. This style was in stark contrast to that in two productions for teenagers I witnessed at the International Festivals of 2001 and 2002. Both plays were highly realistic, involved violence, and were intended to create postperformance discussions about particular incidents.

The Stones, by Australia's Zeal Theatre (see script and sidebars in this issue), is based on an event that took place in Melbourne. Two boys kicked rocks from a freeway overpass for fun, accidentally causing a driver's death, and were charged with manslaughter. The verdict was "not guilty." But here, ultimately, the audience is called upon to deliver the verdict, for the play ends with one of the boys realizing how reckless he had been and the other just relieved that he was "getting off." Two actors play all the roles —the boys, officers, attorneys—in a small space with a minimum change of costume. They never "identify" with their characters, but in good Brechtian fashion demonstrate how small acts of vandalism can lead to tragedy. Going beyond pure documentary, the play calls upon the spectators to reveal what they have learned and to make judgments.

The work of the Teatergruppen Mariehønen of Denmark is also based on the Brechtian *Lehrstück* methodology. Here the set, which can easily be transported into schools or open spaces, acts as a metaphor of life. An equilateral triangle surrounds a box that contains large boxing gloves; a lighting rig at each point of the triangle is the designated space for each character. The spectators are ushered in as if they are going to witness a boxing match. The characters, all in their early teens, are Poul; Stevens, a bully, who makes life hell for Poul; Norman, who has an alcoholic father who beats him and his mother; and Henrietta, whose parents are going through a divorce. The play begins at the end of the school year. Stevens beats Poul up and makes him promise that on the first day of school in the fall he will wear girl's clothing to indicate that he is a "sissy." Poul spends the summer with his friends Norman and Henrietta learning how to box so he can defend himself in the fall. Stevens frequently interferes with the friends, as do their conflicts at home. All their personal problems emerge as they engage in the boxing ring of life. In the end they find a way to stop the turmoil and violence of bullying, confronting it inside and outside their homes.

The actors do not mimic teenagers. Instead, they illustrate the dramatic situations in which teenagers may find themselves. Making full use of the boxing metaphor, they reveal the shifting sides of the different combats that the characters are obliged to enter. What becomes clear is that there are many ways to defend oneself and that solidarity is essential when one is confronted by tyranny.

There are hundreds of tiny groups like Teatergruppen Mariehønen and Zeal Theatre in the Western world, formed by adults with a message for children. Their work varies according to their grasp of the power relations of their social world. Characteristically their best work is unspectacular, enabling their audiences to unravel some of the forces that control their lives. When children and adults play together and learn how to cooperate against these forces, they form unspectacular theater that is dangerous to the theater of the spectacle.

It is crucial to support the kind of educational children's theater that generally takes place unseen in thousands of schools in the Western world. In the United States this comes closest to what Benjamin envisioned as proletarian children's theater. If we don't support it, the unspectacular will not thrive as a subversive force—and I think that is our only hope for it. Fortunately (or, some might say, unfortunately), the society of the spectacle, like the theater of the spectacle itself, feeds off the unspectacular. Both need its life force to make themselves appear interesting as well as interested in their spectators. I will close with a summary of the work that I do with the Children's Theatre Company of Minneapolis. This large, wealthy organization exemplifies how a traditional middle-class theater, while creating spectacles, can transcend itself through subversive unspectacular work.

Neighborhood bridges

Neighborhood Bridges, originally sponsored by a generous grant from the Open Foundation in New York, is now entirely funded by the Children's Theatre Company of Minneapolis. The syllabus is based on my book *Creative Storytelling: Building Community, Changing Lives* (1995). The aim was to set up a year-round program in two inner-city elementary schools in Minneapolis, with storytellers meeting with one class in each school for two hours a week. The children in these schools are mainly African American, Hmong, Somalian, and Native American, with a sprinkling of whites. The two classes were to contact each other during the course of the year, and in May, after exploring different genres of storytelling, writing, drawing, and improvisation, they each would present a play they had created for their own school and parents. They would perform this play for the partner school and then, finally, join the other class in a festival at the Children's Theater. In other words, productions would create bridges within the school, the community, and the theater.

In the spring and summer of 1998, I trained eight actors and taught an intensive summer seminar for teachers and storytellers to prepare them for the first year. Our success in developing the talents and skills of more than one hundred students during the first two years enabled us to obtain more support from other foundations and to expand; by the fall of 2002, Neighborhood Bridges had effective programs in six innercity schools in Minneapolis. More actor-educators have been trained in summer seminars taught in collaboration with the Perpich Center for the Arts and Hamline University. The program, now with thirteen classes of more than three hundred students, involves extensive collaboration with teachers in all the schools, as well as with the Book Arts Center and the College of Education at the University of Minnesota. The children become pen pals with their friends at other schools and meet at the Children's Theater to see performances and learn about the production of plays. To celebrate their work during the school year, they perform their own plays in school festivals in May.

Neighborhood Bridges has three guiding principles:

1. We believe that much harm has been done to children by the mass media in all its forms, and our creative work is in part a means to offset and question this influence. We do not, however, dismiss or denigrate popular culture. We try to expose contradictions instead. For instance, we discuss how wonderful superheroes are as they fight for the disadvantaged, but we prompt the students to ask why the superheroes earn so much money by getting children to buy consumer articles while they, the children, remain poor. Why don't superheroes change the conditions of the children's lives? How can any of us change our lives? Do we need heroes? The actor-educators of Neighborhood Bridges offer not solutions or resolutions but alternative ways of thinking and acting.

2. We know that we cannot fully change children's lives, and we do not want to play the role of therapist. But we do want to engage teachers and children, to animate them, to set them on a path of self-discovery, to provide skills, to strengthen self-confidence. In the process, we learn as much about ourselves and our capabilities as they do about theirs.

3. Our work is not limited to a specific grade level or school. We focus on storytelling as a means to enable people to become storytellers of their lives, a technique that can be used from preschools to universities and elsewhere. We do not believe in one-time workshops, seminars, or performances. Primarily we seek to build community, which means that our work is long-term and that we want to involve not just children but also parents, teachers, administrators, actor-educators, and friends. At times the creative process may even test the conception and self-conception of the institutions within which we work.

To keep ourselves from imposing our method and ideas, we borrowed a slogan from Brecht: Make yourself dispensable, especially when it comes to sharing knowledge. To this end, we make contact with all the schools, teachers, and administrators, hand out a printed syllabus, offer a summer workshop for teachers, hold preparatory meetings each week with the teachers, and hold three meetings a year with teachers from all the schools in our program. Ironically, there is one major problem that we actually hope arises and that we seek to resolve through collaboration: teachers have found that our work makes the writing, reading, and learning that the children do more pleasurable and even more effective than the official programs.

Outside the schools themselves, our collaboration involves the staff at the Children's Theatre Company, parents, and university students and professors at certain stages of our work, and in the spring, each class also has the opportunity to bring in musicians, set designers, costume makers, or dancers to help the children learn about different arts and crafts. In short, our May celebration of nine months' work with the children is a collaborative effort in which the entire community expresses and articulates how the children see and imagine themselves in the world around them.

The children in May are not the same children that we met in September. Obviously, they have grown because of all sorts of biological, psychological, and social factors. Viewed in light of our program, we can note additional individual and collective changes. We encourage and foster transformation in two primary ways: (1) by constantly changing the classroom environment and introducing the children to new environments and (2) by improvising to alter rules and regulations and to shift their expectations, and the audience's. For instance, we begin by playing a game called the fantastic binominal, which is varied throughout the year. It begins with the actor-educator writing prepositions called linking words on the board and asking the class for any two nouns, which she or he also writes on the board. After asking the students to choose a linking word, the actor-educator improvises a story based on the three words (perhaps "bear on ice cream," or "ice cream on the bear"). After that story is done, the actor-educator asks for two volunteers to write two more nouns on the board. The words are to stimulate the students to write and illustrate very short stories. Three or four volunteers read their stories aloud after reading the stories to themselves to make sure they understand what has been written. These stories can serve as the basis for further work during the week, with the teacher helping the students hone their stories and draw pictures. They also serve as scripts for plays that the students develop.

After the children write and perform their stories for the other children, we push the chairs and tables to the side to create a free space. The children, recognizing that the classroom can be changed to their liking, turn found objects—"junk"—into props, people, scenery—things other than they are—just as the children themselves will become other than they think they are. Environmental change leads to personal change. Our initial game with the fantastic binominal animates the children to conceive stories in which two haphazard elements are brought together to form a story, their story. In the same way, movement and taking over terrain in the classroom for storytelling, discussion, and performance can lead to an understanding of how appropriation can work.

We want to suggest to the children (and the teachers) that appropriation can enable them to express their desires and needs. We model change. We tell fairy tales, legends, fables, tall tales, myths, and then similar tales that question the traditional versions. For instance, we tell "Little Red Riding Hood" as a tale of rape in which the girl is blamed for her own violation, and we counter it with Catherine Storr's "Little Polly Riding Hood and the Stupid Wolf" to show how girls can trick and escape predators. We develop plays that contrast heroes like John Henry or Kate Crackernuts with the superheroes of comics and popular films and animate the students to create their own heroes or question heroism. We act these stories out with the students and push them with our suggestions to take over all the tales told during the two hours we are with them. We show that we are not afraid to take risks even when we may make blunders. We adapt to constantly changing conditions in the classroom and in the school. We try to show how change may be linked to tolerance. By forming within the classroom three groups of children that stay together throughout the year, we hope the children will build their own little community and cooperate with one another. We try to foster respect and understanding among the three groups. In the end, they will join together and be changed into one large community to produce a play for other classes and schools.

We have seen shy children step into spaces they had never entered before. We have seen previously uncooperative children join in freely. We have seen children conceive projects that represent changes they have been undergoing and discoveries they are making. In the May 2002 festival of Crossing Bridges, one class turned "The Magic Table, the Gold Donkey, and the Club" into a play about drug dealing. Another class created a story about a soldier bringing peace to an ethnically divided neighborhood through a song contest.

Finally, in all our work, we note changes in the teachers and ourselves—how we become more sensitive to children's needs and our own and how we use conversation to solve problems and to create projects that build on our social awareness and creative designs.

Creative and critical literacy

Neighborhood Bridges is an explicit critique of functional literacy and how schools and politicians hinder learning by testing rote skills. Until the end of the nineteenth century, most people did not know how to read and write, yet they were able to solve problems and build great things. The oral form of transmitting and sharing knowledge was sufficient and, in many cases, still is sufficient to spark imagination and inspire people to think critically about their circumstances. On the other hand, reading and writing are important skills in our advanced technological society, and they can enable children to gain meaningful pleasure out of life and to structure their existence in manifold ways. So we do help children learn how to read and write. Without the requisite oral, literary, and dramatic skills, it is difficult for them to project themselves into the world and to narrate their own lives.

A remark by the psychologist Jerome Bruner encapsulates our approach:

> I conceive of schools and preschools as serving a renewed function within our changing societies. This entails building school cultures that operate as mutual communities of learners, involved jointly in solving problems with all contributing to the process of educating one another. Such groups provide not only a locus for instruction, but a focus for identity and mutual work. Let these schools be a place for the praxis (rather than the proclamation) of cultural mutuality—which means an increase in the awareness that children have of what they are doing, how they are doing it, and why. The balance between individuality and group effectiveness gets worked out within the culture of the group; so too the balancing of ethnic or racial identities and the sense of the larger community of which they are part.[11]

Bruner calls for mutual learning that depends on cooperation and participation because it also enables individuals to develop their talents more fully. The stories and plays that the children create from mutual learning in the Neighborhood Bridges program make the ordinary seem strange, and the strange and fantastic images and words reveal their hopes for a better future. The stories and plays demand close reading, just as each child calls for close reading.

In becoming stimulating and demanding storytellers, the children become risk takers. Their willingness to cross bridges and spread what they have learned, that is, to apply their learning to the world, brings us back to one of the key notions in Benjamin's "Program": "Children who have played theater in this way have become free in such productions. Through play they have fulfilled their childhood."

Certainly, it is impossible to speak about his "Program" today without revising and expanding it. History has changed childhood. But children still play and labor to define themselves; they still struggle against oppression in the family, school, and community, they still seek to articulate their needs. Benjamin saw a specific "proletarian" theater as a way for children (the most oppressed group in society) to come to terms with conditions that were not of their own making. He demanded, perhaps too rigidly, a theater in which children could voice their wants and develop projects that spoke to their needs. This type of theater work is still possible, but it is a theater work that must cut across all social classes in schools and communities, and it should include the unspectacular theater productions of adults. Such unspectacular work by children's theaters and other groups must continue to confront the society of the spectacle if theater's vital, dangerous impulse is to be kept alive.

Notes

1 Jack Zipes, ed., *Political Plays for Children: The Grips Theater of Berlin* (St. Louis: Telos, 1976), 2.

2 For information on Grips, see Zipes, *Political Plays for Children*, a translation of three plays with an introduction about the history of the Grips Theater. Gerhard Fischer has just published an excellent social history of Grips: *Grips: Geschichte eines populären Theaters (1966–2000)* (Munich: Iudicium, 2002).

3 His essays, including "Programm eines proletarischen Kindertheaters," can be found in Walter Benjamin, *Über Kinder, Jugend und Erziehung* (Frankfurt am Main: Suhrkamp, 1970). All the page citations in the text are taken from this volume. For a translation of "Programm," see Susan Buck-Morss, trans., "Program for a Proletarian Children's Theater," *Performance* 1 (March–April 1973): 28–32. I have not used Buck-Morss's translation because there are problems with it. To begin with, the title is wrong. Benjamin did not write a program *for* a proletarian theater; he wrote a program *of* or *about* it. In fact, he was writing about the work that Lacis had already accomplished. I consulted Buck-Morss's translation, but all the translated passages in this article are mine.

4 For information about their relationship, see Jack Zipes, "Building a Children's Theater, 2: Documents: Asja Lacis/Walter Benjamin," *Performance* 1 (March–April 1973): 22–27.

5 For excellent critiques of consumerism, see Charles McGovern, Susan Strasser, and Mattias Judt, eds., *Getting and Spending: European and American Consumer Societies in the Twentieth Century* (Cambridge: Cambridge University Press, 1998); Charles McGovern, *Sold American: Inventing the Consumer, 1890–1945* (Chapel Hill: University of North Carolina Press, 2002); and Gary Cross, *An All-Consuming Century: Why Consumerism Won in Modern America* (New York: Columbia University Press, 2000).

6 Guy Debord, *The Society of the Spectacle*, trans. Donald Nicholson-Smith (New York: Zone Books, 1995), 19; first published as *La societé du spectacle* (Paris: Buchet-Chastel, 1967). Debord, who died in 1994, wrote a preface for the third French edition of 1992, included in the American edition.

7 Ibid., 23.

8 Zygmunt Bauman, *Globalization: The Human Consequences* (New York: Columbia University Press, 1998), 18.

9 I have amply discussed homogenization tendencies in my book *Sticks and Stones: The Troublesome Success of Children's Literature from Slovenly Peter to Harry Potter* (New York: Routledge, 2001).

10 See Alex Molnar, *Giving Kids the Business: The Commercialization of America's Schools* (Boulder, Colo.: Westview, 1996).

11 Jerome Bruner, *The Culture of Education* (Cambridge: Harvard University Press, 1996), 81–82.

99

CARNIVALS, THE CARNIVALESQUE, *THE MAGIC PUDDIN'*, AND DAVID ALMOND'S *WILD GIRL, WILD BOY*

Towards a theorizing of children's plays

Rosemary Ross Johnston

Source: *Children's Literature in Education* 34(2) (June 2003): 131–146.

Children's literature theory and criticism continues to grow, but there is one area in which very little theoretical work has been done—children's plays and children's theatre. I am not referring to educational drama or theatre in education, nor necessarily plays written to be acted by children; rather, this discussion concerns plays written for and performed to audiences who are children. My emphasis here is on plays presented to children commercially, as books are presented to children commercially (that is, through market processes).

In fact, my point of departure is a book. *The Magic Pudding*, written by the Australian artist Norman Lindsay in 1918, is a well-known illustrated text that has been adapted and performed as a play many times, notably on several occasions as a puppet production. Even a brief overview suggests that a productive interpretive hermeneutic through which to view *The Magic Pudding* is the Bakhtinian optic of the carnivalesque, with its emphasis on parody, food, marketplace language, fools and rogues, and the 'laughing truth.' *The Magic Pudding* is in fact a profoundly theatrical text. The visuality of events, visual eccentricity of the characters, and the chronology of story pattern—a rollicking journey—lend themselves to dramatic adaptation, as does the extensive use of the rhythms and rhymes of verse; the characters break out into verse in the same way as the characters of stage musicals break out into song (in fact, many of the verses are called songs). The book is composed mainly of dialogue. Those parts that are not dialogue tend to read as stage directions, describing accompanying actions and how words are said:

> 'Always anxious to be eaten,' said Bill, 'that's this Puddin's mania. Well, to oblige him, I ask you to join us at lunch.'
> 'Delighted, I'm sure,' said Bunyip Bluegum, seating himself. 'There's nothing I enjoy more than a good go-in at steak-and-kidney pudding in the open air.'
> 'Well said,' remarked Sam Sawnoff, patting him on the back. 'Hearty eaters are always welcome.'
> 'You'll enjoy this Puddin',' said Bill, handing him a large slice. 'This is a very rare Puddin'.'
> 'It's a cut—an'-come-again Puddin',' said Sam.
> 'It's a Christmas steak and apple-dumpling Puddin',' said Bill.
> 'It's a—. Shall I tell him?' Sam asked, looking at Bill. Bill nodded and the Penguin leaned across to Bunyip Bluegum and said in a low voice, 'It's a Magic Puddin'.'
>
> (p. 21)

Norman Lindsay's illustrations all face an audience—an implicit auditorium—and are drawn on the one level; the characters are almost caricatures, easily identifiable by costumes and gait; there is considerable language play and parody; the action is slapstick, farce, vaudeville, with the dress-ups and disguises of pantomime, and lots of shouting and fighting and hitting and trouncing; there is also a great deal of eating and talk about stomachs and 'raging tums.' In the words of the penguin Sam Sawnoff, 'songs, roars of laughter and boisterous jests are the order of the day' (p. 48).

Lindsay's story is a performance—a performance not of childhood (as children's books are sometimes described)—but rather an artistically self conscious performance *for* childhood. Conceived at a time of personal and national heaviness (the last year of the World War I) it is a deliberate indulgence in jollity and play, a 'conversation, song and story' (p. 44) set as a journey through an overtly Australian bush context and spiced with irony and political and social satire:

> Bunyip decided to leave home without further ado. The trouble was that he couldn't make up his mind whether to be a Traveller or a Swagman. You can't go about the world being nothing, but if you are a traveller you have to carry a bag, while if you are a swagman you have to carry a swag, and the question is: Which is the heavier?
>
> (p. 11)

The book parodies many social institutions, including the pretentions of the legal system, and even becomes metafictive at the end when Bill warns:

'For the point is, here we are pretty close to the end of the book, and something will have to be done in a Tremendous Hurry, or we'll be cut off short by the cover.'

'The solution is perfectly simple,' said Bunyip. 'We have merely to stop wandering along the road, and the story will stop wandering through the book.'

(p. 168)

Although the language of the whole text has been inflected ironically, it is only at the end that the narrator's presence becomes visible; note however, that the narrator, who emerges from the wings in the final scenes, is a participant rather than an observer:

On winter nights there is always Puddin' and hot coffee for supper, and many's the good go-in I've had up there, a-sitting round the fire.

(p. 171)

The last song, extolling the significance of home, constitutes a brilliant finale to a 'rolling, roaring life,' with 'all hands joining in the chorus':

> Home, home, home,
> That's the song of them that roam,
> The song of the roaring, rolling sea
> Is all about rolling home.

(p. 171)

The journey that is the pattern of so many children's stories has reached journey's end—home, or a new construction of home; the carnival is over.

The notion of performance is significant. It is integral to the study of children's plays, which are written with actual performance in mind and which constitute what can be seen as a real, practical performativity. The topical debate (see for example, Bell, 1999) around this notion of performativity—a term emerging out of linguistic theory (Austin, 1962) to refer to the relationship of *speech* to *act*, but initiated into feminist theory by Butler (1990) to refer to the relationship of *act* to *identity*—provides a provocative backdrop to considerations of children's plays. For Butler, performativity describes the production, through constant repetition, reference, and citation, of subjects or selves as effects. In Spivak's words, this identity—'subject-effect'—is 'the effect of an effect' (1988, p. 204); identity is embodied in dramatic acts. Rather than performance being the effect of identity, identity is the effect of performance. Performance, in Butler's theoretical terms, is a 'bounded act' (1993, p. 24), a form of theatricality; Lloyd points out the Derridean idea that 'everything is in some sense always theatrical' (1999, p. 202). As a way of viewing children's plays, I want to apply (reapply?) the idea of *performance*—the act bounded by the sense of miming [that is, mimicking] and exaggerating existing codes and signifiers (Lloyd, 1999 p. 202), iterating and reiterating cultural practices (sometimes transgressively)—to the play itself, using it to refer to the deliberate creation of subject, space, story, and identity in the context of overt artistic act, theatre. The idea of *performativity* is adopted here to refer to that which is enacted and revealed about the production and performance of identity, but particularly to the idea of performative belonging:

> The performativity of belonging 'cites' the norms that constitute or make present the 'community' or group as such. The repetition, sometimes ritualistic repetition, of these normalised codes makes material the belongings [belongingness] they purport to simply describe.
>
> (Bell 1999, p. 3)

'Acts' derive their binding power (Fortier, 1999, p. 43) through routine and reiteration, but most of all through citationality, that is, 'through the invocation of convention' (Butler 1993, p. 234). Who I am does not shape what I do; what I do shapes who I am. By extension, what I participate in, what I laugh at, especially representations of community seen in community with others, shapes who I am. In this way, children's plays, like children's books but more obviously so, constitute, cross-reference, and make present a community of belonging that is in a sense 'doubled' through the consciousness of the visuality of performance. The invocation of convention is part of the performative utterance (speech to act), which 'confers a binding power on the action performed' (Butler 1993, p. 234). To put it simply, the 'act' of the performance/play, which is culturally coded, constructs identities and communities of belonging; children's plays represent a conscious, theatrical citationality (quotation) of speech, act, identity, and belonging.

That brings me to my next point. Children's books can be critiqued by academics as a text, because children will also read the books (that is, we are looking at the same thing, even though our points of view may be very different); our reading of these books assumes a child audience/implied reader, even if we are not concerned with the response of that audience. Children's plays as texts, on the other hand, cannot with integrity be separated from the play as dramatic presentation, because it is this that children will actually experience. Therefore, I am proposing an idea of *children's plays-as-the-performance-of-texts* rather than play as text. In other words, any theoretical consideration must assume performance and performativity. This of course introduces a huge number of variables, but adjunctively it implies certain defining characteristics. These include:

1. Plays, unlike books, will usually not be read by children or adults. Rather, plays will be viewed and experienced live. (I am not concerned here with plays produced for television.)
2. The experience of the play will involve a performance, and in any performance there will be many variables, including such things as the contributions/interventions of actors and directors, staging, size of theatre, and costumes. The ideologies and commitment (to excellence, to promulgating a particular worldview, to children, to education, to artistic development) of all those involved in the production process will also shape the experience of the audience.
3. A live play is usually a one-off experience; most children will see most plays only once. The play normally has to stand on that one performance, whereas books can be revisited.
4. The play must hold the children's interest.

There are of course ways in which children's books, especially as read to children, can be compared to theatre. As I have written elsewhere:

> [C]hildren's literature in the classroom is a type of theatre.... Every time we read a book with children it is a viewing, as theatre is: a viewing of the text, of the imaginary experience that is the invitation of the text, and of each other's participation in that experience. Like theatre it is a corporate experience of being involved in shared story. The word *theatre* derives from the Greek word *theatron*, meaning a place for viewing or a place for seeing.... A reading event is a metafictional mise-en-scène, a sliding between a present 'real' setting and an imagined 'un-real' setting.... Every turn of the picture book page is a shift in scene; the teacher's hand turning the page is a *stagehand*. Readers are part of the stage crew in this reading event, getting things ready and making links between what is seen and what is unseen and filling in the gaps by running around in the backstage places of the imagination.
>
> (Johnston 2001, pp. 433–434)

This is not to take away from the real—or unreal—experience of theatre, which can present powerfully to the senses: visual, aural, kinaesthetic. And thus we come to four significant characteristics of children's plays:

1. First, although of course children may and do respond individually to the play with very private, important, and nonevident reactions, *theatre is a corporate experience.* Plays not only connect and construct community, they are also seen *in community*—with families, friends, and peers.
2. Second, this corporate communal nature of children's theatre means that the *experience of the play criss-crosses the footlights.* Feedback is

not reflected by how many books are sold, but at the very moment of performance; indeed, feedback as audience response is immediate. There are qualifications to this, however; Fox makes the important point that theatre behaviour is learned behaviour, and sometimes children do not know what is expected of them ('Is it okay to laugh?' 'When do we clap, or don't we?'; 2002; see Acknowledgment).

3. Third, and following on from this, children's plays are essentially an interactive experience (even when they are not designed to be overtly interactive in the modern sense) in that the *audience and its response can change the dynamic of the play as it happens.* Sad parts can become funny not only by how the writer conceives them and the actor acts them but by how the audience as a collective respond to them. In short, plays depend on an audience, and the audience is a fundamental part of performance.

4. And fourth, the distribution of power in children's theatre—like all distributions of power—is complex, involving the varying roles of writers, producers, directors, costume designers, and actors, as well as lighting and sound technicians and so on. But, in the end, I believe that *power—as choice and freedom to respond—resides principally with the child audience.* There is great political power in body language (especially in the communal body language of five hundred children).

Is this different from adult theatre, and if so, in what ways are children's plays distinctive?

Children's plays, like children's books, are part of an artistic continuum. It is obviously difficult to analyse plays-as-performance-of-texts (as I am proposing here), as play text can change with each performance of it. However, some characteristics (if not differences) are:

1. The fundamental rule is that children's plays absolutely must capture children's interest.

2. Again, the essence of the children's play is that it is a shared communal physical experience. Children *perform* audience together, no matter what their interior thoughts may be. This is also true of adult plays, of course, but adult audiences are more independent, likely to be less influenced by peer pressure to perform in a certain way, and likely to be attending the play with a variety of motives and expectations.

3. There is generally, but not exclusively, a great emphasis on action.

4. There may be greater emphasis on the journey of the play rather than on what character development takes place.

5. Children's plays are on the whole fast paced. Even when action is not fast paced, dialogue is (as in the Chorus of Voices in David Almond's *Wild Girl, Wild Boy*). There are variations on this, but the principle holds.

6. Children's plays—although not always those for young adults, which tend to be issue based—contain many different forms of humour, both verbal and visual.

7. Dramatic irony is a very common and pervasive element in children's plays. The audience loves to be 'in the know' and especially enjoys trying to help stage characters who are not (at its most basic level, 'He's over there!' Look, behind you!'). At a more subtle level, and in other genres of plays, dramatic irony works as it does in Shakespeare—to complicate the sense of drama and highlight the inevitability of outcome. Thus, the CREA Productions' adaptation of *The Crucible*, which sought to make an 'adult' play accessible to students who were struggling with the original but who were studying—and 'knew'—the tragic Salem history, introduced the play with a prelude presenting the seduction of gossip and peer pressure as a dimly lit dance around a cauldron, from which words were taken out, breathed on, passed around, and inflamed (a metaphor of Austin's speech to act).

8. The role of fools, rogues, and other rascals is on the whole not that of the Bakhtinian fool or rogue who speaks wise words or 'laughing truths'; rather, fools and rogues are often either downright bad, humorous, or both. The person who tends to speak wisdom in a children's play may be the child or animal figure who is most mocked and marginalised (the Cinderella figure), suggesting not only the contemporary significance of peers but also a change in social attitudes. In some plays the wise person is the Storyteller/Chorus (a little like the Narrator/Chorus who becomes visible at the end of *The Magic Pudding*). In others, such as the Almond play, the Chorus of Voices represents conventional mob 'wisdom' (including the comments of well-meaning schoolteachers).

And that brings me back to the idea of carnival and children's plays. There has been much discussion of the carnivalesque in children's literature (Nikolajeva, 1996, 2000; Stephens, 1992) but one point is often missing. The *carnivalesque* may be a time-out experience, as Stephens suggests, but the intrinsic power of the spirit of *carnival* is community, connection to others. Carnival is a performative event of belonging; it is a performance art, a type of 'citation theatre,' endlessly quoting itself in ritualistic practices. Clark and Holquist note that Bakhtin identified two Rabelaisian subtexts, 'carnival, which is a social institution, and grotesque realism, which is a literary mode' (1984, p. 299). Carnival is a physical coming together, a significant 'suspension of all hierarchical precedence,' a 'feast of becoming, change and renewal' (Bakhtin, 1965/1984, p. 10). Carnival laughter and mockeries are corporate play. Carnival depends on common senses of the ridiculous, in-jokes, and knowledges. Centrifugal language—that is, the everyday slangy language at the margins of the marketplace (and playground)—becomes part of a shared 'laughing word,' which may in turn initiate a moral reorganisation.

Carnival slides into grotesque realism through the body—its apertures and gross flesh, its bellies and appetites. The many pitfalls that happen to bodies—tripping over, silly disguises—become a grotesquerie of slapstick possibilities for all to enjoy together. As Bakhtin notes, 'it is the medieval comic theatre which is most intimately related to carnival' (1965/1984, p. 15). There are many children's plays that seek to teach—about the environment and so on—and there are serious plays with morals, but many at some point, and sometimes as a small episode of relief, involve comic (or drastic) things happening to bodies. *Peter Pan* (1904), which started life as a play rather than a book, is an obvious example, with its Nanny as the body of a dog, the hook of Captain Hook replacing the hand bitten off by a crocodile, and so on. Arguably, the Lost Boys have been 'cut off' from their mother. This is represented against, but as part of, nostalgic nursery images and romantic conceptions of Never-Never Land. One of the *CREA Production* plays, which was very successful and seen by about 7,000 primary school children, was *Stop, Look, Listen: Santa in the City*. It was a performance about Road Safety produced in collaboration with the Road Traffic Authority of New South Wales and three local councils. Written and directed by a postgraduate student in the Master of Arts in Children's Literature and Literacy course, in collaboration with a colleague and myself, it was performed by UTS students from the Faculty of Education. This play revolved around Santa getting lost in the city with a sleighful of presents because the baddies had kidnapped Red Man and Green Man (of traffic light fame). The play contained many carnival elements: a journey, lots of action and humour, irony, dramatic irony and breaking into song, much body grotesquerie and falling over and pouncing on people, and some questionable marketplace (school playground) language. Another CREA play, *Sense and Sustainability*, written by Barbara Poston-Anderson, had a strong environmental message, but Sludge, Slick, and Smog had to undergo considerable amounts of pushing around and pummelling before they were recycled and transformed. And another, a retelling of Andersen's *The Dancing Princesses*, which I adapted into a more mystical story of imagination and desire ('Shadow World/calling me/from across the silver sea'), had some light relief in a carnivalesque interlude, as the invisible Gardener following the princesses stumbled and lost his way.

There are other ways of viewing children's theatre—once called a 'ghetto' by a *Times* critic. Bakhtin claims that the freedom of grotesque realism helped develop the Romantic discovery of what he calls 'the *interior infinite* of the individual' (1965/1984, p. 44). The representation of subjectivity (the interior infinite) in children's plays is at once physical and direct, with little obvious access to inner worlds. However, child audiences are remarkably perceptive in discerning what characters are thinking and feeling through what they say and do. Further, just as Shakespeare uses soliloquies in the revelation of inner worlds, children's plays often use song; thus the oldest Dancing Princess sings out her sorrow about the death of their mother, the subsequent overprotectiveness of their father, and the passing of time:

> *I dreamt last night of times gone by*
> *Of overflowing days, and summer sky*
> *Of rainbow colours bright, like tinted cellophane*
> *I dreamt last night I was a child again.*
> *Why can't the world be like my memories*
> *When roads were long and mountains high?*
> *When just the branches of a blossom tree*
> *Became a fortress reaching to the sky*
> *And I could keep my tryst [sung as 'date'] with destiny*
> *With laughing eyes, as dreams fulfil?*

As we shall see, David Almond uses a contemporary Chorus to allow the audience to hear what his protagonist is hearing all too clearly. Again, developing a concept of children's plays in terms of a proposed *dramatic chronotope* is also theoretically exciting. Briefly, this would explore the dramatic relationship of people and events on the one hand, to time and space on the other. Such a conception highlights in particular the often dense construction of theatrical temporality beyond the obvious temporal-spatial shifts of scene changes, which may imply a simultaneous present anyway. In other words, sometimes scenes/events that happen *after* each other on stage are presented in such a way as to be understood as happening at the same time. Where this is particularly interesting is when an actor/narrator/chorus wraps up at the end invoking another time-space again—a sort of omniscient continuous present, a sense of *dramatic eternal*—that automatically refigures the action of the play in a frame of past. In some cases this happens almost as the quotation, incasement, autothematism, and mirror games of Gide's *mise-en-abyme* (Kowzan, 1976, p. 68), which is described by Rimmon-Kenan as 'a transposition of the theme of a work to the level of the characters' (1983, p. 93). The Narrator at the end of *The Magic Pudding* is an example of this in a novel, and many of the plays we have produced at CREA have a storyteller/narrator figure who moves the chronotope out of the 'play time' and into the 'now time,' also often subtly positioning her/himself alongside the audience's present, describing the play that has just been seen as a *quotation*, more or less placing it in quotation marks. Such figures may provide a frame as an interpretive hermeneutic (*incasement*), or *mirror* the action and ideas of the play. *Autothematism* is related to the concept of metafiction: in some plays, this figure—like Puck—may give an overlay of the play calling attention to itself as performance.

Carnival is one way of performing childhood. Implicit in the idea of carnival is the serious period—the period of abstinence, festival, and feast—

and often sacred time it traditionally precedes, for example, Lent and Easter in the Christian tradition. Ironically, the etymology of the word carnival —*carn* = flesh, and *levare* = to raise, remove, meaning 'the putting away of flesh'—describes what comes after the carnival; what happens during the carnival is the exact opposite (a telling parody). Perhaps in this context, children's plays as carnival celebrate a construction/reconstruction of childhood as the free and uninhibited before-time preceding the economic and social concerns of adulthood. This carnival of childhood is fun, festive, scatological, perhaps part of adapting to bodies that are, in the view of some of their owners, changing quite grotesquely. In this way, the inevitability of growth is expressed, and mediated, in what Bakhtin calls 'the laughing truth'—making fun of what cannot be changed.

Carnival, like childhood, is never (or should never be) an end-state; rather, it is a seductive freedom, a 'kind of existential heteroglossia,' that is, a many-voiced ('heteroglossic'), noisy commentary on issues of life, death and existence. It is something between 'normal' life and sacred, spiritual life. In reality, writes Bakhtin, 'carnival is life itself . . . shaped according to a certain sense of play' (Bakhtin, 1965/1984, p. 7). Children's theatre is also play; like carnival, it 'builds its own world in opposition to the official world . . .' (p. 88), it is parodic, unifying, generative; indeed, while carnival lasts, 'there is no other life outside it' (p. 7).

David Almond's *Wild Girl, Wild Boy* (2002) is a play for older children/ young adults, but it creates exactly such a world of existential heteroglossia, of a many-voiced world that problematises and opposes an inner sacred; it is an imaginative construction of interior worlds that are out of joint with other, larger, more politically powerful worlds. Whereas *The Magic Pudding* ends metafictively; *Wild Girl, Wild Boy* begins metafictively:

ELAINE Wild . . . Girl . . . Wild . . . Boy . . .
That's the title. That's the title.
Once . . . there . . . was . . . a . . . girl . . . called . . . Elaine . . .
Ah. Yes. Phew. That's the start . . .
She . . . lived . . . with . . .

She holds up the paper and looks at her words.
ELAINE Look at it! Look at it! I'm so stupid. No, I'm not! I have
  problems . . . writing. Something to do with the way I . . . see or something.

The play explores the troubled 'interior infinite' of Elaine, the way she sees herself and others in conflicting worlds, times, and spaces that collide in misunderstanding and pain. This misunderstanding is manifest theatrically in the grim chorus of voices—'of neighbours, classmates and teachers' (p. 26)—that reflect attitudes towards difference and the wildness of creative imagination. Elaine is a figure of ridicule, a seeming 'fool,' who huddles within herself, holding her hands around her head as the voices start:

THE CHORUS OF VOICES —Have you seen the way she just stares out the window with her gob hanging open?
—Like she's catching flies.
—Like a little kid.
—Like a baby.
—And the state of her books?
—Like a spider's crawled over them.
—Like somebody's chucked spaghetti on them.
—Hey, Elaine, has somebody chucked spaghetti on your books?
—No, that's her writing, man!
—Now leave Elaine alone. Oh dear, Elaine. We're going to have to do better than that, aren't we?
—Concentrate, girl!
—Keep your mind on your work.
—Elaine has severe difficulty in maintaining concentration on the task in hand.

This choric 'carnival' of voices represents a dialogised phenomenology of mindscapes: a refracted one of Elaine's own inner world, with its confusion and despair and desire for understanding, and those of the community around her. Briefly, the play tells the story of a young girl ('wild girl')—Elaine —whose imaginative father has died, leaving her alone with a more down-to-earth mother. Grieving her father's death, she grieves the concomitant loss of the imaginative spaces and freedoms of the space of the allotment to which he introduced her, where they listened together to what Almond refers to in his Afterword as the 'endless lovely singing of the larks' (p. 86):

ELAINE Then he dies, and there was nothing more to dance for and nothing more to sing for.
Let me out!
No answer.

One day, having truanted from school, and sitting and drawing in the allotment, she is joined by (draws?) Wild Boy, who has fur on his hands and can not speak, only making 'weird' noises. She takes him back home with her:

ELAINE holds WILD BOY in front of her mum.
WILD BOY smiles tenderly into Mum's eyes.
ELAINE realises that MUM sees nothing.

ELAINE Look, Mum. Look. Oh, Wild Boy, she can't see you. She can't see!
MUM moves close to ELAINE, peers into her eyes.
MUM Elaine, what's going in there? What's happened to my little girl?

One of the many ways in which this play can be seen as performance-of-text is to contemplate the different options of designing the allotment space on stage, and of representing and blocking the actors' physical and mental interactions between restraints and freedom. Wild Boy is a carnival figure; Bakhtin notes that the Roman Saturnalia presented images of men 'wearing the skin of wild beasts' (1965/1984, p. 392). In Almond's play, 'spit and horse muck,' bodily excretion and excrement, are used on the fairy seeds to magic the fairy into existence. The allotment—regenerative space, secret garden, other world heterocosm, fertile and imaginative wilderness and wildness—is the place of both death and life; not a Rabelaisian underworld but an overworld:

> [I]t contains the past, the rejected and condemned, as unworthy to dwell in the present. . . . But it also gives us a glimpse of the new life, of the future that is born, for it is this future that finally kills the past.
>
> (Bakhtin, 1965/1984, p. 409)

Wild Girl, Wild Boy slips in and out of ('quotes') times and spaces in a refracted *mise-en-abyme*, inserting and framing the past in the present. Wild Boy mirrors the wild side of Elaine, the side that yearns for faery and daydream. Her mother and Mr. McNamara, a problematic neighbour, decry Elaine's wildness:

MCNAMARA Discipline her. Tame her
It's like gardening . . .
Start getting wild and you cut them back . . .
    Otherwise there's just . . . wilderness.

But at the end of the play, as Elaine coaxes her mother and McNamara into tasting the sweetness of the raspberries, they undergo a moral psychic reorganisation that is part of the essence of carnival:

MCNAMARA The larks so loud. The sun so bright . . .
I brought you these.
MUM Raspberries.

MCNAMARA They were hanging over my allotment.
I reached deep into the thorns.

ELAINE Dad's.

MCNAMARA Yes, your dad's. They're delicious.
Sweeter than any I ever grew.

MUM takes the raspberries from him. She hands one to ELAINE.
MCNAMARA exits.
MUM and ELAINE eat the raspberries.

MUM Delicious

ELAINE Raspberries. Delicious and sweet and wild.

The Magic Pudding is a humorous trip to a safe harbour (or more correctly treehouse). *Wild Girl, Wild Boy* is a difficult traversing through the
complexities of grief, loss, mother and daughter intersubjective relationships,
and the untamed parts of the human psyche. Journey's end for Elaine comes
as she and her mother, 'absorbed in each other and in their memories'—
that is, in both past and present—dance together into the 'delicious and
sweet' wilderness. This represents another version of the arrival home,
and another version of carnival, a human rejuvenation and 'tendency
to duality' (Bakhtin, 1965/1984, p. 323) that is expressed bodily in their
parent/child relationship and invokes images of both birth and death:
'You were once a yolky little salty thing,' Elaine's mother tells her (p. 78).
Carnival, writes Bakhtin, 'celebrates the destruction of the old and the
birth of the new world—the new year, the new spring, the new kingdom'
(p. 410). There is a logic, he goes on to say, about seeing things 'wrong
side out' (p. 411), as Elaine does. The grotesque hairy body of Wild Boy
provokes ambivalence and ambiguity: is he a figment of Elaine's
imagination? delusion? imaginary friend? alter ego? symbol of imaginative
freedom? shadow? metaphor of the fertility of the untamed and the barren-
ness of the safe and ordinary?

ELAINE No wings. Fur on your hands. You're . . . ugly. No, not ugly.

The play relates very clearly to some of Almond's prose work, particularly *Secret Heart* (2001). But as he writes in the Afterword to *Wild Girl,
Wild Boy*, the writer's input is only one part of a play:

> [U]nlike stories in prose that march line by line from top left to
> bottom right, all the space filled in by the writer, a story in play
> form moves down the page in short bursts surrounded by lots of
> space. Dialogue, names, skimpy stage directions, and that's all.
> The space around the words is for the director, the actors and the
> designer to fill.
>
> (pp. 88–89)

Later, Almond describes his feeling on arriving for the first performance
of the text:

A last minute rehearsal was under way. The music played. Beneath the stage lights were the bedroom, the allotment. The moon shone through the window above the bed. Who was that figure that shuffled through the lights, with his wild hair, his ragged clothes, with fur on his hands and feet? Who was that girl, her face transfigured by a weird mixture of despair and delight?

(pp. 92–92)

The playwright concludes his remarks with these words:

In the end of course, none of it exists. There is no Elaine, there is no Wild Boy, there is no allotment, there is no bedroom. The play is a subterfuge, a set of disguises and tricks. It's a pack of lies. . . .

Of course it depends on the creative skills of writer, directors, actors, composers, designers. But it also depends on the creative skills of the audience, those skills of the imagination that allow us all to leap into other minds and other worlds, skills that are at once quite natural, straightforward, commonplace and quite amazing.

(pp. 92–93)

Almond's last point is also, I believe, true to a great extent of reading a book. Nonetheless, children's plays are texts that are mediated by performance, and it is this performance that gives their stories and characters shape, voice, movement, and life. Further, this performance constitutes a performativity and productive power that is overt and that constitutes, through the visuality and citation of theatre, activities and images of community and belonging. Theatre, corporate yet intimate, is a powerful medium of sensual communication. The fleeting ephemerality of the theatrical experience is a carefully constructed performance of human moment that is at once real and unreal. Plays, more so than books, in their immediacy and sensual present, exert a corporate captivity, if only for an hour or two. Writers such as David Almond seek to lay the groundwork for imaginative freedom and a sort of carnivalesque wildness that is subtly encoded as transient. There is a sense of stage as sacred space bound (perhaps protected) by conventions and multiple citations: what is acted there will constitute what is there, and what is. When we consider plays-as-the-performance-of-text, child audiences become part of performance and text, through ceremonials and rituals that help construct them. As adult writers creating plays for children implicitly cite their conceptions of childhood (in a sort of wistful living intertextuality), stage becomes 'the allotment,' where wildness is tested and tasted and, in our ideological climate at least, found to be 'good.'

Acknowledgment

I would like to thank Geoff Fox, whose own experience with children's theatre I respect, for his extremely helpful comments on this article.

References

Almond, D., *Secret Heart*. London: Hodder Headline, 2001.

Almond, D., *Wild Girl, Wild Boy*. London: Hodder Headline, 2002.

Austin, J. L., *How to Do Things with Words*. Cambridge, MA: Harvard University Press, 1962.

Bakhtin, M. M., *Rabelais and his World*. Bloomington: Indiana University Press, 1984. (Original work published 1965)

Bell, V., ed., *Performativity and Belonging*. London: Sage Publications, 1999.

Butler, J., *Gender Trouble: Feminism and the Subversion of Identity*. London: Routledge, 1990.

Clark, K., and M. Holquist, *Mikhail Bakhtin*. Cambridge MA: Harvard University Press, 1984.

Johnston, R. R., Part III, chaps. 16–27 in *Literacy: Reading, Writing and Children's Literature*, G. Winch, R. R. Johnston, P. March, L. Ljungdahl, and M. Halliday, eds., pp. 285–437. Melbourne: Oxford University Press, 2001.

Kowzan, Tadewsz, 'Art "en Abyme'," *Diogenes*. Paris, Librairie Gallimard, No. 96.

Lindsay, N., *The Magic Pudding*. Sydney: Angus & Robertson, 2000. (Original work published 1919)

Nikolajeva, M., *Children's Literature Comes of Age: Towards a New Aesthetics*. New York: Garland, 1996.

Nikolajeva, M., *From Mythic to Linear: Time in Children's Literature*. Lanham, MD, and London: The Children's Literature Association and Scarecrow Press, 2000.

Rimmon-Kenan, S., *Narrative Fiction: Contemporary Poetics*. London: Methuen, 1983.

Spivak, G., "Subaltern studies: deconstructing historiography,' in *Other Worlds: Essays in Cultural Politics*, pp. 197–221. New York and London: Routledge, 1988.

Stephens, J., *Language and Ideology in Children's Literature*. London: Longman, 1992.

INDEX

fictional direction **II** 222
fictional reflexivity: Ommundsen's
position **III** 376
fictional text: active approach **II** 224
fictional words **II** 290
Fictions of Discourse (O'Neill)
III 432–4
Fielder, L. **II** 333
Figgie Robbin (Causley) **I** 179
Filboid Studge **I** 36, 38, 41
film: adaptation **I** 165, 166; ownership
I 166; text **I** 166
final vocabularies **II** 247
Fincke, K. **II** 183
Finnish **IV** 130
Firestone, S. **III** 212
first-person narrative **II** 17–18; **III** 95,
419–22
Fish, S. **II** 219
Five Children and It (Nesbit) **I** 80
Fleischman, P. **II** 195
Flynn, R. **III** 20, 21
folk quatrains **IV** 43
folklore **II** 288–9; textual practice
II 292; written **II** 290, 291
folksongs **IV** 295–8
folktales **II** 171, 362–3; American
Indians **II** 27; and development of
novel **III** 87; revitalization **I** 167
fonts **II** 118
Foreign Affairs (Lurie) **I** 2; **II** 166;
III 208
The Forest Princess (Herman) **IV** 285–6
formalism **II** 235, 327, 332
formatting features **II** 117
Forms of Things Unknown (Lewis)
II 130–1
formulaic fiction: external orientation
in **III** 405; romantic characters in
III 395
formulaic texts **II** 220
Forster, E. M. **II** 215
fort-da game **III** 364
Foucault, M. **III** 23
Foulkes, A. P. **II** 263
France: book translation **IV** 106, 116,
124, 128; role in development of fairy
tale **IV** 220–4, 272
Freeman, M. **II** 194
Freese, H.-L. **IV** 90
French: counting-out rhymes **IV** 46–8;
experiences of translators **IV** 134–5;
translations into **IV** 106, 116, 124, 128

French feminism **II** 234
Freud, A. **III** 361
Freud, S. **II** 28, 194, 330; **III** 24–5, 312,
313, 343–5, 356
Freudian: fantasy theories **I** 186
Friedenberg, E. Z. **I** 87
Froebel, F. **III** 342–3
The Frog King (trad.) **IV** 232
The Frog Prince (trad.) **IV** 282
From Where I Stand (Price) **III** 111, 115
Frye, N. **II** 5; **III** 391–2; **IV** 262
functional literacy **II** 58
fundamental issues **I** 4
Fuss, D. **II** 185, 366
"The Future of the Profession"
(Griswold) **III** 18

Gadamer, H.-G. **IV** 97
Galbraith, M. **II** 183; **III** 19–20
Galgenlieder (Morgenstern) **IV** 109
game: as text **III** 378–82; text **III** 386–8
Game of Dark (Mayne) **I** 80
Gardam, J. **III** 78, 420
the garden: in children's literature
III 91–2
Garden of Forking Paths (Borges)
I 228
Garfield, L. **I** 58
Garner, A. **I** 81; **II** 126; **III** 77–81, 89,
93; **IV** 72
Gavin, J. **IV** 168
Gay, M. **IV** 114
Geertz, C. **III** 17; **IV** 59–60, 62
gender **II** 169, 187, 237, 240, 251,
336; in 18th century publishing
III 188–90; in 19th century
publishing **III** 189, 190–6; adult
book choice and **III** 187; bias **II** 64;
cleansing text **II** 64–5; and dress
III 279–80; in fairy tales **III** 250,
262–4, 278–80; and fairy tales
IV 217, 220–1, 223, 256, 273–4, 284;
feminist challenge to stereotyping
III 249–50; in heroic fantasy **III** 224;
hierarchy of value **III** 199; issues
I 125; nonsexist versions of fairy
tales **IV** 284–7; in picture books
III 37–8; and picture books
IV 286–7; polarization in literature
III 192–6; and reading behaviour
III 196–204; relations **II** 155; and
revisionist readings **IV** 174, 175–6;
rules **II** 28–9; stereotyping **II** 333;